12-12-75

1. *Matrimony*

MATRIMONY

PAPAL TEACHINGS

MATRIMONY

Selected and Arranged

by

THE BENEDICTINE MONKS OF SOLESMES

Translated by

MICHAEL J. BYRNES

ST. PAUL EDITIONS

NIHIL OBSTAT:

Rt. Rev. Alfred R. Julien, J.C.D.
Diocesan Censor

IMPRIMATUR:

✠ **Richard Cardinal Cushing**
Archbishop of Boston

August 27, 1963

FOREWORD

The present volume is one of three dealing with the basic unit of society. Two others, containing papal teaching on the *Christian Family* and on *Education* deal with the specific functions of Christian Spouses. This volume presents the teachings of the Supreme Pontiffs (from Benedict XIV to John XXIII) on that which lies at the basis of all family life, viz. the *Sacrament of Matrimony*.

Probably no other institution over the last two centuries has been attacked so violently as matrimony. This should not surprise us, because enemies of religion would consider the primary cell of society a natural target. By recalling marriage to its original sanctity and elevating it to the dignity of a sacrament, Our Lord, Jesus Christ, made it a vital instrument of His Redemption. Where else would one expect the universal de-christianization and laicization of mankind to begin from than here? How else could mankind be more easily and quickly withdrawn from God's Dominion than by desanctifying Matrimony.

The secularization of matrimony first began with infidels and later was extended by the Protestant Reformation. With the rise of civil divorce the sacred significance of marriage was lost for many peoples and, along with this, the sense that marriage belonged to the Church. After the French Revolution the power of the State over marriage grew apace and, for the first time in a millenium, the Church found Matrimony withdrawn from her dominant control.

Once the breach was made and the idea launched that marriage was mainly a human contract, there followed the adoption of civil legislation pertaining to divorce, contraception, sterilization, and abortion, which struck at the very heart of Christian marriage, even in countries that still call themselves Catholic.

The consequences of these historical developments were foreseen by Pius IX and Leo XIII. They predicted the moral corruption and degradation, so evident in the last fifty years, that would by inexorable law follow upon the repudiation of God's laws for marriage and the married.

We briefly recall these stages of decline because they parallel the stages through which the positive teaching of the Supreme Pontiffs has followed. First there are occasional reminders, sorrowful pleas, rapid condemnations in the hour of first assaults. Then, with Leo XIII comes the beginning of a complete marriage tract. Only the sudden occupation of Rome prevented the promulgation of a constitution on Matrimony.

Fifty years later, *Casti Connubii* took its place among the great papal documents of all time. Here and in another letter entitled *Arcanum* Pius XI defined not only the nature of Matrimony but also the moral duties flowing therefrom. Pius XII, finally in his repeated allocutions, not only clarified and consolidated the truths taught by his predecessors, but corrected the errors which had insiduously entered the Church itself, and gave new authoritative direction to the theology on marriage.

The selections in this book may be called occasional instructions, if by this is meant that the vast majority of these Papal statements are not formally constructed documents. But as Vicars of Christ, the succession of Holy Fathers recorded here are anxious to enunciate for the faithful, those teachings on marriage most suitable to the needs of the moment. Whatever the circumstances of the preaching, however, it can hardly be called transient. Even when changes in Matrimonial discipline are announced, as for example in the form of marriage, the basic doctrine of the Church remains the same. All the Pontiffs from Benedict XIV to John XXIII develop and make more precise the teachings of their predecessors.

But more often they merely repeat it, refer to it, as their assurance of conformity with the doctrine of the Apostles and Jesus Christ.

This schematic approach may help canonists avoid confusing this present volume with a summary of juridical decisions or legislative prescriptions concerning Matrimony. Even where these decisions and prescriptions are quoted, they are only a small part of the substance of this volume. In common with the series to which it belongs, this compendium aims only at putting between two covers all the Papal statements which together describe the Christian view of marriage. May this volume contribute to the restoration of matrimony and the family to Jesus Christ and thus of all society itself.

Solesmes, 1954

INTRODUCTION

HOW THE DOCUMENTS ARE PRESENTED

At the head of each document is found
a title, to facilitate understanding,
the type of document,
the "incipit" if the text is taken from a written document
the address و and the date of origin;
in the body of the text:
subtitles for the longer citations.
in italics in parentheses, a brief summary of those
portions of the original document not cited in the
text, because not referring directly to the subject
being treated.

HOW TO USE THIS VOLUME

To find the texts relating to a given question:
look first in the alphabetical index or else directly in
the analytical index, where the numbers in heavy print
refer the reader to the papal texts.
To clarify a text by placing it in its context in the development of the thought of the Popes, or by comparing it
to parallel texts: the numbers in italics, given in parentheses in the margin of the text, refer to the analytical
index, which in turn summarizes briefly the lines of
papal thought and indicates the relative texts.

THE NUMBERING OF THE TEXT

The numbers in heavy print, refer to the paragraphs of the
papal pronouncements, given in chronological order
in the text.
The numbers in italics, given in parentheses, refer to the
divisions of the analytical index.

CONTENTS

16

18

INDEXES

PAPAL DOCUMENTS

BENEDICT XIV
1740-1758

PERPETUAL UNION

Encycl. *Matrimonii*, April 11, 1741—to the Polish Episcopate.

The lasting and indissoluble bond of marriage—the sanctity of which was declared in the beginning by Adam, and confirmed graciously by Christ with these words: "What God hath joined together, let no man put asunder" (a) so elevating it by evangelical grace and making it a great Sacrament in the Church—has now been brought to our attention as being easily dissolved. This is so in some Catholic regions of the world and especially in that flourishing kingdom of Poland, as if marriage was not contracted under the guardianship of the natural and divine law, the evangelical precepts and the approved canons. There are no tears or words sufficient enough to manifest to you Our concern in this matter and our most bitter sorrow of soul as Pontiff. . . . However, We cannot put aside the obligations We have of conveying to you, Venerable Brethren, Our most just protests, and of studying together the method of checking such a license, and of confining it by salutary laws within the limits prescribed by the Catholic Church.

(Proposals intended to check the abuses).

1a Matt. 19:6.

— 25 —

WHAT GOD HATH JOINED TOGETHER

Apost. Const. *Dei miseratione,* November 3, 1741.

2
(99) Through the goodness of God whose judgments are incomprehensible and whose ways are unsearchable, We have been raised—though not for merits of Our own—to the Supreme Power in the Church in order to guard with anxious care the entire flock of the Lord. We know that it is a duty of the pastoral office entrusted to Us to uproot the abuses resulting from the work of the unceasing cunning of the infernal enemy and of human malice; abuses that hinder the salvation of souls and injure the sacraments of the Church. We must use the power that has been conferred on Us from on high to check human rashness and to preserve the holy authority of the Divine Law.

3
(2,
14,
15,
23,
51) Since the matrimonial contract was instituted by God, inasmuch as it is a natural institution whose aim is the education of the offspring and the conservation of the other benefits of marriage, it is suitable that it be perpetual and indissoluble (a). Inasmuch as it is a Sacrament of the Catholic Church, it can never be dissolved by human presumption: Our Lord so ordained it Himself with these words: "What God hath joined together, let no man put asunder" (b). Now We have been informed that in some ecclesiastical chanceries this bond has been broken through the excessive compliance of the judges; sentences

3a *Si quidem Matrimonii fœdus a Deo institutum, quod, et quatenus naturæ officium est, pro educandæ prolis studio, aliisque Matrimonii bonis, servandis, perpetuum, et indissolubile esse convenit.*
3b Matt. 19:6.

of nullity of matrimony have been issued rashly and without due consideration and liberty has been given to married couples to contract other marriages. It would have been fitting for these imprudent judges to have heeded the warning that came to them from the very qualities of human nature and, in a certain sense, even from its very voice not to violate with such precipitate audacity the bond of holy matrimony; a bond that the first parent of the human race declared perpetual and indissoluble when he declared: "This now is bone of my bones, and flesh of my flesh", and when he added: "Wherefore a man shall leave father and mother, and shall cleave to his wife: and they shall be two in one flesh" (c).

(*Legislative provisions intended to halt the abuses.*)

SOLEMN   FORM

Enc. *Satis vobis,* November 17, 1741.

We do not doubt, Venerable Brethen, that you are well aware, that it was always the anxious care of Holy Mother Church that the sacrament of matrimony, called "great" by the Apostle (a), should be celebrated publicly and with proper notice. So that this might be done in future more diligently than in the past, the sacred council of Trent,—following the pattern of the Lateran Council, which was held under Innocent III,—decreed that in future, before marriage should be contracted the banns should be read three times by the parish priest of the contracting parties, on three consecutive holy days, in Church,

4
(7,
12)

3c Gen. 2:23-24.
4a Ephes. 5:32.

during the Solemn High Mass, and in a public manner. Only then, if no legitimate impediments had been discovered could the marriage ceremony be performed in the Church, before the parish priest, or before another priest with the permission of the parish priest or the Ordinary, and the presence of two or three witnesses. The same holy council of Trent ordered the parish priests to keep a register in which marriages were to be recorded, together with the names of the contracting parties, the witnesses, the date and place of the marriage (b).

The abuse of secret marriages

5
(12)
These prudent laws, put forth so usefully by such a high authority, little by little through the iniquity of the age have fallen into disuse and lost their vigor. Now all too frequently marriages are celebrated in such a way that every trace of them is lost, and the record disappears forever. Another frequent custom is to celebrate marriage, no preliminary public announcement having been made, before the parish priest, or another priest authorized by him, and in the presence of only two witnesses chosen with care by the contracting parties. Matrimony is often celebrated outside the church, or sometimes even in the church but behind closed doors or at a time when it is deserted. Thus no one is aware of the ceremony performed except the parish priest, the contracting parties and the witnesses.

4b Council of Trent, sess. 24, chap. *Tametsi.*—Denz. 990-992.—Cf. C.I.C., can. 1022. — *"Publice a parocho denuntietur inter quosnam matrimonium sit contrahendum"*. Can. 1027. — *"Omnes fideles impedimenta, si qua norint, parocho aut loci Ordinario, ante matrimonii celebrationem, revelare"*.

Consequences of secret marriages

What a far cry these secret marriages, or as they are **6** more commonly called "marriages of conscience", are from *(12,* the dignity of the Sacrament and the legal prescriptions *29)* of the Church is clearly manifested to anyone who reflects on their disastrous consequences. In fact, such marriages are the cause of grave sins, especially for those who, despising divine judgments, abandon their first wife with whom they had been secretly living in order to live with another woman in an adulterous manner, after having deceived her with a promise of a future marriage to be contracted publicly. Others, blinded by passion, dare to contract a second secret marriage, after having already contracted a first secret marriage the bond of which is not yet dissolved by the death of the spouse, thus becoming guilty of the crime of polygamy. Others go still further in their impudence and in their contempt of such a great Sacrament. After having contracted a secret marriage, they contract another marriage, either secret or public, and more audacious than the former, are not in the least concerned at being regarded as polygamists. The great evils that derive from such marriages cannot be tolerated at all. If, in fact, a man lives separated from his wife to avoid arousing any suspicion of marriage, their life in common is impossible and the words of Our Lord: "a man shall cleave to his wife: and they shall be two in one flesh" (a) are despised; on the other hand, if they lead a life in common, everyone will consider it a crime and so detestable a thing that it will be regarded

6a Gen. 2:24.

as a scandal. Such scandal will not be repaired by a secretly celebrated marriage—a marriage hidden in a secret and of which nobody knows anything.

7   No less is the wrong suffered by the children. It of-
(12) ten happens that they are abandoned by their parents and, in particular, by the mother and cannot be educated in a pious and fitting manner. They are left to the mercy of circumstances, when their parents did not seek to kill them by an act contrary to natural law. If the parents have not dared to implicate themselves in such a crime, and human love urged them to nourish and educate their children, the latter will have to suffer for other reasons: they will find themselves deprived of the inheritance and family goods, even if they have the right to them by the bond of paternal blood. They cannot avail themselves of their legitimacy and their filiation, and all this on account of the secrecy of their parents' marriage.

(Call to the Bishops to be less willing to grant dispensations so easily from the publication of the marriage banns.)

8   After the dispensation from the banns, it is necessary
(12) that you use equal vigilance, or indeed even greater vigilance, to prevent the marriage from being celebrated in the presence of the parish priest alone or another priest delegated by him and in the presence of two discreet witnesses, so that notice of the ceremony be not divulged. In order for this to be licit, according to the norms of the sacred canons, an ordinary or trivial excuse is not sufficient; there must be a grave, urgent, even most urgent, cause ... (a). It is the duty of your pastoral

office to study and ponder whether the reason for the dispensation is legitimate and urgent, so that the secretly celebrated marriage may not have those disastrous consequences that We have sorrowfully enumerated.

(*The almost sole reason: the convalidation of a marriage held by all to be legitimate.—The manner of conducting the prescribed inquiry.*)

DISPENSATIONS FROM IMPEDIMENTS

Apost. Const. *Ad Apostolicae servitutis,* February 25, 1742.

To Our Apostolic office belongs the duty to take the greatest care that dispensations be not granted for those degrees of affinity or consanguinity wherein marriage is prohibited, or for other impediments established by the sacred canons, unless for reasonable causes. Let all the pretexts be removed by which the impious are able to damage in any way the name and the dignity of the Roman Church, over which We, through no merit of Our own but by divine mercy, have been placed in authority.

9
(49,
51,
92)

(*Regulations for seeking dispensations from matrimonial impediments, and for granting these dispensations.*)

8a *Id enim, ut ad præscriptum Sacrorum Canonum licite fieri possit, non satis est obvia quævis et vulgaris causa, sed gravis, urgens, et urgentissima requiritur.*—This requirement was ratified by law and fixed by can. 1104 of Canon Law.: *Nonnisi ex gravissima et urgentissima causa et ab ipso loci Ordinario, excluso Vicario Generali sine speciali mandato, permitti potest ut* matrimonium

AN ARTICLE OF FAITH

Letter *Nuper ad Nos,* March 16, 1743, to the Patriarch of the Maronites.

(*Election of the New Patriarch of the Maronites.— The Holy See asks for a profession of Faith*).

10
(7,
76)
The formula of the profession of Faith that you will give is the following: "I, Simon, Patriarch-elect of the Antiochian Church of the Maronite nation, believe with firm faith and profess all and each of the truths contained in the symbol of Faith followed by the Holy Roman Church, in other words: I believe in One God, etc.

I believe that there are seven Sacraments of the New Law, instituted by Christ Our Lord, for the salvation of mankind, even if all of them are not necessary for each single person; that is, Baptism, Confirmation, Eucharist, Penance, Extreme Unction, Holy Orders and Matrimony. . . .

I believe that the bond of the Sacrament of Matrimony is indissoluble, and, even if there is the possibility of a separation from bed and board as a result of adultery, heresy or the like, it is never lawful for a husband and wife to proceed to another marriage. . ."

IN AN INFIDEL COUNTRY

Encycl. *Inter omnigenas,* February 2, 1743, to the Bishops and people of Serbia and nearby regions.

conscientiæ *ineatur, idest matrimonium celebretur omissis denuntiationibus et secreto, ad norman canonum qui sequuntur".*

(Decay of Christian customs among the faithful under the domination of the Turks.—Denunciation of the principal abuses, and measures to be used to remedy them.)

The Form

It is with pain and sorrow that We have learned **11** that the decrees of the Council of Trent regarding the *(12)* Sacrament of Matrimony are not observed by certain persons in those regions where the decrees have long since been duly published, as noted in the Council of Albania itself (a). While we declare that all the faithful of these regions are bound to observe the above mentioned law, we also declare the so-called marriages contracted in the presence of the Turkish judge or *caid,* and those not even contracted before a judge but only by the spouses themselves not adhering to the prescriptions of the aforesaid Council of Trent, to be null and void. We command then that those who contract similar null and clandestine marriages, and who, after having contracted them, live together in an illicit concubinage are to be excluded from participation in the Sacraments unless they repent of the past and are united in a proper marriage before the Church.

Prohibition of the Moslem rite

We do not permit the faithful who have duly con- **12** tracted matrimony, not even if done to remove from *(69)* women the danger of abduction by the Turks, to renew by proxy the Turkish rite before the *caid,* unless the

11a Held in 1703. Cf. Mansi, t. 35, col. 1375.

2. *Matrimony*

Moslem rite be a purely civil matter, not involving any invocation of Mohammed or any other kind of superstition. The married couple cannot be considered less culpable if they go through this rite by proxy rather than in person; the crime is committed by their authorization or command.

13　　As regards the publication of the banns established
(12) by the Council of Trent, We prescribe also that, as far as is possible, this should be done even in Serbia, where it has been said that this practice has not been maintained. In the above-mentioned Council of Albania, in fact, the publications are enjoined upon the parish priests of Serbia, and they have been forbidden the use of the faculty to grant dispensations, except in cases of urgent necessity.

Prohibition of divorce

14　　If the wife of one of the faithful seeks refuge with
(16, the Turks, and dares to contract with one of them a sinful
75) union, it is not lawful for the man to take another wife in the place of the one who fled; for matrimony by divine law is indissoluble while both parties are living and it is not dissolved by a crime such as that perpetrated by the wife. Whoever in such a case weds another woman commits adultery, and, if he does not separate himself definitively from her, he is to be excluded from the Sacraments.

15　　What must be said about the salvation of such
(10, women, if they do not repent, is obvious to all. As re-
26) gards Christian women who are abducted forcibly by the Turks and compelled to wed while still children, and who are not regularly united by any valid bond of sacramental

faith, but persevere in illicit concubinage with the infidels,
We establish the same punishment as has been decreed
in the above-mentioned Council of Albania: namely, that
they be refused the Sacraments of the Church, in spite of
their supposed perseverance in the Christian faith, or the
fact that they, while still children, have been subjected
to the violence of the Turks; or the fact that they are now
regarded by the Turks as the only, or principal and legitimate, wife. These motives do not confer any right to the
reception of the Sacraments upon those who continue to
live in concubinage and fornication; and they do not give
any authority to the priests to administer the Sacrament
to such unworthy persons.   1887655

Conditions for dispensations

As regards matrimonial dispensations, let the Bishops 16
and the missionaries of Serbia be on their guard, when(51)
using the faculties granted them by this Holy See, against
issuing them in a rash manner or in favor of those who
do not merit such dispensations; and let them not exceed
their authority when granting dispensations. We ordain
that no dispensation be granted to those secret Christians,
noted above, who simulate the Moslem rites. Indeed, such
people, ashamed of Christ, make themselves unworthy
of the favors of the Church, which is the Spouse of Christ.
Besides, no dispensation may be granted in those cases
in which it is foreseen that the marriage will not be celebrated validly and in a holy manner according to the rites
of the Catholic Church. In such cases there is no question
of dispensation but of dissoluteness and encouragement to
incontinence; matters against which a good and prudent
minister of Christ is always obliged to guard.

INTRODUCTION OF THE CIVIL FORMALITIES

Letter *Redditae sunt Nobis,* September 17, 1746, to Paul Simon of St. Joseph, Carmelite.

(*Doubts raised about the procedure to follow with Catholics, obliged by the laws of the United Provinces, to present themselves before a civil magistrate or an heretical minister in order to contract marriage.*)

17
(69,
74)
You have explained to Us that several times in your city it happens that Catholics who wish to contract marriage have to appear before the civil magistrate or before an heretical minister—such being the obligation of the laws of the country. The couple express their mutual consent to wedlock before these persons, and then neglect to renew this consent before a legitimate Catholic minister and two witnesses, as the Council of Trent commands; or, in other cases, they defer such a renewal for an indefinite time, during which time they enjoy all the matrimonial privileges as if they were legitimately married.

You have therefore asked Us what must be thought of such mutual consent expressed before a civil magistrate or an heretical minister. Is it sufficient to constitute a valid marriage, at least as far as the contract is concerned? Some of you reply in the affirmative: others hold the opposite opinion. None of you doubt that such a contract is not raised to a sacrament.

(*The principle on which the reply to these divergent opinions is based: In every place where the decree of the Council of Trent has been promulgated, the marriage between Catholics, contracted without observing the prescribed form, is null.*)

The Catholics placed under your care should know **18** that when they appear before a civil magistrate or an *(74)* heretical minister they are performing a purely civil act, by which they show their obedience to the laws of the land; but they do not contract matrimony. They should know that until their marriage is celebrated before a Catholic priest and two witnesses they will never be true and legitimate spouses before God or the Church; and that in the meantime should they have marital relations between them they commit a grave sin. Let it be known also that should there be offspring from such a union, they would be illegitimate before God because they would not be born from a lawful wife; and if the couple do not renew their consent according to the prescriptions of the Church, the offspring will remain illegitimate in the eyes of the Church (a).

It will be your duty, in future, whenever the oppor- **19** tunity presents itself, to give fuller explanations to every *(54)* one, with all the reserve and prudence required in the circumstances; to admonish all that if they have to follow the customs of their country and the ordinances of the civil ruler, they must safeguard the rights of religion. Let them give greater importance to the most holy laws of the Church that regulate the marriage of the faithful.

18a *Sciant, nisi coram Ministro Catholico et duobus Testibus nuptias celebraverint, nusquam se, neque coram Deo, neque coram Ecclesia, veros et legitimos Coniuges fore: nec, si interim coniugalem inter se consuetudinem habueint, eam gravi culpa carituram. Sciant denique, si qua ex husiusmodi coniunctione orietur soboles, eam, utpote ex non legitima uxore natam, in oculis Dei fore illegitimam, et nisi coniuges consensum ex Ecclesiæ præscripto renovaverint, illegitimam perpetuo futuram etiam in Ecclesia foro.*

It is also your duty to see to it that when two Catholics have complied with the civil and merely political ceremony before the heretics, they abstain from excessive familiarity and that they do not live together under the same roof before completing a true and legitimate marriage according to the norms of the Council of Trent. Even if this familiarity can be without sin, it is certainly dangerous and a certain cause of suspicion, danger and suspicion that must be avoided by good and honorable Catholics.

20
(54) To avoid these dangers We know that it would be best for the Catholics to present themselves for the civil ceremony before a civil magistrate or heretical minister only after having celebrated a legitimate Church marriage. But since We gather from your letters that this is not possible without danger and confusion, We exhort you to employ all your powers that the parties, after having completed the formalities according to the customs of the State, do not delay too long the fulfillment of the duties placed upon them by the laws of the Church, and that they contract the matrimonial bond in the prescribed manner and devoutly according to the norms of the Council of Trent (a).

20a Cf. The actual legislation relative to mixed marriages: C.I.C., can., 1063. — § 1. *Etsi ab Ecclesia obtenta sit dispensatio super impedimento mixtæ religionis, coniu-*

THE BILL OF DIVORCE

Apost. Const. *Apostolici ministerii,* September 16, 1747.

(*Duty that is incumbent on the Holy See to suppress abuses.*)

It was recently pointed out to Us, and certain proofs confirm it, that some Jews converted to Catholicism whose wife is unwilling to embrace the Christian truths, after having abjured their Jewish infidelity and after having been baptized and bound by solemn promise to the Faith of Christ, do not hesitate to return with sacrilegious audacity to the encampment of the Jews or to the quarter commonly called the "*Ghetto,*" and there, according to the Rabbinic rite and with Jewish superstitions and unsuitable observances, grant to their wives a bill of divorce. In other cases, in order to give the women the possibility of being united to another man, they give the same bill of divorce to their wives, outside the Jewish quarter, before

ges nequeunt, vel ante vel post matrimonium coram Ecclesiam initum, adire quoque, sive per se sive per procuratorem, ministrum acatholicum uti sacris addictum, ad matrimonialem consensum præstandum vel renovandum.

§ 2. Si parochus certe noverit sponsos hanc legem violaturos esse vel iam violasse, eorum matrimonio ne assistat, nisi ex gravissimis causis, remoto scandalo et consulto prius Ordinaro.

§ 3. Non improbatur tamen quod, lege civili iubente, coniuges se sistant etiam coram ministro acatholico, officialis civilis tantum munere fungente, idque ad actum civilem dumtaxat explendum, effectuum civilium gratia.

a lawyer and Christian witnesses. Moses, indeed, left written in the 24th chapter of Deuteronomy: "If a man takes a wife, and have her, and she find not favor in his eyes, for some uncleanness, he shall write a bill of divorce, and shall give it in her hand, and send her out of his house (a).

22
(80)
It is difficult to know whether this concession was made only to avoid a greater evil, (in such a manner that he who gave and she who received the divorce were certainly exempt from the penalty but not from guilt); or whether the dispensation was a concession made by God, on account of the hardness of the Jews' hearts, (so that both he who sent and she who accepted the divorce were exempted from guilt and penalty and that both were allowed to contract validly and legitimately another marriage). On this point, the older and the more recent theologians do not hold the same opinion; some follow the first opinion, others the second.

Jesus Christ abrogated the Jewish repudiation

23
(4,
15)
But whatever may be the correct opinion on that point, it is certain that Our Redeemer, Jesus Christ, the Son of God, when questioned as to his opinion about the bill of divorce that Moses had permitted, replied, as can be seen from the Gospel of St. Matthew, chapter 19, and in St. Mark, chapter 10: "Because Moses, by reason of the hardness of your heart, permitted you to put away your wives; but it was not so from the beginning. And I say to you, that whoever puts away his wife, except for immorality, and marries another, commits adultery; and

21a Dt. 24:1.

he who marries a woman who has been put away commits adultery"; and Jesus concluded thus: "What therefore God has joined together, let no man put asunder" (a). Theologians deduce from these words the legitimate conclusion that it is no longer permissible for the Jews to repudiate their legitimate spouse, and that the bill of divorce no longer dissolves the marriage bond; for Jesus Christ has returned it to its primitive state, in other words, to indissolubility. He did this not by promulgating a new law, but rather by abolishing the ancient concession or dispensation made against the aforesaid indissolubility. As the matter stands, even if the repudiation is tolerated among the Jewish couples who persist in Jewish beliefs, it certainly must not be permitted at all nor tolerated that a Jew converted to the Faith and purified by sacred Baptism, should grant according to the Jewish rite and custom a bill of divorce to the wife who obstinately retains her Jewish belief.

The use of the Pauline privilege

Therefore, so that in future everything may be done in due order and in a praiseworthy and reasonable manner, We will and decree that a Jew converted to the Faith, if he have a Jewish wife, shall question her in the usual manner to find out if she desires to become a convert and to live together *sine contumelia Creatoris;* i.e., without danger of grave sin against faith or morals. If the woman refuses, he then remains free to contract another marriage, according to the words of the blessed Apostle Paul: "If

24
(15, 16, 49)

23a Cf. Matt. 19:5-9; Mark 10:5-9.

the unbeliever departs, let him depart. For a brother or sister is not under bondage in such cases, but God has called us in peace (a). This truth has already been well emphasized by Our illustrious Predecessor, Innocent III, in his decree that begins with the words: *Quanto de divortio* (b).

(*Controversy among theologians on the moment in which a marriage contracted before conversion is dissolved through the Pauline privilege: the Pope does not wish to determine the question, but promulgates sanctions against those who omit to question the unconverted partner.*)

A CONSTANT TRADITION

Encycl. *Magnæ Nobis,* June 29, 1748—to the Polish Episcopate.

(*Abuse of mixed marriages and of the custom of asking for dispensations from other impediments in favor of those who contract such marriages.*)

25
(84) We certainly have no need to cite all the evidence that would abundantly demonstrate the antiquity of the discipline in virtue of which the Apostolic See has always

---

24a 1 Cor. 7:15.

24b Today the legislation of the Church is regulated on this matter by the C.I.C., can. 1120, § 1.—*Legitimum inter non baptizatos matrimonium, licet consummatum, solvitur in favorem fidei ex privilegio Paulino.*

§ 2. *Hoc privilegium non obtinet in matrimonio inter partem baptizatam et partem non baptizatam inito cum dispensatione ab impedimento disparitatis cultus.*

disapproved marriages between Catholics and heretics. It would be well, however, to mention at least some of the evidence to show that the same discipline and law constantly observed up to now is still actually held to be in force by Us and by the Apostolic See and is religiously observed. We report the testimony that Our Predecessor, Urban VIII, of happy memory, made of himself and of his times in his Apostolic Letter, dated December 30, 1624, which can be read in Cardinal Albizio's book: *De inconstantia in Fide*, where it is written: "Quite justly, we maintain that marriages between Catholics and heretics must be absolutely avoided, and inasmuch as it is in Our power We intend to keep such marriages away from the Catholic Church" (a).

No less decisive were the thoughts of Our Predecessor of holy memory, Pope Clement XI, in the letter dated June 25, 1706 and printed in the collection of Briefs and Letters of the same Pope, which appeared in Rome in the year 1726. On p. 32, we read: "We hold that the rule followed by the Church of God, by the Apostolic See, by Our Predecessors and by the Sacred Canons, to abhor those marriages between Catholics and heretics, is of the greatest importance; a rule to which exceptions must not be allowed save when demanded by the good of the whole Christian Community." In another letter, dated June 23, 1707, found in the same collection, p. 391, it says: "The Church holds in abhorrence such marriages, which bring with them great ills and grave danger for the spirit". **26** *(84)*

25a Cf. Card. Albizio, *De inconstantia in Fide,* c. 37, n. 127.

27   We think that Our judgment on this point is
(82, clearly enough expressed in the rescript issued by Our
84, order on November 4, 1741, and printed among Our
86) Bulls (a). The following words are contained in this document: "His Holiness greatly deplores that there are Catholics who, shamefully maddened by an insane love, do
not abhor with all their hearts nor seek to avoid absolutely similar reprehensible marriages, which have always
been condemned and prohibited by Holy Mother Church.
He praises the zeal of those Bishops who use their powers
most energetically, by inflicting spiritual penalties, in restraining Catholics from uniting themselves with heretics
by means of these sacrilegious bonds. He seriously and
gravely exhorts and admonishes all Bishops, Vicars
Apostolic, Parish Priests, missionaries and all other faithful ministers of God and of the Church, who live in those
countries—namely in Holland and Belgium—to take every
possible opportunity to persuade the Catholics of both
sexes to abstain from such weddings that are the ruin
of their souls, and to apply themselves in every way and
with all the means at their disposal to hinder these marriages and put an end to them" (b). A little further on,
speaking of the marriages already contracted between
the Catholic party and the heretical party, the letter says:
"It is necessary that the Catholic party, whether male or
female, be induced to reflect and to do penance for the
most serious offence that has been committed; to ask God
for pardon; to strive in all possible ways to bring back the

27a It is the declaration *Matrimonia, quae in locis.*—Cf.
    Benedicti Papae XIV Bullarium. Venetiis 1778, c. 1,
    p. 89ss.—Cf. Denz. 1452-1457.
27b *Bullarium,* 1, document n. 34, § 3.—Denz. 1455.

partner that has abandoned the true faith to the fold of the Catholic Church and to win back that soul. That will greatly help to obtain forgiveness of the offence committed. Let it be remembered, however, as has been pointed out above, that he or she will be bound by such a matrimonial bond for ever (c).

The practice of the Holy See

To these statements of principle of the Apostolic See, 28 there also corresponds a constant maintenance of the(85) practice consecrated by custom. In fact, every time that it is necessary to have recourse to the Apostolic See, be it to obtain the simple faculty for contracting marriage between a Catholic and a heretic, or to obtain a dispensation for some degree of relationship or canonical impediment existing between the parties, it is not usual to grant either permission or dispensation unless first the obligation is stipulated or the following condition is formulated: to abjure the heresy. Our Predecessor of happy memory, Pope Innocent X, was even more exacting. He had commanded and taken the necessary precaution that such dispensations should not be finally granted, unless it first had been ascertained by authentic documents that the heretical party had already rejected the odious heresy (a).

Our already mentioned Predecessor, Clement XI, in 29 the Congregation of the Holy Office which was held in (85) his presence on June 16, 1710, ordered that it be com-

27c Ibid.
28a Cf. Card. Albizio, *De inconstantia in Fide*, c. 18, n. 44.

manded by letter to the Archbishop of Malines not to grant further licenses or dispensations for marriages that were to be contracted between a Catholic and a heretic, if first of all there was not the abjuration of the latter. He decreed besides that those theologians who had expressed themselves contrary to such a procedure be severly admonished. (a)

30
(84,
85,
86)
If there have been examples of Roman Pontiffs who have conceded a license to contract matrimony, or even a dispensation in regards to an impediment, without first of all insisting upon the condition of the abjuration of the heresy, We say that these concessions were very rare and that the greater number of them were granted for marriages to be contracted between persons of princely rank, and always for a very serious reason and an urgent case regarding the public good. Even in those cases the appropriate guarantees were always sought; on the one hand to preserve the Catholic party from the danger of being perverted by the heretical party—and after having instructed the Catholic party of the obligation of seriously working for the conversion of the heretical party—and on the other hand to assure to the children born from such a marriage an exclusive education in the holy Catholic religion. It is thus easy to see that in similar concessions no pretext of error can arise for those who execute the rescript of dispensation, unless they knowingly and willingly neglect their duty. In conclusion, from what has been already said, it appears clear that every request addressed to the Apostolic See for faculties or dispensa-

29a Cf. Vincent Petra, Works, t. 4, p. 76, n. 14.

tions for contracting marriage between a Catholic and a heretic must be preceded by an abjuration of the heresy. The same Apostolic See, as We have already said, has always reproved and condemned, and now once again reproves and condemns such marriages not preceded by an abjuration (a).

30a Today the legislation of the Church on this matter is regulated by the following canons of the C.I.C.:

Can. 1060.—*Severissime Ecclesia ubique prohibet ne matrimonium ineatur inter duas personas baptizatas, quarum altera sit catholica, altera vero sectae haereticae seu schismaticae adscripta; quod si adsit perversionis periculum coniugis catholici et prolis, coniugium ipsa etiam lege divina vetatur.*

Can. 1061.—§1. *Ecclesia super impedimento mixtae religionis non dispensat, nisi:*

1º *Urgeant iustae et graves causae;*

2º *Cautionem praestiterit coniux acatholicus de amovendo a coniuge catholico perversioinis periculo, et uterque coniux de universa prole catholice tantum baptizanda et educanda;*

3º *Moralis habeatur certitudo de cautionum implemento.*

§2. *Cautiones regulariter in scriptis exigantur.*

Can. 1062.—*Coniux catholicus obligatione tenetur conversionis coniugis acatholici prudenter curandi.*

Can. 1063.—Cf. above; n. 20, note (a).

Can. 1064.—*Ordinarii aliique animarum pastores:*

1º *Fideles a mixtis nuptiis, quantum possunt, absterreant;*

2º *Si eas impedire non valeant, omni studio curent ne contra Dei et Ecclesiae leges contrahantur;*

3º *Mixtis nuptiis celebratis sive in proprio sive in alieno territorio, sedulo invigilent ut coniuges promissiones factas fideliter impleant;*

4º *Assistetes matrimonio servent praescriptum can.* 1102. Cf. further ahead, n. 90, note (a).

Can. 1065.—1. *Absterreantur quoque fideles a matrimonio contrahendo cum iis qui notorie aut catholicum*

(Practical rules given to the Bishops for completing the document for a request for dispensations.—The Pope hopes that this letter will dissipate misunderstandings and silence the calumniators of the Holy See.)

fidem ebiecerunt, etsi ad sectam acatholicum non transierint, aut societatibus ab Ecclesia damnatis adscripti sunt.

§2. Parochus praedicitis nuptiis ne assistat, nisi consulto Ordinario qui, inspectus omnibus rei adiunctis, ei permittere poterit ut matrimonio intersit, dummodo urgeat gravis causa et pro suo prudenti arbitrio Ordinarius iudicet satis cautum esse catholicae educationi universae prolis et remotioni periculi perversonis alterius coniugis. Can. 1066.—Si publicus peccator aut censura notorie innodatus prius ad sacramentalem confessionem accedere aut cum Ecclesia reconciliari recusaverit, parochus eius matrimonio ne assistat, nisi gravis urgeat causa, de qua, si fieri possit, consultat Ordinarum.

The declaration of the Sacred Congregation of the Holy Office, on the 11th of August 1949, declared that the prescriptions of the Canons 1061 and 1062 were applicable to Communists (cf. AAS 41 (1949) 427).

CLEMENT XIII
1758-1769

DIVIDED FAMILIES

Apost. Let. *Quantopere*, November 16, 1763—to Cardinal de Rohan, Bishop of Strasbourg.

You are certainly not unaware of how much the **31** Catholic Church abhors marriages contracted between *(84)* Catholics and heretics. The eternal salvation of her children is the object of her zealous preoccupation and therefore she has always dissuaded them from forming such unions.

The heretical woman

It is Our conviction that such unions will intro- **32** duce much harm in the midst of the Catholic Church. *(83)* If the mother who has the early education of her children is a stranger to our holy faith, ought we not fear for the religious formation of the children? The maternal instinct will impel the mother to use every solicitude for what has to do with the eternal salvation of her children and therefore she will not lose any occasion of instructing them in the doctrines of her sect, which she judges to be the only true one. If she sees her husband observe fast and abstinence on the days prescribed, approach the Sacrament of Penance in a devout manner to purify his soul from sin, or, again, proceed to the Eucharistic Table, then she will not let slip the opportunity—and the occasion will present itself often enough—of ridiculing these holy observances, as if they were so many useless practices. It will necessarily follow that, little by little, there will take root in the soul of the children a contempt for things most holy. And the principles that inspire their spirit from early infancy will be uprooted only with difficulty, if at all.

The husband

33   If it happens to be the case that the mother professes
(83) the Catholic Faith and the father belongs to a heretical sect, he will before the children ridicule the words and the actions of the wife and everything else that pertains to religion. What will be the effect on the still weak souls of the children? Will not the influence that the authority of the father exerts over them perhaps make them doubt the religion of their mother?

34   Besides, what will happen on the day when a serious
(83) discussion on the question of religion arises between husband and wife? The children's minds excited by the arguments put forward by each parent will become muddled, and they will insensibly fall into religious indifference. Nothing is more contrary to faith, nothing more harmful than this attitude; for it completely ruins any religious faith, be it true or false.

35   It is clear that the Lutheran heresy sees in such mar-
(83) riages the best prospects of spreading its doctrines. In fact, young women well grounded in the Lutheran heresy to whom permission has been given—except in some places—to establish their residence with their husbands, when the latter profess the Catholic Faith, will necessarily follow their husbands wherever he desires to settle. Besides, the young bride will receive in her husband's house many adherents of her sect. One will not be able

to refuse entry to the ministers of this same sect who will come to pay their respects to the woman. And they will use their ministry to confirm their sheep in their own errors and point out to the mother what she must do to destroy the young faith produced by the true doctrine in the souls of her children at the very moment in which this begins to develop.

In vain, therefore, is the Catholics' zeal to extirpate **36** the errors condemned by the Church in the places where (83) they flourish, if afterwards these same errors flourish with impunity among Catholics. Another consideration can be added: if of the two parties the Catholic member dies and leaves young children, the other party who is heretical will have full liberty to contaminate their souls with the insidious doctrines of his sect.

You see, therefore, beloved children, what the Catholic religion can expect from children born of such unions. One could further ask whether from such a marriage entered into with the purpose of propagating the Catholic Faith, there has instead arisen only advantage for heresy and an extension of its dire effects, and what is worse, whether the only result has been an increase in indifference towards all religion; for this disposition more often than not opens the way to impiety.

PIUS VI
1775-1799

ORIGIN OF THE CHURCH'S POWER

Letter *Post factum tibi*, February 2, 1782, to the Archbishop of Treviso.

There is no doubt that the Church has the right to establish impediments to marriage, for the Council of Trent has defined: "If anyone says that the Church has not been able to establish diriment impediments to matrimony, or that by establishing them she has erred: let him be anathema" (a). Even the Catholic teachers most favorable to lay authority never hesitated to recognize in this power a right given to the Church by Christ, and one which she has used from the earliest times right up to the present day. 37 (46, 49)

Very ancient documents could be quoted as regards this usage, referring precisely to the times in which pagan princes never made such a concession to the Church, which often had to suffer the most violent persecutions. Yet the ecclesiastical decrees on this matter are anterior to the imperial constitutions; indeed, the former seemed to have served as a model for the latter. It can be noted in particular that the impediment of affinity in the early centuries was considered as diriment by ecclesiastical law, as can be attested by the letter of St. Basil to Diodorus and by the Council of Neo-Caesarea (a), at which a 38 (46, 49)

37a Council of Trent, sess. 24. 4—Cf. Denz. 974.
38a Council of Neocesarea, can. 2.

celebrated jurist stated in a note on the Council of Granada, that such an impediment had been abrogated by the ancient law of the Romans.

39   Therein is a proof *a fortiori* of the Church's right to
(46, establish such impediments and of the lack of foundation
48) in the arguments of those who seek to evade the definition of the Council of Trent by pretending that the Council did not mean to define whether this power was given to the Church by Christ, or whether it was expressly or tacitly conceded to her instead by the princes. Since the Apostles made effective use of this power as regards the marriages of the faithful; and since it is impossible to pretend that their immediate successors obtained this power through a concession of the State, it must necessarily be concluded that they received it from Our Lord, together with the Power of the Keys. To say that in using this power they were mistaken, involves postulating a mistake consisting in arrogating to themselves a power that they did not have and they then would have usurped the legitimate rights belonging to the civil power. But everyone will easily understand that such an hypothesis is absurd.

40   It is also known that it has been defined in the same
(46, place (a) that the Church has the power of establishing
67) various degrees of prohibiting and diriment impediments. Consequently, since at no moment can a dogma of faith have been or be now false, it follows necessarily that from the beginning of the Church and at all times since it has been true and will be true in the future that the Church possesses in reality the power that the Council

40a Council of Trent, sess. 24, can. 3.—Denz. 973.

attributes to her. Now, on the contrary, if even
a tacit concession on the part of the princes had been
necessary, it would follow that what the Council declares
could not have been verified in the first centuries at the
time of the pagan princes and it could not be verified
today in those regions where Christians are subject to the
dominion of the infidels. Besides, if princes could annul
the impediments sanctioned by the Church with the revo-
cation of a power benevolently conceded by them, then
what was defined at the Council of Trent would no longer
be true and we would find ourselves faced with the monstrous situation of being obliged at a certain point to
deny to the Church a power which had already been
recognized to be hers by the Holy Spirit Himself through
an Ecumenical Council (b).

(*Historical surveys.—Limits of Episcopal power.*)

HERETICAL WOMEN

Letter *Exequendo nunc,* July 13, 1782—to the Archbishop of Malines.

(*Difficulties of the Belgian Bishops as regards mixed
marriages.*)

We must not, however, withdraw from the unani-   **41**
mous opinion of Our Predecessors and from ecclesiastical (82,

---

40b Today the legislation of the Church on this matter
is fixed by the C.I.C., can. 1038.—§ 1. *Supreme tantum
auctoritatis ecclesiasticae est authentice declarare quan-
donam ius divinum matriomonium impediat vel dirimat.
§ 2. Eidem supremae auctoritati privative ius est alia
impedimenta matrimonium impedientia vel dirimentia
pro baptizatis costituendi per modum legis sive univer-
salis sive particularis.*

85) discipline, which do not approve of marriages between
two heretical parties or between a Catholic and a heretic,
and much less so in the case where a dispensation is
necessary for some degree of consanguinity. The question presents itself often enough and among the innumerable decisions, completely uniform, which are opposed to such sacriligious unions, there is to be noted
the special prohibition addressed to one of your predecessors, the Archbishop of Malines, by Pope Clement XI,
which Benedict XIV quotes in his letter dated June 29,
1748 (a). We cannot abandon this line of conduct, because We have not the right to do so. This is because of
the danger of the perversion of the Catholic party, especially if the heretic is a woman; according to the very
wise observations of Cardinal Bellarmine, who, relying
on examples taken from the Sacred Texts—Adam's dis-
obedience at Eve's instigation; Solomon's idolatry provoked by the wiles of his wives; Achab's perversity
aroused by Jezabel's counsels—writes in the thirty-fifth of
his intimate letters: "Woman's nature is such that it is
much easier for them to lead their husbands into error
than for their husbands to lead them to truth".

42   However, we do not wish to increase in any way
(82, your difficulties and those of your Brethren in the Epis-
83)   copate, nor bring on them those inevitable criticisms
which they seem to fear. As regards the question of the
simple permission or concession to be granted, We repeat
what Benedict XIV, quoted above, said in his reply to the
Bishop of Breslau, on September 12, 1750, namely: "that
he could not approve with a positive act that dispensations

41a Cf. above, n. 25-30.

be granted for marriages between heretics, or between heretics and Catholics, but that he could however close his eyes"; and he added: "The fact that We know and tolerate it ought to be sufficient to reassure your conscience, since in this question there is no conflict with the divine and the natural law, but only ecclesiastical law. We testify before you at the feet of the Crucified that what We do at the present time is done so that greater evils may be avoided for religion." He concludes by saying that it is necessary to use all means to prevent the spread of this evil.

(*Reply to the difficulties arising from civil legislation.—Conduct to be followed by parish priests in the case of mixed marriages.*)

COMPETENCE OF THE CHURCH

Letter *Deessemus Nos*, September 16, 1788—to the Bishop of Mottola.

(*Sentence of nullity pronounced by the Bishop without due reason.*)

It is a dogma of Faith that Matrimony, which was only an indissoluble contract before the coming of Christ, became, after the Incarnation, one of the seven Sacraments of the Evangelical Law. This was defined, under pain of excommunication, by the Holy Council of Trent against the heretics and the impious of those times (a). It follows that to the Church alone, the guardian of everything that refers to the Sacraments, belongs every right

43
*(4,
7,
14,
49,
55,
67,
69)*

43a Council of Trent, sess. 24, can. 1.—Denz. 971.

and power to determine the validity of this contract which was elevated to the high dignity of a Sacrament; and in consequence, it belongs to the Church alone to judge the validity or invalidity of marriages. That is so obvious that—wishing to oppose those who recklessly affirmed, either in writing or in speech, as is again so widely done in our days, that this is a practice foreign to the Church's spirit and unheard of at the time of the Apostles,—the Council was induced to add a special canon of condemnation and to put under pain of excommunication whoever dared to say that matrimonial cases are not within the competence of ecclesiastical judges (b).

(*Discussions as regards the cases of fact.*)

44   The spirit and motive of this law are so extensive that
(46, they leave no room for exception or limitation. If these
47, cases are reserved exclusively to the Church's judgment
49) because the matrimonial contract is truly and properly one of the seven Sacraments of the Evangelical Law, and indeed this matter of the sacrament is common to all matrimonial cases, then all these cases must belong exclusively to the ecclesiastical judges, since in all of them there is this matter of the sacrament (a). This is the unanimous opinion of the canonists, even of those less inclined to favor the Church's rights.

43b Ibid., can. 12.—Denz.—This doctrine was continued by the C.I.C., can. 1016.—*Baptizatorum matrimonium regitur iure non solum divino, sed etiam canonico. salva competentia civilis potestatis circa mere civilis eiusdem matrimonii effectus.*

44a *Spiritus vero sive ratio legis adeo patet, ut nullum exceptioni aut limitationi locum relinquant: si enim hae causae non alia ratione pertinent ad unum Ecclesiae iudicium, nisi quia contractus matrimonialis est vere et*

(Discussion of the particular case that occasioned the letter.)

In this matter the Church's authority is so great and **45** of such a nature that it is not possible to issue sentences *(49,* regarding matrimonial cases unless the conditions already *55)* established by the Church are observed, namely, to keep in mind the hierarchical order, which is of divine institution, and by complying with the laws promulgated by the Church herself. Every time that the civil powers make laws regarding these cases, they do so only as simple executors and defenders of ecclesiastical law, following in all things the holy rules by declaring that they do not intend with their sanctions either to touch or include that which concerns "the matter of the Sacrament or the substance of the contract, which is the *materia proxima* of the Sacrament, or the ecclesiastical effects" (a). These are the very words used by the commissioners of Louis XIII, in his name, to the French clergy (b).

(Judgment on the sentence passed by the Bishop.)

proprie unum ex septem legis evangelicae sacramentis, sicut haec sacrimenti ratio communis est omnibus causis matrimonialibus, ita omnes hae causae spectare unice debent ad iudices ecclesiasticos, cum eadem ratio sit in omnibus.

45a *Quoties principes saeculi leges condiderunt quae has causas spectarent, hoc ipsum praestiterint ut meri executores et defensores legum ecclesiasticarum, sacras per omnia sequentes regulas, declarando nolle se suis sanctionibus complecti ac comprehendere id quod respicit "ratio Sacramenti, seu substantiam contractus quae materia Sacramenti proxima est, seu effectus ecclesiasticos".*

45b Natale Alessandro, *Theol. dogm. moral., Tractatus de Sacr. Matrimonii,* 1. II, c. 2, art. 3, pr. 1.

THE PREVALENT INTENTION

Letter *Gravissimam*, July 11, 1789, to the Archbishop of Prague.

(*Résumé of the Episcopal consultation concerning the validity of marriage contracted by Lutherans who admit the possibility of divorce.—Observations on the particulars of the case which motivated the consultation.*)

46
(12) That marriage contracted with a condition contrary to its substance is null and void can be argued from the enclosed decision of Gregory IX and Benedict XIV (a). However, following once again the teaching of the same Pontiff, (b), if it is not a matter of formal condition included in the contract, but only an error on the part of the contracting parties, who are under the impression that divorce can be granted in the case of adultery, it can be presumed that since they wish to contract marriage, they desired to do so in a manner conforming to the prescriptions of Christ, and therefore as an indissoluble contract. Thus their personal error is to a certain extent annulled by their wishing to marry in a manner conforming to the institution of Christ (c).

46a *De Syn. Dioec.*, 1, XIII, c. 22.
46b Ibid.
46c *Locum esse praesumptioni ut dum matrimonium contrahere voluerunt, illud iuxta institutum Christi atque adeo indissolubile inire voluerunt, nimirum generali ea intentione contrahendi iuxta institutionem Christi privatum illum errorem quodammodo absorbente.*
Cf. C.I.C., can. 1082.—§ 1. *Ut matrimonialis consensus haberi possit, necesse est ut contrahentes saltem non*

(*Motives for believing that this interpretation is to be applied to the marriages of Lutherans.*)

If there be no canonical impediment, it must be con- **47** cluded that a voluntary consent to make a contract in *(12)* conformity to Christ's law is required and is sufficient to constitute a valid marriage. However, when a condition contrary to the substance of matrimony is introduced into the contract, the intention of making a contract according to Christ's law is positively excluded, by reason of the opposition between the law of Christ and the condition positively and explicitly posited; the consent then cannot constitute a true marriage.

THE NATURAL LAW

Letter *Litteris tuis*, July 11, 1789, to the **Bishop** of Agra.

(*Summary of the difficulties relative to those marriages contracted in an heretical sect which does not believe in indissolubility of marriage.*)

ignorent matrimonium esse societatem permanentem inter virum et mulierum ad filios procreandos.
§ 2. *Haec ignorantia post pubertatem non praesumitur.*
Can. 1092—*Conditio semel apposita et non revocata:*
1⁰ *Si sit futuro necessaria vel impossibilis vel turpis, sed non contra matrimonii substantiam, pro non adiecta habeatur;*
2⁰ *Si de futuro contra matrimonii substantiam, illud reddit invalidum;*
3⁰ *Si de futuro licità, valorem matrimonii suspendit;*
4⁰ *Si de praeterito vel de praesenti, matrimonium erit validum vel non, prout id quod conditioni subest, exsistit vel non.*

48
(14,
57,
75,
77)
This is the doctrine of the Council of Trent (a): "The first parent of the human race, moved by the Divine Spirit, declared that marriage is a perpetual and indissoluble bond when he stated 'This now is bone of my bones and flesh of my flesh' (b). Christ confirmed the same stability of the bond which had been proclaimed by Adam so long ago when he declared: 'what God hath joined together, let no man put asunder'" (c). Thus marriage in the very state of nature, and certainly long before it was raised to the dignity of a sacrament in the true sense of the word, was divinely instituted in such a manner that its bond was perpetual and indissoluable, so that it cannot be dissolved by any civil law.

49
(10,
12,
14,
55)
Even if this sacramental nature can be separated from marriage as in the case of infidels, nevertheless, in such a marriage there must remain—as there certainly does remain—that perpetual bond which from the very beginning of time is by divine law so inherent in matrimony that it cannot be subject to any civil power. Thus, any marriage which is said to be a contract, or is contracted in such a way as to be a true marriage, will then have at the same time that perpetual bond which by divine institution is the basis of every true marriage. If this were not the case, then there must be supposed a contract without such a perpetual bond; but this would not be true marriage; but an illicit union contrary to divine law and which therefore cannot be lawfully entered into nor maintained (a).

48a Council of Trent, sess. 24.—Denz. 969.
48b Gen. 2:23.   48c Matt. 19:6.
49a *Quodcumque matrimonium contrahi dictatur, vel ita contrahitur, ut reapse sit verum matrimonium tumque*

Therefore, whoever is under the impression that **50** marriage, because it is not a sacrament, is only a purely *(6,* civil contract and as a consequence can be declared null *10,* by the civil law is deceived. Rather, the contrary is true. In *56,* other words, marriage is not a civil contract, but a *57)* natural contract instituted and ratified by divine law prior to any civil society. Besides, there is an essential difference distinguishing it from all other purely civil contracts, namely, that in the latter the consent can be legally supplied, while no human power can validly supply consent in a matrimonial contract.

Consequently, since there arises from every contract **51** a mutual right for the contracting parties, and as the *(10,* nature of matrimony is such that it confers on each party *11,* the right to the body of the other (a), it would not be *12)* possible to attribute the quality of a true matrimonial contract to a union which established a marriage on the condition that it could be dissolved. Such a union would not confer any right to ask for conjugal rights from the partner, but would rather bring with it the obligation of dissolving such an illegimate bond. Such a pact, since it does not confer any matrimonial right, would not even have a title sufficient for it to be called a matrimonial contract.

adiunctum habetit perpetuum illum nexum divino omni matrimonio contrahentem; vel contrahi supponitur sine illo perpetuo nexu, tumque verum matrimonium non est, sed illicita coniunctio, ad divinae legi ex obiecto repugnans, quae proinde nec iniri potest, nec retineri.

51a Cf. C.I.C., can. 1111.—Utrique coniugi ab ipso matrimonii inito aequum ius et officium est quod attinet ad actus proprios coniugalis vitae.

(Application of these principles to the difficulties proposed.)

JANSENIST ERRORS

Apost. Const. *Auctorem fidei,* August 28, 1794—
which condemned the schismatic Council of Pistoia.

Proposition 58—Betrothal

52   As if an act which opens the way to the sacrament is
(49, not under this aspect subject to the laws of the Church,
55) the proposition maintaining that a betrothal properly
so called constitutes a purely civil act, preparing the way
to the celebration of matrimony, and that it is entirely
subject to the prescriptions of civil law is false, damages
the Church's rights as regards the effects deriving even
from the betrothal in virtue of the canonical sanctions
and derogates from the discipline established by the
Church (a).

Proposition 59—Authority of the Civil power over impediments

53   Contrary to canons 3, 4, 9, 12 of the 24th Session of
(46, the Council of Trent, and heretical is the doctrine of the
56) Synod affirming that at least in origin there belongs to
the Supreme Civil Authority the right to establish diriment impediments which render the matrimonial contract null; because the original right is said essentially
to be connected with the right of dispensing; adding,
that the Church, thanks to the consent or connivance of

52a Cf. Denz. **1558.**

the civil powers, had been able to establish impediments that invalidate the very matrimonial contract; as if the Church of her own power has not always been able to establish impediments for Christian marriages, and can still do so, that not only render such marriage illicit but also render it null as regards the bond and which bind Christians in infidel territories; and also to dispense from the same.

Proposition 60

Likewise, the Synod's request to the civil power to eliminate from the number of the impediments the one concerning spiritual relationship and the other called public honesty, whose origins are to be found in Justinian's collections; to restrict the impediment of affinity and of relationship originating from any union, whether licit or illicit, to the fourth degree, according to the civil computation for the lateral and oblique line, so as to leave no hope of obtaining a dispensation; inasmuch as it attributes the right to the civil power either to abolish or to restrict the impediments established and approved by the authority of the Church, and inasmuch as it supposes that the Church can be deprived by the civil power of the right of dispensing from the impediments established and approved by them:—is subversive of the liberty and power of the Church, contrary to the Council of Trent and arises from an heretical principle already condemned (a). **54** *(46, 56)*

53a Cf. Denz. 1559.
54a Cf. Denz. 1560.

PIUS VII
1800-1823

AFTER A DIVORCE SENTENCE

Letter *Etsi Fraternitatis,* October 8, 1803—to the Archbishop of Mainz.

(*Resumé of the difficulties proposed by the Archbishop.*)

To reply to you in a fitting and comprehensive manner, according to the duty of our Pastoral Office, regarding the above mentioned problems, We deem it necessary to present first of all two principles which constitute the foundation of the whole question and which always must be held in mind, especially when the matter is that of entering or dissolving marriages between Catholics and heretics or even between heretics themselves. **55** *(84, 85)*

The principles
(*The Church's abhorrence of mixed marriages.*)

The first principle is that the Church has always prohibited and condemned marriages contracted between Catholics and heretics as harmful and detestable. We could easily prove that by quoting an innumerable number of decrees of Councils and Supreme Pontiffs, if it were not sufficient to call to mind what was written by Our Predecessor of immortal memory, Benedict XIV, both in his Encyclical Letter to the Primate, Archbishops, and Bishops of Poland (a), and later in his memorable **56** *(85)*

56a Cf. above, n. 25-30.

work regarding the diocesan Synod. Even when these marriages are tolerated in certain places, on account of the difficulties of the times, this is only by a permission that must in no way be considered an approval or consent, but rather a tolerance—not given of one's own free will—to avoid further and greater evils. These were the words of Pius VI, of happy memory, not so long ago to the Bishops of Breslau, Rosenau and Zips.

Incompetence of the civil power to dissolve marriage

57
(57,
75,
80)
    The second principle is that the sentence of lay tribunals and non-Catholic assemblies which issue sentences of nullity and attempt to dissolve marriages have no value or effect in the eyes of the Church.

You ask what a parish priest must do when one of the parties, freed from his first marriage and having obtained his liberty by a sentence of a non-Catholic tribunal, wishes to wed a Catholic. You ask if the parish priest can assist at this marriage and give the nuptial blessing, as some have dared to do in your diocese, (as you tell us) you yourselves, by the wisdom that distinguishes you, should understand that such priests commit a very grave crime and betray the sacred ministry, if they approve of such marriages by their presence and ratify them with their blessing! On the other hand, it cannot be called a marriage but an adulterous union, since the impediment—the bond of the first marriage—which persists and remains unaltered—cannot be dissolved or annulled by the sentence of a non-Catholic tribunal. As long as such an impediment remains and persists every other union between the man and the woman is adulterous. Therefore, instead of sweet and persuasive words, it is preferable that the parish priest seriously exhort the person not to commit such a grave crime and sin against the law of God, a law He established from the beginning of the world, and therefore He said: "What God hath joined together, let no man put asunder" (a). If the person obstinately refuses to listen to his parish priest and unites himself with a non-Catholic, thus committing an infamous adultery, and if the parish priest sees that it could be highly dangerous to religion to insist again and oppose his will to such a union, he can then bear in silence such a monstrous crime, but he can never assist at such a union, much less bless it. If the secular power orders, threatens or reproves, "we must obey God rather than men" (b). The priest fo God, according to the words of St. Cyprian, servant of the Gospel and defender of Christ's precepts, can be put to death but he can never be vanquished (c).

Repentant Divorcees

To give a complete answer to the questions which **58** you have proposed to Us, it must still be decided *(81)* whether the wedded parties belonging to the Catholic religion, who after the dissolution of the first marriage by means of the sole authority of a non-Catholic court contract a second marriage before a non-Catholic minister, and then, repentant of the crime committed, humbly ask forgiveness can or cannot be admitted to the sacraments. There can be no doubt at all on the matter, pro-

57a Matt. 19:6.
57b Acts 5:29.
57c Cf. letter to Cornelius "contra haereticos". Migne, P.L., 3, 825.

vided they do the penance imposed on them, and first of all separate from the second party, if the first party is still living. However, if the first husband or wife is dead, and the two parties actually living together are Catholics, it is for the Bishop to decide what must be done so that the marriage can be established sacramentally and according to the law. If it is a case of a Catholic person who wishes to marry a non-Catholic—whether it be the case that the first marriage has been rightly and legitimately dissolved by a double sentence of the Ecclesiastical judge; or whether it be the case that the first marriage has been naturally annulled and dissolved through the death of the partner—the Bishop will have to act with caution and the utmost care.

59   As the Church has always abhorred marriages be-
(81) tween heretics and Catholics and has always forbidden them by most severe laws—because at all times there is hidden therein for the Catholic party the grave danger of perversion and alienation from the faith and also because the Catholic education of the children of both sexes has always been proven to be uncertain and doubtful—let the Bishops reject and refuse such unions as far as they can in all charity and Christian gentleness. If the damage and the perversion of the Catholic spouse can be avoided and the Christian education of the children assured according to the conditions which Benedict XIV, in the above quoted letter to the Bishops of Poland (a), prescribed to be diligently observed, and if you, Venerable Brethren, or your suffragan Bishops ask Us for a dispensation, We will not refuse to heed your prayers

59a Cf. above, n. 25-30.

in certain cases and for a pressing reason whenever the good of religion and the salvation of souls makes it necessary.

DISPARITY OF CULT AND MIXED MARRIAGES

Letter *Que Votre Majesté,* June 26, 1805, to the Emperor Napoleon (a).

(Regret expressed by the Pope at his not being able to declare null the marriage of the emperor's brother, since the arguments brought to light have no true value: summary of the arguments.)

First, disparity of cult, considered by the Church as a diriment impediment, is not verified between two baptized persons, even if one of them does not happen to be in communion with the Church. This impediment is to be found only in those marriages contracted between a Christian and an infidel (b). Marriages between Prottestants and Catholics, no matter how much they are disapproved of by the Church, are recognized by her as valid. **60** *(12, 82, 84)*

It is not exact to say that the law of France, relative to marriages of non-emancipated children and minors contracted without the parents' and guardians' consent, **61** *(12, 54-*

60a André, *Cours alphabétique et métodique de Droit Canon.* Nouvelle edition (Paris 1853) 2. 62.

60b The same legislation has been fixed by the C.I.C, can. 1070.—§1. *Nullum est matrimonium contractum a persona non baptizata cum persona baptizata in Ecclesia catholica vel ad eandem ex haeresi aut schismate conversa.*

56, renders them null as regards the sacrament. The very
108) civil legislative power declared, at the instance of the
clergy assembled in the year 1629, that by establishing
the nullity of these marriages the legislators intended to
speak only of the civil effects of marriage and that the
lay judges could not give any other sense or interpetation
to the law, since Louis XIII, the author of this declaration, knew full well that the secular power had not the
right to establish diriment impediments to matrimony
as a sacrament.

In fact, the Church, far from declaring null the bond
of those marriages made without the parents' and guardians' consent, while reprobating them, has at all times declared them valid and this above all at the Council of
Trent (a).

(*In the marriage discussed there had been neither
abduction nor defect of form.*)

62 Your Majesty ought to understand that the docu-
(16, ments which We have at hand place it outside of Our
48, power to pronounce a sentence of nullity. If, besides the
50, circumstances already alleged, there were other details
81) which could bring to light the proof of some fact which
would constitute an impediment capable of inducing
nullity, We would then be able to base Our judgment on
this proof and pronounce a decree which would conform
to the rules of the Church. However, We cannot Our-

61a Session 24, cap. 1, *Tametsi.*—Cf. Denz. 990.—Cf.
C.I.C., can., 1034.—*Parochus graviter filiosfamilias min-
ores horetetur ne nuptias ineant, insciis aut rationabiliter
invitis parentibus; quod si abnuerint, eorum matrimonio
ne assistat, nisi consulto prius loci Ordinario.*

selves depart from these rules by pronouncing the invalidity of a marriage which, according to the declaration of God, no human power can dissolve.

If We usurped an authority We did not have We would render Ourselves culpable of the most abominable abuse of Our sacred ministry before the tribunal of God and the entire Church.

(*Confidence that the emperor will understand the inability of the Pope and his regret at not being able to satisfy the request.*)

A NECESSARY SEVERITY

Encycl. *Vix nova a Nobis,* February 27, 1809, to the French episcopate.

(*Résumé of the extraordinary powers already conferred on the French episcopate.—New concessions and new demands.*)

Some of you also asked Us for the faculty of dispensing or of allowing marriage to be contracted between two parties, one of whom professes the Catholic Faith and the other heresy. We think that you know very well that the true Catholic Church, the Church of Jesus Christ, has always disapproved of marriage with heretics. The Church holds them in abhorrence as Clement XI, of happy memory, said: "Because they are bound up with innumerable difficulties and manifold spiritual dangers" (a). The Church has almost the same laws both to prohibit Christians from contracting marriage with infidels

63
(82-85)

63a Letter of June 23, 1707.

and to prohibit the sacrilegious union of Catholics with heretics. We must also be bitterly afflicted, as was Our Predecessor of happy memory Benedict XIV, to find Catholics so foolishly entangled by a shameful and criminal passion to such a point that they no longer abhor or feel it their duty to abstain from such detestable unions, unions Our Holy Mother Church has unceasingly condemned and prohibited. Besides the obvious ever present danger of perversion in which the Catholic party and the children who may be born from such a union find themselves, it will also be very difficult for the wedded parties to live together in perfect harmony since they do not share the same faith. Without doubt, in such a union family peace and tranquility will never find its true meaning. The Holy See has always based itself on these very grave and obvious reasons to prevent such danger in as far as it is possible, and it is for these reasons that such permission is not usually granted. When it is granted, it is done unwillingly, with the greatest caution, and only in the gravest circumstances, circumstances which are practically of a public and notorious nature.

(*Impossibility of granting the faculty to dispense from the impediment of mixed religion.*)

PIUS VIII
1829-1830

NEW DIGNITY OF MATRIMONY

Encycl. *Traditi humilitati,* May 21, 1829.

(*On the occasion of his recent election as Supreme Pontiff Pius VIII begs the prayers of the Bishops and offers them various recommendations.*)

But there is another matter, in view of the times in which We live, that We have resolved to recommend to your most ardent zeal for the welfare of souls. It is this, that you also inculcate in your flock the same respectful veneration for the sanctity of matrimony, for this sacred bond, so that nothing be done which may offend its sacramental dignity, or dishonor the purity of the nuptial bed, or permit the least doubt as regards the indissolubility of the marriage bond. The only suitable means for effecting this object is to declare openly and clearly to the Christian people that matrimony is subject not only to human laws but also most certainly to the divine law; that it is not to be classed among earthly matters but among holy matters, and, that therefore it belongs entirely to the Church to regulate it. **64** *(5, 6, 99, 101, 103)*

In fact, the matrimonial union, which had as its first object the propagation of the family, has now been raised by Our Lord Jesus Christ to the dignity of a sacrament and enriched with heavenly gifts (grace perfects nature). The Church rejoices not so much in seeing the succession of the children of men, but rather in educating them in God's ways and in His divine religion, so as to **65** *(22, 24, 101)* increase the number of those who adore the sovereign Lord of the universe. In fact, it is certain that this conjugal union, of which God is the author, represents the sublime and perpetual union of Our Lord Jesus Christ and the Church and that this intimate society which is formed by means of marriage between a man and his bride is a sacrament, a sacred image of the immortal love of Jesus Christ for His Church, His Spouse. It is necessary, therefore, to instruct the people about these matters; to explain to them what has been established and what has been condemned by the canons of the Church and the decrees of the Councils, so that all nations will do everything to assure the effects of the virtue of the sacrament and not dare to do what the Church has rejected.　　　　　(*Another request for prayers.*)

CONDITION FOR DISPENSATIONS

Apost. Letter *Litteris altero,* March 25, 1830—to the Bishops of the province of Cologne.

(*Difficulties arising from mixed marriages caused by the Prussian civil laws.—Hopes for a solution.*)

66
(84-
86)
Coming therefore to the question, We think it unnecessary to teach you what is the rule and practice of the Church as regards the mixed marriages in question. You are aware that she has always abhorred such unions which present so many difficulties and spiritual dangers and it is for this reason that she has always diligently watched over the execution of the canonical religious laws which prohibit them. Cases can be found, it is true, where some Roman Pontiffs have at times waived this prohibition and have dispensed from the observance of the sacred canons, but they did so only reluctantly and

for very grave reasons. Nevertheless, their constant practice was to add an express stipulation and preventative conditions to the dispensations under which they permitted these marriages, namely, that the Catholic party should not be perverted by the non-Catholic party, but rather on the contrary that the former should realize that he was bound to use all the means at his disposal to lead the latter from error; that the children of both sexes born from the union should be brought up exclusively in the sanctity of the Catholic religion.

You know, Venerable Brethren, that these precautions aim at respecting the natural and divine laws on this matter. It is recognized that those Catholics—men and women—who wed non-Catholics in such a rash manner as to expose themselves and their future children to the danger of perversion, not only violate the sacred canons, but directly and gravely sin against the natural and divine law. You fully understand therefore that We would render Ourselves culpable of a serious crime before God and the Church were We to authorize for you or the priests in your dioceses a line of conduct relative to mixed marriages from which it could be argued that if these unions are not approved formally and verbally, yet they are sanctioned at least confusedly in fact and reality. **67 (84, 86, 100)**

While praising the zeal which up to the present has endowed your efforts to keep the Catholics under your spiritual care from the snares of such marriages, We urge you earnestly in the name of the Lord to continue with the same aim "in all patience and doctrine" (a): your labors will be abundantly rewarded in heaven.

67a 2 Tim. 4:2.

Duty of the clergy

68   In the meantime, according to these instructions,
(83, everytime that a Catholic, especially a woman, wishes
84, to wed a non-Catholic, it will be necessary for the Bishop
100) or the pastor to instruct her carefully regarding the canonical regulations about these marriages and to warn
her seriously of the sin to which she would render herself liable before God, were she to violate them. Above
all, it would be best to make her realize that the most
certain dogma of our religion is that "outside of the
Catholic Faith no one can be saved;" and that as a consequence she must admit that her conduct will be cruel
and atrocious towards the children that she expects from
God if she enters a marriage knowing that their education will depend completely on the will of a non-Catholic father.

According as prudence advises it, these salutary
warnings ought to be repeated, particularly with the approach of the wedding day and in the time established
for the publication of the banns, during which there may
come to light other canonical impediments which can
invalidate the marriage. If in certain cases the paternal
warnings of priests are not heeded, one will indeed abstain from signalling out these persons for censure, to
prevent any trouble and preserve the Catholic religion
from further evils; but on the other hand the Catholic
priest will have to keep himself from honoring the marriage with any kind of religious ceremony; he will have
to refrain from any act which could be taken as a consent to such a marriage.

(Practical dispositions.)

GREGORY XVI
1831-1846

MIXED MARRIAGES

Encycl. *Summo jugiter*, May 27, 1832—to the Bishops of Bavaria.

On every occasion the Apostolic See has exercised the greatest care that the canons of the Church which rigorously prohibit marriages of Catholics with heretics be strictly observed. Although at times it has been necessary to tolerate them in certain places in order to avoid a greater scandal, nonetheless Roman Pontiffs have always used every means within their power to bring to the mind of the faithful how dangerous and harmful these unions are for their eternal salvation and of what a crime the man or woman who dares to violate the Church's holy laws in such a matter renders himself blameworthy. If the Popes have sometimes granted a dispensation in some particular cases from these holy and canonical safeguards, it was always done against their wishes and for some very grave reason. When granting such a privilege, however, they have always expressly exacted the necessary guarantees as a preliminary condition to the marriage, not only to avoid the danger of the perversion of the Catholic party—who on the contrary should know that he is obliged to use all means to convert his partner—but also to ensure the Catholic education of all the children. **69** *(84, 86)*

Considering the most holy conduct of Our Predecessors in such matters, We—who notwithstanding Our **70** *(82)*

unworthiness have been raised by divine Providence to
the Chair of Peter—cannot be but profoundly grieved
that in your diocese, according to exact and numerous
reports, there are persons who endeavor to use all means
to propagate the principle of absolute liberty to contract mixed marriages, and bring forward opinions contrary to the Catholic truth to give further authority to
the proposal.

Outline of the errors diffused in Bavaria

71
(75, In fact, We have been informed that these persons
77, dare to affirm that Catholics can freely and lawfully
83) contract such unions, without any need of a dispensation
from the Holy See, although according to the canons a
dispensation must be granted in each individual case.
Again, they assert that it is not necessary to comply with
the preliminary conditions, in particular as regards the
children's education in the truths of the Catholic religion.
Their audacity goes so far as to assert that such a marital
union must be approved even when the heretical party
has been separated by divorce from the wife or husband
who is still living. Furthermore, they strive to intimidate
priests, threatening to cite them before the civil court if
they refuse to announce the mixed marriages from the
pulpit, and to assist at their celebration, or at least grant
to the future contracting parties dismissorial letters, as
they call them. Last but not least, there are to be found
those who would try to persuade themselves—and have
others believe—that a person can be saved even outside
the bosom of the Catholic Church, saying that heretics
who live and die in the heresy can yet obtain eternal
salvation.

*(The attitude of a great number of Bavarian Cath-
olics is a heartfelt consolation for the Pope.—His hope in
the King's dispositions.)*

The foundation of the Church's doctrine:
unity of faith

To consider the present question, it will be neces-   **72**
sary for Us first to treat the question of faith, without *(83)*
which it is impossible to please God (a), and which, as
We have pointed out, is placed in danger by the teaching
of those who wish to extend the liberty of mixed marriages beyond certain limits. Lastly, you know as well
as We, with what persistence the Fathers inculcated this
article of Faith, which these innovators dare to deny,
namely, that faith and union in the Catholic Church is
necessary for salvation.

This is what St. Ignatius Martyr, one of the most   **73**
celebrated disciples of the Apostles, taught in his letter *(83)*
to the Philadelphians: "Do not be deceived," he wrote
them, "he who adheres to the author of a schism will
not enter the kingdom of God" (a). St. Augustine, speaking to the other bishops of Africa at the Council of Cirta,
said: "Whoever is outside the fold of the Catholic
Church, even though his conduct appear praiseworthy,
will not enjoy eternal life and God's anger will pour
down on him because of the crime that he has committed
by being separated from Jesus Christ" (b). Without
delaying further to quote the almost innumerable citations from other of the older Fathers, We shall limit

72a Hebrews 11:6.
73a Migne, P.G., 5, 699.
73b *Epist.* 141.

Ourselves to quoting the words of Our glorious Predecessor, St. Gregory the Great, who expressly attests that
such is the Church's doctrine on this point. "The Holy,
Universal Church", he says, "teaches that God cannot
be truly adored except within her fold: she insists that all
those who are separated from her will not be saved" (c).

74   This same teaching is declared in a decree on Faith
(83) published by another of Our Predecessors, Innocent III,
in accordance with the 4th Lateran Ecumenical Council,
"that there is only One, Universal Church, outside which
absolutely no one will be saved" (a). Finally, the same
dogma is expressed in the Professions of Faith that were
proposed by the Apostolic See: the one that is in use in
the whole Latin Church (b) as well as in the other two,
one of which is accepted by the Greeks (c) and the
other by all the remaining Oriental Catholics (d).

75   If We have quoted these authorities—among the
(83) many others that could be brought forward—it is certainly not to teach you an article of Faith as if you were
ignorant of it. Far be it from us, Venerable Brethren,
such a suspicion injurious to you! But, the strange audacity with which certain innovators have dared to attack one of the Church's most important and evident
dogmas, left Us so perplexed that We could not refrain
from expressing Ourselves on such a question.

73c *Moral in Job*, 14, 5.
74a   Cap. *Firmiter credimus; cf.* Denz. 430.
74b *Professio fidei Tridentina; cf.* Denz. 994 ss.
74c *Professio fidei Graecis praescripta; cf.* Denz. 1083 ff.
74d Benedict XIV, Lett. Nuper ad Nos; cf. above n. 10.

The consequences: *damage of mixed marriages*

Take courage, therefore, Venerable Brethren; arm **76** yourselves with the sword of the spirit, which is the *(83,* word of God, and work unceasingly to eradicate this *84,* deadly error which is so rapidly gaining ground. Let you *100,* and your priests take the necessary measures to induce *101)* the faithful more than ever to greater zeal to defend the faith and Catholic unity as the only means of salvation and consequently to avoid every danger of separation. When the faithful are truly convinced and strongly conscious of the necessity to conserve this unity, then will they take more heed of the warnings and advice you will give them not to contract marriage with heretics. If, nonetheless grave reasons sometimes determine them to wed, let them not proceed to do so before having received the Church's dispensation and religiously fulfilled the conditions that she usually exacts in such cases as We have already said.

No need to expose oneself to danger

You must therefore point out to the faithful who **77** propose to contract such marriages—to their parents and *(24,* guardians—the regulations of the sacred canons in this *33,* matter and exhort them unceasingly not to dare violate *84,* them at the cost of their souls. If it is necessary, you *86,* should remind them of the precept so universally known, *100)* of natural and divine law, which not only imposes the obligation of avoiding sin, but also its proximate occasion, and this other precept of the same law which orders the parents to bring up their children well, to instruct them in God's ways (a), and therefore to teach

77a cf. Eph. 6:4.

them the true worship of God, which is found only in the fold of the Catholic Church.

78   Exhort the faithful to consider seriously how griev-
(83, ously they would insult the Supreme Majesty, how cruel
100) they would be towards themselves and the children who would be born from the marriage, if by contracting it in a rash manner they should expose to the danger of losing the faith not only themselves but even their children.

Celebration of mixed marriages

79   But, if, notwithstanding everything, it happens that
(86) a Catholic man or woman—little impressed by your warnings and advice—persists in his or her design to contract a mixed marriage without having asked for and obtained a canonical dispensation, or without having fulfilled all the prescribed conditions, then the parish priest will consider it his duty not only to abstain from being present at such a union, but not even to make the publication of the marriage or grant the dismissorial letters. Your duty, Venerable Brethren, is to communicate your intentions in such matters to the priests of your dioceses and to demand that they take no part in such kinds of marriages. In truth, any priest who acts in a manner contrary to these directives—especially in the particular circumstances in Bavaria—would make it appear that he approves these illicit unions, and with his consent would favor a liberty which could only hinder the salvation of souls and the interests of the faith.

80   After all that We have said, it is hardly necessary for
(80) Us to deal with other cases of mixed marriages, much more serious than the previous ones, in which the heretical party is divorced from a wife or husband still living.

You know, Venerable Brethren, that by divine law, the conjugal bond is such that no human power can dissolve it. A mixed marriage would be in such a case not only illicit, but even invalid—an adultery—unless of course the first marriage, considered by the heretical party as dissolved by virtue of the divorce, had been contracted invalidly, as would be the case if there were a real diriment impediment. In this last case, and after having observed the above mentioned norms, let no one proceed to a second marriage before a canonical judgment has been given, which having carefully considered the nature of the first marriage declares it null.

THE RESPONSIBILITY OF THE BISHOPS

Encycl. *Mirari vos,* August 15, 1832.

(*Various matters which recall the solicitude of the Pope and the Bishops.*)

The honorable marriage of Christians that is called by St. Paul "a great sacrament in Christ and in the Church" (a) demands our earnest care so that nothing less than the true opinion should be held and that nothing be introduced which is contrary to its sanctity or injurious to the indissolubility of its bond. Our Predecessor, Pius VIII, of happy memory, had already urgently recommended this to you in his letters (b); but nevertheless the wicked attempts of the impious against this sacrament continue to multiply. Therefore, the faithful must be carefully instructed that once matrimony has

81
(16, 35, 61, 68, 99, 101, 103, 107)

81a Eph. 5:32.
81b cf. above, n. 64.

been legitimately contracted it can neved be dissolved, and that God has prescribed for the married couple a bond and a perpetual union of life which can be broken only by death. Keeping in mind that marriage is a sacred matter, and therefore subject to the Church, let the laws established by her be ever present before them, and let these laws be devoutly and carefully fulfilled as a prescription on whose faithful observance depend the force, validity and legitimacy of marriage. For no reason whatsoever can acts be done which are contrary to the canonical regulations and the decrees of the Councils which regard such matters. It is well known what an unhappy ending these marriages have which are contracted against the Church's discipline or without having first implored the blessing of Heaven or again as a result of a blind passion when the married couple give no thought to the sanctity of the Sacrament or to the mysteries that it enfolds.

SACRED DOMAIN

Encycl. *Commissum divinitus,* May 17, 1835, to the clergy of Switzerland.

(*Interference of the Congress of Baden in the ecclesiastical domain.*)

82 Nothing belongs so much to the Church and is more (47) strictly reserved to her ministers—and this by the will of Christ—than the administration of the Sacraments instituted by Him; for such a motive He established His ministers on earth to be sole judges of the discipline that regulates this dispensation.

It is therefore abominable that the civil power **83** should take to itself such an august power; it is an (54, abominable thing that it should take any decision in 55, such a matter or proffer an order to the sacred minis- 69) ters; further it is a crime if, in its legislation, it inserts regulations which are contrary to the principles that rule the administration of the holy mysteries to the Christian people. All these are rules which have been handed down to us either in writing or verbally from the first times of the Church.

"You know," said Our Predecessor, Gelasius, in his letter to the Emperor Anastasius, "you know, most devoted son, that notwithstanding the dignity which grants you authority over the people, you are subject in all divine matters to the religious authority and must entrust yourself to it for everything that regards your salvation. When it is a matter of administering the heavenly sacraments and of the just rules referring to them, realize that the order of religion assigns you a position which is subordinate and not supreme. Know therefore that in all these things you are subject to the judgment of this religious authority and not to your own" (a).

Nonetheless, although it be so incredible and mon- **84** strous, the Congress of Baden's authority has gone so (9, far as to concern itself with the rules that regulate 83) the administration of the sacraments and to confer rights and powers in this domain on the civil power. Thus there are found articles wherein the members of the Congress rashly and boldly have exercised authority

83a St. Gelasius, *Letter VIII to the Emporer Anastasius.—Migne, P.L.*, 59, 41.

over matrimony; this sacrament which is so great in its relation to Christ and the Church. Thus they are clearly seen to have placed mixed marriages in a favorable light, while an obligation is placed upon Catholic priests to bless such marital unions, and not to concern themselves about the disparity of cult between the contracting parties, and most severe punishments are established against those who do not conform to such regulations.

85
(55,
82,
83,
84,
86)
These regulations must not only be condemned—and rightly so—because the civil power assumes to itself the right of establishing laws concerning the celebration of a divinely instituted sacrament and dares in such a grave matter to impose its authority upon the sacred ministers; but also and above all because these laws favor that most absurd and impious opinion which is called indifferentism, and, what is worse, they are based on this opinion as if it were an indisputable principle. These laws must be also condemned, because they are in open conflict with Catholic truth and with the Church's doctrine which has always held in abomination and prohibited mixed marriages, whether it be on account of the profanation of holy things resulting from this union, or whether it be on account of the great danger of perversion in which the Catholic party places himself and the deplorable education reserved for the children, who will be born from such a union. All these reasons impose the duty of authorizing the celebration of such marriages only under certain very precise conditions established for the avoidance of discord and danger.

Apost. Letter, *Quas Vestro,* April 30, 1841—to the Bishops of Hungary.

(The Pope has the duty to watch over doctrine and discipline.)

The Church's views on marriages between Catholics and non-Catholics are quite sufficiently known. She has always considered such unions as illicit and highly dangerous; on acount of the unworthy communion in sacred matters which they involve, and again on account of the danger of perversion in which the Catholic party is placed, which is followed then by the bad education of the children.   **86** *(82-84)*

(The Pope calls to mind the condemnations already issued by the Sovereign Pontiffs as regards mixed marriages.)

It follows then that if this Holy See has sometimes mitigated the severity of the canons and has authorized such marriages: it has done so reluctantly, for grave reasons; and always with the expresed condition of obtaining the necessary guarantees before marriage not only to avoid the perversion of the Catholic party by the heretic (the Catholic on the contrary must use all his means to convert the heretical party) but also to assure the Catholic education of all the children—male and female—born from such a marriage. He who rashly exposes himself or his future children to the danger of perversion sins gravely against the divine law and the natural law, which also exact these guarantees (a).   **87** *(82, 86)*

87a *Quae cere cautiones in ipsa divina et naturali lege fundantur, in quam procul dubio gravissime peccat quisque se vel futuram sobolem periculo temere committit.*

(The situation in Hungary.—Practical Provisions.)

88
(85,
86)
If therefore, in the dioceses of this kingdom, it occasionally happens that on account of the special conditions of the times, places and persons, it becomes absolutely impossible to avoid the marriage of a Catholic and a non-Catholic without causing a greater scandal or danger to the Catholic religion and the conditions requested by the Church are not forthcoming, and if at the same time (to use the same words of Pius VII in his letter to the Bishops of Mainz) (a), it appears useful to the Church and the common good that such marriages, even though prohibited and illicit, be celebrated in the presence of the parish priest rather than the heretical minister, to whom the parties will more than likely go, then in this case the parish priest or his delegate may assist at the marriage. However, it must be only a material presence—every ecclesiastical rite is to be excluded—as simply a witness, qualified or authorized according to the term in use, so that after having heard the consent of the one and the other party, he can then according to his function write the validly accomplished act in the marriage registry.

89
(85)
However, once again following the opportune recommendations of Our Predecessor, in similar circumstances, bishops and priests will be required to use greater efforts to see that the Catholic party is not a victim of perversion and that the Catholic education of the children is assured. Finally they must seriously admonish the Catholic party of the duty to undertake the conversion of the partner and this will also serve as an opportune means of obtaining God's pardon for the sin.

88a cf. above, n. 5ss.

(The Pope once again declares his displeasure at being bound to tolerate such abuses, and the only motive which induces him to do so is the desire to avoid still greater evils for the Church.)

THE BLESSING OF MIXED MARRIAGES

Brief, *Non sine gravi*, May 23, 1846—to the Bishop of Fribourg.

(Résumé of the teachings of the Encycl. Summo jugiter (see above nos. 69ff) relative to mixed marriages.)

As regards the nuptial blessing, you know full well that the Church usually refuses it even for the mixed marriages which have been authorized by the Holy See and for which have already been assured the required guarantees. Even if there is tolerated the practice introduced in certain places of allowing the blessing to be given at those marriages which enjoy the benefit of a dispensation and for which the required guarantees have been given, this blessing must never be given in the case in which a most grave sin is committed in the very act of the celebration of marriage, because the dispensation and the necessary guarantees are lacking. In practice it must never be tolerated that the sacred rite be associated with these sacrilegious contracts and that God's priests appear as supporting by their action that which they condemn as illicit in their words and preaching. Our enemies are quick to note such action. Certainly they would not care in the least about the blessing of the Catholic priest if it were not for the fact that it is a means for them to make the Christian people forget the canons that condemn these mixed marriages and an opportunity to weak-

90
(84,
86)

en the constant zeal of the Church to restrain her children from such unions which are contracted at the risk of their birthright. Our enemies know that if their wishes were realized it is most likely that Catholic women in particular would be inclined to think that such marriages are not prohibited or at least are not so culpable, seeing that the Church honors them with her rites and the priest's blessing (a).

(*Universal character of these regulations.—Practical provisions.*)

90a The actual legislation on this point is to be found in the C.I.C., can. 1102.—§1. *In matrimoniis inter partem catholicam et partem acatholicam interrogationes de consensu fieri debent secundum praescriptum can. 1095, §1, n. 3.*
2.*Sed omnes sacri ritus prohibentur; quod si e hac prohibitione graviora mala praevideantur, Ordinarius potest aliquam ex consuetis ecclesi   caeremoniis, exclusa semper Missae celebratione,   ittere.*

PIUS IX
1846-1878

SACRAMENT AND CONTRACT

Apost. Letter *Ad Apostolicæ Sedis,* August 22, 1851.
(*Condemnation of the work of John Nepomucene Nuytz entitled*s Institutions de Droit ecclésiastique, *and the* Traité de Droit ecclésiastique, *of the same author.*)

Other errors as regards Matrimony are also main- **91** tained by the author: "that it cannot be demonstrated *(7,* with any proof that Jesus Christ elevated matrimony to *8,* the dignity of a sacrament; that the sacrament is only *46,* an accessory to the marriage contract from which it *49,* can be separated, and that the sacrament itself consists *55,* only in the nuptial blessing; that the matrimonial bond *56,* is not indissoluble by natural law; that the Church does *63)* not have the right to introduce diriment impediments, but that this right belongs to the State, which alone can annul the existing impediments; that matrimonial causes and those concerning betrothals depend of their nature on the civil court; that the Church, as time went by, began to introduce diriment impediments, not of her own right, but in virtue of a prerogative received from the State; that the canons of the Council of Trent (a) which excommunicate those who dare to deny the Church's rights to introduce diriment impediments are either not dogmatic or must be intended in the sense that this right is conferred on her by the State".

He goes on to say "that the form defined by the **92** Council of Trent does not oblige under pain of nullity *(12,* when the civil power prescribes another form and de- *63)* sires that the marriage contracted in this new form be

91a *Sess.* 24, *Canones de sacramento matrimonii*—Cf. *Denz.* 971-982.

valid; that Boniface VIII was the first to assert that the vow of chastity pronounced in Ordination annulled Matrimony".

(*Other errors.*)

93   Therefore, it is clear that by asserting such teach-
(67) ing and similar propositions, the author aims to destroy the constitution and government of the Church, and to undermine the Catholic Faith completely, since he deprives the Church of her exterior jurisdiction and coercive power which was given to her to bring back those who had strayed from the path of justice; that he admits and professes false principles as regards the nature and bond of matrimony; that he denies the Church's power to establish and remove diriment impediments, maintaining that this power belongs instead to civil authority; and finally that in a complete upheaval he subordinates the Church to this same civil power to the point of attributing to the latter directly or indirectly all that which in the government of the Church as regards persons, sacred things and ecclesiastical jurisdiction is of divine institution or sanctioned by canonical laws, thus renewing the impious system of protestantism which reduces the society of the faithful to being the slave of civil authority.

(*Sanctions.*)

ROYAL CONSULTATION

Letter *La Lettera*, September 19, 1852, to King Victor Emmanuel.

(*Acknowledged receipt of the King's letter of July 25, in which the Pope was asked his opinion on the proposed law relative to civil matrimony, following the law of April 9, 1850.*)

It is a dogma of Faith that matrimony has been raised to the dignity of a Sacrament by Our Lord Jesus Christ, and it is a doctrine of the Catholic Church that the Sacrament is not an accidental quality added to the contract, but is the very essence of matrimony so much so that the conjugal bond is not legitimate if there is not the Matrimony-Sacrament, but a mere concubinage. A civil law which supposes that for Catholics the sacrament can be separated from the matrimonial contract and pretends to regulate its validity contradicts the Church's doctrine, invades her rights and practically puts concubinage on the same plane as the Sacrament of Matrimony, sanctioning as legitimate both the one and the other (a).

94
(67,
69,
71,
74)

Insufficient guarantees

Neither the Church's doctrine would be saved, nor its rights sufficiently guaranteed should the two conditions—alluded to by Your Majesty in the Senate's discussion—be adopted. The first condition is that the Law hold as valid those marriages which are regularly celebrated in the Church; the second, that when a marriage which the Church does not recognize as valid is cele-

95
(73)

94a *Una legge civile che supponendo divisibile per i Cattolici il Sacramento dal contratto di Matrimonio, pretende di regolarne la validità, contraddice alla dottrina della Chiesa, invade i diritti della medesima, e praticamente parifica il concubinato al Sacramento del Matrimonio sanzionando legittimo l'uno come l'altro.*

brated, the party that later on wishes to conform to
the Church's precepts is not bound to continue living
in a union condemned by the Church.

96   With regard to the first condition, either marriages
(73) regularly celebrated before the Church are regarded as
valid, and in this case the regulation of the law is superfluous; there would be an even greater usurpation
of legitimate power if the civil law were to pretend to
take notice of and decide whether the Sacrament of
Marriage had been validly celebrated *"in faciem Ecclesiæ";* or it is wished to regard as valid in the Church only
those matrimonial contracts which are "regular", i.e.,
according to civil law, and again in this case there would
be a violation of a right which belongs exclusively to
the Church (a).

97   As regards the second condition, which gives one
(73) of the parties the liberty of not living in an illicit union,
on account of the nullity of the marriage because it was
not celebrated *in faciem Ecclesiæ* nor in conformity with
her laws, a union would be permitted which as regards
the civil power is legitimate but condemned by the
Church.

98   Both conditions then—since they do not abandon
(54, the hypothesis on which the law depends in all its regu-
73) lations, that is of separating the Sacrament from the
contract—allow the above mentioned opposition to exist
between the law itself and the Church's doctrine regarding Matrimony.
          Nevertheless, there is another means of concilia-
tion which, while giving to Caesar what is Caesar's,
leaves to the Church what belongs to her. While the
Civil Power may legislate concerning the civil effects

which derive from marriages, let it leave to the Church the question of its validity among Christians. Let the Civil Power base its action on the validity or the invalidity of Matrimony as shall have been determined by the Church and basing itself on these principles, the determination of which is outside its sphere, let it then establish the civil effects.

(*The condemnation of the law does not hinder the Pope's love for Catholics.—Reply to the King's complaints against some members of the Piedmontese clergy.*)

If, however, the writings which on the part of the clergy have appeared in opposition to the proposed Law of Matrimony have been regarded as a stimulus to revolt, let Us say that, leaving out of consideration the means that some may have used, the clergy did its duty. We wrote to Your Majesty that the law is not Catholic and, if a law is not Catholic, the clergy are obliged to warn the faithful despite the danger incurred (a). **99** *(73, 99, 100)*

Your Majesty, We speak to you in the name of Jesus Christ, Whose Vicar We are, however unworthy, and in His Holy Name We bid you not to sanction this law which will only give rise to a thousand disorders.

(*The Press' viewpoint; appeal to the King.*)

99a *Se mai però si intendesse per eccitamento alla rivolta gli scritti che per parte del Clero sono comparsi per opporsi al progetto di Legge sul Matrimonio, diremo che, prescindendo dai modi che qualcuno avesse potuto adoperare, il Clero ha fatto il suo dovere ... Se una legge non è cattolica, è obbligato il Clero di avvertirne i fedeli anche di fronte al pericolo che incorre.*

"CIVIL MATRIMONY" IN NEW GRANADA

Consistorial All., September 27, 1852.
(*Laws contrary to the Church in New Granada.*)

100
(56,
67,
69,
71,
75,
77)
Let us not mention the other decree which—holding in no account the mystery, dignity and sanctity of the sacrament of Matrimony, ignoring its institution, radically altering its nature and completely scorning the Church's power over this sacrament—was proposed in conformity with the already condemned errors of heretics and against the Catholic Church's doctrines, that Matrimony was to be considered as a civil contract, and that divorce properly so-called was to be sanctioned in various cases, and that all matrimonial cases were to be brought before lay tribunals and judged by the same (a).

101
(7,
8,
47,
74)
No Catholic is ignorant of, or can be ignorant of, the fact that Matrimony is truly and properly one of the seven Sacraments of the evangelical law, instituted by Jesus Christ Our Lord. It necessarily follows that: 1) among the faithful there cannot be a marriage which is not at the same time a sacrament; every other union between Christians outside of the sacrament, made in virtue of any civil law, is none other than disgraceful and base concubinage, repeatedly condemned by the Church; 2) the sacrament can never be separated from the marriage contract, and only the Church has the power to regulate those matters which pertain to matrimony (a).

100a Cf. *Denz.* 1640.
101a Cf. *Denz.* 1640.

(Joy in seeing those laws proposed by the deputies rejected by the Senate.—Solemn condemnation of the impious laws.)

A REVEALED TRUTH

Letter *Verbis exprimere,* August 15, 1859, to the Bishops of the province of Fogaras and Weissenburg. *(Urgent invitation to teach the Catholic doctrine.)*

Among other matters, do not forget to expound **102** and to inculcate in the faithful under your care the doc- *(15,* trine of the Catholic Church on marriage and especial- *16,* ly on the indissolubility of its bond. You are well aware *99,* that, according to the doctrine of the Catholic Church, *101)* marriage once contracted can be dissolved, before it has been consummated, through the religious profession of one of the parties or through a canonical dispensation which can be granted only by the Sovereign Pontiff, and which is given very rarely and for very serious reasons. Again, you know full well that the same Church, basing itself on the Gospel and the Apostles, teaches very clearly that the matrimonial bond can never be dissolved by one of the parties neither because of adultery committed by the other, nor because of lapse into heresy, deliberate absences or the difficulties of common life. The Church declares that such a bond is perpetual, firm and indissoluble, in conformity with Adam's declaration, well known and uttered under divine inspiration; in conformity with the revelation of Christ Our Lord, the teaching of the Apostles and ecclesiastical tradition: all these are authorities well known by you.

103   The perpetual and indissoluble strength of the
(14) marriage bond does not have its origin in ecclesiastical discipline. For the consummated marriage is solidly based on divine and natural law: such a marriage can never be dissolved for any reason—not even by the Pope himself—and not even in the case where one of the parties may have violated conjugal fidelity by committing adultery.

104   Nothing must be more dear to your priestly au-
(15, thority and your episcopal zeal for the defense and
99, propagation of the Catholic doctrine than to see that
100) the faithful entrusted to your care profess and observe these truths. If there are persons in your dioceses who err on this point and think that marriage can be dissolved in the case of adultery, you must undertake to eradicate and eliminate totally from their souls this error so contrary to Catholic doctrine, with all zeal, authority, vigilance, prudence and constancy. You will understand in your wisdom that in a work of such a kind it is necessary to overcome every difficulty—no matter what its nature—that is likely to present itself, with all patience and instruction, because it is a question of a divinely revealed Catholic truth which all the members of the Church are firmly obliged to profess and observe. With all your zeal, knowledge and solicitude as bishops, it will be your office to explain, inculcate and teach clearly the Church's doctrine in such matters, to all those who come to you for explanations of their difficulties. Point out that these difficulties cannot be absolutely brought forward as arguments against or opposed to Catholic doctrine.

(Invitation to the Bishops to ensure similar teaching by their clergy.)

LEGAL CONCUBINAGE

Consistorial All., December 17, 1860.

(Various attacks on the Church's rights; aim of the adversaries.)

What they are looking for, the aim of all their intrigues, is the destruction of the very foundations of our most holy religion. **105** *(64, 65, 69)*

(List of the measures taken in this direction.)

It is always for the same purpose (and We cannot recall it to mind without bitter anguish) that Protestant Churches have been constructed in several Italian cities, that public schools have been opened wherein are taught with impunity the most perverse doctrines to the great detriment of the Catholic religion. Again, in Umbria a decree has been published in virtue of which Matrimony —called by the Apostle a great Sacrament (a)—becoming a bond established by civil law, is almost withdrawn from ecclesiastical power, with the apparent purpose that later on it will be reduced to a state in which it will depend only on human law, thus establishing (may God forbid!) with great danger to souls, legal concubinage.

(Hope that the culpable will realize their errors.— Persecutions in the Far East.)

105a Cf. Eph. 5:32.

THE SYLLABUS

Syllabus, or résumé of the principal contemporary errors, December 8, 1864.

VIII—Errors relative to Christian marriage.

106
(7)
65. In no way can it be proved that Christ raised Matrimony to the dignity of a Sacrament.

107
(8)
66. The Sacrament of Matrimony is an accessory to and separable from the contract and the whole Sacrament lies only in the nuptial blessing.

108
(14,
77)
67. The marriage bond by natural law is not indissoluble and in various cases divorce properly so-called can be sanctioned by civil authority.

109
(49,
56)
68. The Church has not the power to introduce impediments which invalidate marriage, but such a power belongs to civil authority, which can set aside the existing impediments.

110
(46)
69. The Church began to introduce diriment impediments in later centuries not through its own authority, but using the right which she had taken from the civil power.

111
(49)
70. The canons of the Council of Trent, in which excommunication is inflicted on those who dare to deny the Church's power to establish diriment impediments, are either not dogmatic or must be understood as referring to this derived power.

112
(12)
71. The marriage form of the Council of Trent does not oblige under pain of nullity when the civil law pre-

scribes another form and desires that the marriage be valid when it be celebrated with this new civil form.

72. Boniface VIII was the first to assert that the vow of chastity pronounced in ordination renders a marriage null. **113** *(46, 63)*

73. A true marriage can exist between Christians in virtue of a simple civil contract; and it is false that the marriage contract between Christians is always a sacrament, or that the contract is null if the sacrament is excluded. **114** *(8, 74)*

74. Matrimonial cases and those concerning betrothals are by their nature within the competence of the civil authority (a). **115** *(49, 55, 56)*

ABUSE OF MARRIAGE BETWEEN RELATIVES

Speech to Italian Youth, January 6, 1875.

(*Divine protection over the Church.—The Pope's counsels regarding the present disorders: in particular.*)

I am speaking of those marriages between relatives which over the last twenty or twenty-five years have not only doubled but quadrupled. When the right moment arises, therefore, I would wish you to speak to the friend or relative who is inclined to this kind of marriage and deter them from such. It is true that it can sometimes happen that a dispensation must be granted on account of the number of canonical causes involved; but this extraordinary increase is to be condemned because it is **116** *(12, 49, 92)*

115a The *Syallbus* can be read in *Denz*. 1701-1780.—The errors regarding Christian matrimony are in Denz. 1765-1774.

contrary to the health of the body, and here the doctors may speak; and at other times it is contrary to morals, and in this matter I am competent myself to speak and teach (a).

117 I know well that it will be said it would be easier to
(56, prevent this disorder by denying a dispensation. But a
92) great difficulty lies herein, because governments have permitted such marriages and this beguiles weak souls. Rather than prepare themselves to receive the sacrament, because they are either caught up in a blind passion, or enticed by the greed of money, or, worse still, because they lack the Faith, they prefer to live even in an incestuous concubinage. Thus the contracting parties are deprived of the grace which God would grant them to live peacefully and charitably, and of that necessary zeal to be able to educate their children in His holy fear.

118 If the governing powers had the patience to inter-
(73) vene only after the Church had exercised her rights, as justice demands, they could then and not before proceed with the civil acts, thus preventing the contracting parties from staining their consciences; a stain

116a The ecclesiastical legislation as regards the impediments of consanguinity is today fixed by the C.I.C., can. 1076.—§1. *In linea recta consanguinitatis matrimoniul irritum est inter omnes ascendentes et descendentes tum legitimos tum naturales.*

§2. *In linea collaterali irritum est usque ad tertium gradum inclusive, ita tamen ut matrimonii impedimentum toties tantum multiplicetur quoties communis stipes multiplicatur.*
§3. *Nunquam matrimonium permittatur, si quod subsit dubium num partes sint consanguineae in aliquo gradu lineae rectae aut in primo gradu lineae collateralis.*

which is extended to all those who have co-operated in such matters (a).

(*Request for the free exercise of worship.*)

PRIORITY OF CIVIL FORMALITIES

Letter *Tuae litterae*, December 1, 1875.—to the Bishop of Ghent.

(*Pope's amazement at the Bishop's approval of the law which prohibits a religious marriage before the civil formalities are completed.*)

It will appear evident at once that this law is contrary to Catholic doctrine, if one considers that its basis rests on the mistaken opinion which considers a civil contract of marriage for the faithful separable from the sacrament of Matrimony. This law then considers religious marriage only to punish the parties if it is contracted before the civil prescriptions have been completed; for, according to the same law, the whole value of the matrimonial contract depends on the civil regulations. On the contrary, however, the Church does not and cannot recognize in all these civil actions, considered apart from the sacrament, anything but a pure formality which conceals a shameful concubinage. **119** *(69, 70, 73, 74)*

It follows that the dangers that derive from the above mentioned law are repugnant to a sane rule of morals. It can happen, in fact, that the parties, or one of them, after having completed the civil formalities, re- **120** *(73)*

118a The complete text of the discourse can be found in *La Civiltà Cattolica*, a. 26 (1875): vol. 5, series 9, pp. 469-472.

fuse to fulfill the religious rite of marriage and thus they live together or may be forced to live together in a deplorable concubinage; or at least it can happen that the parties, before being united in the sacred rite of the Catholic Church, live in an excessive intimacy or dwell together in the same house, as has been shown by the very deplorable experience in those countries where the law is in force.

121
(73)   Besides, it is clear that this same law gravely offends the necessary and salutary liberty of the pastoral ministry, for in numerous cases, depending on circumstances and persons, the prescriptions of the civil law cannot be fulfilled, and a Christian matrimony can in no way be delayed. Such cases would be: the need to quieten those souls who are held in the grip of passion, to avoid an imminent scandal, to reconcile families at enmity through continuous and grave discord, or to provide for the salvation of a Christian soul who is to present itself at the judgment seat of God. It is with great pain that We have heard of an episode which recently happened in Belgium: a parish priest was judged and condemned for having provided for the eternal salvation of a dying person by the celebration of a Christian marriage. What can be more shameful than seeing Catholic magistrates in a Catholic country condemn a pastor of souls for the sole reason that he did his duty, impelled to fulfill an act of sacred ministry relative to the sanctity of the Sacrament, in such circumstances that he could not postpone it to a later date without rendering himself guilty of a grave crime? Venerable Brother, such is the motive of the speech, to which you also allude in your letter, which We addressed on the third of October last to the distinguished group of Belgians who came to Rome to pre-

sent the homage of their filial devotion and to gain the Jubilee indulgence.

We exhorted them to petition the government to ob- **122** tain the priority of the sacrament of matrimony in respect *(105)* to the civil contract. If this is the motive of the petition of which you speak and which some members of a diocese have addressed to the King, We certainly do not see any reason which could condemn their manner of proceding. It is not as if they were aiming to change the constitution or overthrow it. The futility and weakness of such an accusation is so much more evident when the same law recognizes the rights of citizens to present similar requests. If the impious have used such a right so many times to damage the Church, why should the faithful be denied the right to use it for their utility and their welfare?

Leo XIII

1878-1903

THE FAMILY IN PERIL

Encycl. *Inscrutabili,* April 21, 1878.

(The evils of society are caused by the contempt for the Pope's authority.—Consequences.)

(The family) in our days is miserably upset and can- **123** not otherwise be recalled to its dignity, unless it be sub- **(4,** jected to the laws by which it was instituted in the **7,** Church by its Divine Founder. When Christ elevated **11,** Matrimony to the dignity of a Sacrament, a symbol of **46,** His union with the Church, He not only sanctified the **69,** nuptial contract, but likewise supplied most efficacious **103)** aid to parents and children so that they could the more easily attain their temporal and eternal happiness in the performance of their respective duties.

But since iniquitous laws—the religious character of **124** marriage being misunderstood—reduced it to the condi- **(72,** tion of a purely civil contract, thus debasing the nobility **103)** of Christian marriage, it followed that married couples live together in a legal concubinage, give no care to their reciprocally sworn fidelity, children deny the respect and obedience due to their parents, the bonds of domestic charity are weakened, and, what is worse and highly dangerous to the honesty of public morals, very often lamentable and disastrous separations are the result of insane love. Venerable Brethren, such deplorable and grave disorders must make you zealous to admonish the faithful committed to your care with kindly insistence. Let them be ever ready to heed the teachings regarding the sanctity of Christian marriage and to obey the laws with which the Church regulates the duties of married persons and their children.

125   Another most desired effect will be gained by these
(43, means: the improvement and reform of the individual
53, man; because as weak branches and rotten fruit are the
105) result of a poisoned plant, so corruption which contaminates the family reaches out to taint and infect individual citizens. On the contrary, when the family is established in a Christian life, the individual members little by little become accustomed to love religion and piety, to abhor false and harmful doctrines, to grow in virtue, to respect their elders and to restrain that sentiment of selfishness which so degrades and enfeebles human nature.

(*Hopes for the future.*)

SOCIALISM AND MATRIMONY

Encycl. *Quod apostolici,* December 28, 1878.
(*Socialist and communist errors.*)

126   This beneficial power of the Church, which has in-
(14, fluence upon the best ordered regime and upon the pres-
36, ervation of civil society, is necessarily felt and experienced
39, by domestic society, the foundation of every city and
42, kingdom. In fact, Venerable Brethren, you know well
43, that this society, according to the demands of natural
53, law, is based principally on the indissoluble union of man
66, and woman and has its fulfillment in the reciprocal du-
68) ties and rights of father and children, employer and employees. You know, too, that these principles are under-

mined by socialist teachings, because once society loses its inherent stability resulting from Christian Matrimony, it necessarily follows that the father's authority over his children and the children's respect towards their parents are weakened in an extraordinary manner.

The Church, on the other hand, teaches that mat- **127** rimony—"to be held in honor by all" (a)—instituted by *(2,* God as indissoluble from the beginning of the world, to *4,* propagate and preserve the human race, took on a more *7,* holy and permanent condition when Christ deigned to *9,* elevate it to a Sacrament, representing it as the image of *14,* His union with the Church. According to the teaching of *39)* the Apostle (b), as Christ is the head of the Church, so the husband is head of the wife, and as the Church is subject to Christ, Who nourishes a most pure and eternal love for her, so it is expedient that wives be subject to their husbands, who in their turn must love them with faithful and constant affection.

In like manner the Church tempers the power of fa- **128** thers and employers which, without surpassing just meas- *(11,* ure, places sons and employees within the bounds of *40)* respect. Basing ourselves on Catholic teaching we see that the authority of the Father and Heavenly Master is transmitted to the parents and employers. Therefore the apostle exhorts children "to be obedient to their parents, to honor their father and mother,—such is the first commandment with a promise—"(a). To parents he adds: "And you, fathers, do not provoke your children, but raise them in the discipline and teaching of the Lord" (b). Again, speaking to the slaves and their masters, the

127a Hebrews 13:4.   127b Eph. 5:23.
128a Eph. 6:1 ff.   128b Eph. 6:4.

divine commandment is again inculcated by the Apostle, that slaves obey their masters "according to the flesh, as you would Christ ... doing the will of God"; to the masters in their turn, he says: "give up threatening, knowing that their Lord who is also your Lord is in heaven, and that with Him there is no respect of persons" (c).

(*Other social problems.*)

CIVIL MATRIMONY IN PIEDMONT

Letter *Ci siamo,* June 1, 1879, to the Episcopate of the Ecclesiastical provinces of Turin, Vercelli and Genoa.

(*Congratulations to the Bishops of Piedmont for the letter of protest against the new law which prohibits the celebration or a religious matrimony before the civil formalities are completed.*)

129
(7,
69,
72)
Not without reason, Venerable Brethren, you lament as disastrous to religious morality such a reform which, having deprived Christian marriage of every juridical value, hinders its celebration and submits it with penal sanctions to the exigencies of a civil procedure. To affirm that matrimony is a State institution and nothing more than an ordinary civil contract and completely a social relationship is to ignore entirely the fundamental principles of Christianity, and, let Us say, the most elementary notions of natural law.

130
(1,
2,
4,
6,
The conjugal union is not the work or invention of man; God Himself, the Supreme Author of nature, from the beginning of creation, ordained such a union for the propagation of the human race and the constitution of the family. In the order of grace, He willed this union

128c Eph. 6:5, 6, 7, 8, 9.

be further enriched by imposing on it the divine seal 7, of a sacrament (a). Therefore, insofar as the substance 36, and sanctity of the bond are concerned, marriage for 46) Christian jurisprudence is an essentially sacred and religious act, the regulation of which naturally belongs to the religious power, not by a delegation of the State, nor by consent of the Princes, but by mandate of the Divine Founder of Christianity and Author of the sacraments.

You well know, besides, Venerable Brethren, that to 131 justify the intrusion of a civil power in the Christian leg- (70) islation of marriage, there has been openly advocated— proposed as a consequence of modern progress—the concept of the separation of the contract from the sacrament. Thus, considering marriage in isolation as a contract, there are those who would subject it in all things to the dominion of the State; leaving to the Church the right to interfere only by giving a ritual blessing. To give force then to such a theory recourse is had to the authority of foreign Codes, or to the fact that in a few Catholic nations marriage is today governed by legislation which is wholly civil and secular.

Judgment on the law

But no matter what non-Catholic jurists or adher- 132 ents of the autocracy of the State may say, it is certain (8, that those who are sincere Catholics cannot in conscience 63, accept this doctrine as a foundation for a Christian law 71,

130a *La connubiale unione non è opera o invenzione dell'uomo Iddio stesso, supremo Autore della natura, sin dalle prime con detta unione ordinò la propagazione del genere umano e la costituzione della famiglia: e nella legge di grazia, la volle di più nobilitare con imprimerle il divino suggello del Sacramento.*

74) of matrimony. The reason is that this doctrine is founded on a dogmatic error which has been condemned several times by the Church, that is, the reduction of the Sacrament to an extrinsic ceremony and to the condition of a simple rite. This is a doctrine which overthrows the essential concept of Christian marriage, in which the bond, sanctified by religion, is identified with the sacrament and constitutes inseparably with it but one object and one reality (a). In truth, to divest marriage of its sacred character in the midst of Christian society is the same as to degrade it, to scorn the religious faith of the subjects and to devise a harmful deceit, since the bare legal formality of the civil act without the sacrament is of no value and can give no virtue to such unions, nor happiness to their families.

133   Nor can it avail to rely upon the example of those
(70) Catholic nations which, already profoundly afflicted by division over principles and social upheavals, find themselves constrained to undergo a reform of such a kind, either inspired by heretical doctrines and influences, or established by the arrogance of the rulers. Nevertheless, the reform, besides bearing bitter fruits, was never

132a *Ma checché dicano giuristi acattolici o ligii all'auto-crazia dello Stato egli è certo che la coscienza di quanti sono sinceramente cattolici non può accogliere questa dottrina come base d'una legislazione cristiana sul matrimonio per la ragione che fondasi sopra un errore dommatico più volte condannato dalla Chiesa, quale é quello di ridurre il Sacramento ad una estrinseca cerimonia e alla condizione di un semplice rito; dottrina che sovverte l'essenziale concetto del matrimonio cristiano, nel quale il vincolo connubiale santificato dalla religione, s'identifica col Sacramento e costituisce inseparabilmente con esso un solo soggetto ed un sola realità.*

peacefully accepted, but was constantly disapproved by conscientious Catholics and the legitimate teaching authority of the Church.

Here it would be well to note how unjustly the Church is blamed for wanting to perform an action which, they say, intrudes into matrimonial legislation to the damage of the prerogatives of the State and public authority. The Church intervenes to protect only that which is under the authority of the Divine law and which was inalienably committed to her, that is the sanctity of the marriage bond and the religious adjuncts proper to it. **134 (46, 49)**

The State's Duty

No one can question the State's rights to regulate the temporal aspects of matrimony for the common welfare and to regulate justly its civil effects. But not so when the State, entering the sanctuary of religion and conscience, sets itself up as arbiter and reformer of the intimate consequences of a sacred bond which God Himself ordained and which the powers of the world, since they have no power to effect it, can never dissolve or change. **135 (54, 55, 57)**

Hence you will understand, Venerable Brethren, what judgment can be passed on a Catholic State which, putting aside the holy principles and wise discipline of the Christian law of marriage, sets itself to the sorry task of creating a matrimonial morality wholly human, under merely judicial forms and guarantees. The State—insofar as it is able—imposes this by force on its citizens, substituting it for the religious and sacramental form, without which marriage between Christians cannot be either lawful, honored or stable. Venerable Brethren, **136 (71, 103)**

We confess to you Our sadness to see the fate that the
present rulers are preparing for Catholic Italy, and to
see how the injurious and ill-fated design is maturing
in this very metropolis of Catholicism.

The consequences

137   Such a design in itself and in its consequences re-
(71, veals itself unfortunately injurious and disastrous to
72) religion, the priesthood, liberty of conscience and public
morals.

138   Therefore, when the State boldly invades the field
(73) of religion and exercises a right which does not belong
to it, the State recognizes the Sacrament for the sole
reason of hindering its administration and subjugating
it to the rule of the Civil Code and the exigencies of
judicial formalism.

139   Moreover the State draws from the Sacrament a
(73) title of guilt in order to inflict pecuniary and penal fine
on the sacred ministry and the contracting parties. It
regards the sacramental union as illegitimate and value-
less, no matter how blessed it be by God, unless it is
preceded by the civil formalities. The infrequency of
civil celebrations and the neglect of legal procedure—
which is the natural effect of the education of religious
convictions of the Italian people—are unjustly blamed on
the Church and the clergy. The State hinders the priest
even when his duty obliges him to provide readily and
opportunely at times of great difficulties the sacramental
celebration for those who are distressed in conscience
and for the peace and compromised honor of families.

140   As regards the subjects, the State unjustly con-
(71, strains their faith and religious liberty by its prohibition

of using the Sacrament unless it be in dependence on the State. It imposes on their conscience only the morality of the Civil Code as regards married partnership and the procreation of the children, and this before God and religion cannot be justified. At the same time it authorizes a sinful concubinage which can grow and spread with impunity under the guise of civil marriage (as statistics show), by eluding Christian duties and the very prescriptions of the civil Code. What is more dangerous is that it places a legal weapon in the hands of fraudulent men to betray the conscience of God-fearing young girls and honest parents by refusing the religious celebration after the civil ceremony is completed.

73, 74)

The law-makers' aims

As you can see, Venerable Brethren, there naturally arises doubt whether the present reforms of religious marriage have been dictated by a desire for order and social justice or rather by an intention to bring new difficulties upon the Church and the clergy and to increase incentives to perversion for the Italian people. The doubt gains weight, unfortunately, when it is noticed that the said reform aims to strike the sacred ministry more than the principal transgressors; leaving to these latter a time limit in which they can escape penal action, but not so to the priest; and again when one recalls the ignoble comments and irreligious speeches which were made to promote this reform among the people, not without offense and sorrow to every Catholic heart.

141 (64)

(*Résumé of the attacks against the Catholic Church in the speeches of the time.—Prayer to God to protect the Church.*)

142   At the same time, Venerable Brethren, We do not
(1, cease from encouraging the faithful with suitable ex-
6, hortations on the great Catholic truth, that from God
12,
101) marriage has its origin and sanctification and that outside of the forms established by God and the Church,
there is no honesty, sanctity of the marriage bond or
grace of the Sacrament.

    (*The accusations launched against the Church are
refuted by recalling past Pontifical teaching.—The holy
cause of Christian matrimony must be protected more
than ever.*)

CHRISTIAN MARRIAGE

    Encycl. *Arcanum Divinæ Sapientiæ,* February 10,
1880.

The Divine Plan

143   The hidden design of the divine wisdom which
(48) Jesus Christ the Savior of men came to carry out on
earth had this end in view; that, by Himself and in
Himself, He should divinely renew the world, which
was sinking as it were with length of years into decline.
The Apostle Paul summed this up in words of dignity
and majesty when he wrote to the Ephesians, thus:
"That He might make known unto us the mystery of
His will . . . to re-establish all things in Christ that are
in heaven and on earth" (a). In truth, Christ Our Lord,
setting Himself to fulfill the commandment which His
Father had given Him, straightway imparted a new
form and fresh beauty to all things, taking away the
effects of their time-worn age. For He healed the
wounds which the sin of our first father had inflicted

143a Eph. 1:9-10.

on the human race; He brought all men, by nature children of wrath, into favor with God; He led to the light of truth men wearied out by longstanding errors; He renewed to every virtue those who were weakened by lawlessness of every kind; and, giving them again an inheritance of never-ending bliss, He added a sure hope that their mortal and perishable bodies should one day be partakers of immortality and of the glory of heaven.

In order that these unparalleled benefits might last **144** as long as men should be found on the earth, He en- *(48)* trusted to His Church the continuance of His work; and, looking to future times, He commanded her to set in order whatever might have become deranged in human society, and to restore whatever might have fallen into ruin.

The Church's mission

Although the divine renewal We have spoken of **145** chiefly and directly affected men as constituted in the *(48,* supernatural order of grace, nevertheless some of its *53)* precious and salutary fruits were also bestowed abundantly in the order of nature. Hence, not only individual men, but also the whole mass of the human race, have in every respect received no small degree of worthiness. For, so soon as Christian order was once established in the world, it became happily possible for every man to learn what God's fatherly providence is, and to dwell in it habitually, thereby fostering that hope of heavenly help which never confoundeth. From all this flowed fortitude, self-control, constancy, and the evenness of a peaceful mind, together with many high virtues and noble needs.

146
(36,
53)
Wondrous, indeed was the extent of dignity, stead-fastness, and goodness which thus accrued to the State as well as to the family. The authority of rulers became more just and revered, the obedience of the people more ready and unforced, the union of citizens closer, the rights of property more secure. In very truth, the Christian religion thought of and provided for all things which are held to be advantageous in a State; so much so, indeed, that, according to St. Augustine, one cannot see how it could have afforded greater help in the matter of living well and happily, had it been instituted for the single object of procuring or increasing those things which contribute to the conveniences or advantages of this mortal life. Still, the purpose We have set before Us is not to recount in detail benefits of this kind; Our wish is rather to speak about that family union of which marriage is the beginning and the foundation.

The origin of Matrimony

147
(2,
65)
The true origin of marriage, Venerable Brethren, is well known to all. Though the revilers of Christian faith refuse to acknowledge the never-interrupted doctrine of the Church on this subject, and have long striven to destroy the testimony of all nations and of all times, they have nevertheless not only failed to quench the powerful light of truth, but even to lessen it. We record what is known to all, and cannot be doubted by any, that God, on the sixth day of creation, having made man from the slime of the earth, and having breathed into his face the breath of life, gave him a companion whom he miraculously took from the side of Adam while he was asleep (a). God thus, in His most far-reaching fore-

147a Cf. Gen. 2:18-24.

sight decreed that this husband and wife should be the natural beginning of the human race, from whom it might be propagated and preserved by an unfailing fruitfulness throughout all futurity of time (b).

And this union of man and woman, that it might **148** answer more fittingly to the infinitely wise counsels of *(2,* God, even from that beginning manifested chiefly two *14-* most excellent properties—deeply sealed, as it were, and *16)* signed upon it—namely, unity and indissolubility. From the Gospel we see clearly that this doctrine was declared and openly confirmd by the divine authority of Jesus Christ. He bore witness to the Jews and to His Apostles that marriage, from its institution, should exist between two only, that is, between one man and one woman; that of two they are made, so to say, one flesh; and that the marriage bond is by the will of God so closely and strongly made fast that no man may dissolve it or rend it asunder. "For this cause shall a man leave father and mother, and shall cleave to his wife, and they shall be two in one flesh. Therefore now they are not two, but one flesh. What, therefore, God hath joined together, let no man put asunder" (a).

Decadence

This form of marriage, however, so excellent and so **149** preeminent, began to be corrupted by degrees and to dis- *(3)* appear among the heathen, and became, even among the Jewish race clouded in a measure and obscured. For in

147b *Qua in re hoc voluit providentissimus Deus, ut illud par coniugum esset cunctorum hominum naturale principium, ex quo scilicet propagari humanum genus, et, nunquam intermissis procreationibus, conservari in omne tempus oportet.* 148a Matt. 19:5-6.

their midst a common custom was gradually introduced, by which it was accounted as lawful for a man to have more than one wife; and eventually, when, "by reason of the hardness of their heart" (a), Moses indulgently permitted them to put away their wives, the way was open to divorce.

150
(3) But the corruption and change which fell on marriage among the Gentiles seem almost incredible, inasmuch as it was exposed in every land to floods of error and of the most shameful lusts. All nations seemed, more or less, to have forgotten the true notion and origin of marriage; and thus everywhere laws were enacted with reference to marriage, prompted to all appearance by State reasons, but not such as nature required. Solemn rites, invented at will by the lawgivers, brought about that women should bear either the honorable name of wife or the disgraceful name of concubine; and things came to such a pitch that permission to marry, or the refusal of the permission, depended on the will of the heads of State, whose laws were greatly against equity and even to the highest degree unjust. Moreover, plurality of wives and husbands and divorce caused the nuptial bond to be relaxed exceedingly.

151
(3) Hence, too, sprang up the greatest confusion as to the mutual rights and duties of husbands and wives, inasmuch as a man assumed right of dominion over his wife, ordering her to go about her business often without any just cause, while he himself was at liberty (as St. Jerome says) "to run headlong with impunity into lust, unbridled and unrestrained, in houses of ill-fame and amongst his female slaves, as if the dignity of the persons sinned with

149a Cf. Matt. 19:8.

and not the will of the sinner, made the guilt" (a). When the licentiousness of a husband thus showed itself nothing could be more piteous than the wife, sunk so low as to be reckoned only as a means for the gratification of passion, or for the production of offspring. Without any feeling of shame, marriageable girls were bought and sold just like so much merchandise (b), and power was sometimes given to the father and to the husband to inflict capital punishment on the wife. Of necessity the offspring of such marriages as these were either reckoned among the stock-in-trade of the commonwealth, or held to be the property of the father (c); and the law permitted him to make and unmake the marriages of his children at his mere will, and even to exercise against them the monstrous power of life and death.

The restoration of Matrimony

So manifold being the vices and so great the ignominies with which marriage was defiled, an alleviation and a remedy was at length bestowed from on high. Jesus Christ, who restored our human dignity and who perfected the Mosaic law, applied early in His ministry no little solicitude to the question of marriage. He ennobled the marriage in Cana of Galilee by His presence, and made it memorable by the first of the miracles which He wrought (a): and for this reason, even from that day forth, it seemed as if the beginning of new holiness had been conferred on human marriages. Later on he brought back matrimony to the nobility of its prime- **152**
(3,
4)

151a St. Jerome, *Lett.* 77 *ad Oceano,*—Migne, P.L., 22, 691.   151b Cf. Arnobius, *Adv. Gent.*, 4.
151c Cf. Denis d'Alic., 1. 2, cc. 26, 27.
152a Cf. John 2.

val origin by condemning the customs of the Jews in
their abuse of the plurality of wives and of the power
of giving bills of divorce, and still more by commanding most strictly that no one should dare to dissolve that union which God Himself had sanctioned by
a perpetual bond.

Hence, having set aside the difficulties which were
adduced from the law of Moses, He, in the character of
Supreme Law-giver, decreed as follows concerning husbands and wives: "I say to you, that whosoever shall
put away his wife, except it be for fornication, and shall
marry another, committeth adultery; and he that shall
marry her that is put away committeth adultery" (b).

The Sacrament

153   But what was decreed and constituted in respect to
(4,   marriage by the authority of God has been more fully
7,   and more clearly handed down to us by tradition and
29,   the written Word through the Apostles, those heralds
34,   of the laws of God. To the Apostles, indeed, as our mas-
46,   ters, are to be referred the doctrines which "our holy
104) Fathers, the Councils, and the tradition of the Universal
Church have always taught" (a); namely that Christ
our Lord raised marriage to the dignity of a Sacrament;
that to husband and wife, guarded and strengthened by
the heavenly grace which His merits gained for them,
He gave the power to obtain holiness in the married
state; and that, in a wondrous way, making marriage an
example of the mystical union between Himself and His
Church, He not only perfected that love which is according to nature (b), but also made the natural union of

153a Council of Trent, Sess. 24 *in prol.*   152b Matt. 19:9.
153b Council of Trent, Sess. 24, cap. I, *de reform. matr.*

one man with one woman far more perfect through the bond of heavenly love (c). Paul says to the Ephesians: "Husbands love your wives, as Christ also loved the Church, and delivered Himself up for it, that He might sanctify it . . . So also ought men to love their wives as their own bodies . . . For no man ever hated his own flesh, but nourisheth and cherisheth it, as also Christ doth the Church; because we are members of His body, of His flesh, and of His bones. For this cause shall a man leave his father and mother, and shall cleave to his wife, and they shall be two in one flesh. This is a great Sacrament; but I speak in Christ and in the Church" (d).

Indissolubility

In like manner from the teaching of the Apostles we learn that the unity of marriage and its perpetual indissolubility, the indispensable conditions of its very origin, must, according to the command of Christ, be holy and inviolable without exception. Paul says again: "To them that are married, not I, but the Lord commandeth that the wife depart not from her husband; and if she depart, that she remain unmarried or be reconciled to her husband" (a), and again "a woman is bound by the law as long as her husband liveth; but if her husband die, she is at liberty" (b). It is for these reasons that marriage is "a great Sacrament" (c), "hon- **154 (4, 7, 13, 14)**

153c *Atque in eo, ad exemplar mystici connubii sui cum Ecclesia mire conformato, at amorem qui est naturae consentaneus perfecisse, et viri ac mulieris individuam suapte natura societatem divinae caritatis vinculo validus coniunxisse.*

153d Eph. 5:25 ff.   154a 1 Cor. 7:10-11.
154b 1 Cor. 7:39.   154c Eph. 5:32.

orable in all" (d); holy, pure, and to be reverenced as a type and symbol of most high mysteries.

The new end of Matrimony

155
(5,
22)
Furthermore, the Christian perfection and completeness of marriage are not comprised in those points only which have been mentioned. For, firstly, there has been vouchsafed to the marriage union a higher and nobler purpose than was ever previously given to it. By the command of Christ it not only looks to the propagation of the human race, but to the bringing forth of children for the Church, "fellow-citizens with the saints, and the domestics of God" (a); so that "a people might be born and brought up for the worship and religion of the true God and Our Savior Jesus Christ (b).

Conjugal society

156
(29,
32,
34,
39,
40,
Secondly the mutual duties of husband and wife have been defined, and their several rights accurately established. They are bound, namely, to have such feelings for one another as to cherish always very great mutual love, to be ever faithful to their marriage vow, and to give to one another an unfailing and unselfish

154d Hebrews 13:4.
155a Eph. 2:19.
155b *Nam primo quidem nuptiali societati excelsium quiddam et nobilius propositum est, quam antea fuisset; ea enim spectare iussa est non modo ad propagandum genus humanum sed ad ingenerandam Ecclesiae sobolem, cives Sanctorum et domesticos Dei; "ut nimirum, populus ad veri Dei et Salvatoris nostri Christi cultum et religionem procrearetur atque educaretur"* (*Catechismus Romanus, c.* 8.)

help. The husband is the chief of the family, and the *41,* head of the wife. The woman, because she is flesh of *103)* his flesh and bone of his bone, must be subject to her husband and obey him; not, indeed as a servant, but as a companion, so that her obedience shall be wanting in neither honor nor dignity. Since the husband represents Christ, and since the wife represents the Church, let there always be, both in him who commands and in her who obeys, a heaven-born love guiding both in their respective duties. For "the husband is the head of the wife; as Christ is the head of the Church... Therefore, as the Church is subject to Christ, so also let the wives be to their husbands in all things" (a).

As regards children, they ought to submit to their **157** parents and obey them, and give them honor for con- *(11,* science's sake; while, on the other hand, parents are *23)* bound to give all care and watchful thought to the education of their offspring and their virtuous bringing-up: "Fathers,... bring them up (children) in the discipline and correction of the Lord" (a). From this we see clearly that the duties of husbands and wives are neither few nor light; although to married people who are good these burdens become not only bearable but agreeable, owing to the strength which they gain through the Sacrament.

Matrimony entrusted to the Church

Christ, therefore, having renewed marriage to such **158** and so great excellence, commended and entrusted all *(46,* the discipline bearing upon these matters to His Church. *52,*

156a Eph. 5:23-24.
157a Eph. 6:4.

99) The Church, always and everywhere, has so used her power with reference to the marriages of Christians that men have seen clearly that it belongs to her as of native right; not being made hers by any human grant, but given divinely to her by the will of her Founder. Her constant and watchful care in guarding marriage, by the preservation of its sanctity, is so well understood, as not to need proof. That the judgment of the Council of Jerusalem reprobated licentious and free love (a), we all know, as also that the incestuous Corinthian was condemned by the authority of blessed Paul (b). Again, in the very beginning of the Christian Church were repulsed and defeated, with the like unremitting determination, the efforts of many who aimed at the destruction of Christian marriage such as the Gnostics, Manicheans, and Montanists; and in our own time Mormons, St. Simonians, Phalansterians, and Communists.

159
(46,
49,
52)
In like manner, moreover, a law of marriage just to all, and the same for all, was enacted by the abolition of the old distinction between slaves and free-born men and women (a); and thus the rights of husbands and wives were made equal: for as St. Jerome says, "with us that which is unlawful for women is unlawful for men also, and the same restraint is imposed on equal conditions" (b). The self-same rights also were firmly established for reciprocal affection and for the interchange of duties; the dignity of the woman was asserted

158a Cf. Acts 15:29.
158b Cf. Cor. 5:5.
159a Cf. c. I *de coniug serv.*
159b *Lett. 77 ad Oceano.*—Migne P.L., 22, 691.

and assured; and it was forbidden to man to inflict capital punishment for adultery (c), or lustfully and shamelessly to violate his plighted faith.

It is also a great blessing that the Church has **160** limited, so far as it is needful, the power of fathers of *(46,* families, so that sons and daughters wishing to marry *49,* are not in any way deprived of their rightful free- *53)* dom (a); that, for the purpose of spreading more widely the supernatural love of husbands and wives, she has decreed marriages within certain degrees of consanguinity or affinity to be null and void (b); that she has taken the greatest pains to safeguard marriage, as much as is possible, from error and violence and deceit (c); that she has always wished to preserve the holy chastity of the marriage bed, personal rights (d), the honor of husband and wife (e), and the security of religion (f).

Lastly, with such power and with such foresight of legislation has the Church guarded this divine institution, that no one who thinks rightfully of these matters can fail to see how, with regard to marriage, she is the best guardian and defender of the human race; and how her wisdom has come forth victorious from the lapse

159c Cf. *Interfectores,* e can. *Admonere,* q. 2.
160a Cf. c. 30, q. 3; c. 3 *de cognat. spirit.*
160b Cf. c. 8, *de consang. et affin.;* c. I *de cognat. legali.*
160c Cf. c. 26, *de sponsal.;* cc. 13, 15, 29, *de sponsal. et matrim., et alibi.*
160d Cf. c. I, *de convers. infid.;* cc. 5, 6, *de eo qui duxit in matrim.*
160e Cf. cc. 3, 5, 8, *de sponsal. et matrim.*—Council of Trent, Sess. 24, c. *de reform. matrim.*
160f Cf. c. 7, *de divort.*

of years, from the assaults of men, and from the countless changes of public events.

Modern emancipation

161
(4,
63,
67,
69)
    Yet, owing to the efforts of the arch-enemy of man-
kind, there are persons who, thanklessly casting away so
many other blessings of redemption, despise also or utterly ignore the restoration of marriage to its original
perfection. It is the reproach of some of the ancients that
they showed themselves the enemies of marriage in many
ways; but, in our own age, much more pernicious is the
sin of those who would fain pervert utterly the nature of
marriage, perfect though it is, and complete in all its details and parts.

162
(36,
63-
65,
69)
    The chief reason why they act in this way is because
very many, imbued with the maxims of a false philosophy and corrupted in morals, judge nothing so unbearable as submission and obedience, and strive with all
their might to bring about that not only individual men,
but families also, nay indeed, human society itself, may
in haughty pride despise the sovereignty of God (a).

    Now, since the family and human society at large
spring from marriage, these men will on no account
allow matrimony to be subject to the jurisdiction of the
Church. Nay, they endeavor to deprive it of all holiness,
and so bring it within the contracted sphere of those

162a *Atque huius rei causa in eo praecipua sita est, quod
imbuti falsae philosophiae opinionibus corriptaque con-
suetudine animi plurimorum, nihil tam moleste ferunt,
quam subesse et parere; acerrimeque laborant, ut non
modo singuli homines, sed etiam familiae atque omnis
humanas societas imperium Dei superbe contemnant.*

rights which, having been instituted by man, are ruled and administered by the civil jurisprudence of the community.

Wherefore it necessarily follows that they attribute **163** all power over marriage to civil rulers, and allow none *(63,* whatever to the Church; and when the Church exercises *70)* any such power, they think that she acts either by favor of the civil authority or to its injury. Now is the time, they say, for the heads of the State to vindicate their rights unflinchingly, and to do their best to settle all that relates to marriage according as to them seems good.

Hence come *civil marriages,* commonly so called; hence laws are framed which impose impediments to marriage; hence arise judicial sentences affecting the marriage contract, as to whether or not it has been rightly made. Lastly, all power of prescribing and passing judgment in this matter is, as we see, of set purpose denied to the Catholic Church, so that no regard is paid either to her divine power or to her prudent laws. Yet under these, for so many centuries, have lived the nations which received the light of civilization together with Christianity.

Refutation of naturalism: *true nature of Matrimony*

Nevertheless, all they who reject what is supernat- **164** ural, as well as all who profess that they worship above *(6,* all things the divinity of the State, and strive to disturb *48,* whole communities with such wicked doctrines, cannot escape the charge of delusion. Marriage has God for its author, and was from the very beginning a kind of foreshadowing of the Incarnation of His Son; and therefore there abides in it something holy and religious; not extraneous, but innate; not derived from men, but implanted by nature. Innocent III (a), therefore, and Honorius (b), Our Predecessors, affirmed not falsely nor rashly that marriage was ever among the faithful and unbelievers alike a sacred thing. We call to witness the monuments of antiquity, as also the manners and customs of those people who, being the most civilized, had the greatest knowledge of law and equity. In the minds of all of them it was a fixed and foregone conclusion that, when marriage was thought of, it was thought of as conjoined with religion and holiness. Hence among those peoples marriages were commonly celebrated with religious ceremonies, under the authority of Pontiffs and with the ministry of priests. So mighty, even in the souls ignorant of heavenly doctrine, was the force of nature, of the remembrance of their origin, and of the conscience of the human race. As, then, marriage is holy by its power, in its own nature, and of itself, it ought not to be regulated and administered by the will of civil rulers, but by the divine authority of the Church, which alone in sacred matters professes the office of teaching.

165
(4,
7,
47,
55)
Next, the dignity of the Sacrament must be considered; for through the addition of the Sacrament the marriages of Christians have become far the noblest of all matrimonial unions. But to decree and ordain concerning the Sacrament is, by the will of Christ Himself, so much a part of the power and duty of the Church, that it is plainly absurd to maintain that even the very smallest fraction of such power has been transferred to the civil ruler.

164a C. 8 *de divort.*   164b C. II *de transact.*

History

Lastly, there has to be borne in mind the great **166** weight and crucial test of history, by which it is plainly *(46)* proved that the legislative and judicial authority of which We are speaking has been freely and constantly used by the Church, even in times when some foolishly suppose the reason was that the head of the State either consented to it or connived at it. It would, for instance, be incredible and altogether absurd to assume that Christ Our Lord condemned the long-standing practice of polygamy and divorce by authority delegated to Him by the procurator of the province, or the principal ruler of the Jews. And it would be equally extravagant to think that, when the Apostle Paul taught that divorces and incestuous marriages were not lawful, it was because Tiberius, Caligula, and Nero agreed with him or secretly commanded him so to teach. No man in his senses could ever be persuaded that the Church made so many laws about the holiness and indissolubility of marriage (a), and the marriages of slaves with the free-born (b), by power received from the Roman Emperors most hostile to the Christian name, whose strongest desire was to destroy by violence and murder the rising Church of Christ. Still less could any one believe this to be the case, when the law of the Church was sometimes so divergent from the civil law that Ignatius the Martyr (c), Justin (d), Athenagoras (e), and Tertullian (f), pub-

166a Cf. *Can. Apost.*, 16, 17, 18.
166b Cf. *Philosophum. Oxon.* 1851.
166c Cf. *Epist. ad Polycarp.*, c. 5.
166d Cf. *Apolog. mai.*, n. 15.
166e Cf. *Legal. pro Christian.* nn. 32, 33.
166f Cf. *De coron. milit.*, c. 13

licly denounced as unjust and adulterous certain marriages which had been sanctioned by imperial law.

167
(46)
Furthermore, after all power had devolved upon the Christian emperors, the Supreme Pontiffs and Bishops assembled in council persisted, with the same independence and consciousness of their right, in commanding or forbidding in regard to marriage whatever they judged to be profitable or expedient for the time being, however much it might seem to be at variance with the laws of the State. It is well known that, with respect to the impediments arising from the marriage bond through vow, disparity of worship, blood relationship, certain forms of crime, and from previously plighted troth, many decrees were issued by the rulers of the Church in the Councils of Granada (a), Arles (b), Chalcedon (c), the second of Milevis (d), and others, which were often widely different from the decrees sanctioned by the laws of the Empire.

168
(46,
49)
Furthermore, so far were Christian princes from arrogating any power in the matter of Christian marriage, that they, on the contrary, acknowledged and declared that it belonged exclusively in all its fullness to the Church. In fact, Honorius, the younger Theodosius, and Justinian (a) also, hesitated not to confess that the only power belonging to them in relation to marriage was that of acting as guardians and defenders of the holy canons.

167a Cf. De Aguirre, *Conc. Hispan.*, t. I, can. 13, 15, 16, 17.
167b Cf. Harduin., *Act. Council.*, t. I, can. II.
167c Cf. Ibid., can. 16.   167d Cf. Ibid., can. 17.
168a Cf. *Novel.* 137.

If at any time they enacted anything by their edicts concerning impediments of marriage, they voluntarily explained the reason, affirming that they took it upon themselves so to act, by leave and authority of the Church (b), whose judgments they were wont to appeal to and reverently to accept, in all questions that concern legitimacy (c) and divorce (d); as also in all those points which in any way have a necessary connection with the marriage bond (e). The Council of Trent, therefore, had the clearest right to define that it is in the Church's power "to establish diriment impediments of matrimony" (f), and that "matrimonial causes pertain to ecclesiastical judges" (g).

Vain excuses of the lawyers

Let no one then be deceived by the distinction, which some court lawyers have so strongly insisted upon—the distinction, namely, by virtue of which they sever the matrimonial contract from the sacrament, with intent to hand over the contract to the power and will of the rulers of the State, while reserving questions concerning the Sacrament to the Church.

169
(8, 10, 12, 55, 70)

A distinction, or rather severance, of this kind cannot be approved: for certain it is that in Christian marriage the contract is inseparable from the Sacrament, and that, for this reason, the contract cannot be true and legitimate without being a Sacrament as well. For

168b Cf. Feier, *Matrim. ex instit. Cristi*, Pest, 1835.
168c Cf. c. 3 *de ordin. cognit.*
168d Cf. c. 3 *de divort.*
168e Cf. c. 13 *qui filii sint legit.*
168f Council of Trent, Sess. 24, can. 4.
168g Ibid., can. 12.

Christ Our Lord added to marriage the dignity of a Sacrament; but marriage is the contract itself, whenever that contract is lawfully concluded (a).

170 Marriage, however, is a Sacrament, because it is a
(8- holy sign which gives grace, showing forth an image of
10, the mystical nuptials of Christ with the Church. But the
46) form and image of these nuptials are shown precisely by the very bond of that most close union in which man and woman are bound together in one, which bond is nothing else but the marriage itself. Hence it is clear that among Christians every true marriage is, in itself and by itself, a Sacrament; and that nothing can be further from the truth than to say that the Sacrament is a certain added ornament, or outward endowment which can be separated and torn away from the contract at the caprice of man. Neither therefore by reasoning can it be shown, nor by any testimony of history be proved, that power over the marriages of Christians has ever been lawfully handed over to the rulers of the State. If, in this matter, the right of anyone else has ever been violated, no one can truly say that it has been violated by the Church.

169a *Nec quemquam moveat illa tantopere a Regalistis praedicata distinctio, vi cuius contractum nuptialem a sacramento disjungunt, eo sane consilio, ut, Ecclesiae reservatis sacramenti rationibus, contractum tradant in potestatem arbitriumque principum civitatis.—Etenim non potest hujusmodi distinctio, seu verius distractio, probari; cum exploratum sit in matrimonio christiano contractum a sacramento non esse dissociabilem; atque ideo non posse contractum verum et legitimum consistere, quin sit eo ipso sacramentum. Nam Christus Dominus dignitate sacramenti auxit matrimonium; autem est ipse contractus, si modo sit factus jure.*

Consequences of Naturalism

Would that the teaching of those who reject what is **171** supernatural, besides being full of falsehood and injus- *(68)* tice, were not also the fertile source of so much detriment and calamity! But it is easy to see at a glance the greatness of the evil which unhallowed marriages have brought, and ever will bring, on the whole of human society.

From the beginning of the world, indeed, it was di- **172** vinely ordained that things instituted by God and by *(68)* Nature should prove to be the more profitable and salutary the more they remain unchanged in their full integrity. For God, the Maker of all things, well knowing what was good for the institution and preservation of each of his creatures, so ordered them by his will and mind that each might adequately attain the end for which it was made (a). If the rashness or the weakness of men ventures to change or disturb the order of things most providently instituted, then designs of the greatest wisdom and usefulness begin either to be hurtful or cease to be profitable—either because through the change undergone they have lost their power of benefiting, or because God chooses to inflict punishment on the pride and audacity of man.

172a *Principio quidem lev est provisa divinitus, ut quae Deo et natura auctoribus instituta sunt, eo tanto plus utilia ac salutaria experiamur, quanto magis statu nativo manent integra atque incommutabilia; quandoquidem procreator rerum omnium Deus probe novit quid singularum institutioni et conservationi et expediret, cunctasque voluntate et mente sua sic ordinavit, ut suum unaquaeque exitum convenienter habitura sit.*

173
(67) Now those who deny that marriage is holy, and who relegate it, stripped of all holiness, to the class of common things, uproot thereby the foundations of Nature; not only resisting the designs of Providence, but, so far as they can, destroying the order that God has ordained. No one, therefore, should wonder if from such insane and impious attempts there spring up a crop of evils pernicious in the highest degree both to the salvation of souls and to the safety of the commonwealth.

174
(2,
11,
29,
42) If, then, we consider the end of the divine institution of marriage, we shall see very clearly that God intended it to be a most fruitful source of individual benefit and of public welfare. Not only, in strict truth, was marriage instituted for the propagation of the human race, but also that the lives of husbands and wives might be made better and happier. This comes about in many ways: by their lightening each other's burdens through mutual help; by constant and faithful love; by having all their possessions in common; and by the heavenly grace that flows from the Sacrament.

175
(36,
42) Marriage also can do much for the good of families: for, as long as it is conformable to nature and in accordance with the counsels of God, it has power to strengthen union of heart in the parents; to secure the holy education of children; to temper the authority of the father by the example of the divine authority; to render children obedient to their parents, and servants obedient to their masters. From such marriages as these the State may rightly expect a race of citizens animated by a good spirit and filled with reverence and love of God, recognizing it as their duty to obey those who rule justly and lawfully, to love all, and to injure no one.

These many and glorious fruits were ever the prod-   **176**
uct of marriage, so long as it retained those gifts of   *(43,*
holiness, unity and indissolubility from which proceeded   *68)*
all its fertile and saving power; nor can any one doubt
but that it would always have brought forth such fruits,
at all times and in all places, had it been under the
power and guardianship of the Church, the trustworthy
preserver and protector of these gifts,

But now there is a growing wish to supplant natural
and divine law by human law; and hence has begun a
gradual extinction of that most excellent ideal of marriage which Nature herself had impressed on the soul of
man, and sealed, as it were, with her own seal; nay, even
more, even in Christian marriages this power, productive of so great good, has been weakened by the sinful-
ness of man.

Of what advantage is it, if a state can institute   **177**
nuptials estranged from the Christian religion which is   *(63,*
the mother of all good, cherishing   all sublime virtues,   *68,*
quickening and urging us to everything that is the glory   *75,*
of a lofty and generous soul? When the Christian reli-   *104)*
gion is rejected and repudiated, marriage sinks of necessity into the slavery of man's vicious nature and vile
passions, and finds but little protection in the help of
natural goodness. A very torrent of evil has flowed from
this source, not only into private families, but also into
States. For the salutary fear of God being removed, and
there being no longer that refreshment in toil which is
nowhere more abounding than in the Christian religion,
it very often happens, as from facts is evident, that the
mutual services and duties of marriage seem almost un-

bearable; and thus very many yearn for the loosening of the tie which they believe to be woven by human law and of their own will, whenever incompatibility of temper, or quarrels or the violation of the marriage vow, or mutual consent, or other reasons induce them to think that it would be well to set them free. Then, if they are hindered by law from carrying out this shameless desire, they contend that the laws are iniquitous, inhuman and at variance with the rights of free citizens; adding that every effort should be made to repeal such enactments, and to introduce a more humane code sanctioning divorce.

Naturalism leads to divorce

178 Now, however much the legislators of these our
(61, days may wish to guard themselves against the impiety
64, of men such as We have been speaking of, they are un-
68, able to do so, seeing that they profess to hold and
75) defend the very same principles of jurisprudence; and hence they have to go with the times, and render divorce more easily obtainable. History itself shows this; for, to pass over other instances, we find that, at the close of the last century, divorces were sanctioned by law in that upheaval, or rather, as it might be called, conflagration in France, when society was wholly degraded by the abandoning of God. Many at the present time would fain have those laws reenacted, because they wish God and His Church to be altogether exiled and excluded from the midst of human society, madly thinking that in such laws a remedy must be sought for that mortal corruption which is advancing with rapid strides.

Evils that flow from divorce

Truly, it is hardly possible to describe how great **179** are the evils that flow from divorce. Matrimonial con- *(78,* tracts are by it made variable; mutual kindness is weak- *79)* ened; deplorable inducements to unfaithfulness are supplied; harm is done to the education and training of children; occasion is afforded for the breaking up of homes; the seeds of dissension are sown among families; the dignity of womanhood is lessened and brought low, and women run the risk of being deserted after having ministered to the pleasures of men. Since, then, nothing has such power to lay waste families and destroy the mainstay of kingdoms as the corruption of morals, it is easily seen that divorces are in the highest degree hostile to the prosperity of families and States, springing as they do from the depraved morals of the people, and, as experience shows us, opening out a way to every kind of evil-doing alike in public and in private life.

Further still, if the matter be duly pondered, we shall **180** clearly see these evils to be the more especially danger- *(79)* ous, because, divorce once being tolerated, there will be no restraint powerful enough to keep it within the bounds marked out or pre-established. Great indeed is the force of example, and even greater still the might of passion. With such incitements it must needs follow that the eagerness for divorce, daily spreading by devious ways, will seize upon the minds of many like a virulent conta- gious disease, or like a flood of water bursting through every barrier.

The teachings of history

These are truths that doubtlessly are all clear in **181** themselves; but they will become clearer yet, if we call *(79)* to mind the teachings of experience. So soon as the road to divorce began to be made smooth by law, at once quarrels, jealousies, and judicial separations largely increased; and such shamelessness of life followed, that men who had been in favor of these divorces repented of what they had done, and feared that if they did not carefully seek a remedy by repealing the law, the State itself might come to ruin.

182
(75,
79)
The Romans of old are said to have shrunk with horror from the first examples of divorce; but ere long all sense of decency was blunted in their soul, the meagre restraint of passion died out, and the marriage vow was so often broken that what some writers affirmed would seem to be true—namely, women used to reckon years not by the change of consuls, but of their husbands.

In like manner, at the beginning, Protestants allowed legalized divorce in certain restricted cases; and yet, from the affinity of the circumstances of like kind, the cases for divorce increased to such extent in Germany, America, and elsewhere, that all wise thinkers deplored the boundless corruption of morals, and judged the recklessness of the laws to be simply intolerable.

Even in Catholic States the same evil existed. For whenever at any time divorce was introduced, the abundance of misery that followed exceeded all that the framers of the law could have foreseen. In fact, many set about to contrive all kinds of fraud and device, and by accusations of cruelty, violence and adultery, to feign grounds for the dissolution of the matrimonial bond of which they had grown weary; and all this with so great havoc to morals that an amendment of the laws was deemed to be urgently needed.

Can any one, therefore, doubt that laws in favor of divorce would have a result equally baneful and calamitous were they to be passed in these our days? There exists not, indeed, in the projects and enactments of men any power to change the character and tendency which things have received from nature. Those men therefore show but little wisdom in the idea they have formed of the well-being of the commonwealth, who think that the inherent character of marriage can be perverted with impunity, and who, disregarding the sanctity of religion and of the Sacrament, seem to wish to degrade and dishonor marriage more basely than was done even by heathen laws. Indeed, if they do not change their views, not only private families, but all public society will have unceasing cause to fear lest they should be miserably driven into that general confusion and overthrow of order which is even now the wicked aim of Socialists and Communists. **183 (78-80, 98)**

Thus we most clearly see how foolish and senseless it is to expect any public good from divorce, when, on the contrary, it tends to the certain destruction of Society.

The Church's merit for her treatment of marriage

It must consequently be acknowledged that the Church has deserved exceedingly well of all nations by her ever watchful care in guarding the sanctity and the indissolubility of marriage. Again, no small amount of gratitude is owing to her for having, during the last hundred years, openly denounced the wicked laws which **184 (12, 53)** have grievously offended on this particular subject (a); as well as for her having branded with anathema the baneful heresy among Protestants regarding divorce and separation (b); also for having in many ways condemned the practice of the Greeks of dissolving marriages (c); for having declared invalid all marriages contracted upon the understanding that they be at some future date dissolved (d); and lastly, for having from the earliest times repudiated the imperial laws which disastrously favored divorce (e).

As often, indeed, as the Supreme Pontiffs have resisted the most powerful rulers, in their threatening demands that divorces be carried out by them should be . confirmed by the Church, so often must we account them to have been contending for the safety, not only of religion, but also of the human race. For this reason all generations of men will admire the proofs of unbending courage which are to be found in the decrees of Nicholas I against Lothair; of Urban II and Paschal II against Philip I of France; of Celestine III and Innocent III against Alphonsus of Leon and Philip II of France; of Clement VII and Paul III against Henry VIII; and lastly,

184a Cf. Pius VI, *Ep. ad Episc. Lucion,* May 23, 1783.—
Pius VII, *Apost. Lett.,* Feb. 17, 1809; *Const.,* July 19, 1817.—Pius VIII, *Enc. "Traditi humilitati",* May 24, 1829 (cf. n. 64).—Gregory XVI, *Const.,* Aug. 15, 1832. —Pius IX, *Alloc.,* Sept. 22, 1852.

184b Council of Trent, Sess. 24, can. 5 and 7.

184c Council of Florence and *Istr. Eugenii IV ad Armenos.*—Benedict XIV, *Const. "Etsi pastoralis",* May 26, 1742.   184d Chap. 7 *de condit. appos.*

184e St. Jerome, *Lett.* 79 *ad Oceano.*—St. Ambrose, *lib.* 7 *in cap.* 16 *Lucae,* n. 5.—St. Augustine, *de nuptiis,* c. 10.

of Pius VII, that holy and courageous Pontiff, against Napoleon I at the height of his prosperity and in the fullness of his power.

Cooperation between Church and State

This being so, all rulers and administrators of the State who are desirous of following the dictates of reason and wisdom, and anxious for the good of their people, ought to make up their minds to keep the holy laws of marriage intact, and to make use of the proffered aid of the Church for securing the safety of morals and the happiness of families, rather than suspect her of hostile intention, and falsely and wickedly accuse her of violating the civil law. **185** *(67, 98)*

They should do this the more readily because the Catholic Church, though powerless in any way to abandon the duties of her office or the defense of her authority, still very greatly inclines to kindness and indulgence whenever they are consistent with the safety of her rights and the sanctity of her duties. Wherefore she makes no decrees in relation to marriage without having regard to the state of the body politic and condition of the general public; and has besides more than once mitigated, as far as possible, the enactments of her own laws, when there were just and weighty reasons. **186** *(42, 53, 54)*

Moreover, she is not unaware, and never calls in doubt, that the Sacrament of marriage, being instituted for the preservation and increase of the human race, has a necessary relation to circumstances of life, which, though connected with marriage, belong to the civil order, and about which the State rightly makes strict inquiry and justly promulgates decrees.

187
(54) Yet no one doubts that Jesus Christ, the Founder of the Church, willed her sacred power to be distinct from the civil power, and each power to be free and un-shackled in its own sphere: with this condition, however, —a condition good for both, and of advantage to all men —that union and concord should be maintained between them; and that on those questions which are, though in different ways, of common right and authority, the power to which secular matters have been entrusted should happily and becomingly depend on the other power which has in its charge the interests of heaven.

188
(98) In such arrangement and harmony is found not only the best line of action for each power, but also the most opportune and efficacious method of helping men in all that pertains to their life here, and to their hope of sal-vation hereafter. For, as We have shown in former Encyclical Letters (a), the intellect of man is greatly ennobled by the Christian Faith and made better able to shun and banish all error, while faith borrows in turn no little help from the intellect; and in like manner, when the civil power is in friendly terms with the sacred authority of the Church, there accrues to both great in-crease of usefulness. The dignity of the State is exalted, and so long as religion is its guide government will never rule unjustly; while the Church receives help of protec-tion and defense for the public good of the faithful.

Invitation to Governments

189
(98) Being moved, therefore, by these considerations, as We have exhorted rulers at other times, so still more

188a Enc. *Aeterni Patris,* Aug. 4, 1879.

earnestly We exhort them now to concord and friendly feeling; and We are the first to stretch out Our hand to them with fatherly benevolence, and to offer to them the help of Our supreme authority—a help which is more necessary at this time when, in public opinion, the authority of rulers is wounded and enfeebled. Now that the minds of so many are inflamed with a reckless spirit of liberty, and men are wickedly endeavoring to get rid of every restraint of authority, however legitimate it may be, the public safety demands that both powers should unite their strength to avert the evils that are hanging, not only over the Church, but also over civil society.

Invitation to the Bishops

But, while earnestly exhorting all to a friendly un- **190** ion of will, and beseeching God, the Prince of Peace, to *(99)* infuse a love of concord in all hearts, We cannot, Venerable Brethren, refrain from urging you more and more to fresh earnestness, and zeal, and watchfulness, though We know that these are already very great. With every effort and with all authority, strive, as much as you are able, to preserve whole and undefiled among the people committed to your charge the doctrine which Christ Our Lord taught us; which the Apostles, the interpreters of the will of God, have handed down, and which the Catholic Church has herself scrupulously guarded, and commanded to be believed in all ages by the faithful of Christ.

Instruction for the people

Let special care be taken that the people be well **191** instructed in the precepts of Christian wisdom, so that *(99,*

100) they may always remember that marriage was not instituted by the will of man, but, from the very beginning by the authority and command of God; that it does not admit of plurality of wives or husbands; that Christ, the Author of the New Covenant, raised it from a rite of nature to be a Sacrament, and gave to His Church legislative and judicial power with regard to the bond of marriage. On this point the very greatest care must be taken to instruct them, lest their minds should be led into error by the unsound conclusions of adversaries who desire that the Church should be deprived of that power (a).

192
(8,
74,
101)
In like manner all ought to understand clearly, that, if there be any union of a man and woman among the faithful of Christ which is not a Sacrament, such union has not the force and nature of a true marriage (a); that although contracted in accordance with the laws of the State, it cannot be more than a rite or custom introduced by the civil law. Further, the civil law can deal with and decide those matters alone which in the civil order spring from marriage, and which cannot possibly exist, as is evident, unless there be a true and lawful cause for them, that is to say, the nuptial bond.

> 191a *Quo in genere cavendum magnopere est, ne in errorum mentes inducantur a fallacibus conclusionibus adversariorum, qui ejusmodi potestatem ademptam Ecclesiae vellent.*
> 192a *Similiter omnibus exploratum esse debt, si qua conjunctio viri et mulieris inter Christifideles citra sacramentum contrahatur, eam vi ac ratione justi matrimonii carere.*

It is of the greatest consequence to husband and **193**
wife that all these things should be known and well *(16,*
understood by them, in order that they may conform to *54,*
the laws of the State, if there be no objection on the *57,*
part of the Church; for the Church wishes the effects *100,*
of marriage to be guarded in all possible ways, and that *101)*
no harm may come to the children.

In the great confusion of opinions, however, which
day by day is spreading more and more widely, it should
further be known that no power can dissolve the bond of
Christian marriage whenever this has been ratified and
consummated; and that, of a consequence, those husbands and wives are guilty of a manifest crime who plan,
for whatsoever reason, to be united in a second marriage before the first one has been ended by death (a).

When indeed, matters have come to such a pitch **194**
that it seems impossible for them to live together any *(76,*
longer, then the Church allows them to live apart, and *101,*
strives at the same time to soften the evils of this separa- *103,*
tion by such remedies and helps as are suited to their *107,*
condition; yet she never ceases to endeavor to bring *108)*
about a reconciliation, nor despairs of doing so.

But these are extreme cases; and they would seldom
exist if men and women entered into the married state
with proper dispositions, not influenced by passion, but
entertaining ideas of the duties of marriage and of its

193a *Id quoque est cognitu necessarium, solvere vinculum
conjugii inter christianos rati et consummati, nullius in
potestate esse; ideoque manifesti criminis reos esse, si
qui forte coniuges, quaecumque demum causa esse di-
catur, novo se matrimonii nexu ante implicare velint,
quam abrumpi primum morte contigerit.*

noble purpose; neither would they anticipate their marriage by a series of sins drawing down upon them the wrath of God.

195 To sum up everything in a few words: there would be
(103) a calm and quiet constancy in marriage, if married people would gather strength and life from the virtue of religion which imparts resolution and fortitude; for religion would enable them to bear tranquilly and even gladly the trials of their state—such as, for instance, the faults they discover in one another, the difference of temper and character, the weight of a mother's cares, the wearing anxiety about the education of children, reverses of fortune, and the sorrows of life.

Mixed marriages

196 Care must be taken that they do not easily enter
(83, into marriage with those who are not Catholic; for when
88, minds do not agree as to the observances of religion,
108) it is scarcely possible to hope for agreement in other things. Other reasons also proving that persons should turn with dread from such marriages are chiefly these: that they give occasion to forbidden association and communion in religious matters; endanger the faith of the Catholic partner; are a hindrance to the proper education of the children and often lead to a mixing up of truth and falsehood, and to the belief that all religions are equally good.

Charity towards those who have gone astray

197 Lastly, since We well know that none should be
(99, excluded from Our Charity, We commend, Venerable
101) Brethren, to your fidelity and piety those unhappy

persons who, carried away by the heart of passion, and being utterly indifferent to their salvation, live wickedly together without a bond of lawful marriage. Let your utmost care be exercised in bringing such persons back to their duty, and, both by your own efforts and by those of good men who will consent to help you, strive by every means that they may see how wrongly they have acted; that they may do penance; and that they may be induced to enter into a lawful marriage according to the Catholic rite.

You will at once see, Venerable Brethren, that the **198** doctrine and precepts in relation to Christian marriage, *(53)* which We have thought good to communicate to you in this letter, tend no less to the preservation of civil society than to the everlasting salvation of souls. May God grant that by reason of their gravity and importance, minds may everywhere be found docile and ready to obey them! For this end let us all suppliantly with humble prayer, implore the help of the Blessed and Immaculate Virgin Mary, that our hearts being quickened to the obedience of faith, she may show herself our Mother and our Help. With equal earnestness let us ask the Princes of the Apostles, Peter and Paul, the destroyers of heresies, the sowers of the seed of truth, to save the human race by their powerful patronage from the deluge of errors that is surging afresh.

DIVORCE IN FRANCE

Letter *Les événements,* May 12, 1883 to the President of the French Republic (a).

199a *Lettres Apostoliques de Leon XIII (Paris, Bonne Presse)* 6. 245.

(Remonstrances relative to various laws contrary to to the Church.)

199
(43,
53,
69,
77-
79)
Mr. President, We cannot delay to point out to you other grave dangers which seem to endanger the Catholic Church in France. We refer to two proposed laws, one of which concerns the sacred bond of matrimony and the other, the obligation of military service for the clergy. The political tact and wisdom of the men who hold power will certainly not permit that such projects—advanced by persons hostile to the Church and to the true welfare of society—become an integral part of the legislation of a country which has had nothing more at heart than to conserve the stability and harmony of the family, the foundation stone of the State's power and prosperity, and to protect and guarantee the formation of its patriotic clergy. We cannot now believe that the present intention is to abandon these noble and ancient traditions so as to introduce in France an innovation relative to the nature and character of matrimony, which besides being contrary to the doctrine of the Catholic Church—a doctrine which allows no compromise, since it was established thus by its Divine Founder—has had very sad results in non-Catholic countries. The result has been an increase in family disruptions, woman is no longer in honor, children suffer the greatest injury, domestic society is weakened and there is an increase in the corruption of morals.

(Other regulations contrary to the Church.)

PROJECTS OF FREEMASONRY

Encycl. *Humanum genus*, April 20, 1884.

(*Errors of Freemasons.*)

As regards domestic society, here in brief is the **200** Naturalists' doctrine. Matrimony is only a civil contract. *(63,* It can be rescinded legitimately by the free will of the *65,* partners. To the State belongs the power over the *70,* matrimonial bond. No religion is to be imposed on the *75)* children when educating them. When they are older, each one is free to choose that religion which pleases him most.

Now the Freemasons accept these principles without reserve. Not only do they accept them, but for a long time now they have studied a method which will make these principles part of custom and the way of life. In many countries, which do not hesitate to declare themselves Catholic, marriages which are not celebrated according to the civil law are declared null; in other places divorce is allowed; again in other countries everything is under way to obtain this permission as soon as possible. Everything is done in haste with the intenton of altering the nature of matrimony, to reduce it to a mutable and fleeting union which can be formed and broken at will.

(*Other errors*).

Likewise the other undertaking, to which Freemasons **201** give themselves wholeheartedly, consists in undermining *(65,* the foundation of morality, thus making itself an accom- *72,* plice and cooperator of those who would like everything *78)* to be lawful that is pleasing. This is nothing else than pushing human nature to the most abject and ignominious degradation.

Evil is increased by all the dangers which threaten both civil and domestic society. As We pointed out on another occasion, in matrimony there is a sacred and religious character, as witnessed the unanimous consent of peoples and ages. Besides, the conjugal union is indissoluble by divine law. If this union is now desecrated, if divorce is juridically permitted, the inevitable consequences will be confusion and discord in the family sanctuary, woman will lose her dignity and the children will lose the security of their very welfare.

(*False pretexts adopted by the Freemasons.—Means to be adopted against them*).

THE BOND OF THE FAMILY

Encycl. *Immortale Dei,* November 1, 1885.

(*Merits of the Church's social doctrine relative to the family and the State.*)

202
(*17,*
103) Domestic society has its solid foundation in the sanctity of a marriage which is one and indivisible. The husband's and wife's rights and duties are regulated with the wisest justice and equity. The husband's authority is based on that of God, the fatherly power is rightly tempered to the dignity of the wife and children: for the latter there must be provided maintenance, health and education.

203
(*43*) Augustine spoke admirably, as usual, in several of his works, of the value of these benefits, but especially so where he turns to the Catholic Church with these words: "You guide and instruct those who are children with arguments adapted for children; youth with magna-

nimity, old age with solemn calm, not according to the age which appears evident in the state of the body but that which is discerned in the spirit. You make wives remain subject to their husbands in chaste and faithful obedience, not for satisfying their passions, but for bearing children and working together in the management of the family. You place husbands over their wives not so they may use the weakess of their sex as the subject of their amusement, but so that they may be bound to their wives with a bond of sincere love. By means of such an ingenious subordination you submit the children to their parents, and place the parents over the children by means of an authority full of tenderness" (a).

MATRIMONY AND SOCIETY

Encyl. *Quod multum*, August 22, 1886 to the Bishops of Hungary.

(*The ancient glories of Hungary.—Actual problems.*)

With regard to that which concerns family life, **204** Venerable Brethren, study the best means to inculcate *(46,* into the people's minds the Catholic doctrine of the *82,* sanctity, unity and indissolubility of marriage. Endeavor *84)* to remind them as often as possible that marriages between Christians are, by their very nature, subject to ecclesiastical authority alone. Remind them often what the Church thinks and teaches on what is called "civil marriage" and with what a spirit and with what dispositions Catholics are bound to obey the law on such matters. Let them remember that it is unlawful for Catholics to

203a *De moribus Ecclesiae catholicae,* c. 30, n. 63.

contract marriage—and this for most serious reasons—
with those Christians who are separated from the
the Catholic Faith, and should they dare to do so, without the tolerant authorization of the Church, they sin
against God and against the Church. As this question
has all the importance which you well attribute to it, it is
necessary that all those whose duty it is should watch
with all attention and care, so that no one departs from
the rules laid down on this matter, no matter what the
reason. This is of importance, since on this point more
than on others, obedience to the Church is linked up
necessarily and fundamentally with the very salvation
of society.

205
(36,
43,
68,
83)
In fact, domestic society contains and strengthens
the principles and, so to speak, the best elements of
public life; in fact on the family depends, in large part,
the conditions for the peace and prosperity of the nation.
Now domestic society is what marriages make it, with
their happy or unhappy consequences. Marriages then
cannot bear good fruit if they are not regulated by God
and the Church. The marriage which is deprived of
these conditions, reduced to a servitude of capricious
passions, concluded against God's will and therefore deprived of the very necessary heavenly assistance, lacking
that intimacy of the religious life which is essential
above all else, cannot but bear very bitter fruits, to the
complete ruin of the family and the nation.

It is therefore necessary to consider as praiseworthy
not only by Religion but also by the Country those
Catholics who, two years ago, when the legislative as-
semblies of Hungary were urged to approve and prescribe the legality of marriages between Christians and

Jews, dismissed the proposal with a free and unanimous vote and obtained the confirmation of the previous law regarding marriages.

(*Education.—Clergy.—Press.*)

THE SUPREME LAW

Encycl. *Sapientiæ christianæ*, January 10, 1890.

(*Urgent need for a return to Christian principles.— God must be the Goal, and the supreme law of man's life is to direct himself towards Him.*)

What is said of individuals must be understood to be said of domestic and civil society. Nature did not beget society so that man might follow it as an end in itself, but rather that in it and by it he might find help suitable for his own perfection. **206 (37, 44)**

(*Civil duties of Christians.*)

This is a suitable moment for Us to exhort especially heads of families to endeavor to govern their households according to these precepts, and to educate well their children until they reach maturity. The family may be regarded as the cradle of civil society, and it is in great measure within the circle of family life that the destiny of the State is fostered. And so it is that they who would break away from Christian discipline are working to corrupt family life, to destroy it utterly, root and branch. From such an evil purpose they do not allow themselves to be restrained or deterred by reflecting that this cannot be achieved without inflicting cruel outrage on the parents, who hold from nature their right of training the children to whom they have given birth, with the **207 (23, 24, 37, 43, 65)**

additional obligation of shaping and directing the
education of their little ones to the end for which they
had these children from the goodness of God. It is then
incumbent on parents to make every effort to avert such
an outrage, and to strive manfully to have and to hold
exclusive authority to direct the education of their offspring, as is fitting, in a Christian manner; and first and
foremost to keep them away from schools where there is a
risk of their absorbing the poison of impiety.

(*Final exhortation.*)

SECULARIZATION

Encycl. *Dall'alto*, October 15, 1890 to the Italian
Episcopate.

(*Freemasonry's attacks on the Church and Catholic
Institutions.*)

208
(65,
72)
Every inspiration and religious idea is systematically
banished from official life when it is not directly attacked:
public manifestations of faith and Catholic piety are either
prohibited or interfered with by vain pretexts in a thousand different ways. By proclaiming what they call "civil
matrimony" and "all secular" instruction from elementary
grades to University level, the very foundation and
religious constitution of the family is undermined. Thus it
is that the new generations, in so far as the State has influence, are obliged to grow up without any idea of
religion, and ignorant of the primary and essential duties
towards God.

This is to put the axe to the root. Nor could one imagine a more universal and efficacious means of with-

drawing society, the family and individuals, from the influence of the Church and the Faith: "Undermine clericalism (by every means possible) in its foundations and at the very source of life, that is, in the school and in the family" is the authentic declaration of masonic writers.

... Whenever Freemasonry exerts its impious and disastrous action this system is adopted and put into use; and since Freemasonry is widely diffused, this anti-Christian system is also widely applied.

(*Meaning of the struggle: Faith or free-thinking.— Measures to be adopted.*)

Society receives its life, increase and strength from **209** the family firmly constituted on its natural foundations. *(43,* Without religion and morality domestic society has no *68)* stability and family bonds are weakened and broken.

NATURAL RIGHTS

Encycl. *Rerum Novarum*, May 15, 1891.

(*Errors of Socialism regarding private property.*)

The rights here spoken of, belonging to each in- **210** dividual man, increase in strength when considered in *(19,* relation to man's social and domestic obligations. In *38,* choosing a state of life, it is indisputable that all are *44,* at full liberty to follow the evangelical counsel to ob- *56,* serve virginity, or to bind themselves by the marriage *109,* bond. No human law can abolish the natural and original *110)* right of marriage, nor in any way limit the chief and principal purpose of marriage ordained by God's authority from the beginning: "Increase and multiply" (a). Hence we have the family; domestic society—a society very small, true, but none the less a true society, and one older than any State. Consequently it has rights and duties peculiar to itself which are quite independent of the State.

Family and property

211
(23,
25,
37,
38)
That right to property, therefore, which has been proved to belong naturally to individual persons, must likewise belong to a man in his capacity as head of the family; rather, that right is all the stronger in proportion as the human person receives a wider extension in the family group. It is a most sacred law of nature that a father should provide food and all necessaries for those whom he has begotten; and, likewise, by an impulse of the same nature that makes him see in his children an image of himself—an expression and continuation of his personality—that he should provide them with all that is necessary to enable them to keep themselves decently from want and misery amid the uncertainties of this mortal life. Now in no other way can a father effect this than the ownership of productive property, which he can transmit to his children by inheritance.

Family and State

212
(38,
44)
The family, no less than the State, is, as We have have pointed out, a true society, governed by an authority peculiar to itself, namely, by the authority of the father. Provided, therefore, the limits which are prescribed by the very purposes for which it exists be not

210a Gen. 1:28.

transgressed, the family has at least equal rights with the State in the choice and pursuit of what it needs for its preservation and just liberty. We say, at least equal rights; for inasmuch as the domestic household is antecedent—in logic and in fact—to the gathering of men in a community, the family must necessarily have rights and duties which are prior to those of the community, and founded more immediately in nature. If a man, if his family, on entering into civil society, were to experience at the hands of the State hindrance instead of help, and were to find their rights attacked instead of being upheld, then association in the State would be an object of detestation rather than of desire.

The contention, then, that the civil government should at its option intrude into and exercise control over the family and household is a great and pernicious error. Indeed, if a family finds itself in exceeding distress, utterly deprived of the counsel of friends, and without any prospect of extricating itself, it is right that extreme necessity be met with public aid, since each family is a part of the social body. In like manner, if within the precincts of the household there occur grave disturbances of mutual rights, public authority should intervene to force each party to yield to the other its proper due; for this is not depriving citizens of their rights, but safeguarding and strengthening them in a just and fitting manner. But the rulers of the State must go no further: here nature bids them stop. Paternal authority can be neither abolished nor absorbed by the State; for it has the same source as human life itself. "The child belongs to the father", and is, as it were, the continuation of the father's personality; and speaking

213
(23, 25, 40, 42, 44)

strictly, the child takes its place in civil society, not of its own right, but in its quality as a member of the family in which it is born. And for the very reason that "the child belongs to the father", it is, as St. Thomas Aquinas says, "before it attains the use of free will, under the power and charge of its parents" (a). The Socialists, therefore, substituting for the care of the parent that of the State, act against natural justice, and break up the stability of all family life.

(*Exposition of the Christian social order.*)

THE HOLY FAMILY

Apost. Let. *Neminem fugit,* January 14, 1892.

214 No one is unaware that private and public prosperity
(*43,* depend principally on the constitution of the family.
106) The community's welfare will be measured by the virtues which have taken root in the family and by the extent of the parents' zeal for inculcating in their children—by doctrine and example—the precepts of religion. For it is of the greatest importance that domestic society not only be firmly constituted, but also that it be ruled by holy laws and that the religious spirit and the principles of Christian life be carefully and constantly developed. It is evidently for this purpose that the merciful God—wishing to accomplish the work of the restoration of humanity which had long been awaited—so prepared the details and the manner of Redemption that from the beginning this work would present to the world the august form of a divinely constituted family, in which all men could

213a St. Thomas, *Summa Theologica,* 2a 2ae, q. 10, a. 12.

contemplate the most perfect model of family life and an example of every virtue and sanctity.

Such was the family of Nazareth, wherein was hid- **215** den, before presenting Himself to the world in the mag-*(106)* nificence of His splendor, the Sun of Justice, Christ, God Our Savior, together with the Virgin Mary and St. Joseph, her most holy Spouse and foster father of Jesus. Without doubt, the perfection which results in civil society and domestic life from reciprocal fidelity to the duties of charity, from sanctity of morals and the practice of the virtues, shone with the greatest light in this holy Family, which was to be the model of all other families. Thus, by a benevolent disposition of Providence, this family is constituted in such a manner that all Christians, of every condition and race, can with a little attention, easily find therein a motive for practicing every virtue and an invitation to do so. In fact, fathers of families have an excellent example of vigilance and fatherly protection in Joseph; the Most Holy Mother of God is an admirable example and pattern of love, modesty, of the spirit of submission and perfect faith for mothers; in the person of Jesus, who "was subject to them" (a), children have a divine model of obedience to be admired, venerated and imitated.

(*Devotion to the Holy Family.—Foundation of an Association in honor of the Holy Family.*)

CIVIL MATRIMONY IN ITALY

Letter *Il divisamento,* February 8, 1893 to the Italian Bishops.

215a Luke 2:51.

216   The project to sanction a new law, which imposes
(69) the precedence of the civil rite to the celebration of Christian marriage has rightfully aroused your pastoral vigilance, and you are to be praised for your decision not
to take any steps before you had called upon this Apostolic See, to which *"propter potiorem principalitatem
necesse semper fuit omnem convenire Ecclesiam"* (a).

217   Concerned as We always are, by reason of the bur-
(6, den of Our supreme office, for the safety of the Christian
38, flock, We never hesitated amidst Our grave and incessant
64, cares, to inculcate many times, the necessity of retaining
67, the holy character of Christian marriage impressed on it
70) by its Divine Founder, and this the more strongly as on
it depend the holiness of the family, peace of conscience,
the proper education of the chldren and the welfare of
civil society. We particularly explained with the greatest
care and completeness the Catholic doctrine on such
an argument especially in Our Encyclical Letter *Arcanum Divinae Sapientiae* (a). At the same time We kept
in mind what had been done by the Church during its
history to achieve and maintain the Christian dignity of
the marriage union, and in addition what can be legitimately allowed to the civil power in respect of this union.
If all those who heard Our discourse had been men of
good will, or even of good faith, We would have justly
hoped that once the truth was known, thus illuminating
the mind, it would have induced them, if not to repair
immediately the wrongs already done to the Church with
unjust interference in the marriage of her children, at
least to cease from worse outrages.

216a Cf. St. Irenaeus, *Adv. Haer.*, 1. 3, c. 3. 2.—Migne.
P.G., 7, 849.   217a Cf. n. 143 and ss. of this volume.

But so obstinate is the rancor in some persons that they oppose anything that is Christian and continue in the sad work, already commenced, of laicizing, as they say, society,—this means, to render it independent of Jesus Christ and deprive it of the immense benefits of the Redemption—and far from compensating for the damage publicly done, they threaten it further with this proposed law well known to all.

The Christian dogma

It is not necessary to repeat here word by word the teachings already given, since they are accessible to you and your faithful. Yet it is not inopportune to declare once again that the civil power may regulate the civil effects of marriage, but it must leave to the Church that which regards Matrimony in itself. Let the State admit the fact of true and legitimate matrimony, as instituted by Jesus Christ and practiced by the Church, and then take steps to concede or deny it the effects which follow in the civil community. It is a dogma of Faith that the marriage of Christians was raised by Our Lord Jesus Christ to the dignity of a Sacrament, nor can this dignity, according to Catholic doctrine, be treated as an accidental quality added to the matrimonial contract, but rather it is intimately essential to it, so much so that the very contract became a Sacrament by divine institution. Vain distinction between the contract and the sacrament from which one would infer therefore, is that distinction that between Christians there can exist a valid marriage contract which is not a Sacrament. Since the administration of the Sacraments belongs exclusively to the Church, every interference of political authority in the matrimonial contract—not confined merely to its civil effects—is a sacrilegious usurpation.

218
(7,
8,
47,
54,
55,
56,
70)

The sense of the law

219
(16,
56,
70,
73)

Now a law that would prescribe the precedence of the civil rite to the true marriage which is contracted in the Church would really have as its object the matrimonial contract itself and not merely its civil effects. Thus the State would pretend to administer a Sacrament. No other power, except that to which belongs such an administration, can or ought to judge the conditions necessary for celebrating marriage, as regards the attitude and the capacity of the contracting parties, and the other circumstances on which depend the lawfulness and the validity of the marriage contract. Nor is it right to say that the civil power by its law of the precedence of the civil rite does not affect the Sacrament administered by the Church, that it does not deny it and it does not recognize it, leaving to the free will of the contracting parties the right to celebrate the religious service afterwards if they wish to do so.

In truth, this law would punish a religious marriage, that is a true marriage, by declaring it implicitly illicit if it is not preceded by the civil rite, for one does not pretend to punish a lawful act. The punishment that the prescribed law threatens and which would be sanctioned were the law transgressed would certainly not render null a matrimony contracted according to the Church's laws. Here it is a matter of the divine and natural law, against which no power on earth can prevail. The law would, however, use every means to ensure that such a marriage was considered as null, to impede the obligations and to frustrate the effects that legitimately follow such a contract.

If this were not sufficiently clear in itself, it would **220** become fully obvious upon consideration of an unjust *(73)* and sacrilegious provision recently enacted with regard to the marriages of soldiers, upon whom separation from their wives has been enjoined after they had been legitimately united. Thus, in these days of such vaunted civil progress, we would return to an ancient and barbarous tyranny which dared to deprive men of a right given to them by nature, a tyranny which the Church labored so hard to dispel. The only difference would be that formerly slaves were refused the right of lawful marriage, while today this right would be denied to soldiers and other classes of persons, despoiling them of their freedom and making slaves of them.

Moral consequences

But this is not the only injury which the Church **221** must suffer as the result of such a law. There is another *(48,* equally serious. Everyone knows that Our Divine Savior *71)* committed to His Church the judgment and regulation not only of those matters which regard the Faith, but also of those concerning morality. The Church was instituted by Him so that it might be a sure and infallible guide in the way of eternal salvation. Since it is not sufficient to believe rightly, but is necessary also to act according to the faith, thus to the Church belongs—since she is the depository of the Faith—the judgment of the moral law and its practice. Now it is precisely a matter of morality and practice to ascertain if in certain cases it is better to marry or to abstain from marriage.

The state of virginity is of itself more perfect than **222** the married state, and those who inspired by grace em- *(12,* brace such a state are worthy of the highest praise. But *110)* this grace of perfect continence is not given to all, so that, according to the Apostle, *melius est nubere quam uri* (a). It can likewise happen through the malice and weakness of corrupted nature that reprehensible practices between two persons have gone so far that marriage alone will save one of the parties from grave injury and harm or remove the danger to the eternal salvation of both parties. At other times, to prevent scandal and discord in the families or even between the families, it will be necessary to celebrate marriage with haste and secrecy, leaving its publication to a later date and more favorable circumstances.

223
(56, 61, 64, 73, 110)
These and other most just considerations are not taken into account by a State which, pretending to absorb in itself every right of the family and the individual, does not hesitate to place everyone in its grip, under the pretext of providing for itself: and it would provide in truth very unwisely. To a State which desires to prescind from every divine and Christian law, it little matters that sins are multiplied or that illicit relations are sought after and persevered in; even if reason, faith and history evidently show that the corruption of moral customs weakens, wastes and consumes society.

224
(73)
Such is the blindness and hatred of these new legislators, that even at the very point of death, when a soul is about to present itself at the judgment seat of God, they would bind his minister, by not allowing him to exercise his ministry of reconciliation, peace and salvation; or if he were permitted to do so, it is under such severe conditions that, were they followed to the letter, they would expose a soul to eternal damnation.

222a 1 Cor. 7:9.

The Church's duty

The Church, no matter what an earthly power may decide, will never fail in her divine mission, and cannot be content to see the souls redeemed by the blood of Jesus Christ perish, for which she must render a very strict account. Nor, to tell the truth, has the State anything to fear if it leaves the Church to act with the liberty that belongs to her sacred ministry. If she willingly permits at times secret marriages, or, as they are called, marriages of conscience, she only does so in most urgent and serious cases, as is demanded by the Supreme Law—the good of souls. But the Church herself has fixed the conditions, so as to limit them as much as possible. She has prescribed remedies so that neither the contracting parties nor the offspring suffer and has minutely regulated the matter to prevent other difficulties. **225 (12, 46, 48, 53, 73)**

On the other hand, she deplores both in her legislation and in practice, the existence of such cases, and uses every means possible to ensure that marriages be contracted publicly and with solemnity.

Sufficient proof of this is found in the Constitution *Satis Vobis* (a) of Our illustrious Predecessor, Benedict XIV. After having pointed out what the Councils and the Pontiffs have wisely established for the public solemnity of marriage and enumerated the evils that arise from neglecting these provisions, he admits nevertheless that there are some rare necessary exceptions; but turning to the Bishops, he exhorts them: "An equal, and even perhaps greater vigilance must be used by you lest, after the omission of the banns, the marriage be **226 (12)**

226a Cf. above nn. 4-8.

celebrated in the presence of the Pastor alone or his delegate and two discreet witnesses in order to prevent any publicity or knowledge. In order for this to be licit according to the prescripts of the Sacred Canon, it is not enough to have any ordinary reason, but a serious, urgent reason is required. . . . Part of your pastoral office is to carefully investigate the legitimacy and urgency of the reason for the dispensation in order that marriages secretly celebrated will not have sad results, as with great sorrow, we have noted" (b).

Masonic origin of the law

227 As matters stand, it can be rightly asked what rea-
(73) son the State can possibly have to impose the precedence of the civil rite. Since the marriage contracted in the eyes of the Church is generally public it cannot go unnoticed by the State. The latter, with the laws already in force, has already provided, even excessively, for the civil effects which alone are its concern. Not being content with the so-called civil marriage, why then does it now want to claim its precedence? To hinder perhaps the very rare cases of marriages of conscience, marriages which the Church herself does not permit unless forced to do so for very grave reasons? But the law, ordained of its nature to the common welfare, would be wrongly occupied in concerning itself with those singular cases, which certainly would not disturb public peace and tranquillity, the goal of public authority. Since the law is in ordinance of reason, it would never be just to prevent the doing in those very rare cases of what morality and the eternal salvation of souls demand.

226b The English translation can be found in n. 8 cited above.

If the very essence of the threatened law did not **228** of its nature manifest its final end, it would be sufficient *(64,* to observe those who inspire and encourage it. It is not *65)* a mystery, but a notorious public fact, that the Masonic sect has for a long time meditated this new blow against the Church, and now that the time is ripe imposes upon its members the duty of effecting it. The aims of this evil-intentioned sect are always and everywhere the same, namely, direct hostility to God and his Church. Little or nothing does it concern this sect that souls are lost, we do not say) that society decays more day by day and falls to ruin and that the boasted liberty is suppressed, provided the Church is chained and oppressed with it, and that Christian sentiment be gradually weakened and eradicated from the people.

Irony of the freedom offered by the law

The word liberty in the mouth of those who would **229** pretend to regulate at their pleasure a right given by *(36,* nature whose exercise is anterior to the constitution of *42,* civil society is but bitter irony. Civil society has as *56,* its immediate elements the families which are formed and *65,* constituted by the conjugal bond (a). Still greater is the *109)* damage done to consciences when such a law is forced on a Catholic nation. Such a nation, faithful to the tradition handed down to it, and, through a singular privilege, closer to the center of unity, feels all the more

229a *Per fermo non resta ormai che una amara ironia la parola di libertà in bocca a coloro che pretendono regolare a discrezione un diritto che ogni uomo ha da natura, l'esercizio del quale precede la costituzione della società civile essendochè questa ha per immediati elementi le familglie, le quali vengono formate e costituite dal legame coniugale.*

strongly the damage done to its most sacred convictions and its faith.

230
(73, 74) Nothing can be gained by repeating that the State leaves the persons free to celebrate matrimony even in the Church, since this would leave an equal freedom to the parties of abstaining from such an act, thus introducing by way of practice the erroneous opinion that persons married by the civil rite live in legitimate marriage, while it is obvious that their state is only an abominable concubinage. Again, if the Church, for just reasons, were not able to join in matrimony those who were already bound by civil law, these couples would be constrained to a celibacy for which they have neither desire nor vocation, or on the other hand, to live in an illicit and scandalous union.

231
(73) Not only is violence done to the liberty of the contracting parties, but even to that of the witnesses. This violence is all the more hateful because friends and intimates who are chosen at a time of necessity would be turned into despicable informers, betraying friendship. Tyranny is at its height when it is exercised against the ministers of the Church. They are arrested and punished solely for having assisted at an act which belongs exclusively to the Church; for having safeguarded the most sacred laws of morality and the salvation of souls; in other words, they are accused of doing wrong because they acted according to their conscience and their duty. And all this as if it were a minor offense to common liberty arising from the very provisions of the law, yet it would now be increased by an unheard of severity which manifests itself as partisan and hostile when exercised by a State which pretends, in the rest of its legis-

lation, to show itself lenient in accordance with the customs of the age.

The very State that abolishes or mitigates punishment due to the gravest crimes shows itself willing to oppress the faithful and the priests who, following the voice of their conscience, obey Jesus Christ and His Church. The affected ignorance and self-contradictions of the legislators with reference to Pastors will not go unnoticed by anyone. At the time the legislators appear to show compassion for their poverty and promise to better their condition, they deliberate how to subject them to enormous fines which can never be paid.

This, then, in brief, is the judgment which must be brought against the new law in question. It usurps the rights of the Church, hinders its salutary work and places the salvation of souls in danger. It opposes the true liberty of the faithful and the citizens, promotes and sanctions sacrilegious unions, opens the path to new scandals and moral disorders. It troubles peaceful consciences, renders more acute the conflict between Church and State, a conflict which is completely contrary to the order established by the Creator, is rightly censured and deplored by all honest minds, and of which the Church has certainly not been the cause. 232 (71, 72, 74)

EVILS OF MIXED MARRIAGES

Encycl. *Constanti Hungarorum*, September 2, 1893 to the Bishops of Hungary.

(*New laws contrary to ecclesiastical rights*).

Furthermore, to impede the violence of several evils it is most necessary for the pastors of souls continually to remind the people of the duty they have of avoiding 233 (82, 84) marriage with non-Catholics. Let the faithful be aware of and remember at all times the need of avoiding such relationships which are so detested by the Church, especially for those reasons which We have already pointed out in Our letters (a) "that they give occasion to a forbidden communion of life and religion; endanger the faith of the Catholic partner; are a hindrance to the proper education of the children; and often lead to a confusion of truth and falsehood, and to the belief that all religions are of equal value, without distinction of truth and falsehood."

(*Other harmful laws.—Remedies to use.*)

SANCTITY OF MATRIMONY

Encycl. *Caritatis,* March 19, 1894 to the Bishops of Poland.

(*Social influence of the Church.*)

234
(17,
23,
32,
36,
43)
The integrity and honesty of family life, which is the lifeline of civil society, must be sought in the sanctity of matrimony established according to the precepts of God and the Church, one and indivisible. It is therefore necessary that the duties and the rights between husband and wife be maintained inviolate, and that they perform these duties in all charity and harmony. Let parents provide for the care and upbringing of the children, especially in the matter of education, and let them be first of all teachers by their conduct—no means could be more efficacious or important.

(*Formation of the clergy.—Religious Orders.*)

233a Cf. Enc. *Arcanum divinaae Sapientiae;* n. 196 in this volume.

DIVORCE IN THE UNITED STATES

Letter *Longinqua oceani,* January 6, 1895 to the Bishops of America.

(American legislation and the Church.)

The Christian dogma of the unity and indissolubil- **235** ity of marriage ... offers a most solid guarantee of se- *(17,* curity, not only to family life, but even to civil society. *75,* Many of your fellow citizens, among them those who *79)* disagree with us in other matters, admire and approve the Catholic doctrine and practice on this point, worried as they are by the license of divorce. They are moved to do so as much by love of their country as by correctness of judgment. One cannot imagine a greater evil for society than the attempt to dissolve that bond which God designed as perpetual and indissoluble.

(There follows a citation from the Encyclical "Arcanum", which is quoted above, n. 179.—Workers' associations.—Problems of the laity.)

"CIVIL MARRIAGE" IN HUNGARY

Consistorial All., March 18, 1895.

(Reference to the letters sent to the Bishops of Hungary, quoted above nn. 204; 233.—New law of marriage.)

The law instituted the so-called "civil marriage"; **236** divorce was allowed; Catholic marriage was prohibited *(69,* before the civil ceremony was completed. *71,*

Bishops have acted in all possible ways, tried to use *72,* all the means at their disposal, as was their duty, to save *79)* the Church and the nation from such disastrous evil; the clergy have done everything in their power to help their bishops; the representatives of both Houses of Parliament who wished to preserve the Faith of their forefathers have vigorously attacked the bill. However, these efforts, united in such a just and holy cause, have been in vain. Those who for so long used all means to corrupt public morality and to hasten Hungarian affairs along the road of dangerous innovations have been the victors.

(The Pope recalls the previous teaching on such matters.)

237
(36,
42,
47,
54,
78,
79)
Let those who are principally interested in this affair consider how dangerous and contrary to justice it is to impose on a Catholic nation a form of marriage condemned a thousand times by the Church. The Heads of State have the competence and the right to regulate the civil effects that result from marriage; but to the Church belongs legislation about the conjugal bond, because Our Lord Jesus Christ conferred this power on His Church, elevating Matrimony from a natural institution to the dignity of a Sacrament. Here it is sufficient to recall the Christian dogma of the unity and the perpetuity of marriage. When these qualities disappear the principal foundation on which Jesus Christ ordained the family and the State to be established disappears. No man can hinder the divine will of Him who came to restore and perfect both civil and domestic society.

(Difficulty with the Italian government over the nomination of Bishops.)

"CIVIL MARRIAGE" IN PERU

Letter *Quam religiosa*, August 10, 1898 to the Bishops of Peru.

It grieves Us to see that the recently promulgated law in your country under the pretext of regulating marriages contracted by non-Catholics introduces in fact the so-called civil marriage, even if such a law is not extended to all citizens. Furthermore, the authority of the Church being despised, such civil marriage is permitted for mixed marriages, even if the Apostolic See, for grave reasons and having in view the eternal salvation of the Christian family, does not believe it opportune in some cases to grant a dispensation from the law which prohibits marriage by reason of disparity of cult. **238** *(69, 71, 83)*

Sorrowfully affected by these measures contrary to the submission which is due to Us and to the power which is conferred on Our Supreme ministry, We raise Our Apostolic voice, Venerable Brethren, and excite your zeal, that, keeping watch over the safety of the faithful of Peru, you secure that the Catholic doctrine of marriage be preserved intact and unaltered. **239** *(69)*

Preoccupied with the whole Christian people, as the burden of Our Apostolic See requires, We have never let slip the numerous opportunities to give instruction and regulations regarding the sanctity of marriage. We have taught that a natural function transformed by Jesus Christ, the Author of the New Covenant, into a Sacrament, cannot be separated from religion and put into the category of profane matters. We have pointed out that the life of the contracting parties entered upon with the sacred rite is more peaceful and happy; that family unity is reinforced; that the children are better brought up and that the good of the State is happily assured. We have treated this theme at greater length **240** *(11, 55)* most carefully in Our Apostolic Letter, *Arcanum Divinae Sapientiae* (a), in which We pointed out to the faithful: 1) the vigilant diligence which the Church, the best guardian and protector of the human race, has employed to preserve the honor and sanctity of matrimony; 2) the part that falls to the government of the State and about which it can legitimately legislate and judge. We do not intend, and there would be no need to do so, to repeat here all this teaching which you already know.

241
(7,
8,
47,
49,
54,
55,
56)
However, it would be well for Us to recall once again that if those who govern the State have power over the human questions deriving from matrimony, such as are purely civil matters, they have no right nor any authority over Christian Matrimony in the strict sense. They must allow a matter not established by human authority to be subject to the jurisdiction of the Church. Once the marriage contract is legitimately made, namely, in the manner it was instituted by Jesus Christ, their only concern is to see if there is something which affects the civil order. Since Catholic doctrine, from which no one can stray without sacrificing his Faith, declares that Matrimony contracted between Christians is clothed with the dignity of a Sacrament, no authority other than the divine authority of the Church can govern and regulate it; and no conjugal union can be held valid if it is not contracted according to the law and the discipline of the Church.

CONSEQUENCES OF DIVORCE

Consistorial All., December 16, 1901.

240a Cf. above, nn. 143-198.

(Of all the Church's sufferings, the Pope wishes to call to mind here the attempts made in Italy against the sanctity of Matrimony.)

...We do not admonish but beg all those on whose deliberation depends the present law of *divorce*, that they desist from the enterprise for the sake of all that they hold dear and sacred. Let them not refuse to note and consider seriously, how holy, indivisible and perpetual by divine law is the matrimonial bond of Christians; and how such a law can never, by any human law, be abrogated or derogated. It is a great and dangerous error to wish to reduce Christian marriage to a matter that can be contracted and resolved by civil law.

For the Redeemer and Restorer of human nature, Jesus Christ, the Son of God, having abolished the use of divorce, brought Matrimony back to the primitive state in which it had been authoritatively constituted by God Himself. Elevating it to the dignity and virtue of a Sacrament, He placed it above the type of ordinary contract and above the jurisdiction of civil power, even above ecclesiastical power itself. The civil powers may regulate the civil effects which flow from the bond of matrimony: but to go further is forbidden by God's will.

Every law then that ratifies divorce, is iniquitous, and openly unjust before God, the Creator and Supreme Legislator: therefore it can only give rise to adulterous unions, not to legitimate marriage (a).

242
(4,
54,
55,
57,
75,
77,
80)

242a *Ultro progredi, Dei nutu prohibetur. Omnis ergo lex quae rata esse divortia iubeat, iubet contra fas; apertaque cum iniuria creatoris summique legumlatoris Dei; proptereque causam dare adulterino foederi potest, coniugio iusto non potest.*

243   Culpability increases when it is realized that to re-
(53, strict divorce within foreseen bounds is as difficult in
76, practice as to confine wthin set limits the flames of the
77, most ardent passions.
79)   It is vain, besides, to draw support from foreign
examples in a matter undoubtedly criminal. Can the
multitude of those who sin ever diminish sin itself or
even excuse it? It is all the more obvious when one considers that divorce was never given legal sanction without the Church having ever opposed it whenever possible
with all its authority as guardian and defender of divine
law. Let no one dare to hope that today she is less mindful than in the past of her duties never to connive in
such evil. She will not pass over in silence nor tolerate
submissively the injury done to God and to herself.

244   A great source of evils is enclosed in this iniquity,
(78, and so among these very men who do not fully accept
79) Catholic institutions, or who do not recognize any of
them, there are many, nevertheless, who moved by a
desire for public welfare, fight courageously and wisely
in favor of the indissolubility of matrimony.
        The lawfulness of breaking the matrimonial bond
having in fact been established, the constant and stable
nature of matrimony is upset by law. For this reason
those consequences which We Ourselves have at another time deplored, came on in swift succession: the
weakening of mutual affection on both sides; the opportunity for pernicious incitement towards infidelity;
the endangering of the upbringing and education of
children; the fostering of the germs of discord between
families; the radical disturbing of all things; the reducing of the status of women to the lowest degradation.

Since both the prosperity of family life and the well-being of the State are increased by good morals, and ruined by corrupt ones, it is easy to understand how ruinous are divorces for both public and private order, proceeding as they do from the degradation of morals and leading in turn to ultimate licence.

IMPIOUS LAWS

Encycl. *Annum ingressi sumus*, March 19, 1902.

(*The struggle against the Church.—Its History.— Its result: practical atheism.*)

From such a system of practical atheism there must derive, as there did derive a profound disturbance in the moral order. . . . Each member of the social body had to suffer gravely beginning with the family.

When the secular State, overstepping its boundaries and the essential scope of its power, extended its hand to desecrate the conjugal bond, depriving it of its religious character, it invaded to the full the natural right of parents to educate their children and weakened in various places the stability of matrimony by sanctioning the law of divorce.

Everyone can see what are its fruits. An innumerable number of marriages are made on the basis only of ignoble passions and in a short time they break up or degenerate with tragic consequences or scandalous infidelities. What then of the innocent children, neglected and perverted by the parents' bad example, or by the poison abundantly administered by a State officially secular?

(*Remedies: a return to the Catholic Church.—Value of its doctrine.*)

245
(64,
65,
68,
69,
75)

246
(53) Knowing full well this divine virtue, We have, from the very beginning of our Pontificate, deliberately used every means to bring to light and emphasize the benefits of the Church, and to extend as far as possible its salutary action with the treasure of her doctrines. The more important Acts of Our Pontificate were directed to this end and especially so the Encyclicals on Christian philosophy, human liberty, Christian Matrimony, freemasonry, public powers, Christian constitution of the State, socialism, the workers' question, the principal duties of Christian citizens and on other arguments related thereto.

(*Calumnies against the Church.—Her present battles.—Exhortation.*)

THE WORK OF JESUS CHRIST

Letter *Dum multa,* December 24, 1902, to the Bishops of Ecuador.

(*Legislation contrary to religion in Ecuador.*)

247
(4,
7,
8,
15,
46,
54,
69, After Jesus Christ, the Son of God, the Redeemer and Restorer of human nature, elevated Matrimony to the dignity of a Sacrament, every marriage between Christians is by that very fact a Sacrament, nor can the contract be in any way separated from the Sacrament (a). It follows that—having excepted the rights which the State has over what are called the civil effects— Matrimony falls under the authority of the Church.

247a *Omne apud christianos matrimonium idem sacramentum illico est, nec ratio contractus a sacramenti ratione sejungi nullo modo potest.*

Besides, it is certain that Jesus, the Redeemer of all peo- 75)
ples, abolished the bill of divorce, and gave back to
Matrimony, which was strengthened by a new sanctity,
its indissolubility which it had received in the beginning
through the will of God Himself.

It follows that the marriage of Christians in the   **248**
same moment that it is completed acquires its sanctity, *(14,*
unity and perfection. It cannot be dissolved for any   *48,*
reason whatsoever, save the death of one of the partners, *53,*
in conformity to the words of Sacred Scripture: "What   *71,*
God hath joined together, let no man put asunder" (a).   *77)*
Jesus Christ had in mind the numerous interests of mankind: in practice nothing better assures the preservation
and restoration of good morality, and nothing could be
thought to be more useful and efficacious to nourish the
reciprocal love between husband and wife, and to procure for the family the stability of divine power, to give
back to the children the blessing of the protection and
the education of former times, to safeguard woman's
dignity and to assure the honor and prosperity of the
family and the State.

Therefore, in virtue of Our office of Supreme
Teacher, constituted as We are guardian and defender
of divine and ecclesiastical law, We raise Our voice to
reprove in full the recently promulgated laws in this
republic: the so-called law of civil marriage, and the
law of divorce, and at the same time We reject all that
has been attempted among you against Church discipline.

(*Invitation to defend the Church's rights.*)

248a Matt. 19:6.

ST. PIUS X
1903-1914

EXTENSION OF THE CANONICAL FORM

Decree *Provida sapientique,* January 18, 1906.

The Holy Church has always used her wisdom and her solicitous care to regulate those matters relating to the stability and sanctity of Christian marriage, making it the subject of her laws. And there must be mentioned firstly that law which the Council of Trent adopted to abolish clandestine marriages and eradicate that very real evil from Christian peoples. Everyone knows that this decree was and still is of the greatest value throughout Christendom. In certain places, however, especially in the German Empire on account of its deplorable and numerous religious divisions, of its daily more intricate intermingling of Catholics and heretics, it happens that, as happens in all things human, some grave inconveniences result from the aforesaid law. In fact the Council desired that the chapter *Tametsi* (a) should not have legislative force in any Parish until it had been regularly promulgated. Since, on the other hand, in many places there is a doubt of fact about such promulgation and about the extension of the obligation to non-Catholics

249

(12,

46,

52)

249a The chapter *Tametsi* of Sessio 24 of the Council of Trent, declared clandestine marriages invalid (that is contracted with only a consensual exchange between the parties) and rendered obligatory the canonical-form, exacting the presence of the parish priest and two witnesses.

living in one or another of these places, it follows that a great and difficult diversity and confusion of law exists in several parts of the German Empire. The numerous and thorny problems perplex the judges themselves; so much so that there has arisen among Christian people and non-Catholics irreverence towards the law and nev-erending arguments and accusations.

(*Attempts made by the Holy See to regulate the question.—New norms which extend the Canonical form to the whole of Germany, but for Catholics only; mar-riages of Protestants will remain valid even without this form.*) (b)

"CIVIL MARRIAGE" IN BOLIVIA

Letter *Afflictum propioribus*, November 24, 1906, to the Bishops of Bolivia.

(*Draft of laws contrary to the Church's right.*)

250
(*46,*
65,
69,
71,
72)
Christian matrimony, then, the character and dig-nity of which is held in such high honor by this nation, together with the natural and proper right of the Church over Christian marriages, which she surrounds with re-spect, are now the objects of iniquitous attempts aimed at tearing away from the Church this her exclusive right, to make way for and impose the so-called civil marriage.

Certainly, you and your people can easily see that these laws are injurious to the Church, an obstacle to

249b These prescriptions were a step ahead towards the legislation of the Code of Canon Law. See can. 1094 and 1099. Cf. n. 254, note (a).

good morals and virtues; a step backwards on the road of true and salutary progress for nations and peoples. We are sure that you have done everything possible to avoid this scourge for your country and for your religion and that at present individually or collectively you will protest against these laws and projects. The duty of Our office, which is to rule all nations, earnestly binds us to watch with diligence that the Christian community does not have to suffer in any way at all.

Therefore, it belongs to Us in the first place to re- **251** call the most holy rights of the Church, to confirm them *(63,* regardless of any power, to recommend and protect *99)* them. As there is at stake the supreme interest of the public and of individuals and as by these means the source of the great evils which threaten society and the family can be dried up, We believe it Our duty to explain the principles of Christian matrimony, since they seem to be unknown and to have been replaced by fallacious errros by those who hold the powers of government.

In fact they must have forgotten the sacred character of Christian matrimony and have been filled with erroneous opinions, since they wished to make themselves master of the reserved field of matrimony, proposing laws which are full of snares (a).

It is impossible, in fact, for the Christian people to **252** doubt that matrimony, instituted by God as a function of *(2,*

251a On July 3, 1907, the Holy Office in the Decree *Lamentabili*, the following proposition: (51): *"Matrimonium non potuit evadere legis nisi serius in Ecclesia; siquidem, ut matrimonium pro sacramento heberetur, necesse erat, ut praecederet plena doctrinae de gratia et sacramentis theologica explicatio"* (Denz. 2051).

4,   nature, was elevated to the dignity of a Sacrament by
8,   Jesus, the Savior and Redeemer of mankind; so much
47,   so that matrimony properly so called is for Christians
55,   not to be separated from the idea of Sacrament. Now
74)   the administration of the Sacraments, the law that regulates them, as is the case with all other sacred matters,
is under the Church's power. That is clearer than day-
light. Therefore, the laws regarding matrimony, far
from being within the competence of the civil government, are under the exclusive dominion of the Church.
The wish, therefore, of those who preside in civil affairs
to promulgate laws as regards the marriage of Christians is an invasion of another's right and the performing
of an act afflicted with nullity. On the other hand, Christians who dared to contract a civil marriage would only
go through a form of marriage, and not receive the
Sacrament,—the only and true matrimony—and would,
unjustly, obtain civil effects by relying on an act of
itself null and of no value.

In such circumstances, faced by this injustice and
sacrilege, We cannot help but deplore and reprove them,
and defend, inasmuch as lies in Our power, the Church's
holy rights which are damaged by a government which
pretends to call itself Catholic.

(*Hope for a reform of the projects.*)

CANONICAL FORM

Decree *Ne temere*, August 2, 1907 of the Sacred
Congregation of the Council

253   So that clandestine marriages which the Church of
(12)   God has always detested and prohibited for very serious

reasons might not be rashly contracted, the Council of Trent took the following wise measure: "those who attempt to contract marriage without the presence of the Parish priest—or another priest authorized by the Parish priest himself or the local Bishop—and two or three witnesses, are rendered unable to do so by the Holy Synod, which decrees that the contracts thus made are null and void" (a).

But since the same Holy Council commanded that such a decree be published in all the parishes, and that it should only have force in those places where it had been promulgated, it followed that in several places where the publication was not made the benefits of the Tridentine law could not be used, and even today they are deprived of it and remain subject to the hesitations and inconveniences of the ancient discipline.

Even where the new law is in force, not every difficulty has been swept aside. It often happens, indeed, that a serious doubt arises when determining the parish priest in whose presence marriage must be contracted. The canonical discipline establishes that the parish priest intended is the one in whose parish one or both of the contracting parties have their domicile or quasi-domicile. Since it was sometimes difficult, however, to establish if there existed a certain quasi-domicile, many marriages were exposed to the danger of being invalid, while many others, either through ignorance or fraud, were discovered to be illegitimate and null. **254** *(12)*

We see these things, which have been deplored for so long, happen in Our own days, and the more so when

253a Council of Trent, c. 1, sess. 24, *de reform. matrim.*

the means of communication between distant peoples have become easier and more rapid. For this reason, wise and learned men have judged it useful to bring about some juridical change as regards the form of celebrating marriage. Also many Bishops from all parts of the world, especially from the more important Sees, where such necessity appears more urgent, have addressed supplicant prayers with this purpose to the Apostolic See.

(*The Pope's solicitude.—New rules to make uniform the discipline for the whole Church.*) (a)

254a These dispositions are today substituted by the following canons of the C.I.C.:

"Can. 1094.—*Ea tantum matrimonia valida sunt quae contrahuntur coram praocho, vel loci Ordinario, vel sacerdote ab alterutro delegato et duobus saltem testibus, secundum tamen regulas espressas in canonibus qui sequuntur, et salvis exceptionibus de quibus in can. 1098, 1099.*

Can. 1098.—*Si haberi vel adiri nequeat sine gravis incommodo parochus vel Ordinarius vel sacerdos delegatus qui matrimonio assitant ad norman canonum 1095, 1096:*

1⁰ *In mortis periculo validum et licitum est matrimonium contractum coram solis testibus; et etiam extra mortis periculum, dummodo prudenter praevideatur eam rerum conditionem esse permensem duraturam;*

2⁰ *In utroque casu, si praesto sit alius sacerdos qui adesse possit, vocari et, una cum testibus, matrimonio assistere debet, salva coniugii validitate coram solis testibus.*

Can. 1099.—§ 1. *Ad statutam superius formam servandam teneturs*

1⁰ *Omnes in catholica Ecclesia baptizati et ad eam ex haeresi aut schismate conversi, licet sive hi sive illi ab eadem postea defecerint, quoties inter se matrimonium ineunt;*

2⁰ *Idem, de quibus supra, si cum acatholicis sive bap-*

tizatis sive non baptizatis etiam post obstentam dispensationem ab impedimento mixtae religionis vel disparitatis cultus matrimonium contrahant;
3° Orientales, si cum latinis contrahant hac forma adstrictis.
§2. Firmo autem praescripto §1, n. 1, acatholici sive baptizati sive non baptizati, si inter se contrahant, nullibi tenentur ad catholicam matrimonii formam servandam; (item ab acatholicis nati, etsi in Ecclesia catholica baptizati, qui ab infantili aetate in haeresi vel schismate aut infidelitate vel sine ulla religione adoleverunt, quoties cum parte acatholica contraxerint)".

The last part of can. 1099, which is between parenthesis () was abrogated by the *Motu Proprio* of Aug. 1, 1948; cf. further ahead, n. 538.

"Can. 1101.—*§1 Parochus curet ut sponsi benedictionem sollemnem accipiant, quae dari eis potest etiam postquam diu vixerint in matrimonio, sed solum in Missa, servata speciali rubrica et excepto tempore feriato.*
§2. Sollemnem benedictionem ille tantum sacerdos per ipse vel per alium dare potest, qui valide et licite matrimonio potest assistere".

BENEDICT XV
1914-1922

NATURALISM

Motu proprio *Bonum sane*, July 25, 1920.

(Fiftieth anniversary of the proclamation of St. Joseph, Patron of the Universal Church).

It is now necessary to consider another source of **255** anxiety, a source which is even more serious since it has *(68)* penetrated into the arteries and to the very heart of human society. In fact the scourge of war came upon the nations when they became profoundly inflicted by naturalism, namely by that great disease of the century, which, wherever it takes root, weakens the desire for heavenly benefits, dwarfs the flame of divine charity and draws men away from the healing and elevating grace of Christ, thus taking from them the light of Faith and leaving them only to the corrupt forces of nature, abandoning them to the mercy of the most insane passions.

(Consequences: class hatred.)

Let it be added, that the sanctity of conjugal faith **256** and the respect for paternal authority have been not *(68)* lightly damaged for many people as a result of the war. One reason is that the absence of either husband or wife has diminished in the other party the bond of duty, or again that the absence of watchful care has given a pretext for carelessness, especially among young women, in living too freely. We must therefore confess with true sorrow that public morality is now much more depraved and corrupt than before and that the so-called "social question" is aggravated to such a point as to threaten irreparable ruin.

(Remedy: devotion to St. Joseph.)

PIUS XI
1922-1939

FAMILY PEACE

Encycl. *Ubi arcano*, December 23, 1922.
(*Picture of the social disorder.*)

And it is truly sad to see how this poisonous evil has **257**
penetrated to the very roots of human society, that is, *(42,*
into the family, the process of breaking up which, begun *60,*
some time since, has been accentuated by the terrible *68)*
scourge of the war, with the taking away of fathers and
sons from the home and with corruption of morals in
many ways. The respect due to paternal authority is
often forgotten, as is also that due to blood relationship;
masters and servants look on themselves as adversaries;
the conjugal bond is often violated, the duties which
the conjugal relationship imposes towards God and civil
society are forgotten.

The causes

And it has now, too, come to be held that no longer **258**
God, nor the Lord Jesus would rule over the constitution *9,*
of the family, and marriage has been reduced to a mere *42,*
civil contract—that marriage which Christ made a "great *72)*
Sacrament" (a) and ordained to be for ever the holy and
sanctifying symbol of the bond by which his Church was
united with Him. So We see everywhere among people

258a Eph. 5:32.

the obscuring of all that elevates and sanctifies the idea and the sentiments with which the Church had surrounded this basic cell of civil society which is the family; parental authority and domestic peace overthrown; its stable communiy of life destroyed, its sacred character so frequently violated by the flaring up of sordid passions or by the deadly desire of gain, poisoning the very founts of life not only of the family but of peoples.

(*Remedies.—Reign of Christ*).

259
(36,
40,
44,
101,
106)
Jesus Christ reigns in the family when that family, formed by the Sacrament of Christian matrimony, keeps inviolate its sacred character, where the authority of the parents is modeled on the Divine fatherhood whence it gets its origin and name (a), where the children emulate the example of the Child Jesus and all life is filled with the holiness of the Family of Nazareth.

(*What remains to be done.—Establish the peace of Christ in the reign of Christ*).

FAMILY SANCTIFICATION

Letter *Quod novas*, April 25, 1923 to the Episcopate of Venezuela.

(*Principle objects of attention and teaching of the Bishops*).

260
(35,
43,
63)
We desire above all that you dedicate your whole care to family sanctification: if it is really true that society will be a reflection of the family, it is certainly clear that if God no longer reigns in the family and no longer

259a Cf. Eph. 3:15.

showers down his blessings with the Sacrament of Matrimony, the union is ruined, mutual duties between parents and children are diminished, public morals themselves are in danger! It is inevitable that after having put aside the commandment of God and of His Church, everything collapses and all is in confusion: justice, charity, the union of classes. Now these are precisely the virtues which you must certainly safeguard for your country, so that, sheltered from discord and civil wars, it can enjoy the benefits of peace and every social progess.

(*The mission in infidel territories*).

THE ITALIAN CONCORDAT

Chirograph *Ci si è domandato,* May 30, 1929 to Cardinal Gasparri.

(*Interpretation of the Lateran pacts and the Italian Concordat which recognize the legal value of religious matrimony.*)

In the matter of Matrimony the Concordat procures **261** for the family, for the Italian people, for the country *(52,* still more than for the Church, such a great benefit that *98)* We would have willingly sacrificed Our very life for that alone (a). It was well said: "that there is no doubt that morally and before a religious conscience the practicing

261a The first paragraph of art. 34 of the *Italian Concordat,* signed on Feb. 11, 1929, states: "The Italian State, in wishing to give back to the institution of Matrimony, which is the foundation of the family, the dignity conforming to the catholic traditions of its people, recognizes the civil effects of the sacrament of Matrimony, disciplined by Canon Law."

Catholic will have to celebrate canonical matrimony."
But not so well was added at the same time: "juridically
no one can constrain him to do it" (b). The Church,
a society perfect in its own order, can and must do this
with the means which belong to her; and she will do it;
she does it from this moment by declaring excommuni-
cated those of her members who would neglect or omit
a religious matrimony and give preference to a civil
one only.

(*Guarantees of the agreement.*)

THE NEXT ENCYCLICAL

All. to the Sacred College, December 24, 1930.

(*The actual crisis.—Conditions for a Christian peace.
—Wishes—Christmas gift.*)

262
(42,
48)
... It will be an Encyclical on a very important
subject and one which interests more than ever the family, States, indeed the whole human race. It will be on a
theme of perennial importance which more than ever
presents today deplorable and disturbing aspects; so disturbing in fact that Our intervention is not only opportune and necessary, but even urgent. The Encyclical will
treat of "Christian Marriage in relation to the conditions,
needs and present disorders of the family and society".
It is evident, and it will be even more so after it has
been read, that a work of such gravity and importance
has necessarily demanded long meditation and prepara-

261b An allusion to a misleading interpretation of the
Concordat given by Benito Mussolini, in one of his
discourses.

tion, and had already made much progress in Our spirit long before a royal marriage came to make it even more opportune and necessary than had the general conditions of the world.

More opportune, We say, because We have a duty to all, rich and poor, weak and powerful, great and small, arising from the fact that God, blessed in the mystery of His counsel, has willed Us to be guardian, interpreter and steward of doctrine and of laws divine and ecclesiastical; to this doctrine and to these laws belongs indeed whatever the Church teaches and ordains about marriage, and in particular about mixed marriages.

(The incident of the royal marriage in Bulgaria.)

THE HOLINESS OF MATRIMONY

Encycl. *Casti Connubii*, December 31, 1930.

The dignity of chaste wedlock will be best appreciated, Venerable Brethren, if we consider that when Christ Our Lord, the Son of the Eternal Father, assumed the nature of fallen man He was not content with giving a special place to marriage (the source and foundation of the family and therefore of human society) in the loving plan by which He restored completely our race; He did more: having reestablished it in the perfection in which it had originally been instituted by God He raised it to the rank of a true and "great" Sacrament (a) of the New Law, and accordingly entrusted the entire regulation and care of it to His bride, the Church. **263 (4, 7, 46)**

263a Eph. 5:32.

264
(101,
103)
If this renovation of matrimony is to yield its desired fruits among the nations of the whole world in all ages, it is necessary first that the minds of men should be enlightened on the true doctrine of Christ concerning marriage; and then that married Christians, with the inner grace of God to strengthen their weakness, should conform their views and conduct to the most pure love of Christ, and so assure for themselves and their families true happiness and peace.

265
(61,
63,
99)
But, as We gaze out upon the world from the watch-tower of this Apostolic See, We observe—and you, Venerable Brethren, cannot but share Our sorrow as you also observe—that there are many unmindful of this divine work of renewal, who are totally ignorant of the sanctity of marriage, who impudently deny it, who even allow themselves to be led by the principles of a modern and perverse ethical doctrine to repudiate it with scorn. As these pernicious errors and degraded morals have begun to spread even among the faithful, and, almost imperceptibly, are daily tending to strike deeper roots, We consider it Our duty as Christ's Vicar on earth and as Supreme Shepherd and Teacher to raise Our voice of warning to the flock committed to Our care, to keep them away from poisoned pastures and, as far as We are able, to save them from harm.

266
We have accordingly decided to address you, Venerable Brethren, and through you the universal Church of Christ and indeed the whole human race, on the nature of Christian marriage and its high excellence, on the advantages and benefits that flow from it to the family and to human society, on the errors opposed to this most important point of Gospel teaching, on the vices contrary

to conjugal life, and finally on the chief remedies to be applied. In this We shall follow in the footsteps of Leo XIII, Our predecessor of happy memory, whose Encyclical *Arcanum* on Christian marriage (a), issued fifty years ago, We hereby endorse and confirm; if We deal more fully with certain matters according to the conditions and needs of our times, yet We declare that the doctrine of Leo XIII, far from being obsolete, still retains its full force today.

Divine institution of matrimony

Taking our starting point from that Encyclical, which is concerned almost entirely with vindicating the divine institution of matrimony, its dignity as a Sacrament, and its perpetual stability, let us first recall this immutable inviolable, and fundamental truth: Matrimony was not instituted or reestablished by men but by God; not men, but God, the Author of nature, and Christ our Lord, the restorer of nature, provided marriage with its laws, confirmed it and elevated it; and consequently those laws, can in no way be subject to human wills or to any contrary pact made even by the contracting parties themselves. This is the teaching of Sacred Scripture (a); it is the solemnly defined doctrine of the Council of Trent, which uses the words of Holy Scripture to proclaim and establish that the perpetual indissolubility of the marriage bond, its unity and its stability, derive from God Himself (b). **267** *(1, 5, 6, 12, 13, 14)*

But although matrimony by nature is of divine institution, yet the human will has a part, and a very noble **268** *(1,*

266a Feb. 10, 1880; cf. nn. 143-198.
267a Cf. Gen. 1:27-28, 2:22-23; Matt. 19, 3 ff; Eph. 5:23 ff.   267b Council of Trent, sess. 24.

10,
12)
part, to play in it. Each individual marriage, in so far as it is a conjugal union between a particular man and a particular woman, arises only out of the free consent of the two parties, and this free act by which each yields and receives the specifically marital right (a) is so necessary for the constitution of a true marriage that "no human power can supply its place" (b).

269
(10,
12)
But the only function of this human freedom is to decide that each of the contracting parties in fact wishes to enter the state of matrimony, and to marry this particular person. The freedom of man has no power whatever over the nature of matrimony itself, and therefore when once a person has contracted matrimony he becomes subject to its essential laws and properties. Hence St. Thomas Aquinas, treating of conjugal fidelity and the procreation of children, points out that "in marriage these things are implied by the matrimonial contract itself, and therefore if anything contrary to them were expressed in the consent which makes the marriage, it would be no true marriage at all" (a).

270
(1,
(10,
11)
It is thus seen that marriage, before being a union of bodies, is first and more intimately a union and harmony of minds, brought about not by any passing affection of sense or heart but by a deliberate and resolute decision

268a C.I.C., can. 1081, §2.—"*Consensus matrimonialis est actus voluntatis quo utraque pars tradit et acceptat ius in corpus, perpetuum et exclusivum, in ordine ad actus per se aptos ad prolis generationem*".
268b C.I.C.., can. 1081, §1.—*Matrimonium facit partium concensus inter personas iure habiles legitime manifestatus; qui nulla humana potestate suppleri valet*".
269a St. Thomas, *Summa Theologica*, Suppl. 49, 3.

of the will; and from this cementing of minds, by God's decree, there arises a sacred and inviolable bond.

The peculiar and unique character of this contract differentiates it totally from the unions which animals form among themselves under the impulse of a blind natural instinct, and in which reason and deliberation have no part; it also distinguishes marriage entirely from those irregular unions of human beings in which there is nothing of a true and honorable bond of wills, and which are devoid of any legitimate domestic status.

Consequently the lawful authority has clearly the right and therefore also the duty to prevent, forbid, and punish shameful unions which are contrary to reason and to nature. But at the same time, since this is a matter touching the nature of man itself, the warning of Leo XIII (a) must be borne in mind: "There is no doubt that in deciding upon a state of life every person has the right to make his free choice between following Christ's counsel of virginity and entering upon the state of matrimony. No human law can deprive a human being of his natural and primordial right to marry, or restrict in any way what is the chief cause of wedlock established in the beginning by God's authority: "Increase and multiply" (b). **271 (19, 54, 56, 57, 108, 110)**

The sacred partnership of genuine wedlock is therefore established both by the will of God and by the will of man. From God comes the institution of marriage, its ends, laws and blessings; human beings, by the generous **272 5, 12, 29)**

271a Encycl. *Rerum Novarum,* May 15, 1891, see nn. 210-213.—Cf. can. 1035, of the C.I.C.,—*"Omnes possunt matrimonium contrahere, qui iure non prohibentur".*
271b Gen. 1:28.

and lifelong surrender which they make of their person to each other, become, through God's gift and help, the authors of each particular marriage, with the duties and blessings which the Creator has annexed to it.

I. *The blessings of true marriage*

273
(5,
18,
26,
27,
32,
33)
    As We begin to expound the nature and excellence of the blessings which God has attached to true marriage, We recall the words of that glorious Doctor of the Church of whose death We recently commemorated the fifteenth centenary with the Encyclical *Ad salutem*: (a) "These," writes St. Augustine, "are the blessings which make matrimony itself a blessing: OFFSPRING, FIDELITY, SACRAMENT" (b). The saintly Doctor shows that the whole doctrine of Christian wedlock is excellently summarized under these three heads: "*Fidelity* signifies that outside the matrimonial bond there shall be no sexual intercourse; *Offspring* signifies that children shall be lovingly welcomed, tenderly reared, and religiously educated; *Sacrament* signifies that the bond of wedlock shall never be broken, and that neither party, if separated, shall form a union with another, even for the sake of offspring. Such is the law of marriage, which gives luster to the fruitfulness of nature and sets a curb upon shameful incontinence" (c).

Offspring

274
(5,
    Among the blessings of marriage offspring holds the first place (a). The Creator of the human race Himself,

273a April 20, 1930.
273b St. Augustine, *De boon coniug.*, c. 24, n. 32.
273c St. Augustine, *De Gen. ad litt.*, 1,9,c.7, n. 12.
274a *Itaque primum inter matrimonii bona locum tenet proles.*

who in His goodness has willed to use human beings   *19,*
as His ministers in the propagation of life, taught us   *26)*
this truth when in instituting matrimony in the Garden
of Eden He bade our first parents, and through them all
married persons who should come after them: "Increase
and multiply and fill the earth" (b). St. Augustine
rightly draws the same conclusion from the words of the
Apostle St. Paul to Timothy (c): "The Apostle testifies
that procreation is the purpose of matrimony when, having said, 'I will that younger women should marry', he
adds immediately, as though he had been asked the
reason, 'so that they may bear children and become
mothers of families' " (d).

To appreciate the greatness of this divine gift and   **275**
blessing of marriage it is enough to contemplate the dig-   *(20,*
nity of man and his sublime destiny. Even his rational   *22)*
nature alone sets man above all other visible creatures.
Add to this that God's purpose in willing human beings
be born is not merely that they may exist and occupy
the earth, but far more, that they may worship Him, and
that they may know and love Him and finally enjoy Him
forever in heaven. This destiny, by reason of man's
wondrous elevation to the supernatural order, surpasses
anything that "eye has seen or ear heard, or the heart of
man been able to conceive" (a). Clearly, therefore, the
offspring begotten by God's almighty power with the
cooperation of husband and wife is a very noble gift of
His goodness and a most excellent fruit of marriage.

274b Gen. 1:28.
274c 1 Tim. 5:14.
274d St. Augustine, *De bono coniug.*, c. 24, n. 32.
275a 1 Cor. 2:9.

276
(21,
22)
    Christian parents should understand, moreover, that their duty is not only to propagate and maintain the human race on earth; it is not even merely to rear worshippers of the true God. They are called to give children to the Church, to beget fellow-citizens of the Saints and members of the household of God (a), in order that the worshippers of our God and Savior may increase from day to day (b). It is true that Christian parents, even though themselves in the state of grace cannot transmit their supernatural life to their offspring: indeed the natural generation of life has become the path of death by which original sin is communicated to the children. Nevertheless they do share to some extent in the privilege of the primordial marriage of Paradise, for it is their function to offer their children to the Church so that she, the fruitful Mother of the sons of God, may beget them anew to supernatural righteousness in the waters of baptism, make them living members of Christ, sharers of immortal life, and heirs, finally, of that eternal glory to which we all fervently aspire.

277
(22,
23,
27,
100)
    The truly Christian mother who ponders these things will understand that the words of our Redeemer are spoken of her in a sublime and consoling sense: "A woman . . . when she hath brought forth the child remembereth no more the anguish, for joy that a man is born

276a Cf. Eph. 2:19
276b *Christiani vero parentes intelligant praeterea se non iam solum ad genus humanum in terra propagandum et conservandum, immo vero, non ad quoslibet veri Dei cultores educandos destinari, sed ad pariendam Ecclesiae Christi sobolem, ad cives sanctorum et domesticos Dei procreandos, ut populus Dei et Salvatoris nostri cultui addictus in dies augeautur.*

into the world" (a). Rising superior to all the pains, cares, and responsibilities of her maternal office, she will have far better right to glory than that famous Roman matron, the mother of the Gracchi, for she will glory with a holy joy in the Lord as she contemplates the group of splendid children that surrounds her. These little ones, eagerly and gratefully received from the hand of God, will be considered by both father and mother as a talent entrusted to them, not merely to be used for their own advantage or for that of any earthly kingdom, but to give back to God in the day of reckoning, together with the fruit that has accrued.

Education

But the blessing of offspring implies more than the begetting of it; its proper education is also required (a). God, for all His wisdom, would have made insufficient provision for the begotten child (and therefore for the whole human race) if those who had received from Him the power and the right to beget it had not also received from Him the right and the duty to educate it. Clearly, even in the matter of its natural life the child is not self-sufficient; it is still less so in regard to supernatural life. For many years it will need to be helped by others, to be instructed and educated. And there can be no doubt that, by natural and divine law, the right and duty of educating offspring belong primarily to those who, having begun the work of nature by begetting children, are absolutely forbidden to leave unfinished the work they

278 *(17, 23, 31)*

277a John 16:21.
278a *Procreationis autem beneficio bonum prolis haud sane absolvitur, sed alterum accedat oportet, quod debita prolis educatione continetur.*

have begun and so expose it to inevitable ruin. For this most necessary task of education the best possible provision has been made in marriage, where the indissoluble bond between the parents ensures that their collaboration and mutual help in that work will be always available.

279
(91,
23)
Since we have dealt at length elsewhere with the Christian education of youth (a) We may be content to summarize the matter here in the words of St. Augustine which We have already quoted: "Offspring signifies that children shall be lovingly welcomed . . . and religiously educated" (b). As the Code of Canon Law succinctly expresses it: "The primary end of matrimony is the procreation and education of offspring" (c).

280
(26)
In conclusion We must not omit to observe that since this twofold function, so honorable and so important, has been entrusted to the parents for the benefit of the offspring, it follows that the lawful use of the power given by God for the procreation of life is reserved, by the divine and natural law, as the exclusive right and privilege of the married state, and must be restricted entirely within the sacred limits of wedlock.

Conjugal fidelity

281
(33)
The second of the blessings of matrimony mentioned by St. Augustine is Fidelity, that is, the mutual faithfulness of husband and wife in observing the matrimonial

279a Encycl. *Divini illius Magistri,* Dec. 31, 1929.
279b St. Augustine, *De Gen. ad litt.,* 1. 9, c. 7, n. 12.
279c C.I.C., can. 1013, §1.—"*Matrimonii finis primarius est procreatio atque educatio prolis; secundarius mutuum adiutorium et remedium concupiscentiae*".

contract. This implies that the right which in virtue of this divinely ratified agreement belongs exclusively to each companion will neither be denied by the one to the other nor granted to any third party; and, moreover, that no concession will be made even to one of the contracting parties if it is contrary to the rights and laws of God and incompatible with matrimonial fidelity itself. For such concession can in no circumstances be permitted.

Unity

Hence conjugal fidelity requires in the first place **282** that absolute unity of wedlock (a) of which the Creator *(3,* furnished us with the first example in the marriage of *13,* our first parents, when He decreed that it should subsist *18,* between one man and one woman only. And, although *29,* later this original law was to some extent relaxed for a *32)* time by God the supreme Lawgiver, yet there is no doubt that the primordial and perfect unity of marriage was completely restored, and every dispensation from it abrogated, by the law of the Gospel. This is abundantly clear from the words of Christ and from the constant teaching and practice of the Church. Therefore the Council of Trent solemnly defined: "That only two are united and made one by this bond was clearly taught by Christ our Lord when He said: *'Therefore now they are not two but one flesh'* " (b).

Our Lord thus condemned every form of polygamy **283** or polyandry, whether simultaneous or successive, as well *(13,*

282a Cf. C.I.C., can. 1013, §2.—*"Essentiales matrimonii proprietates sunt unitas ac indissolubilitas, quae in matrimonio christiano peculiarem obtinent firmitatem ratione sacramenti".*   282b Council of Trent, sess. 24.

33) as every external act of impurity. But He went further. In order to preserve the frontiers of marriage perfectly inviolable He also forbade any thoughts or voluntary desires concernng such things: "But I say to you that whosoever shall look on a woman to lust after her hath already committed adultery with her in his heart" (a). These words of Our Lord cannot be made void even by the consent of one of the partners; they are the promulgation of a divine and natural law which no human will can infringe or modify (b).

284
(33) Indeed, the blessing of conjugal fidelity will only possess all its due splendor if the intimate intercourse of husband and wife also bears the imprint of chastity; in all things they must shape their conduct according to the divine and natural law, endeavoring always to follow the wise and holy will of their Creator, and inspired with a deep reverence for the work of God.

Conjugal charity

285
(34) This "faithfulness in chastity", as St. Augustine appropriately calls conjugal fidelity, will flourish more readily with more luxuriant bloom under the radiance of another most noble influence, namely that of marital love, which pervades all the duties of married life and holds in Christian marriage a sort of primacy of honor. "Conjugal fidelity requires husband and wife to be united by a special kind of love; they must love each other not as adulterers love, but as Christ loved the Church. This is the rule prescribed by the Apostle when

283a Matt. 5:28.
283b *Decr. S. Officii*, March 2, 1679, propos. 50.—"*Copula cum coniugata, conseniente marito, non est adulterium*".

he says: '*Husbands, love your wives as Christ also loved the Church*' (a). Now Christ certainly loved the Church with a boundless charity, and not for His own personal advantage but solely for the good of His Bride" (b). Charity is not an attachment founded on a mere carnal and transitory desire, or limited to words of affection; it is a deep-seated devotion of the heart, which, since true love shows itself in works (c), is manifested in action.

This action in the home is not confined to mutual help; it must have as its higher and indeed its chief objective that of shaping and perfecting the interior life of husband and wife. Their life-partnership must help them to increase daily in the practice of virtue, and above all to grow in the true love of God and their neighbor, in that charity on which "depends the whole Law and the Prophets" (a). All human beings, no matter what their condition of life or honorable calling, are able and bound to imitate the perfect model of all sanctity which God has set before them in the person of Christ Our Lord, and, with the help of God, to reach the summit of Christian perfection—as the example of many Saints abundantly proves. **286** *(29. 35)*

This mutual interior formation of husband and wife, this persevering endeavor to bring each other to the state of perfection, may in a true sense be called, as the Roman Catechism calls it, the primary cause and reason of **287** *(29, 35)*

285a Eph. 5:25; Col. 3:19.
285b *Catech. Rom.*, 2, c. 8, q. 24.
285c Cf. St. Gregory the Great, *Homil. XXX in Evang.*, (John 14:23-31), n. 1.
286a Matt. 22:40.

matrimony, so long as marriage is considered not in its stricter sense, as the institution destined for the procreation and education of children, but in the wider sense as a complete and intimate life-partnership and association (a).

287a *Haec mutua coniugum interior conformatio, hoc assiduum sese invicem perficiendi studium, verissima quadam ratione, ut docet Catechismus Romanus, etiam primaria matrimonii causa et ratio dici potest, si tamen matrimonuim non pressius ut institutum ad prolem rite procreandam educandamque, sed latius ut totius vitae communio, consuetudo, societas accipiatur.*—Following is the text of the Roman Catechism to which the allusion is made. "*Vir et mulier coniugi cur debeant.—Sed quibus de causis vir et mulier coniugi debeant explicandum est. Prima igitur ratio est, haec ipsa diversi sexu naturae instinctu expetita societas, mutui auxilii spe conciliata, ut alter alterius ope adiutus vitae incommoda facilius ferre, et senectutis imbecillitatem sustentare queat.— Altera est procreationis appetitus, non tam quidem ob eam rem, ut bonorum et divitiarum haeredes relinquantur, quam ut verae fidei et religionis cultores educentur. Quod quidem maxime sanctis illis Patriarchis, cum uxores ducerent, propositum fuisse, ex sacris Litteris satis apparet. Quare Angelus, cum Tobiam admoneret, quo pacti mali daemonis vim posset repellere "Ostendam, inquit, tibi, qui sunt, quibus praevalere potest daemonium, ii namque, qui coniugum ita suscipiunt, ut Deum a se, et a sua mente excludant, et suae libidini ita vacent; et sicut equus et mulus, quibus non est intellectus habet potestatem daemonium super eos*" (Tobias 6:16-22). *Atque una haec etiam causa fuit cur Deus ab initio matrimonium instituerit. Quare fit, ut illorum sit scelus gravissimum qui matrimonio iuncti, medicamentis vel conceptum impediunt, vel partum abigunt. Haec homicidarum impia conspiratio existimanda est*" (Catech. Rom., p. 2, c. 8, q. 13).

The same charity must rule and regulate all the other rights and duties of husband and wife; and so in the prescription of the Apostle: "Let the husband render the debt to the wife, and the wife also in like manner to the husband" (b), we must see a rule of charity as well as a law of justice.

The "order of love"

Finally, the bond of charity having thus set its seal upon the home, there must reign in it what St. Augustine calls "the order of love". This implies the primacy of the husband over his wife and children, and the ready submission and willing obedience of the wife, according to the commandment of the Apostle: "Let women be subject to their husbands as to the Lord, because the husband is the head of the wife as Christ is the head of the Church" (a).   **288** *(31, 35)*

The submission of the wife neither ignores nor suppresses the liberty to which her dignity as a human person and her noble functions as wife, mother, and companion give her the full right. It does not oblige her to yield indiscriminately to all the desires of her husband, which may be unreasonable or incompatible with her wifely dignity. Nor does it mean that she is on a level with persons who in law are called minors, and who are ordinarily denied the unrestricted exercise of their rights on the ground of their immature judgment and inexperience. But it does forbid such abuse of freedom as would neglect the welfare of the family; it refuses, in this body which is the family, to allow the heart to be separated   **289** *(39-41)*

287b 1 Cor. 7:3.
288a Eph. 5:22-23.

from the head, with great detriment to the body itself and even the risk of disaster. If the husband is the head of the domestic body, then the wife is its heart; and as the first holds the primacy of authority, so the second can and ought to claim the primacy of love.

290
(39, 41)
Moreover, the wife's submission to her husband admits of degrees; it may vary according to circumstances of persons, places, and time. Indeed, should the husband neglect his duty in the government of the family, it will devolve upon the wife to supply his place. But the structure of the family itself, and its fundamental law divinely instituted and established, may at no time and in no place be violated or changed.

291
(39, 40, 41)
On the observance of this relation between husband and wife Leo XIII, Our predecessor of happy memory, gives the following wise rules in his Encyclical on Christian marriage: "The husband is the ruler of the family and the head of the wife; but the wife, because she is flesh of his flesh and bone of his bone, will submit to him and obey him, not as a servant but as a companion; and thus her obedience will not be wanting in either honor or dignity. But in him who commands and in her who obeys, since they bear respectively the image of Christ and His Church, divine charity must ever be the regulating standard of their reciprocal duties" (a).

292
(32, 33)
The blessing of conjugal fidelity thus comprises unity, chastity, charity, and a noble and honorable obedience; four advantages arising out of the conjugal union, four benefits for the husband and wife which

291a Enc. *Arcanum*, Feb. 10, 1880.—Cf. nn. 143-198.

guarantee and promote peace, dignity and happiness in marriage. No wonder that conjugal fidelity has always been counted among the most precious blessings of matrimony.

The Sacrament

But the complement and crown of all is the blessing **293** of Christian marriage which, following St. Augustine, *(7,* We have called "Sacrament". It denotes both the indis- *18)* solubility of the matrimonial bond and the consecration of this contract by Christ, Who elevated it to the rank of a sign which is a cause of grace (a).

Indissolubility

The indissolubility of the marriage contract is em- **294** phatically declared by Christ Himself when He says, *(15,* "What God hath joined together let no man put asun- *16)* der" (a), and "Every man that putteth away his wife and marrieth another committeth adultery; and he that marrieth her that is put away committeth adultery" (b).

And this attribute of marriage is assigned by St. Augustine to the blessing called Sacrament in the following passage: "*Sacrament* signifies that the bond of wedlock shall never be broken, and that neither party, if separated, shall form a union with another, even for the sake of offspring" (c).

293a *Attamen tantorum beneficiorum summa completur et quasi cumulatur illo christiani coniugii bono, quod Augustini verbo nuncupavimus Sacramentum, quo denotatur et vinculi indissolubilitas et contractus in efficax gratiae signum per Christum facta elatio atque consecratio.*
294a Matt. 19:6.   294b Luke 16:18.
294c St. Augustine, *De Gen ad litt.,* 1, 9, c. 7, n. 12.

295
(2,
3,
4,
14,
15)
But this inviolable stability, though not always in equal measure nor always with the same degree of perfection, is the attribute of every true matrimonial bond; for the words of the Lord, *"What God hath joined together let no man put asunder"*, were spoken concerning the nuptial union of our first parents, the prototype of all future marriages, and are consequently applicable to every true marriage. It is true that before the coming of Christ the perfection and strictness of the original law were modified to the extent that Moses, because of the hardness of their hearts, allowed even the members of God's people to give a bill of divorce for certain reasons. But Christ, in virtue of His power as supreme Lawgiver, revoked this concession and restored the law to its original perfection by those words which must never be forgotten: *"What God hath joined together let no man put asunder"* (a).

296
(12,
14,
57)
"Wherefore, it is evident," wrote Pius VI, Our predecessor of happy memory, to the Bishop of Agria, "that even in the state of nature, and at all events long before it was raised to the dignity of a Sacrament properly so called, marriage was divinely constituted in such a way as to involve a perpetual and indissoluble bond, which consequently cannot be dissolved by any civil law. Therefore, although a marriage may exist without a Sacrament, as in the case of marriage between infidels, even so, being a true marriage it must and does retain the character of a perpetual bond, which from the very beginning has been by divine law inseparable from marriage and over which no civil power has any authority. Therefore if a

295a Matt. 19:6.

marriage is said to be contracted, either it is so contracted as to be a true marriage, in which case it carries with it that perpetual bond which by divine law is inherent in every true marriage; or else it is deemed to be contracted without this perpetual bond, in which case it is not a true marriage at all, but an illicit union objectively contrary to the divine law, which consequently may not be entered upon or maintained" (a).

If the stability of marriage appears in some rare cases to be subject to exception—as in certain natural marriages contracted between infidels, (a) or between Christians, in the category of marriages ratified but not consummated (b)—such exception does not depend upon the will of man or of any merely human power, but upon the divine law, of which the Church of Christ is the sole guardian and interpreter. But no such dissolving power can ever, or for any cause, be exercised upon a Christian marriage ratified and consummated. In such a marriage the matrimonial contract has attained its final perfection, and therefore by God's will exhibits the highest degree of stability and indissolubility, which no human authority can put asunder (c). **297** **(15, 16)**

296a Pius VI, *Rescript. ad Episc. Agriens.*, July 11, 1789; cf. nn. 48-51.

297a Cf. C.I.C., can. 1120; cf. note 24b.

297b C.I.C., can. 1119.—"*Matrimonium non consummatum inter baptizatos vel inter partem baptizatam et partem non baptizatam, dissolvitur tum ipso iure per sollemnem professionem religiosam, tum per dispensationem a Sede Apostolica ex iusta causa concessam, utraque parte rogante vel alterutra, etsi altera sit invita*".

297c C.I.C., can. 1118.—"*Matrimonium validum ratum et consummatum nulla humana potestate nullaque causa, praeterquam morte, dissolvi potest*".

The sacramental mystery

298
(9,
16)
If we seek with reverence to discover the intrinsic reason of this divine ordinance, Venerable Brethren, we shall easily find it in the mystical significance of Christian wedlock, seen in its full perfection in consummated marriages between Christians. The Apostle, in the Epistle to the Ephesians, which We quoted at the beginning of this Encyclical (a), tells us that Christian wedlock signifies that most perfect union which subsists between Christ and the Church: "This is a great sacrament; but I speak in Christ and the Church"; and this is a union which certainly, as long as Christ lives and the Church lives by Him, can never cease or be dissolved. The same teaching is thus set forth by St. Augustine: "This is what is observed in Christ and in the Church: married persons must never break their married life by any divorce. This Sacrament is esteemed so highly in the City of our God, that is in the Church, that when women marry or are married for the purpose of procreating offspring it is not lawful to a leave a wife, even though she be sterile, to marry another who may bear children. If anyone were to act in this way he would not be condemned by the law of this world, which by divorce permits him to contract another marriage. Indeed Our Lord tells us that the holy Lawgiver Moses made the same concession to the Israelites by reason of the hardness of their hearts. But according to the law of the Gospel such a man is guilty of adultery; and so too is his wife, if she marry another man" (b).

298a Eph. 5:32.
298b St. Augustine, *De. nupt. at concup.*, 1. 1, c. 10.

The benefits of indissolubility

The many precious benefits which flow from the **299** indissolubility of matrimony will be understood if we *(17)* consider, even superficially, the welfare of husband and wife, of their children, and of society as a whole. In the first place, husband and wife find in it a guarantee of that enduring stability which their reciprocal and generous surrender of their persons and of the deepest love of their hearts naturally requires; for true charity "never falleth away" (a). To chastity it affords a bulwark against temptations to infidelity, whether from within or from without. It banishes the fear of being deserted in adversity or old age, and establishes instead a quiet feeling of security. It provides an effective safeguard to the dignity of each party and ensures that they will always be at hand to help each other, the indissoluble bond which unites them serving as a constant reminder that it is not for the sake of transitory goods, nor for the mere satisfaction of desire, but in order to obtain for each other higher and everlasting goods, that they have contracted this matrimonial union which can be dissolved only by death. Excellent provision is also made for the instruction and education of the offspring, which has to be prolonged over many years: a task involving weighty and enduring responsibilities which the united efforts of both parents will make easier to bear.

Equal advantages are afforded to the whole of so- **300** ciety, for experience shows that the inviolable indissolu- *(17,* bility of marriage is a most fruitful source of upright *42,*

299a 1 Cor. 13:8.

43) living and of moral integrity. If this is observed the happiness and prosperity of the State are secured; for the State is what it is made to be by the individuals and families which compose it, as a body is composed of its members. Consequently those who strenuously defend the permanent stability of matrimony render a great service to the individual welfare of married persons and their children, and to the public welfare of society.

The signs of grace

301
(11,
18)
But in addition to this, permanent indissolubility, the blessing of which We are speaking, includes other far greater advantages, which are most aptly designated by the word Sacrament. For on the lips of a Christian this is no empty word. When Our Lord, Who "instituted and perfected the Sacraments" (a), raised the marriage of His faithful ones to the dignity of a true and real Sacrament of the New Law, He really made it the sign and the source of that special interior grace "by which natural married love is perfected, the indissoluble unity of marriage secured, and the married parties sanctified" (b).

302
(8,
10)
And because Christ has made the valid matrimonial consent among the faithful to be a sign of grace, the essence of the Sacrament is so closely bound up with Christian wedlock that there can be no true marriage between baptized persons "which is not at the same time a Sacrament" (a).

301a Council of Trent, sess. 24.   301b Ibid.
302a *Et quoniam Christus ipsum coniugalem inter fideles validum consensum signum gratiae constituit, ratio*

When the faithful, therefore, give that consent with **303** a sincere heart they open for themselves the treasury of *(11)* sacramental grace, from which they can draw supernatural strength enabling them to fulfil their obligations and functions faithfully, holily, and perseveringly until death.

For this Sacrament, if its fruit is not frustrated by any obstacle, not only increases in the soul sanctifying grace, the permanent principle of supernatural life, but also adds special gifts, good impulses, and seeds of grace, amplifying and perfecting the powers of nature, and enabling the recipients not only to understand with their minds, but also to relish intimately, grasp firmly, will effectively, and fulfil indeed all that belongs to the state of wedlock and its purposes and duties; it also gives them the right to obtain the help of actual grace whenever they need it for the discharge of their matrimonial tasks.

But it must not be forgotten that, according to the **304** law of Divine Providence in the supernatural order, *(11,* Sacraments, received after the use of reason has been *104)* reached, do not produce their full fruits unless the recipients correspond with grace; and therefore the grace of matrimony will remain, to a great extent, like a useless talent hidden in a field if husband and wife to not exert their supernatural strength and cultivate and develop the seeds of grace that they have received. But if they

Sacrimenti cum christiano coniugio tam intime coniungitur, ut nullum inter baptizatos verum matrimonium esse possit," quin sit eo ipso Sacramentum". C.I.C., can. 1012, §1.—"Christus Dominus ad sacramenti dignitatem evexit ipsum contractu matrimonialem inter baptizatos". §2.—"Quare inter baptizatos nequit matrimonialis contractus validus consistere, quin sit eo ipso sacramentum".

do what lies in their power and if they are docile to grace, then they will be able to support the burdens and duties of their state, and from this Sacrament they will derive strength, and a kind of consecration. St. Augustine tells us that, just as by Baptism or by Holy Orders a man is called and aided to lead a Christian life or to fulfil the priestly function, and is never deprived of sacramental grace for these ends, so in a similar way (though not through the sacramental character) the faithful united by the ties of matrimony can never be deprived of its sacramental help or loosened from its bond (a). Indeed, he adds, even if they should become adulterers they would still bear that bond forever with them, though not for the glory of grace, but for the guilt of sin: "just as an apostate soul—one that has divorced itself from Christ, as it were—though it has lost the faith, yet does not lose the Sacrament of faith received in the regenerating waters of Baptism" (b).

305
(5,
33,
34)

Let Christian husband and wife, therefore, not fettered but adorned with the golden chains of this Sacrament, not hampered by them but helped and strengthened, strive earnestly so that their union, not only in virtue of the Sacrament and its significance but also by their own spirit and conduct, may be and always remain the image of that most fruitful union of Christ with His Church which is without doubt the venerable mystery of the most perfect charity.

304 C.I.C., can. 1110—"*Ex valido matrimonio enascitur inter coniuges vinculum natura sua perpetuum et exclusivum; matrimonium praetera christianum coniugibus non ponentibus obicem gratiam confert*".
304b St. Augustine, *De nupt. et concup.*, 1. 1, c. 10.

Anyone who considers this with attentive mind and with lively faith, Venerable Brethren, anyone who views in their proper light these excellent blessings of marriage (Offspring, Fidelity, Sacrament), cannot but admire the wisdom, sanctity, and goodness with which, in the chaste and sacred union of wedlock, God has made such abundant provision at once for the dignity and happiness of husband and wife, and for the maintenance and propagation of the human race.

II. *Errors and sins contrary to Matrimony*

The high excellence of chaste wedlock, Venerable **306** Brethren, makes it all the more lamentable to find this divine institution, especially in our own day, so frequently scorned and so widely degraded.

It is not now only in secret or in the darkness, but **307** openly and without any sense of shame, that the sancti- (54, ty of marriage is treated with derision and contempt. 55) The spoken and the written word, theatrical performances of every kind, novels, love-stories, humorous tales, cinematograph films, broadcast talks—all the latest inventions of modern science are used to this end. On the other hand, divorce, adultery, and the most shameful vices are glorified or, at any rate, depicted in such colors as to make them appear free from all blame or infamy. Books are published, impudently advertised as scientific works, but often in reality having nothing more than a veneer of science to recommend them more easily to the notice of the public. The doctrines they contain are proffered as the marvellous products of the modern spirit, a spirit described as single-minded in its search for the truth and emancipated from the prejudices of former times. And among these old-fashioned prejudices they count the doctrine which We have expounded on Christian marriage.

308 And these ideas are being instilled into every cate-
(61, gory of mankind: rich and poor, workers and employers,
101) learned and unlearned, single and married, believers and unbelievers, old and young. For these last, because they offer an easy prey, the worst snares of all are laid.

Not all the advocates of the new doctrines allow themselves to be led to the extreme consequences of unbridled lust; some of them try to steer a middle course and consider that it is only on a certain number of points that concessions ought to be made to the modern age. But even these are the more or less conscious emissaries of that enemy of ours who is forever seeking to sow cockle among the wheat (a).

309 This is the reason why We, whom the Father of the
(99, family has set to guard His field, and upon whom rests
100) the sacred duty of preventing the good seed from being choked with weeds, regard as spoken to Ourselves by the Holy Spirit those solemn words with which the Apostle Paul admonished his beloved Timothy: "Be thou vigilant ... fulfil thy ministry.... Preach the word; be instant in season, out of 'season, reprove, entreat, rebuke in all patience and doctrine" (a).

308a *Sunt qui medio quasi itinere consistere enisi, in quibusdam tantum divinae naturalisque legis praeceptis aliquid nostris temporibus concedendum putent. Sed hi quoque, plus minusve conscii, emissarii sunt illius inimici nostri, semper conatur zizania superseminare in medio tritici.*—Cf. Matt. 13, 25.
309a 2 Tim. 4, 2:5.

If the enemy's wiles are to be foiled they must first be exposed; above all it is expedient to denounce his deceits to the unsuspecting. Therefore, although We should prefer not even to name these crimes, "as becometh saints" (b), yet the welfare and salvation of souls will not suffer Us to pass them over in complete silence.

The source of the errors

To begin, then, with the source of these evils; **310** their main root lies in a theory according to which mat- *(63)* rimony was not instituted by God, the Author of nature, nor raised by Christ our Lord to the dignity of a true Sacrament. It was invented, they say, by man. Some maintain that in nature and its laws they find no vestige of matrimony whatever: nothing but the power to procreate life and a strong impulse towards satisfying this instinct in some way. Others acknowledge that man's nature reveals some beginnings and rudiments of the true wedlock, in the sense that without some permanent bond between human beings there would be no adequate provision for the dignity of the parties or for the natural function of propagating and educating offspring. Nevertheless these also hold that since matrimony is something more than these rudiments, it must, under the influence of various causes, have been invented only by the mind of man and instituted only by his will.

How mistaken and immoral these views are has **311** already been proved by what We have said in this Letter *(63,* of the origin and nature of wedlock, of its ends, and of *67,* the blessings which belong to it. That they are also per- *68)*

309b Eph. 5, 3.

nicious may be seen in the conclusions which their advocates draw from them. They claim that the laws, institutions, and customs by which marriage is regulated, having been established only by the will of men, are subject to that will alone, and therefore can and ought to be made, changed, and abrogated at man's desire and in accordance with the varying fortunes of human affairs. The power of generation, they maintain, since it is rooted in nature itself, is more sacred and wider in its scope than marriage; it can therefore be used outside the limits of wedlock as well as within them, and without any regard to the ends of matrimony. It follows that the licentiousness of an unchaste woman would enjoy practically the same rights as would the chaste motherhood of a lawful wedded wife.

312
(68)   Following the lead of these principles, some have gone to the length of inventing new types of union which they suggest as being more suited to the conditions of the modern man and the present age. In these they see so many new kinds of marriage: the *temporary* marriage, the *experimental* marriage, the *companionate* marriage; and they claim for them the full freedom and complete rights of matrimony, eliminating the indissoluble bond, however, and excluding the offspring, unless the parties choose later to transform their cohabitation and intimacy into a fully legalized marriage.

313
(68)   There are some even who demand legal recognition of these monstrosities, or at least want them to be tolerated by public usage and institution. It does not seem to occur to their minds that in such things there is nothing of that modern "culture" which they vaunt so highly;

that they are, in fact, abominable corruptions which would result even in civilized nations adopting the barbarous customs of certain savage tribes.

The attack upon Offspring

Turning now, Venerable Brethren, to treat in detail the vices which are contrary to each of the blessings of matrimony, We must begin with the consideration of offspring, which many nowadays have the effrontery to call a troublesome burden of wedlock—a burden which they urge married folk carefully to avoid, not by means of a virtuous continence (which is permissible even in marriage with the consent of both parties) but by vitiating the act of nature. This criminal abuse is claimed as a right by some on the ground that they cannot endure children, but want to satisfy their carnal desire without incurring any responsibility. Others plead that they can neither observe continence, nor, for personal reasons or for reasons affecting the mother, or on account of economic difficulties, can they consent to have children. *314 (5, 87)*

But no reason whatever, even the gravest, can make what is intrinsically against nature become conformable with nature and morally good. The conjugal act is of its very nature designed for the procreation of offspring; and therefore those who in performing it deliberately deprive it of its natural power and efficacy, act against nature and do something which is shameful and intrinsically immoral. *315 (19, 87)*

We cannot wonder, then, if we find evidence in the Sacred Scriptures that the Divine Majesty detests this unspeakable crime with the deepest hatred and has sometimes punished it with death, as St. Augustine observes: "Sexual intercourse even with a lawful wife is unlawful and shameful if the conception of offspring is prevented. This is what Onan, the son of Juda, did, and on that account God put him to death" (a).

Promulgation of the Christian teaching

316
(48,
87)
Wherefore, since there are some who, openly departing from the Christian teaching which has been handed down uninterruptedly from the beginning, have in recent times thought fit solemnly to preach another doctrine concernng this practice, the Catholic Church, to whom God has committed the task of teaching and preserving morals and right conduct in their integrity, standing erect amidst this moral devastation, raises her voice in sign of her divine mission to keep the chastity of the marriage contract unsullied by this ugly stain, and through Our mouth proclaims anew: that any use of matrimony whatsoever in the exercise of which the act is deprived, by human interference, of its natural power to procreate life, is an offence against the law of God and of nature, and that those who commit it are guilty of a grave sin (a).

315a St. Augustine, *De coniug. adult.*, 1. 2, n. 12.—Cf. Gen. 38, 8:10; Decrees of the Sacred Penitentiary, April 3, and June 3, 1916.

316a *Cum igitur quidam, a christiana doctrina iam inde ab initio tradita neque umquam intermissa manifesto recedentes, aliam nuper de hoc agendi modo doctrinam sollemniter praedicandam censuerint, Ecclesia Catholica, cui ipse Deus morum integritatem honestatemque docedam et defendendam commisit, in media hac morum ruina posita, ut nuptialis foederis castimoniam a turpi hac labe immunem stervet, in signum legationis suae di-*

A charge to confessors

Therefore, priests who hear confessions and others **317**
who have the care of souls are admonished by Us, in the **(87)**
exercise of Our sovereign authority and Our care for the
salvation of the souls of all, that they must not allow the
souls committed to their charge to be in error concerning this most serious law of God, and, what is much more
important, that they must themselves be on their guard
against these false doctrines and in no way connive at
them. Should any confessor or pastor of souls himself—
which God forbid!—lead into error the faithful committed to his care, or at least, by his approval or by a misleading silence, confirm them in holding such doctrines,
then let him know that he will have to render to God,
the Sovereign Judge, a strict account of this betrayal of
his trust; and he must consider as addressed to himself
the words of Christ: "They are blind and leaders of the
blind; and if the blind lead the blind, both fall into
the pit" (a).

Frequently the motives alleged in defence of the il- **318**
licit use of marriage are—to say nothing of those that are **(27,**
shameful—fictitious and exaggerated. Nevertheless the **87)**
Church, who is a loving Mother, hears with sympathetic
understanding the plea urged for the ailing mother
whose very life may be endangered. Who can fail to be
moved with pity at such a thought? And who can refuse

vinae, altam per os Nostrum extollit vocem atque denuo
promulgat: quemlibet matrimonii usum, in quo exercendo,
actus, deindustria hominum, naturali suae proceandae vi
destituatur, Dei et naturae legem infringere, et eos, qui
tale quid commiserint, gravis noxae labe commiserint.
317a Matt. 15, 14.

a tribute of the highest admiration for the mother who with heroic courage exposes herself to almost certain death in order to preserve the life of the child she has conceived? The sufferings which she has endured in order completely to dischage her natural duty, God alone out of His rich and bountiful mercy can reward; and He will do so most surely with full measure and overflowing (a).

319
(19,
29,
30,
87)
Holy Church is also well aware that in many cases one of the partners is more sinned against than sinning, reluctantly allowing a perversion of right order for a truly grave reason. Such a partner is guiltless, so long as the law of charity even then is remembered, and every effort made to dissuade and prevent the other partner from sin. Nor are husband and wife to be accused of acting against nature if they make use of their right in a proper and natural manner, even though natural causes (due to circumstances of time or to certain defects) render it impossible for new life to originate. Both matrimony and the use of the matrimonial right have secondary ends—such as mutual help, the fostering of reciprocal love, and the abatement of concupiscence—which husband and wife are quite entitled to have in view, so long as the intrinsic nature of that act, and therefore its due subordination to its primary end, is safeguarded.

320
(60,
87,
104)
We feel deep sympathy also with the unfortunate condition of married persons who for reasons of extreme poverty experience the greatest difficulty in rearing children.

But external conditions, however calamitous, must not be allowed to provide occasion for an error more

318a Luke 6, 38.

calamitous still. No difficulty that arises can ever detract from the binding obligation of divine commandments which forbid acts intrinsically evil (a); there are no circumstances in which husband and wife are unable, with the strength given by God's grace, to discharge their duty faithfully and preserve their chastity in the married state from this shameful stain. This is a truth of faith proclaimed by the teaching authority of the Council of Trent: "Let no man make the rash assertion, condemned by the Fathers, that it is impossible for a man in the state of grace to observe God's commandments. God does not command the impossible. When He lays a command upon you He bids you do what you are able, and pray for what is beyond your power; and He helps you to have it in your power" (b).

The same doctrine was solemnly asserted and con- **321** firmed by the Church in the condemnation of the Jan- *(104)* senist heresy, which had dared to utter this blasphemy against the goodness of God: "There are some divine commandments which it is impossible for the just, with the present strength, to observe even though they may wish and strive to do so; moreover they lack the grace which would render their fulfillment possible" (a).

Another crime: against the living but unborn child

We must also allude to another very serious crime, **322** Venerable Brethren, that which attacks the life of the *(89)*

320a *Nullae enim exsurgere possunt difficultates quae mandatorum Dei, actus, ex interiore natura sua malos, vetantium, obligationi derogare queant.*
320b Council of Trent, sess. 6, c. 11.
321a Ap. Cost. *Cum occasione,* May 31, 1653, prop. 1.

offspring while it is yet hidden in the womb of its mother. Some hold this to be permissible, and a matter to be left to the free choice of the mother or father; others hold it to be wrong only in the absence of very grave reasons, or what are called "indications" of the medical, social, or eugenic order. With regard to the penal laws of the State which forbid the destruction of the begotten but unborn child, they are unanimous in requiring that the various indications which they severally defend shall be recognized by the law of the land and made immune from any penalty. There are even some who demand the active assistance of the public authorities in these lethal operations, and it is a lamentable and notorious fact that there are places where this is frequently afforded.

323
(89) As "for the medical and therapeutic indication", We have already said, Venerable Brethren, how deeply We feel for the mother whose fulfilment of her natural duty involves her in grave danger to health and even life itself. But can any reason ever avail to excuse the direct killing of the innocent? For this is what is at stake.

The infliction of death whether upon the mother or upon the child is against the commandment of God and the voice of nature: "Thou shall not kill" (a). The lives of both are equally sacred and no one, even the public authority, can ever have the right to destroy them.

323a Exodus 20, 13; cf. *Decret. S.C.S. Officii*, May 4, 1898; July 24, 1895; May 31, 1889, to the Archbishop of Lyons: *Ad dubiums "An tuto doceri possit in scholis catholicis, licitam esse operationem chirurgicam, quam craniotomiam appellant, quando scilicet, ea ommissa, mater et infans perituri sint, ea e contra admissa, salvanda sit mater, infante pereunte?"* the reply given was: *"Tuto doceri non posse".*—The same reply was given

It is absurd to invoke against innocent human beings **324** the right of the State to inflict capital punishment, for *(89)* this is valid only against the guilty. Nor is there any question here of the right of self-defence, even to the shedding of blood, against an unjust assailant, for none could describe as an unjust assailant an innocent child. Nor, finally, does there exist any so-called right of extreme necessity which could extend to the direct killing of an innocent human being. Honorable and skillful doctors are therefore worthy of all praise when they make every effort to protect and preserve the life of both mother and child. On the contrary, those who encompass the death of the one or the other, whether on the plea of medical treatment or from a motive of misguided compassion, act in a manner unworthy of the high repute of the medical profession.

This teaching is in full accord with severe strictures **325** of the Bishop of Hippo upon those depraved married *(89)* persons who, having attempted unsuccessfully to forestall the conception of offspring, criminally and ruthlessly put it to death. "Their licentious cruelty," he writes, "or their cruel licentiousness, sometimes goes to such lengths as to procure sterilizing poisons, and if these are unavailing, in some way to stifle within the womb and eject the fetus that has been conceived. They want their offspring to die before it comes to life, or, if it is already living in the womb, to perish before it is born. Surely, if they are both of such a mind, they do not deserve the

to the Archbishop of Cambrai, Aug. 19, 1889, with this precision: "*. . .et quamcumque chirurgicam operationem directe occisivam foetus vel matris gestantis*" (Denz. nn. 1889, 1890).

name of husband and wife; and if they have been of such a mind from the beginning, it was not for wedlock but for fornication that they became united. If they are not both of such a mind, then I will venture to say that either the woman is the mere mistress of the husband or the man is the paramour of the wife" (a).

326 It is permissible and even obligatory to take into
(88, account the evidence alleged in regard to the social and
89) eugenic "indication" so long as legitimate and proper means are used and due limits observed; but to attempt to meet the needs upon which it is based by the killing of the innocent is an irrational proceeding and contrary to the divine law; a law promulgated also by the Apostle when he says that we must not do evil that good may come (a).

327 Governments and legislatures must remember that
(89, it is the duty of the public authority to protect the life of
98) the innocent by appropriate laws and penalties, especially when those whose life is attacked and endangered are unable to protect themselves, as is particularly the case with infants in their mother's womb. If the State authorities not only fail to protect these little ones, but by their laws and decrees suffer them to be killed, and even deliver them into the hands of doctors and others for that purpose, let them remember that God is the Judge and Avenger of the innocent blood that cries from earth to heaven (a).

328 In conclusion We must mention a pernicious prac-
(56, tice which, though directly touching upon a man's natural

325a St. Augustine, *De nupt. et concupisc.*, c. 15. 15
326a Rom. 3, 8.   327a Cf. Gen. 4, 10.

right to marry, in a true sense also concerns the blessing   58,
of offspring. We refer to those who in their excessive   88)
preoccupation with eugenic considerations are not content
to give salutary advice for the improvement of the health
and strength of the unborn child—which is certainly quite
reasonable—but want to set these considerations above
all other end, even those of a higher order, and would
have the public authority forbid marriage to any persons
who, in the light of the laws and the conjectures of
eugenic science, are deemed likely through heredity to
beget defective offspring, even though they may be in all
essential respects fit to marry. They even demand legislation to deprive such persons of that natural faculty by
medical action, even against their will. They are not
asking the public authority to inflict corporal punishment
for some crime that has been committed or, as a preventive measure to forestall future crimes of guilty persons;
they are simply arrogating to the State, against all right
and justice, a power which it has never had and can never
legitimately possess.

Those who act in this way, commit the error of for-   329
getting that the family is more sacred than the State   (22,
and that human beings are born primarily for Heaven   44,
and eternity, not for earth and time. Those who on other 88,
counts are capable of marriage, even though, granted 109)
every care and attention, it is surmised that they will
only beget defective offspring, are certainly not to be
accused of a serious crime if they enter the married
state; though it is often well to dissuade them from doing so.

The public authorities have no direct power over   330
the bodily members of the subjects and therefore, in the (56,

58,   absence of any crime or any cause calling for corporal
88)   punishment, they can never directly injure or attack the
       integrity of the body on any ground whatever, eugenic
       or otherwise. St. Thomas Aquinas teaches the same doc-
       trine, when inquiring whether human judges are allowed
       to inflict harm upon a man in order to forestall future
       evils, he answers affirmatively in regard to certain kinds
       of harm, but rightly denies it in regard to any lesion of
       the body: "A human tribunal may never condemn an in-
       nocent man to physical punishment, such as death, mu-
       tilation, or flogging" (a).

331   It is to be observed also that even the individual
(88)   human being—as Christian doctrine teaches and the light
       of reason clearly shows—has no power over the members
       of his own body except so far as he uses them for their
       natural purpose; he cannot destroy or mutilate them, or
       in any other way render himself incapable of his natural
       functions except when there is no other way of providing
       for the welfare of the body as a whole.

The attack upon conjugal fidelity

332   Passing now to consider another set of errors, those
(5,   which concern conjugal fidelity We may observe that, in
32,   a sense, any sin committed against the offspring is also
92)   in consequence a sin against fidelity in wedlock, since
       the one blessing of Matrimony is connected with the
       other. But there are, besides, several other errors and
       vicious practices contrary to conjugal fidelity, correspond-
       ing in number exactly to the domestic virtues which that
       fidelity implies, and respectively opposed to them: the

330a Summa Theol., 2.a 2.ae, q. 108, a. 4, ad 2.

virtues thus attacked are, the chaste mutual fidelity of husband and wife, the honorable obedience of wife to husband, and the true and unfailing charity between them.

Conjugal fidelity is attacked in the first place by **333** those who countenance the modern ideas and outlook *(93)* concerning a false and far from harmless friendship with third parties. Husband and wife, they claim, should be allowed greater freedom of feeling and action in their relations with others, especially because many are naturally endowed with a sexual temperament which cannot find satisfaction within the narrow sphere of monogamous marriage. The rigid attitude of good married folk, which condemns and banishes any sensual feeling or action in regard to a third person, is accounted by them an old fashion narrowness of mind, or a contemptible form of jealousy. They therefore consider that any penal laws of the State for the safeguarding of marital fidelity are obsolete, or ought to be annulled.

The decent feeling of every chaste husband and wife **334** needs only to listen to the voice of nature, to repudiate *(93)* these opinions as both groundless and shameful; and the voice of nature is corroborated by God's commandment: "Thou shalt not commit adultery" (a), and by the words of Christ, "Whosoever shall look upon a woman to lust after her, hath already committed adultery with her in his heart" (b). No human customs, no bad examples, no vaunted human progress, can deprive this divine commandment of its binding force. Just as Jesus Christ

334a Exodus 20, 14.
334b Matt. 5, 28.

is one, "yesterday and today and the same forever" (c) so the teaching of Christ remains forever one and the same, and not one jot or tittle of it shall pass away until all is fulfilled (d).

The emancipation of woman

335　　The same false teachers, who by the spoken and the
(95) written word seek to dim the luster of marital fidelity and chastity, attack also the loyal and honorable obedience of the wife to her husband, which some of them even describe as an ignominious servitude of one partner to the other. All rights between husband and wife, they say, are equal, and since the servitude of one of the partners is a violation of this equality, they blatantly proclaim or demand the emancipation of woman. This, in their view, is threefold: *social,* regarding the government of the home; *economic,* regarding the administration of property, and *physiological,* regarding the prevention or suppression of offspring. Physiological emancipation would free women at will from the wifely and maternal responsibilities—and this, as we have seen, is not emancipation but an abominable crime; economic emancipation would authorize the wife, without the knowledge of her husband and even against his will, to conduct and administer her own affairs without any regard to the welfare of children, husband, or family; social emancipation, finally, would free the wife from the domestic cares of children and family, enabling her, to the neglect of these, to follow her own bent, and engage in business and even in public affairs.

334c Heb. 13, 8.
334d Cf. Matt. 5, 18.

This is no true emancipation of woman, nor is it the **336**
reasonable and exalted liberty which is due to the high *(95)*
office of a Christian woman and wife. On the contrary it
is a degradation of the spirit of woman and of the dignity of a mother; it is a total perversion of family life,
depriving the husband of his wife, the children of
their mother, and the home and the family of their ever-
watchful guardian. The wife herself cannot but suffer
damage from this unnatural equality with her husband. If
she abdicates the royal throne upon which the Gospel
has set her in the home, she will soon find herself reduced (in reality if not in appearance) to the slavery
of ancient days, and will become, what she was among
the heathen, nothing more than the tool of her husband.

Such demands for equality of rights between hus- **337**
band and wife are pretentious and exaggerated. But there *(39,*
is a true equality between them, which is to be recog- *41)*
nized in all that pertains to the person and dignity of
a human being, and in all that is implied by the marriage
contract and is inherent in wedlock itself. Here, admittedly, each party enjoys exactly the same rights and is
bound by the same obligations. In all else, however,
there must be a certain inequality and adjustment, demanded by the welfare of the family and by the unity
and ordered stability which must reign in the home.

So far as the changed circumstances and customs **338**
of human intercourse may render necessary some modi- *(39,*
fication in the social and economic condition of the *95)*
married woman, it rests with the public authority to adapt
the civil rights of the wife to the needs and requirements
of modern times; but with the stipulation that regard
must be had always to the needs of woman's special tem-

perament, to moral rectitude and to the welfare of the family, and provided also that the essential order of the home remains inviolate. This order was constituted by an authority higher than man's, that is, by the authority and wisdom of God Himself, and neither the laws of the State nor the good pleasure of individuals can ever change it.

339
(32,
96)
But the modern enemies of wedlock go even further than this. They repudiate that true and solid love which is the foundation of married happiness and tender intimacy, substituting for it an unreasoning compatibility of temperament and disposition which they call sympathy. When this ceases, they maintain that the only bond uniting hearts is broken and completely dissolved. But what else is this than to build a house upon sand? No sooner is it exposed to the waves of adversity than it will totter and collapse, as Our Lord says: "And the winds blew and they beat upon that house; and it fell; and great was the fall thereof" (a). On the other hand, the house which has been built upon a rock, that is, upon the mutual charity of husband and wife, and reinforced by the deliberate and unfaltering union of their hearts, will not ever be shaken by adversity, still less will it ever fall.

The attack upon the Sacrament

340
(5,
18,
63,
69,
So far, Venerable Brethren, We have been vindicating the first two great blessings of Christian marriage against the attacks of the modern enemies of society. The third of these blessings, the Sacrament, far surpasses the other two, and it is therefore not surprising that they

339a Matt. 7, 27.

attack it with even greater violence (a). They begin by representing matrimony as an absolutely profane and purely civil affair, to be in no way entrusted to the care of a religious society, the Church of Christ, but only to that of the State. They go on to say that the nuptial contract should be freed from any indissoluble bond, and that the separation of husband and wife by divorce ought to be not only tolerated but legally sanctioned. The final consequence is that wedlock is entirely stripped of its sacred character and reduced to the level of profane and civil affairs.

70, 75, 78)

They establish their first point on the ground that the civil act itself is to be regarded as the real matrimonial contract (civil marriage, as it is called); the religious act being a mere accessory, or, at the most, a concession to be made to a common and superstitious folk. Moreover, they say, no blame ought to attach to Catholics for marrying non-Catholics without any regard to religion and without asking the consent of religious authority. Their second point, which is really a consequence of the first, consists in vindicating complete divorce, and in praising and promoting legislation which favors the dissolution of the marriage bond.

341 (70, 75, 82)

The religious character of wedlock in general, and of Christian wedlock and the Sacrament of Matrimony in particular, is treated very fully and proved by weighty

342 (a)

340a *Praestantissima quidem hactenus duo priora christiani coniugii bona vindicamus, Venerabiles Fratres, quibus hodierni societatis eversores insidiantur. Sed sicut haec bona tertium, quod sacramenti est, longe antecellit, ita nil mirum quod hanc imprimis excellentiam multo acrius videmus ab iisdem oppugnari.*

arguments in the Encyclical of Leo XIII which We have often mentioned and expressly endorsed. We therefore refer you to that document, contenting Ourselves here with recalling only a few points.

343
(1,
6,
22,
29)
That even natural wedlock has within it something that is sacred and religious can be established on grounds of natural reason alone, as shown in ancient historical documents, in the unvarying conscience of peoples, and in their institutions and customs. And this religious character of marriage is "not adventitious but inherent in it, not humanly invented but naturally intrinsic to it," because "It has God as its author and because from the very beginning it has been a foreshadowing of the Incarnation of the Word of God" (a). The sacred character of marriage, intimately connected with the sphere of religion and holy things, arises from its divine origin already described; it arises also from its purpose, which is to beget and form children of God and to unite husband and wife with God by charity and mutual help; it arises, finally, from the natural function of marriage, instituted by the wise Providence of God the Creator to be a vehicle for the transmission of life, wherein parents act as ministers of the divine omnipotence (b).

342a Enc. *Arcanum,* 10th February 1880; cf. nn. 143-198.
343a Enc. *Arcanum,* 10th February 1880; cf. nn. 143-198.
343b *Consurgit enim sacra coniugii ratio, quae intime cum religione et sacrarum rerum ordine coniuncta est, cum ex origine illa divina, quam supra commemoravimus, tum ex fine ad ingenerandam educandamque Deo sobolem, ac Deo item coniuges christiano amore mutuoque adiumento addicendos; tum denique ex eiusdem naturali coniugii officio, providentissima Dei Conditoris mente*

To all this a new dignity is added by the Sacrament, **344** by reason of which Christian wedlock has become by *(6,* far the noblest marriage of all, being raised to such lofty *7,* eminence that the Apostle sees in it "a great mystery", *103)* and a thing "honorable in all" (a). The fact that marriage is a religious thing, that it is a sublime symbol of grace and of the union of Christ with His Church, makes it the duty of those contemplating marriage to treat Christian wedlock with holy reverence and to strive earnestly to make their future union approximate as closely as possible to its prototype.

Mixed marriages

Serious blame, not unattended sometimes with dan- **345** ger to their eternal salvation, attaches to those who rash- *(83,* ly contract mixed marriages, against which the maternal *84,* love and foresight of the Church, for very weighty rea- *86)* sons, warns her children. This may be seen in many documents, which are summarized in the following canon of the Code: "The Church everywhere and most strictly forbids the contracting of marriage between two baptised persons one of whom is a Catholic and the other a member of an heretical or schismatical sect. If there is danger of perversion for the Catholic party and the offspring, such a union is forbidden by the divine law itself (a). If the Church sometimes, for reasons touching time, circumstances, or persons, does not refuse to dispense in these strict precepts (saving always the law of

instituto, ut quoddam sit transvehendae vitae quasi vehiculum, quo parentes divinae ominpotentiae velut administri inserviunt.
344a Cf. Eph. 5:32; Hebrews 13:4.
345a C.I.C., can. 1060.

God and with all the possible precautions against the danger of perversion), yet even so it will be difficult for the Catholic party to avoid suffering some detriment from such a union.

346 A frequent result of these marriages is that the chil-
(82, dren unhappily fall away from religion altogether, or at
83) least rapidly lapse into a negligence and indifference regarding it which is not far removed from infidelity and impiety. It should also be remarked that in mixed marriages the living harmony of souls between husband and wife, which, as We have said, is to be modelled upon the mysterious union between Christ and His Church, becomes much more difficult of attainment.

347 Such marriages will not easily exhibit that intimate
(29, union of hearts which, as it is the sign and the mark of
82) the Church of Christ, ought also be the sign, the glory, and the adornment of Christian wedlock. The bond between hearts is usually broken, or at least endangered, when mind and will are at variance concerning the ultimate realities which a man holds most sacred, that is, concerning matters of religious truth and sentiment; and this may easily lead to an estrangement between husband and wife, to the great detriment of domestic peace and happiness, which depends so much upon their mutual charity. "Marriage," as the old Roman law defined it many centuries ago, "is a union between a man and a woman, an association for the whole of life, in which both are under the same law, divine and human" (a).

347a Modestinus (in Dig., 1:23,2: De ritu nuptiarum), 1:1, Regularum.

Divorce

But the chief obstacle to the renovation and rehabil- **348** itation of marriage willed by Christ the Redeemer lies, *(75,* as We have already observed, Venerable Brethren, in the *100)* constantly increasing facility of divorce. The advocates of the new paganism, undeterred by the lessons of a sad experience, persist in an unrelenting spirit of hostility to the sacred indissolubility of wedlock and to the legislation which protects it. They are untiring in their efforts to obtain the legal authorization of divorce, and to substitute for the out-of-date legislation of the past a law which will be more humane.

The grounds suggested for divorce are many and **349** varied. Some they call subjective (due to the defect or *(76)* fault of the partners), others objective (due to circumstances); briefly, they consist in anything which may render a permanent association difficult or disagreeable. Various arguments are advanced to justify these grounds and the corresponding legislation. First there is the benefit of husband and wife: one of the parties is either innocent, and in that case has the right to be freed from the guilty companion; or else guilty, and therefore ought to be separated from a partner to whom an enforced association is unwelcome. Or appeal is made to the welfare of the offspring, deprived of a proper education, or failing to derive any benefit from it, since the scandal of their parents' disagreements and misdeeds must easily lead the children astray from the paths of virtue. The common welfare of society also provides them with an excuse. This, they claim, calls for the total suppression of marriages which are incapable of fulfilling their natural function. In the interests of the public good, moreover, separations should be legalized to prevent crimes which may easily result from the continued cohabitation or association of husband and wife. Such legislation would also put an end to the growing frequency of certain cases in which the Courts and the laws' authority are brought into contempt. For there are married persons, who, to obtain the coveted decree of divorce, either purposely commit those crimes for which the law empowers the judge to dissolve their marriage, or else perjure themselves in accusing each other of them before a judge who is perfectly well aware of the true facts of the case.

350
(*68,*
75,
76)
Their conclusion is that the laws must be adjusted to meet all these needs and to conform to the changed conditions of the times, the opinions of mankind, and the institutions and customs of States. Anyone of these reasons, it is maintained, would alone be sufficient, but taken cumulatively they are thought to provide over-whelming proof that, in certain determined cases, divorce ought to be allowed.

Others, with an effrontery which is astonishing, contend that marriage is a purely private contract and, like all other private contracts, ought to be left absolutely to the consent and private decision of the two contracting parties; it ought therefore to be rescindible for any cause whatever.

Answer to the objections

351
(*16,*
57,
80)
Opposed to all these aberrations, Venerable Brethren, there stands one irrefragable law of God, amply endorsed by Christ, a law against whose force no human decree, nor ordinance of peoples, nor lawgiver's will can prevail: "what God hath joined together, let no man put asun-

der" (a). If anyone in spite of that law makes such a separation his act is null and void, with the consequence which Christ Himself has clearly proclaimed: "He that putteth away his wife and marrieth another committeth adultery; and he that marrieth her that is put away from her husband committeth adultery" (b). And these words of Christ apply to any marriage whatsoever, even to a legitimate marriage of the natural order. Indissolubility is the attribute of every true marriage, and therefore so far as the dissolution of the bond is concerned it is independent of the will of the parties themselves and of every secular power.

We may also recall the solemn judgment of the **352** Council of Trent, anathematizing anyone who asserts *(77)* that "the bond of marriage can be dissolved on the ground of heresy, or the irksomeness of conjugal life, or systematic desertion (a); also its condemnation of those who assert "the Church to be in error when she has taught and teaches that, according to the doctrine of the Gospel and of the Apostles, the bond of matrimony cannot be dissolved by reason of the adultery of one of the parties; and that neither party, even the innocent party not guilty of adultery, is able during the lifetime of the other to contract another marriage; and that adultery is committed by him who dismisses an adulterous wife and marries another woman, and by her who dismisses an adulterous husband and marries another man" (b).

If the Church was not, and is not now, in error when **353** she taught and still teaches this doctrine; and if, conse- *(16)*

351a Matt. 19:6.   351b Luke 16:18.
352a Council of Trent, sess. 24, can. 5.
352b Council of Trent, sess. 24, can. 7.

quently, it is certain that the marriage bond cannot be dissolved even on the ground of adultery, then clearly all the other grounds of divorce, much less serious, which are commonly advanced, have even less validity, and are to be entirely dismissed.

Separation

354
(49,
57,
76)
    As for the objections, under three headings, which We have heard against the indissolubility of marriage, these are easily answered. All the difficulties therein alleged are removed, and all the dangers eliminated, if in such cases a separation between husband and wife is allowed which leaves the bond of marriage intact; and this is authorized in clear terms by the Church in the canons which deal with separation from bed, board, and dwelling (a). Touching the grounds, conditions and manner of this separation; the precautions to be taken in regard to the education of the children and the security of the family; remedies to forestall the evils arising out of such a separation for the married parties, for the children, and for the civil community itself—it will be for the laws of the Church to make provision for all this as far as possible. To a limited extent this will rest also with the State, in regard to the civil aspects and effects of such separation.

Consequences of divorce

355
(17,
58,
78,
79)
    The arguments, outlined above, which are commonly used to establish the indissolubility of the marriage bond are, evidently, valid against the necessity or the facility of divorce and also against any power on the part

354a C.I.C., can. 1128-1132.

of a civil authority to grant it. To every advantage which stands in favor of indissolubility there is a corresponding disadvantage attaching to divorce; and these disadvantages are as injurious to the State as to individuals.

Our Predecessor, Leo XIII, clearly showed how divorce is as pregnant a source of evils as the indissolubility of marriage is fertile in blessings. If the bond is inviolate, we see husband and wife living in peace and security; if it is not, the prospect of an early separation, or, still more, the danger of an eventual divorce renders the conjugal union precarious; at the very least these must give cause for anxiety and suspicion. In the one case there is mutual good will and the complete assurance of possessions shared in common; in the other, both of these suffer considerably from even the possibility of separation. In the one case there are appropriate safeguards of chaste marital fidelity; in the other, harmful temptations to a breach of conjugal faith. The willing acceptance of children, their care and education, are in the one case effectively secured; in the other they are subject to the gravest detriment. In the one case many possibilities of discord between families and relatives are precluded; in the other there are manifold occasions of it. The seeds of dissension in the one case are easily stifled; in the other, sown more widely and abundantly. Finally, the dignity and the function of womankind are in the one case happily restored and rehabilitated; in the other, humbled and degraded, wives being confronted with the prospect that "having served their purpose of satisfying the desires of their husbands, they will be cast aside and abandoned" (a).

356
(17,
78,
79)

356a Enc. *Arcanum*, 10th February 1880; cf. nn. 143-198.

357   And because (to conclude with the authoritative
(61, words of Leo XIII) "nothing contributes so effectively
68, to destroying the family and to sapping the strength of
79) the State as the corruption of morals, it is easy to see
that divorce is the greatest enemy of the family and of the
State. For divorce is the fruit of depraved public morality, and, as experience shows, it opens the way to the
worst vices in private and public life. The seriousness
of the situation becomes more evident still if it is considered that when once facility for divorce has been
granted no curb will avail to restrict its use within definite and prearranged limits. The force of example is
great, and the force of passion greater still. This stimu-
lated, the morbid desire for divorce will take hold on the
souls of mankind, daily spreading like a contagious disease, or like a mighty flood which breaks its banks and
overflows" (a).

358   And therefore, the Encyclical adds, "unless there is
(78, a change of heart, family and State must feel themselves
79) in constant danger of a general and complete collapse"
(a). How far these prophecies, now fifty years old, have
been fulfilled may be seen in the daily increasing corruption of morals and the unparalleled degradation of
the family in those regions where Communism holds
full sway.

III   *Return to the divine idea of Matrimony*

359   Hitherto, Venerable Brethren, We have reverently
(59, admired the wise provisions of Our Creator and Redeem-

357a Enc. *Arcanum,* 10th February 1880; cf. nn. 143-198.
358a Enc. *Arcanum,* 10th February 1880; cf. nn. 143-198.

er concerning human wedlock, and We have seen with   98)
sorrow how that loving ordinance of the divine goodness
is now on every side being frustrated and repudiated by
the passions, errors, and sins of mankind. It is therefore
fitting that We should now with fatherly solicitude turn
to find suitable remedies for the distastrous abuses We
have mentioned, and indicate means for the restoration
of marriage to the place of honor which is its due.

We may well begin by recalling a truth which is an   **360**
axiom of sound philosophy, and therefore also of sacred   (5,
theology. It is to the effect that when a thing has dete-   59,
riorated, it can only be restored to its original and natural   99,
state by return to the divine ideal, which, as the Angelic 100)
Doctor teaches, is the model of all that is right and
orderly (a). This principle was effectively invoked by
Leo III against the Naturalists: "It is a law of divine
Providence," he wrote, "that the institutions which have
God as their author prove the more useful and salutary
according as they remain more true to their original and
natural state, inviolate and unchanged. God, the Creator
of all things, knew well what was best suited for the
establishment and maintenance of each of His works,
and by His will and understanding so ordained them that
each might properly attain its purpose. But if men recklessly and maliciously set about altering or disturbing
the order thus providentially established, then even the
wisest and most beneficent institution begins to be harmful, or at least ceases to be useful, either because such
change has deprived it of its beneficent power, or else
because God Himself has willed in this way to punish

360a St. Thomas, *Summa Theologica*, 1. a 2. ae, q. 91, a.
  1-2.

men for their pride and their audacity" (b). If marriage, then, is to be restored to its normal condition, all must meditate upon the divine plan concerning it and endeavor to shape their conduct accordingly.

Obedience to divine laws

361   The chief obstacle in the way of this endeavor is the
(61, violence of rebellious concupiscence, certainly the
103) principal source of sins against the laws of matrimony; and since man cannot acquire mastery over his passions unless he is submissive to God, obedience to his Creator must consequently be his first care, according to the order divinely established. For it is an invariable law that he who submits his will to God has the joy of being able, with the aid of grace, to master his passions and concupiscence; whereas, on the contrary, he who rebels against God has painful experience of the interior conflict which the violence of his desires lets loose in his soul.

362   How wisely it has been so decreed St. Augustine
(103) shows in these words: "It is appropriate that the lower should be subject to the higher; therefore he who would have control over that which is below him must himself be subject to what is above him. Observe this order if you would find peace: 'Serve God and your flesh will serve you.' Could anything be more just, more harmonious? Obey your superior and your inferior will obey you. Serve Him Who made you, so that you yourself may be served by that which was made for you. The reverse order we do not acknowledge, nor do we

360b Enc. *Arcanum,* 10th February, 1880; cf. nn. 143-198.

commend it to you: 'Let your flesh serve you, and you serve God.' No. 'Serve God and your flesh will serve you.' But if you neglect the first you will not have the second. If you do not obey God you will be tortured by your own slave" (a).

The glorious Apostle of the Nations, under the **363** inspiration of the Holy Spirit, bears witness to this *(11,* ordinance of the divine Wisdom. Alluding to the *61,* philosophers of antiquity who, although they had clearly *103)* known the Creator of all things, had refused to adore Him or to do Him honor, he says: "Wherefore God gave them up to the desires of their heart, to uncleanness, to dishonor their own bodies among themselves," and again, "For this same reason, God delivered them up to shameful affections" (a). And St. James tells that "God resists the proud and gives grace to the humble" (b), that grace, without which, according to St. Paul, it is impossible for man to subdue the rebellion of the flesh (c).

Since, therefore, man cannot achieve the needful **364** restraint of unruly passion unless he himself first yields *(104)* to his Creator the humble homage of piety and reverence which is due to Him, it follows that the first necessity in those who unite themselves in the sacred bonds of matrimony is an inner, genuine piety towards God, a piety which will pervade their whole lives and fill mind and will with the deepest reverence for the divine Majesty.

362a St. Augustine, *Enarrat. in Ps.* 143.
363a Rom. 1:24, 26.
363b Rom. 1:24. 26.
363c Cf. Rom. ch, 7 and 8.

365 And so pastors of souls are acting rightly and in
(104) accordance with the true Christian spirit when, in order
to ensure that married persons observe God's law in
marriage, they exhort them to be faithful to their pious
and religious practices, to surrender their wills entirely
to God, constantly to ask His help, to frequent the
Sacraments, and to foster and preserve in their hearts a
sincere devotion to Almighty God.

366 It is a serious error, on the contrary, to suppose that
(104) men can be brought to curb their carnal desires if they
neglect or despise these supernatural means, and content
themselves with using the latest discoveries of natural
science—biology, the science of heredity, and the like.
This is not to say that these natural means are to be
regarded as unimportant. God is the Author of nature
as well of grace, and He has made the good things of
both orders for the service and the use of mankind;
therefore, the faithful may and ought to make use also
of natural means. What is wrong is to consider these in
themselves sufficient to secure chastity in the conjugal
state, or to attribute to them a greater efficacy than to
the help of supernatural grace.

Obedience to the Church

367 The observance of the divine laws in marriage and
(61, in married life, without which the effective restoration
101, of wedlock is impossible, supposes that all men are able
103) with ease, with certainty and without any admixture of
error to ascertain what these laws are. But it is evident
that many illusions would be invited, and many errors
mingled with the truth, if everybody were left to discover these laws by the light of reason alone, or if they

had to be discerned by each one's private interpretation of revealed truth. This consideration holds in regard to many other truths of the moral order; but it calls for particular attention in regard to marriage, where frail human nature is so easy a prey to carnal passion and can be so readily deceived and corrupted by it. This is especially the case because the observance of God's law sometimes requires of married persons difficult and enduring sacrifices, sacrifices which, as experience shows, the weak man is apt to invoke as so many excuses for not keeping with the divine law.

Accordingly, if the minds and the conduct of mankind are to be guided, not by some imaginative or adulterated conception of the divine law, but by a true and authentic knowledge of it, it is necessary that devotion to God and the desire to serve Him should be accompanied by a sincere and humble obedience to the Church. For Christ Himself has constituted the Church as the teacher of truth also in matters touching the guidance and regulation of moral conduct, although in this sphere there is much which, absolutely speaking, is accessible to the human reason unaided. In the case of natural truths of religion and morality God added revelation to the light of reason in order that "even in the present state of the human race all men might with ease, with firm certitude, and without any admixture of error" (a) know what is right and true; and with the same end in view He has appointed the Church to be the guardian and teacher of all truth concerning Faith and morals. **368** *(48, 103)*

368a Vatican Council, sess. 3, c. 2.

369 Let the faithful obey the Church, therefore, if they
(103) would keep themselves safe from error and moral corruption. Furthermore, if they are not to deprive themselves of the help so generously provided by God, they
must yield their obedience not only to the more solemn
definitions of the Church but also, in due measure, to
the other constitutions and decrees by which certain
opinions are proscribed and condemned as dangerous
and vicious (a).

370 So, too, in the questions which are raised at the
(103) present day concerning marriage, let the faithful not
trust too much in their own judgment or surrender to
the allurement of a false freedom or so-called independence of thought.

371 It is alien to the true Christian spirit such unwean-
(103) ing confidence in one's own mind as to accept only what
one has discovered from a direct examination of the
subject; or to restrict one's assent and obedience to the
prescriptions laid down in those more solemn definitions
above mentioned, as though one might prudently consider the other decisions of the Church to be wrong or
insufficiently grounded in truth and moral rectitude (a).

369a Cf. Vatican Council, sess. 3, c. 4; C.I.C., can. 1324.
371a *Alienissimum enim est ab omni veri nominis christiano
suo ingenio ita superbe fidere, ut iis solum, quae ipse
ex interioribus rerum visceribus cognoverit, assentiri
velit, et Ecclesiam, ad omnes gentes docendas regendas-
que a Deo missam, rerum et adiunctorum recentium
minus gnaram existimare, vel etiam iis tantum, quae
per somemniores quas diximus definitiones ea iusserit,
assensum et obedientiam praestare, preinde ac si opinari
prudenter liceat cetera eius decreta aut falso laborare
aut veritatis honestatisque causa niti non satis.*

The true Christian, whether learned or unlearned, will allow himself in all matters pertaining to faith and morals to be ruled and guided by the Holy Church of God, through its Supreme Pastor, the Roman Pontiff, who himself is guided by Our Lord Jesus Christ.

Doctrinal instruction on marriage

Since the universal and enduring rehabilitation of marriage calls for a return to God's law and plan, it is of the first importance that the faithful should be well instructed concerning marriage; instructed by the spoken and written word, not once nor superficially but frequently and thoroughly, and with clear and weighty arguments, so that these truths may take hold of their minds and move their hearts. The faithful must be brought to meditate upon the great wisdom, sanctity, and benevolence towards mankind which God has shown in instituting matrimony and securing it with holy laws; and especially by raising it so marvellously to the dignity of a Sacrament, thus opening to married persons a fountain of grace abundant enough to enable themselves chastely and faithfully to fulfill its noble purposes, for the benefit and salvation of themselves, their children, the State, and the whole of humanity.

372
(11,
101)

If the modern subverters of marriage spare no pains— by discourses, writings, books, pamphlets and other means without number—to mislead the minds of men, to corrupt their hearts, to cast ridicule upon matrimonial chastity, to belaud the more shameful vices, then much more ought you, Venerable Brethren, whom "the Holy Ghost has placed as Bishops to rule the Church of God which He purchased with the price of His own

373
(62,
99)

Blood" (a), to devote all your efforts to meet their attack. You yourselves, with the help of the priests subject to your authority, and also through those chosen laity who are called as helpers of the hierarchical apostolate in the movement called *Catholic Action* (so much commended and desired by Us), must use every appropriate means to oppose error with truth, vice with the radiance of chastity, the servitude of the passions with the liberty of the sons of God (b), iniquitous facilities for divorce with the unfailing stability of a true charity in marriage, and with the sacrament of conjugal troth preserved inviolate until death.

374 Christians will then render heartfelt thanks to God
(68, for the gentle yet firm strength of His commandment
103) which binds them, and keeps them as far as possible aloof from all idolatry of the flesh and from the degraded slavery of the passions. They will shrink in horror from, and use every means to avoid those abominable opinions which, to the shame of human dignity are at this moment being advertised under the name of "the perfect marriage"—a "perfect marriage" which, it has been truly said, is nothing but a marriage depraved.

375 This salutary teaching, this religious science of
(107) matrimony, bears no resemblance to that exaggerated physiological education which the so-called reformers of our day offer as a beneficent service to married folk. They debate much upon these questions of physiology; but what they teach by it is more that art of skilful sinning than the virtue of chastely living.

373a Acts 20:28.
373b Cf. John 8:32 ff.; Gal. 5:13.

And so, Venerable Brethren, We heartily endorse **376** the words which Leo XIII, Our Predecessor of happy *(101)* memory, addressed to the Bishops of the whole world in his Encyclical on Christian Marriage: "Use all your efforts and all your authority so that among the peoples entrusted to your care you may preserve undiminished and untarnished the doctrine which Christ Our Lord and His Apostles, interpreters of the Divine Will, have delivered to us, which the Catholic Church also has religiously maintained, and has commanded to be observed by all Christians throughout all ages" (a).

Cooperation with the graces of the Sacrament

But the teaching of the Church, however excellent, **377** does not alone suffice to re-establish Matrimony in its *(103,* perfect conformity with the Divine law. Even when *104)* married persons are fully instructed concerning the Christian doctrine of marriage, they still need a firm purpose to observe the holy laws of God and of nature regarding it. Whatever the theories sustained and propagated by certain persons, husband and wife must make and keep this sacred and solemn resolution: that in all things concerning marriage they will without any hesitation keep the commandments of God; help each other always in mutual love; preserve the honor of chastity; never violate the indissolubility of the marriage bond; and use their matrimonial rights always in a Christian and sacred way, especially in the early days of wedlock, so that should circumstances subsequently require them to observe continence, their habit of self-restraint will help them more easily to do so.

376a Enc. *Arcanum,* 10th February 1880; cf. nn. 143-198.

378   For forming, maintaining, and fulfilling this resolu-
(11, tion, Christian husbands and wives will find a great
104) assistance in frequent meditation upon their state and in
an effective remembrance of the Sacrament they have
received. Let them be constantly mindful that they have
been consecrated and strengthened for the duties and
the dignities of their state by a Sacrament, whose
efficacy, though it does not confer a character remains
none the less in perpetuity. In this connection they will
do well to ponder these consoling words of the saintly
Cardinal Bellarmine, who thus expressed an opinion
shared with him by other eminent theologians: "The
Sacrament of Matrimony may be considered in two ways:
in the moment of its accomplishment, and its perman-
ency afterwards. This Sacrament, in fact, is similar to
the Eucharist; which is a Sacrament, not only in
the moment of its accomplishment, but also as long as
it remains. For as long as husband and wife live, their
fellowship is always the Sacrament of Christ and the
Church" (a).

379   But if the grace of this Sacrament is to exert the
(104) whole of its efficacy, husband and wife must cooperate
with it. Of this cooperation We have already spoken
and it consists in their strenuous endeavor to discharge
their duties as faithfully as possible. Just as in the natural
order the strength that God gives will yield its full
efficacy only if men make use of it by their own effort
and industry, and will remain without fruit if these are
wanting; so also the powers of grace, infused into the
soul by the Sacrament and remaining in it, must be exer-

378a St. Robert Bellarmino, *De controversiis*, t. 3, *De
Matr.*, contr. 2, cap. 6.

cised by the recipients through their own efforts and activity. Let not married persons neglect the sacramental grace which is in them (a). Let them attend zealously to the discharge of their duties, however hard they may find them, and they will feel the efficacy of that grace growing every day.

At times the difficulties of life and the married state **380** may weigh upon them more heavily than usual. But *(104)* let them not be discouraged, but consider as in a manner addressed to themselves those words which St. Paul wrote concerning the Sacrament of Holy Orders to his beloved disciple Timothy, when difficulties and contumely had brought him to the brink of discouragement: "I admonish thee that thou stir up the grace which is in thee by the imposition of my hands. For God hath not given us the spirit of fear; but of power, and of love, and of sobriety" (a).

Preparation for marriage

But all this, Venerable Brethren, depends in great **381** measure upon the suitable preparation, remote as well *(107)* as proximate, of the parties for marriage. Indeed it can hardly be denied that the firm foundation of a happy marriage and the ruin of an unhappy one have been prepared already in the souls of men and women during the days of their childhood and youth. Those who before marriage, were in all things self-seeking, and indulged their passions, will, it is to be feared, be the same in marriage as they were before it; they will reap

379a Cf. 1 Tim. 4:14.
380a 2 Tim. 1:6-7.

what they have sown (a), and in their home will reign unhappiness, lamentation, mutual disdain, misunderstandings, and boredom with each other's company—worst of all they may even find themselves with their passions still untamed.

382
(103,
107)
Let young men and women, therefore, approach wedlock well disposed and well prepared, so that they may be able to help each other to face the adversities of life side by side, and, what is far more important, attain their eternal salvation and shape their interior life according to the age of the fullness of Christ (a). This will also enable them the more easily to be to their children parents such as God wants them to be to their little ones: a father who is truly a father, a mother who is truly a mother; parents whose loving care will cause their children, even in spite of great poverty and amidst this vale of tears, to find in their home some likeness of that happy Paradise of delights in which the Creator of the human race placed its first members. In this way, too, they will make their children perfect men and perfect Christians, inspiring them with a truly Catholic spirit, and training them to that noble love of country which piety and gratitude require of us.

383
(107)
Therefore those who intend at some time to enter the holy state of Matrimony, as well as those who are concerned with the education of Christian youth, will attach great importance to these counsels, thus preparing the way for blessings and forestalling evils. They will also bear in mind the warning which We gave in

381a Cf. Gal. 6:9.
382a Eph. 4:13.

Our Encyclical on Education: "From childhood, inclinations which are evil must be repressed and inclinations which are good must be fostered and encouraged. The minds of children must above all be imbued with the doctrines that come from God, and their hearts strengthened with the assistance of Divine grace. Without these none will be able to master his own desires, nor will it be possible to expect the full and perfect results of a teaching and training of the Church, whom God has provided with heavenly doctrines and with divine Sacraments, precisely in order that she may be the effective Teacher of all mankind" (a).

The choice of a partner

Of the first importance in the proximate preparation for matrimony is the careful choice of a partner.(108) **384** On this, indeed, depends for the most part the happiness or unhappiness of marriage, because each partner may be to the other either a great help or else a great danger and a hindrance in the leading of a Christian married life. An imprudent choice may be the source of a lifetime of regrets, and therefore those about to marry ought to reflect carefully before choosing the person with whom they will have to spend the remainder of their lives. In this reflection they should give the first place to the consideration of God and the true Religion of Christ; then they should consider themselves, their future offspring, and also the human race and the nation, of which Matrimony is the source.

Let them fervently ask God's help to make their **385** choice with Christian prudence; not under the influence (108)

383a Enc. *Divini illius Magistri*, 31st December, 1929.

of an unreasoning and unbridled passion; not out of the sole desire of monetary gain or any other less noble motive; but guided by a true and upright love and sincere affection towards their partner, and seeking in marriage the ends for which God instituted it. Let them not forget, finally, to ask the prudent advice of their parents. To this advice they should attach great value, since their mature judgment and experience may save them from making a disastrous mistake in this matter. They will thus enter upon the sacred right of Matrimony hallowed abundantly with the blessing of the fourth commandment: *"Honor thy father and thy mother* (which is the first commandment with a promise) *that it may be well with thee and thou mayest be long-lived upon the earth"* (a).

Economic difficulties

386
(60) Not infrequently the perfect observance of God's commandments and the proper use of matrimony are attended with great difficulty because married persons are in straitened circumstances or in great poverty. The needs of such families must, obviously, be relieved in the best way possible.

387
(60,
97) In the first place, every effort must be made to implant the wise provisions set forth by Our Predecessor, Leo XIII (a), namely, that economic and social conditions in a country should make it possible for every father of a family to earn such a wage as suffices, in the condition and in the locality in which he lives, for the support of himself, his wife, and his children:

385a Eph. 6, 2-3; cf. Exod. 20:12.
387a Enc. *Rerum Novarum,* 15th May, 1891; cf. n. 210.

"the laborer is worthy of his hire" (b). To refuse this wage, or to pay less than what is right, is a grave injustice, and is numbered in Holy Scripture among the greatest of sins (c). Moreover, it is forbidden to fix a rate of wages so low that, in the circumstances, they are insufficient for the support of a family.

But steps should also be taken to ensure that the parties themselves, long before entering upon the state of matrimony, make careful provisions in advance to meet, at any rate partially, the expenses and the needs of the future; and they should take advice from experts as to how this can effectively and honestly be done. Those who cannot do this by their own unaided efforts should be encouraged to join with others similarly situated in private or public associations in order to make provision for the necessities of life (a). **388** *(105, 107)*

If the means which We have indicated do not suffice to enable a family, especially one which is unusually large or helpless, to balance its budget, then the love of Christians for their neighbors absolutely requires that the wants of the needy should be supplied by Christian charity. The rich, especially, should help the poor, and those who have superfluous possessions should not squander them in luxury or in useless expenditure, but to devote them to supporting the life and health of those who lack necessities. Those who give of their substance to Christ in the person of His poor will receive an abundant re- **389** *(97)*

387b Luke 10:7.
387c Cf. Deut. 24:14, 15.
388a Cf. Enc. *Rerum Novarum*, 15th May, 1891; cf. n. 210.

ward from the Lord when He comes to judge the world, and those who do not give will be punished (a). The Apostle's words are no empty warning: "He that hath the substance of this world and shall see his brother in need, and shall shut up his bowels from him: how doth the charity of God abide in Him?" (b).

Duty of the public authority

390
(43,
60,
97,
98)
If private contributions are not enough for this purpose it is the duty of public authority to supplement the individual resources, especially in a matter of such importance to the common good as that of assuring to families and married persons conditions which befit the dignity of man.

If families, especially those with many children, have no home fit to live in; if the husband cannot find work and livelihood; if commodities of daily use can only be purchased at exorbitant prices; if the mother, to the great detriment of the home, is compelled by need to earn money by her labor; and if in the ordinary or even extraordinary labors of childbirth she is deprived of suitable nourishment, medicine, the assistance of a skilled physician, and other necessities; then it is obvious that if husband and wife lose heart, married life and the observance of God's commandments become very difficult indeed. The danger to public security, to the welfare and even the very life of the State, becomes evident. When human beings are reduced to such straits, counsels of despair may prompt them to the thought that, having now nothing to lose, they will have much to gain by stirring up a general revolution in the country.

389a Matt. 25:34 ff.   389b 1 John 3:17.

Consequently, those who have care of the State and **391** of the common good cannot neglect such needs of married *(97,* people and their families without great injury to the *98)* public welfare. In their legislation, therefore, and in their allocation of public funds they should regard as a primary object that of relieving the want of needy families.

One thing in this connection We observe with re- **392** gret: it often happens that the right order of things is *(68)* reversed, and the unmarried mother and her child (who admittedly must be succored, if only to avoid greater evils) receive readily and in abundance that assistance which is either refused or else granted only sparingly and grudgingly to legitimate mothers.

But it is not only in the temporal order, Venerable **393** Brother, but in the spiritual order as well that the interest *(68,* of the State is concerned in firmly establishing the *98)* foundations of marriage and their family; it is to the advantage of the civil community that just laws regarding conjugal fidelity and reciprocal help should be made and faithfully observed. For history attests that the safety of the State and the prosperity of its citizens are precarious if the moral order on which they rest is upset, and if the very life-spring of the State (marriage and the family) is obstructed by the vice of its citizens.

The preservation of the moral order, however, can- **394** not be secured only by State coercion and penalties; nor *(98)* is it enough to set before men's minds the beauty and the necessity of virtue. A religious authority is needed too, to direct the will of man and to strengthen human frailty with the help of Divine grace; and that religious authority is none other than the Church instituted by Christ. Most earnestly in the Lord, therefore, We exhort all who are

charged with the supreme power in the State to initiate
and maintain relations of harmony and friendship with
the Church of Christ, so that the two powers may unite
their efforts and their zeal in order effectively to elimi-
ate the grave evils threatening both Church and State
as a consequence of the wanton liberties by which marriage and the family are being assailed.

395   The State can be of great assistance to the Church
(74,   in the discharge of these duties if its legislation takes
98)   account of the laws of God and the Church and inflicts
penalties upon those who offend. For there are some
who consider themselves morally justified in doing anything, so long as the law of the State allows it or at any
rate does not punish it; and even if their conscience forbids it, they will do these things because they have no
fear of God, and apparently have nothing to fear from the
laws of men. And this is attended with disastrous results
both to themselves and to many others.

396   Such association with the Church will in no way
(98)   endanger or diminish the rights and integrity of the
State. How groundless such fears are was shown by
Leo XIII: "Nobody doubts that Jesus Christ, the Divine
Founder of the Church, intended religious authority to
be distinct from the civil power, so that each might be
free to fulfil without hindrance the task allotted to it; but
with this added provision, that it is to the common interest of both powers and of humanity as a whole that
they should be associated in harmony.... If the civil
power acts in friendly understanding with the sacred
authority of the Church it will necessarily be to the great
advantage of both. The dignity of the State will be
enhanced and, with Religion as its guide, its authority

will never be unjustly exercised. The Church on the other hand will receive the advantage of State support and protection, which is to the public good of the faithful" (a).

A recent and striking example of this is seen in the **397** solemn treaty happily concluded between the Holy See *(98)* and the Kingdom of Italy. By this, in accordance with the above principles and with the law of Christ, a peaceful and friendly arrangement has been reached in particular regarding marriage—an agreement well in keeping with the glorious history of the Italian nation and its ancient religious traditions. Among the Lateran agreements is the following decree: "The State, desiring to restore to the institution of matrimony, which is the basis of the family, a dignity which conforms with the traditions of its people, recognizes civil effects for the Sacrament of matrimony celebrated according to Canon Law" (a); and this rule and principle are applied in subsequent clauses of the Concordat which accompanies the Treaty.

This example may serve to show that, even in an **398** age which advocates the absolute separation of the civil *(98)* authority from the Church, and indeed from Religion altogether, if it is possible for the two Sovereign powers, without any detriment to their respective rights and sovereignty, to unite and associate in mutual harmony and friendly collaboration for the common good of both; and that both can assume a joint responsibility for Matrimony and thus defend the Christian home against the pernicious dangers and even imminent ruin which threaten it.

396a Encycl. *Arcanum,* Feb. 10, 1880; cf. nn. 143-198. 198. 397a *Concordat,* art. 34; cf. AAS 21 (1929) 290.

The Holy Father's prayer

399
(99)
All these considerations, Venerable Bretheren, which Our pastoral solicitude has prompted Us to set before you, We desire to be widely promulgated—conformably always with the rules of Christian prudence—among all Our beloved children, over whom you have immediate charge, among all the members of Christ's great family. We desire them to be explained so that all may fully understand the sound doctrine on Matrimony and be carefully on their guard against the dangers advocated by the preachers of error, and above all so that "denying ungodliness and worldly desire, they may live soberly and justly and godly in this world, looking for the blessed hope and coming of the glory of the great God and Our Savior Jesus Christ" (a).

400
(9,
99)
May the Almighty Father, "of Whom all paternity in Heaven and earth is named" (a), Who gives strength to the weak and courage to the timid and faint-hearted; may Christ Our Lord and Redeemer "Who instituted and perfected the venerable Sacraments" (b), and willed to make Matrimony an image of His ineffable union with the Church; may the Holy Spirit, God Who is Love, the Light of hearts and the Strength of the mind—grant that Our teaching in this Encyclical on the Holy Sacrament of Matrimony, on the admirable will and law of God concerning it, on the errors and dangers which threaten it, and on the remedies by which they are to be met, may be understood by all, be received by all with generous dispositions, and by all, with the help of God's grace, be put into practice, so that the marriages of

399a Titus 2:12-13.   400a Eph. 3:15.
400b Council of Trent, sess 24.

Christians may exhibit a renewed and vigorous life of fertility consecrated to God, of untarnished fidelity, and of unfailing stability, and be hallowed by the holiness and fullness of grace which is the fruit of the Sacrament.

FAMILY WAGES

Encycl. *Quadragesimo Anno*, May 15, 1931.
(*The social doctrine of the Church.—Determining the wages.*)

... It is not possible to estimate a just wage (for **401** work) nor what would be an adequate return to be made *(60,* for it, where its social and individual nature is not taken *97)* into account.

From this double aspect, naturally inherent in human work, follow important conclusions for the regulation and determination of wages.

In the first place, the wage paid to the worker must be sufficient for the support of himself and his family. It is right indeed that the rest of the family contribute according to their ability towards the common maintenance, as indeed we see it done among the families of peasants and among those of many artisans and small tradesmen. But it is wrong to exploit children while still of a tender age, or the weakness of woman. Mothers should carry on their work chiefly at home, or near to it, occupying themselves in caring for the household. A great disorder and one to be eliminated at all costs is the abuse whereby mothers of families, because of the insufficiency of the father's wages, are forced to engage in gainful occupations outside the home, to the neglect of their own proper cares and duties, particularly the upbringing of their children.

402
(97) Every effort must therefore be made to ensure that fathers of families receive a wage sufficient adequately to meet normal domestic needs. If under present circumstances this is not always feasible, social justice demands that reforms be introduced without delay to guarantee such a wage to every adult worker. In this connection We praise those who have most prudently and usefully attempted various methods by which an increased wage is paid in view of increased family burdens, and special provision made for special necessities.

(Necessity for reform of institutions and methods.)

THE HOLY FAMILY

Encycl. *Lux veritatis,* December 25, 1931
(Fifteenth centenary of the Council of Ephesus and of the definition of the dogma of the Divine Motherhood of Mary.)

403
(106) We hold it to be a good sign that it has fallen to Us to celebrate this fifteenth centenary; to Us, who have defended the dignity and sanctity of Christian marriage against every kind of error (a); who have solemnly upheld the Church's most holy rights in the education of the young, affirming and explaining the methods and principles which best serve to this end (b). Thus these two subjects of Ours find both in the divine Motherhood and in the family of Nazareth a singular model to be held up as an example to everyone. "Indeed," to use the words of Our Predecessor Leo XIII of happy memory, "Joseph is for fathers of families an excellent example of

403a Encycl. *Casti connubii,* December 31, 1930.
403b Encycl. *Divini illius Magistri,* December 31, 1929.

paternal and vigilant protection; the Most Holy Mother of God is an admirable example and pattern to mothers of love, modesty, of the spirit of submission and perfect faith; in the person of Jesus, Who was subject to them, children have a divine model of obedience to be admired, venerated and imitated" (c).

To those mothers of modern times, who, weary of children and the conjugal bond, have debased and violated the duties that were imposed on them, nothing could be more helpful than to look at Mary and consider seriously to what great dignity the most important duty of motherhood has been raised by her. Indeed, it is to be hoped that with the grace of the Heavenly Queen they will be induced to blush with shame for the disgrace inflicted on the great Sacrament of Matrimony and be so inspired that they will use all possible means to imitate Mary's admirable virtues.   **404** *(42, 87, 103, 106)*

Whenever all this that we have desired should come to pass, if, that is, domestic society—the basis of all human society—were to be led back to this most worthy pattern of integrity, then without doubt we would be able to withstand and finally put an end to that frightening accumulation of evils that surrounds us.

CRIMES OF DIVORCE

Encycl. *Dilectissima nobis,* June 3, 1933 to the Spanish Episcopate.

(*Duties of the Bishops during religious persecution.— Religious instruction of children.*)

403c Apost. Letter *Neminem fugit,* January 14, 1892; cf. above, nn. 214-215.

405		This is all the more necessary, as We see it, because
(75,	in Spain laws have been recently promulgated whose
77,	aim is to sully the family sanctuary by unjustly introducing
78,	divorce in the territory of the Republic (a). Having
79)	opened the way to family disintegration, these laws have
sown the seeds of the greatest evils that can beset civil
society.

(*Invitation to unity in defence of the Faith.*)

STERILIZATION

All. to the Sacred College, December 23, 1933.

(*General expectation of an important disourse of the Pope.*)

406		Now, in that general expectation there must be
(88,	distinguished immediately one aspect that merited
107)	particular regard. Indeed, there was not only the desire
to know what the Holy Father thought of the general
conditions of the world, international and global, but
there was that which had the character of a filial consultation. The Pope, the Vicar of Christ the Master, is
asked what the believer, the faithful, the Catholic must
think—among so many and different opinions—of that
most repulsive subject called sterilization. This is a word
which expresses a procedure already in use in foreign
countries and which had already had some preparation
not so far away, but which has now been an object of
the provision of notorious laws (a).

405a *Id sane vel maiorem necessitatem habere consemus,
quod proxime in Hispania editae leges, divortio in rem
publicam inique inducto, familae sacrarium polluere
conantur.*

406a The discourse is reported in third person.

The more repulsive the subject, so much the more **407**
were We happy to be able to satisfy, at least initially and *(88,*
with detail, that filial expectation and consultation.   *107)*

There was in 1931 a decree of the Holy Office (a),
of which Congregation, as all know, the Pope is Prefect
and for which, therefore, he is evidently a little, nay
more than a little, responsible, and there was the 1931

407a Decree of the Holy Office on "Sex Education" and
"Eugenics", March 21, 1931:
"In the general meeting of the Holy Office, held on
March 18, 1931, the following questions were presented:
1. May the method called "sex-education" or even "sex
initiation" be approved?
2. What should be said about the Eugenic method,
whether positive or negative, and about the means it
advocates to better the human race, while violating
natural, divine, and ecclesiastical laws pertaning to matrimony and the rights of individuals?
The most eminent Cardinals in charge of safeguarding
the integrity of faith and morals, discussed these matters
and carefully analyzed them. Then, considering the vote
of the Most Reverend Consultants to the meeting,
they determined to answer thus:
The answer to the *first question* is *no*. In the education
of youth the method to be followed is that hitherto observed by the Church and the Saints as recommended
by His Holiness, the Pope, in the encyclical dealing with
the Christian education of youth, promulgated on December 31, 1929. The first place is to be given to the full,
sound and continuous instruction in religion of the youth
of both sexes. Esteem, desire and love of the angelic
virtue must be instilled into their minds and hearts. They
must be made fully alive to the necessity of constant
prayer, and assiduous frequenting of the Sacraments of
Penance and the Holy Eucharist; they must be directed
to foster a filial devotion to the Blessed Virgin as Mother
of holy purity, to whose protection they must entirely
commit themselves. Precautions must be taken to see

Encyclical "Casti connubii" (b) which has had, thanks to God and to men of good will, such a kindly reception everywhere and which will be of great advantage to all: two documents wherein is contained what must be thought and held on this matter. The statements contained in them are fairy clear; and it seems in truth to Us that both the faithful and Pastors can find in these documents at least in substance and in general outline, what should provide the object of their thinking and teaching.

(*General situation of humanity.—Christmas greetings.*)

EVILS OF THE CINEMA

Encycl. *Vigilanti cura,* June 29, 1936.
(*Importance and dangers of the cinema.*)

408
(62) Everyone knows what damage bad films cause to souls. They become occasions of sin; they lead youth to the practice of evil because they are the glorification of the passions; they present life in a false light; obscure ideals; destroy true love, respect for matrimony and affection for the family.   (*Other dangers.—Remedies.*)

that they avoid dangerous reading, indecent shows, conversations of the wicked, and all other occasions of sin. Hence no approbation whatever can be given to the advocacy of the new method even as taken up recently by some Catholic authors and set before the public in printed publications.
The reply to the *second question* was that the Eugenic method is definitely not to be approved. Rather it must be considered false and condemned, as it was in fact declared in the Holy Father's Encyclical on Christian matrimony, *Casti conubii,* of December 31, 1930." Cf. AAS 23 (1931), 118.   407b Cf. above, n. 263

COMMUNISM

Encycl. *Divini Redemptoris, March* 19, 1937.

(The danger of Communism.—Doctrine: denial of human dignity.)

In a system which denies to human life all that is **409** of a sacred and spiritual nature, it follows as a matter of *(6,* course that matrimony and the family are considered to *12,* be a purely civil and artificial institution, originating in *14,* a particular set of economic conditions; and as the theory *66,* refuses to recognize any matrimonial bond of the jurid- *69,* ical and moral order not completely dependent on the *75,* will of the individual or the community, it likewise as a *95)* necessary consequence denies the indissolubility of matri- mony. The complete emancipation of women from any ties with home or family is a special characteristic of the commmunist theory. Held to be totally free from the pro- tective authority of her husband, the wife is withdrawn from the home and the care of her children and, equally with her husband, thrust into the turmoil of public life and communal industry, her home and her children be- ing handed over to the custody of the State. Parents, finally, are denied the right to educate the children; this right is claimed exclusively for the community and is therefore allowed to be exercised only in its name and by its mandate.

What does human society become, based on these **410** materialistic principles? It becomes an association of hu- *(66)* man beings, with no other hierarchy than that of the economic system. Its sole function is to produce wealth by communal labor; and its sole aim is the enjoyment of material goods in a paradise where each man "gives labor according to his strength and receives wealth according to his needs." It is to be noted also that this system grants the community the right, indeed the practically unlimited and arbitrary power, to direct individual citizens into communal industry regardless of their personal welfare, and even to constrain the unwilling by force. The only moral code, the only law acknowledged in this society, is that which has its origin in the economic system of the time; earthly in origin, therefore, and subject to constant change. Briefly, the object is to introduce a new order and a new civilization, evolved from the hidden forces of nature, and culminating in a godless human society.

(*Communist propaganda.— The Church's doctrine.*)

411
(1,
29,
38,
109)
As marriage and the natural use of marriage are of divine institution, so the constitution of the family and its chief functions have their origin in the sovereign Creator of all, and not in the will of man or in any economic system. These are matters which We have explained fully enough in Our Encyclical on the sanctity of Christian Marriage (a) as well as in the aforesaid Encyclical on Christian Education (b).

(*Remedies.*)

IN DEFENCE OF THE FAMILY

Apost. Let. *Con singular complacencia*, January 18, 1939 to the Episcopate of the Philippine Islands.

(*Means to restore the Faith and Christian life.*)

412
(36,
In the first place it is necessary for you to work unceasingly for the restoration of the reign of Christ in the

411a Enc. *Casti connubii*, 31st December, 1930.
411b Enc. *Divini illius Magistri*, 31st December, 1929.

heart of the family. "Jesus Christ reigns in the family,"   *38,*
We said in the Encyclical *Ubi Arcano*, "when that family,   *42,*
formed by the Sacrament of Christian Matrimony, keeps   *99,*
inviolate its sacred character" (a). Catholic Action must   *104)*
tend to this Christian restoration of the family which is
the source of human life, an institution organized by God
Himself, a place where the supernatural life of God's
children receives its first development.

We are well aware that, even in the midst of this   **413**
people whom We love, God's enemies seek every means   *(75,*
to debase the divine institution of the family. They know   *87)*
no obstacle when it comes to propagating doctrines contrary to the indissolubility of the marriage bond, new
theories and abominable practices which suppress life
at its very beginning.

As a consequence, it is imperative that Catholic   **414**
Action and in particular the associations of men and of   *(99,*
women react in an appropriate manner against such   *101,*
great evils. They will react principally and above all by   *103,*
living themselves in a holy manner in the married state;   *105,*
then by making known in their circle the Church's teach-   *107)*
ings on Matrimony, as We expounded it fully in Our
Encyclical "*Casti connubii*" (a); by enlightening and assisting parents with spiritual aid in the fulfilment of their
duties; by preparing for new families with a profoundly
Christian formation of youth, so that on entering the
married state the latter may be already instructed in the
responsibilities they undertake. To this end, it is fitting
to spread the devotion towards the holiest of families,

412a Pius XI, *Ubi arcano*, December 23, 1922; cf. above
     nn. 257-259.
414a Cf. above, nn. 263-400.

the Family of Nazareth, proposing it as a model to parents and children, consecrating the family to it, according to the desire (which is also Our own) of Our Predecessor, Leo XIII (b).

415
(99,
105)
In this vast field for high endeavors—the restoring of family life—a large part of the apostolate belongs to the woman: here We wish to praise especially and to encourage all the more her zeal for Catholic Action. For this reason We make a paternal plea to all Catholic women without distinction of social condition or age: to girls, young women, mothers of families, widows. Let all of them cooperate in all good works according to their own strength, their own place, and their own abilities. Let them enter the battle, as powerful auxiliaries, to reinforce Christ's army of Apostles who are working to save souls; let them contribute especially in teaching Christian doctrine, in strengthening persons of their own sex in the practice of true Christian piety or leading them back to it. In this way these women will contribute to build the foundations of the restored family life and will continue the glorious tradition of the first Christian women, who, on account of their apostolic zeal, merited to be remembered with honor by the Apostle: "I beseech thee also . . . help them, for they have toiled with me in the gospel" (a).

We do not doubt that Our appeal will be welcomed readily. In such a way the domestic sanctuary together with all civil society will reap undoubted advantage from the growing organizations of women.

414b Ap. Lett. *Neminem fugit,* 14th June, 1892; cf. above nn. 214-215.
415a Phil. 4:3.

PIUS XII

1939-1958

THE MISSION OF THE NEWLY WEDS

All. to newlyweds, May 24, 1934.

From the moment of your marriage you have **416** become founders of new families ... designed to nourish *(22,* a future which is lost in the mysteries of divine Provi- *43)* dence; designed to nourish civil society with good citizens, eager to provide for society itself that salvation and security of which it never, as now, felt so much the need; destined also to increase the Church of Jesus Christ, because it is from new families that the Church awaits new children of God, who will be obedient to her most holy laws; designed, lastly, to prepare new citizens for the heavenly country, when this temporal exile shall have been completed.

(*Necessity of living in a Christian manner to fulfill this mission.*)

THE SACRAMENT

All. to newly weds, July 12, 1939.

Reflect ... on what the Catechism itself teaches, and **417** which We desire to call to your mind at this audience: *(11,* at the base of every Christian family there is a Sacra- *36)* ment. This means that it is not a mere contract, a simple ceremony or a purely external rite to mark an important date in one's life, but a true and proper religious act of supernatural life, from which flows an almost constant right to obtain from God all those graces, those divine aids, which are necessary for and useful to sanctify married life, to fulfill the duties of the married state, to overcome its difficulties, to maintain its resolves and to reach its highest ideals (a).

God, on His part, has assured us of His aid, elevating Christian marriage to a permanent symbol of the indissoluble union of Christ and the Church.

(*Divine blessings on the Christian family.*)

THE FAMILY ABOVE ALL ELSE

Encycl. *Summi Pontificatus*, October 20, 1939.

(*New paganism.—Principles of social order.—The State must respect private activities.*)

418
(38,
44,
66)
If the State takes over and claims for itself all private enterprises it forgets that those enterprises are regulated by a multiplicity of rules and standards which are peculiar and private to themselves, and contribute to the due achievement of their purposes. The result is public loss, arising from the damage done to these private enterprises when they are removed from their natural sphere, which is that of private responsibility.

A special danger arises from such habits of thought and action. Domestic life, the primary and indispensable cell of human society, with all its claims and interests, is thrown into the background; it is regarded exclusively from the standpoint of national power. Men come to forget that they and their families have a priority over the

417a *Dal quale profluisce quasi un diritto costante ad impetrare tutte quelle grazie tutti quegli aiuti divini che sono necessari ed opportuni a santificare la vita matrimoniale, a compiere i doveri dello stato coniugale, a superarne le difficoltà, a mantenere i propositi, a raggiungere i piu alti ideali.*

State in the natural order, and that a divine Creator has endowed both with their own rights and powers, destined both for their several functions, corresponding to the unchanging exigencies of nature.

(*Civic virtues are not the only ones.*)

We see, then, growing up under Our eyes the dangers, the crises, which We have good reason to fear for the future as well as for Our own age. They spring from the weakening and the gradual abolition of all the privileges of family life. And We hold it to be Our office, out of respect for the duty which Our responsible position places upon Us, to defend those privileges loyally and unmistakably. It is the life of the family, beyond doubt, that suffers most from the great poverty of our times, whether in material or in spiritual things, and from the countless errors which are its miserable consequence. Men suffer under a daily burden of difficulties and hardships, under a want of means which threatens to exceed all the experience of the past; and the reasons for it are often past detection. Such inflictions could not be borne without a strength and nobility of mind which must provoke universal admiration. **419** *(44, 60, 66, 99)*

Those who have the pastoral care of souls and can see into the hearts know well the many tears shed by mothers in secret, the hidden griefs and countless anxieties experienced by many fathers of families, matters of which no statistics speak, or are able to speak. Such priests are watching with apprehensive eyes the formidable growth of this load of human misery. And no one knows better than they what hidden forces of wickedness there are, whose one aim is to exploit these hardships in the interests of revolution; forces that are only **420** *(37, 105)* waiting their opportunity to carry out the godless designs that they have set themselves. No prudent and sensible man, in these desperate conditions, would deny to the civil authority ample and extraordinary powers to deal with this situation and to remedy the miseries of the poor. But God's law, imposed in the moral order, bids us carefully distinguish, in the interests of common good, what is the right and what is the wrong way of meeting the needs of the moment, what necessity does and what it does not demand of us.

(*Absolutism.—Remedies.—Catholic Action.*)

421
(21,
24)

In the promotion of this collaboration of the laity, so important at the present time there is a special mission for the family. The tone of the family can have a great influence on the mental development of the children. So long as the sacred fire of the Christian Faith burns on our domestic hearths, so long as fathers and mothers instil that Faith into the minds of their children, We have no reason to doubt that the rising generation will recognize, readily and actively, the royal power of Jesus Christ; it will do its utmost to offer a determined resistance to those who seek to banish Our Redeemer from public life, and impiously infringe His rights over us. In countries where churches are closed, where the crucifix is removed from schools and colleges, the family circle remains as the one impregnable citadel of our Christian culture. (*Salvation comes from the Church.*)

EXPERIENCE IN THE U. S. A.

Encycl. *Sertum lætitæ,* November 1, 1939.

(*The Church in the United States.—Evils caused by naturalism in education.*)

Domestic life flourishes with true happiness if the **422**
law of Christ is observed, and by the same token, where *(32,*
the Gospel is abandoned it miserably perishes and is cor- *103)*
rupted by vices. "He that seeketh the law, shall be filled
with it, and he that dealeth deceitfully shall meet with a
stumbling block therein" (a). What is to be found on
earth more joyful and unperturbed than the Christian
family? Living near the Altar of God, where love has
been proclaimed a holy, unbreakable bond, it is strengthened and increased by that same love, which supernatural grace nourishes. "Let marriage be held in honor
with all, and let the marriage bed be undefiled" (b).
The peaceful home does not resound with quarrels nor
is it the witness of secret suffering caused by the revelation of the deceits of infidelity. The firmest trust keeps
distant the thorn of suspicion; in reciprocal kindness
sorrows depart and joys increase. There, children are not
considered as a heavy burden but a heavenly gift; nor can
an evil utilitarian motive or the demands of sterile licentiousness hinder the gift of life and cause the tender
names of brother and sister to be forgotten.

(*Preaching: a means for forming Christian families.*)

... It must also be remembered that the dogma of **423**
the unity and indissolubility of marriage should be *(13,*
known by all those who enter married life, especially its *15,*
importance for religion, and that it should be fully res- *17,*
pected in a holy manner. Quite a number of people—even *57,*
if far from our Faith, but noted for their political wisdom *75,*
—admit that such a fundamental point of Catholic doc- *79,*

422a Eccles. 32:19.
422b Heb. 13:4.

82,
101)
trine has valid efficacy for ensuring firm family union, for the continuing prosperous future of civil society, for the sanctity of the people and for a civilization whose light be not false and purposeless.

Oh! if your country had known from the experience of others and not from its own the immense damage caused by divorce! Let reverence towards religion and love for the great American people counsel energetic action to cure this perverse disease at its very root. The consequences of this evil have been described by Pope Leo XIII with words both energetic and accurate . . .

(*Quotation of the Encyclical* "Arcanum"; *cf. nn.* 143-198.)

424
(83)
As regards those marriages in which one or the other party dissents from Catholic dogma or has not received the Sacrament of Baptism, We are sure that you will observe exactly the prescriptions of the Code of Canon Law. These marriages, in fact, as you are convinced by experience, are rarely happy and are usually a cause of many losses for the Catholic Church.

(*Remedies suggested.*)

GOD'S PLACE

All. to newlyweds, November 8, 1939.
(*New duties imposed by marriage.*)

425
(11,
20)
Matrimony is not, for you, . . . a purely natural alliance, a merely human pact; it is a contract in which God has His place, which in truth is the first place. You were united before His altar, not only to lighten each other's burden during this life, but further still to collaborate

with God Himself for the continuation of His creative, preservative and redemptive work. Receiving and blessing your promises, God, at the same time, conferred on you a special grace to make all the more easy the fulfilment of new and special duties.

CONJUGAL CHASTITY

All. to the newlyweds, December 6, 1939.

(*Beauty of purity; purity of Christ.*)

Jesus Christ, to continue His work, wished His **426** Church, His Mystical Bride, to be "without spot or *(33,* wrinkle ... but holy and without blemish" (a). Dear *108)* young people just married, this is the model which the great Apostle, St. Paul, proposes to you: "Husbands, love your wives, just as Christ also loved the Church" (b), because what makes the greatness of the Sacrament of Matrimony is its relation to the union of Christ and the Church.

Perhaps you think that the idea of a purity without **427** stain is to be applied exclusively to virginity, the sublime *(33,* ideal to which God does not call all Christians, but only *108)* some privileged souls. You know these souls, but, even admiring them, you did not think that such was your calling. Without going to the summit of a total renunciation of earthly joys, you can, by following the ordinary way of the commandments, have the legitimate desire to see yourselves surrounded by a glorious crown of

426a Eph. 5:27.
426b Eph. 5:25.

children, the fruit of your union. Yet the matrimonial state, willed by God for the greater part of mankind, can and must have its stainless purity.

428
(11,
33,
108,
109)
Whoever carries out faithfully and without faltering the obligations of his own state is immaculate in the eyes of God. God does not call all His children to the state of perfection, but invites each one of them to the perfection of his own state: "You therefore are to be perfect," Jesus said, "even as your Heavenly Father is perfect" (a). You know the duties of conjugal chastity. They exact a real courage, sometimes even heroic, and a filial Faith in Providence; but the grace of the Sacrament has been given you exactly that you may face these duties. Do not therefore be led astray by arguments unfortunately in vogue and by all too frequent disgraceful examples.

(The purity of Mary Most Holy.)

OMNIPOTENCE OF GRACE

All. to newlyweds, January 17, 1940.

(The Pope, as the successor of St. Peter, puts them on their guard against false teachers.)

429
(11)
You will sometimes hear religion treated as an accessory matter, if not at times harmful.... There will, perhaps, be extolled before your eyes a religious sentimentality without dogmas; errors and prejudices contrary to what you learned from the Catechism will be asserted...; you will hear it said that Christian marriage

428a Matt. 5:48.

imposes excessive obligations on the wedded parties, which are impossible to be fulfilled. Impossible, it is true, for mere human power; but it is for this very reason that the Sacrament has placed and preserved in you, with the state of grace, divine aids. Nothing that God prescribes is above these supernatural aids, present and cooperating in you: "I can do all things in him who strengthens me" (a), exclaimed the Apostle of the Gentiles. "But by the grace of God, I am what I am" (b).

(*Intercession to St. Peter for firmness of Faith.*)

THE FAMILY, CELL OF SOCIETY

All. to the newlyweds, June 26, 1940.

(*If society is to be saved, the family must be Christianized again.*)

The family is the basis of society. As the human **430** body is composed of living cells, which are not placed *(65)* only one beside the other, but by their intimate and constant relationship constitute an organic whole, so society is formed not by a conglomeration of individuals, sporadic beings, who appear for an instant and disappear the next, but by the economic community and by the moral solidarity of families, which, transmitting from generation to generation the precious inheritance of a common ideal, civilization and religious faith, guarantee the cohesion and continuity of social ties. St. Augustine noted it fifteen centuries ago, when he wrote that the family ought to be the initial element and like

429a Phil. 4:13.
429b 1 Cor. 15:10.

a cell (*particula*) of the city. Since each part is ordained to the purpose and integrity of the whole, he concluded that peace in the family between who commands and who obeys helps to maintain harmony between the citizens (a). Well they know it who, in order to expel God from society and throw it all into disorder, use every means to deprive the family of respect and take away even the remembrance of the divine laws, by exalting divorce and free union, by obstructing the providential duty given to parents towards their children, by instilling in married couples the fear of the material efforts and moral responsibilities which accompany the glorious burden of numerous children.

(*As an antidote: The Holy Father urges devotion to the Sacred Heart.*)

SPIRITUAL HEREDITY

All. to newlyweds, July 3, 1940.
(*The price of blood.*)

431 One of the most important cares of parents is to
(21) transmit to their children a blood which is not altered or impoverished by internal sickness, by external contamination or by progressive degeneration.

Above all, remember that when you call your children heirs of your blood, you must refer to something which is much greater than corporal generation only. You are, and your children ought to be, the source of a race of saints, according to the words of Tobias to his

430a *De civitate Dei,* I. 10, c. 16.

young bride: *"Filii Sanctorum sumus"* (a), which means men sanctified and raised up to participate in the divine nature by means of supernatural grace. The Christian, by virtue of Baptism, which has opened up to him the merits of the Divine Blood, is a son of God, one of those, according to St. John: "who believe in His name; who were born not of blood, nor of the will of the flesh, nor of the will of man, but of God" (b).

As a consequence, in baptized people, when one **432** speaks of transmitting inherited blood to descendants, *(21)* who will live and die not as animals deprived of reason, but as men and as Christians, there is no need to limit the sense of those words to a purely biological and material element, but it may be extended to that which is, as it were, the nutritive liquid of the intellectual and spiritual life: the patrimony of faith, virtue, and honor transmitted by parents to their posterity is a thousand times more precious than the blood—be it ever so rich— infused into their veins.

The members of a noble family are proud of being **433** of illustrious blood; and this luster, based on the merits *(21)* of their ancestors, implies in the heirs much more than mere physical advantages. But all those who have received the grace of Baptism, can call themselves "princes of the blood," not only of a regal but of a divine blood. Inspire therefore . . . in the children God will grant you, such an esteem of this supernatural nobility that they will be ready to suffer everything rather than lose such a precious treasure.

431a   Tob. 8:5.   431b John 1:12-13.

THE SACRED BOND

All. to the Tribunal of the Holy Roman Rota, October 1, 1940.

(*Truth and justice.—The Tribunal's duty.*)

434
(10)
Since matrimonial cases predominate in your forum, the Sacred Roman Rota has the glory of being the Tribunal of the Christian family—rich or poor, humble or great—in which justice enters to make the divine law of the marriage union triumph, as the vindicator of the indissoluble bond, of complete liberty of consent in the unity of life, of the sanctity of the sacrament. . . .

In the family circle human society takes its origin, the names of mother and father receive their strength and greatness, the family tree finds its branches, the country its champions, the Church her ministers. Hence the Rota shines in the juridical order as the guardian of holy matrimony. . . .

435
(49,
51,
81)
But if the Sacred Rota is the guardian and protector of the indissolubility of matrimony, it also knows how to distinguish from such indissolubility an invalidly contracted marriage, and therefore a marriage which (in truth) never really existed. Indeed, in such a case, there belongs to the married couple *iure naturæ* the right to accuse such a marriage—provided they have not been guilty of causing the impediment or the nullity. To this their right, there corresponds on the judge's part, who shall have reached the conclusion with moral certainty *ex actis et probatis* of the invalidity of the marriage, the obligation to declare it null when passing his sentence.

(The sufferings of the war.—God is the Judge of the nations.)

CHRISTIAN LOVE

All. to newlyweds, October 23, 1940.

(Man, masterpiece of God's love.—Beauty of human love.)

But what new and inexpressible beauty is added to **436** this love of two human hearts, when there is harmonized *(35)* the hymn of two souls vibrating with supernatural life! Here, too, there is verified a mutual exchange of gifts; and then, with sensible tenderness and its healthy joys, with natural affection and its impulses, with a spiritual union and its delights, the two beings who love each other become one in all that is most intimate, from the unshaken profundity of their beliefs to the highest summit of their hopes. *Consortium omnis vitæ, divini et humani iuris communicatio (a).*

Such is Christian marriage, modelled, according to **437** the famous expression of St. Paul (a), on the union of *(10,* Christ with His Church. In the one as in the other, the *13,* gift of self is total, exclusive, irrevocable; in the one *39)* and in the other the husband is the head of the spouse, who is subject to him as to the Lord; in the one and in the other the mutual gift becomes a principle of expansion and source of life.

436a I., D., *De ritu nupt.,* 23:2.
437a Eph. 5:32.

438
(20, 21) God's eternal love created the world and humanity from nothing; the love of Jesus for the Church generates souls for the supernatural life; the love of the Christian husband for his wife partakes of these two divine effusions, when, according to the explicit will of the Creator, the man and the woman prepare the dwelling place of a soul in which the Holy Spirit will abide with His grace. Thus, married couples, in the providential mission assigned them, are truly the collaborators of God and of Christ. Their very works have something of a divine nature, so that they may call themselves *divinæ consortes naturæ* (a).

HOLY ORDERS AND MATRIMONY

All. to newlyweds, January 15, 1941.

(*Priesthood and married life are the only states of life consecrated by a Sacrament.*)

439
(7) Holy Orders and Matrimony, as you well know, crown and complete the number of the Sacraments. But why did God give in His Church such a special place to the Priesthood and to Matrimony? It would certainly be rash for us to ask the Creator the reasons of His work and His preferences by questioning Him: "Quare hoc fecisti?" Nevertheless, following in the footsteps of the learned Doctors, and in particular of St. Thomas, we are allowed to seek and delight in the harmonies and the mysteries hidden in the divine thought and elections, whence to draw a more loving faith and to raise ourselves to a higher idea of the grace received.

438a 2 Peter 1:4.

When the Son of God deigned to become Man and **440** the Savior of mankind, His word restored to its former *(4,* splendor the marriage bond of man and woman, which *7)* through human passions had degenerated from the nobility of its institution. He raised it to a great Sacrament in the union of Himself with His Bride, the Church, Our Mother, made fertile by His Divine Blood, "cleansing it by the laver of water in the word of life" (a), and to those who believe in His name He gives them the power to become the sons of God; because they are born not of blood, nor of the will of the flesh, nor of the will of man, but of God (b).

(*These words of St. John indicate a dual fatherhood in the Church, that of the priesthood and that of matrimony.—The role of priests and bishops in building up the kingdom of God.*)

But what could they ever do, if they did not have **441** other workers at their side to hew the rock, to cut and *(22,* square it as the building requires? Who are these *24)* workers? They are the married couples, who give to the Church her living stones, which they tend with skill. Beloved sons and daughters, you are those workers.

But note well that, with the motherhood and fatherhood that comes to you, you must not be content to hew and to collect together with your labors only rough hewn stone. You must cut it, prepare it and give it the shape that best suits it for the building: for this double duty has the great Sacrament of Matrimony been instituted by God.

440a Cf. Eph. 5:26.
440b John 1:12-13.

442 It is the clear doctrine of the Angelic Doctor,
(22, St. Thomas that this sacrament, which has consecrated
23, your union, makes you "propagators and preservers of the
24) spiritual life according to a ministry which is at the same
time corporal and spiritual," which consists in "the conception of children and bringing them up for divine
worship" (a). You are, always under the guidance
of the priest, the first and closest educators and teachers
of the children of God entrusted and given to you. In
building the Church's temple, composed not of inert
stones but of souls living a new and heavenly life, you
are as it were the spiritual precursors, priests yourselves
of the cradle, infancy and childhood, for you must point
out to the children the way to heaven.

443 Your place in the Church as Christian couples is
(11, not then merely to beget children and offer living stones
24, for the work of priests, the highest ministers of God. The
25) exceedingly abundant graces which flow from the sacrament of matrimony have not been given you merely for
the sake of remaining fully and constantly faithful to
God's law in the august moment of calling your children
to life and for facing and supporting with Christian
courage the pain, sufferings and worries that very often
follow and accompany marriage. But such graces have
been given you rather as a sanctification, light and help
in your corporal and spiritual ministry; for together with
natural life it is your sacred duty, as God's instruments,
to propagate, preserve and contribute to the development in the children given you by Him of that spiritual
life infused in them by the washing of holy Baptism.
(*Education of children.*)

442a St. Thomas, *Contra gentes,* 4:58.

SUPERNATURAL AFFECTION

All. to newlyweds, January 29, 1941.
(*The teaching of St. Francis of Sales.*)

A mutual affection, born solely in the inclination **444** that attracts man towards woman, or even from the mere *(34)* pleasure for the human gifts which one sex discovers with such satisfaction in the other—such an affection, no matter how beautiful and deep-rooted it may prove to be and no matter how it echoes in the intimacy of the loving conversations of the newly married, would never of itself suffice, nor could it fully achieve that union of your souls which the loving Providence of God has intended and willed when leading you one towards the other. Only supernatural charity, a bond of friendship between God and man, can tie knots strong enough to resist all the shocks, all the vicissitudes, all the inevitable trials of a long life spent together; only divine grace can make you superior to all the daily miseries, all the multiple contrasts and disparities of tastes or of ideas, springing, like weeds, from the root of weak human nature. And this charity and grace, is it not the strength and virtue which you went to ask of the great Sacrament you received? The world, society and the family have need of a divine charity, greater than faith and hope!

(*Charity does not take away anything from the intimacy of human life.*)

MINISTERS OF THE SACRAMENT

All. to newlyweds, March 5, 1941.

Are you perhaps ignorant that in every Sacrament **445** the minister is but a simple instrument in God's hand? *(10)* Yes, even man has his part: he performs a symbolic ceremony, pronounces words which signify the grace proper to the Sacrament; but it is God alone Who produces such a grace, using man only as a minister acting in His name. This minister can be likened to a brush, which an artist uses to execute and paint on the canvas the image of his mind and his art. And so it is that God is the principal Cause, Who works with a power proper to Himself, while the servant or minister is only the instrumental cause working as moved by God's power, in such a manner that grace, which the Sacrament confers and causes, and which makes us partakers of the divine nature, is ascribed as an effect to the divine cause and not to the minister (a). Hence the spiritual power of the Sacrament cannot be contaminated by the minister: it is as sunlight which is received pure by that which it illuminates (b).

446   Now, in the great Sacrament of Matrimony who was
(10)   God's instrument to produce grace in your souls? Was it perhaps the priest who blessed and joined you in matrimony? No. The Church truly insists that those who are to be married,—except in determined and exceptional cases (a)—in order that their bond and

445a Cf. St. Thomas, *Summa theologica*, p. 3, q. 62, a. 1.
445b Cf. St. Augustine, *In Joannis Evang.*, tr. 5, n. 15.—Migne, P.L., 35, 1422.
446a *Ora, nel gran sacramento del matrimonio, chi è stato lo strumento di Dio, che ha prodotto nelle anime vostre la grazia? E' stato forse il sacerdote che vi ha benedetti e congiunti in matrimonio? No. La Chiesa prescrive bensì agli sposi—salvo in determinati casi eccezionali,—acciocchè il loro vincolo e i lori mutui impegni siano validi e procurino loro le grazie sacramentali, di affermarli e scambiarseli dinanzi al sacerdote, il quale la rappresenta come testimonio qualificato, ed è il ministro delle sacre*

mutual obligations be valid and that they may receive
the sacramental graces, should affirm and exchange these
before the priest, who represents the Church as a
qualified witness, and is the minister of the sacred
ceremonies which accompany the matrimonial contract.
But in his presence, you yourselves have been constituted
by God as ministers of the Sacrament, you, whom He
has used to bind your indissoluble bond and infuse into
your souls the graces which render you constant and
faithful to your new obligations. To what great honor
He has raised you! Does it not perhaps seem that Our
Lord wished you, from the first step you made from the
altar with the priestly blessing, to begin and continue
the office of cooperators and instruments of His work,
to which He has opened and sanctified the way?

In the Sacrament of Matrimony, the reciprocal **447**
acceptance of each other, the verbal consent you mani- *(10,*
fested, was an exterior action which has drawn down *20)*
divine grace upon you. In your married life you will be
instruments of the divine art in forming the material
body of your children. You will call into the flesh of your
flesh the spiritual and immortal soul which God will
create at your request, the same God Who faithfully
produced grace at the call of the Sacrament. When
you give birth to your first child, the new Eve will
repeat with the first mother of mankind: *Possedi
hominem per Deum* (a); I have gotten a man through

> *ceremonie che accompagnano il contratto matrimoniale;
> ma, in sua presenza, voi stessi siete stati costituiti da Dio
> ministri del sacramento, voi, di cui Egli si è servito per
> stringere l'indissolubile unione vostra ed effondere nelle
> vostre anime le grazie che vi rendano costanti e fedeli
> ai vostri nuovi obblighi.*   447a Gen. 4:1.

God. God alone can create souls; God alone can produce grace; but He will deign to avail Himself of your ministry to create souls from nothing, He Who in like manner used your ministry to infuse grace in you.

God awaits the "yes" of the spouses

448
(10,
20)
In both these collaborations, God awaits your "yes" to use His creative omnipotence. He, Who, "being master of power, judges with tranquillity and with great favor disposes of us" (a), does not wish to treat you as inert things or as instruments deprived of reason, as is the brush in the painter's hand. He wants you to place freely the act which He awaits to complete His creative and sanctifying work.

449
(20)
Beloved sons and daughters, you stand before the Creator as the appointed preparers of His ways yet free and intimately responsible. It will depend on you also whether those "innocent souls, who know nothing" (a) shall come to the threshold of life, whom the embrace of infinite Love desires to call from nothing to make of them one day His chosen companions in the eternal happiness of Heaven. But if, alas! they remain but magnificent images in God's mind when they could have been rays of Sun that illuminate every man who comes into this world, they will forever be but lights extinguished by men's cowardice and selfishness.

450
(20,
25)
Did you not freely unite yourselves in the Sacrament before God as His ministers, humbly and freely—according to the command given to our first parents—to ask for the souls which He desires to confide to you?

448a Wisd. 12:18.   449a Dante, *Purgatorio*, 16:87.

Before the altar, only your free will has enabled you to join yourselves with the bond of the sacrament of marriage, and no other consent could be a substitute for yours. Other Sacraments—those, that is, which are more necessary—when the minister is not available, can be supplied by the power of divine mercy, and grace is granted to the heart without the external sign: to the catechumen who has no one to pour water over his head, to the sinner who finds no one to absolve him, God will benignly grant to their desire and love that grace which makes them His friends and sons even without their receiving actual Baptism and Confession.

Sublime responsibilities

But in the Sacrament of Matrimony there is no supplying the ministers, just as there is no substitutes for the parties. Here is the triumph of the incomparable grandeur of the greatest gift, namely, free will, and the terrible responsibility given to intelligent man to be the master of his own life and that of others, of the life that reaches unto eternity. He can halt its course in others by rebelling against God. For if life's continuation is assured by blind instinct in the animal species, in the human race—this race descended from Adam, fallen, redeemed and sanctified by the Word Incarnate, Son of God,—the cold and malicious calculations of pleasure loving and unnatural egoism exert themselves to cut off the flowering of a bodily life aspiring to open out and expand itself. Such a crime will restrain the arm of the Lord from calling into existence the smile of innocent souls, which would have animated those bodies and elevated those members as instruments of the spirit and of grace, until one day they should have participated in

451
(10,
20,
87)

the reward of their virtues and in the eternal joy of saintly glory.

452
(19, 27)
Beloved newlyweds, conscious of the inviolable purpose of the Sacrament which you have undertaken, you will prepare a crib for the gifts of God's omnipotence, even if sometimes Divine Providence will permit your ardent desires and your prayers to go unheard, leaving empty the crib which had been prepared with so much love. Undoubtedly, more than once, you will see grace inspire generous souls to renounce family joys in order to make them mothers with a larger heart and a higher supernatural fecundity. But you, in the beautiful and holy union of Christian matrimony, have in your power the ability of transmitting life, not only on a natural plane but further still on a spiritual and supernatural plane, as you also have the dreadful power of arresting its course.

453
(27, 87)
While this power of transmitting life exalts you, it subjects you in its use to the law of God, whose severity towards those who culpably deviate from its high and true end must not surprise you. Let these be afraid (a); but you, who are sincere and obedient Christians need not be afraid, for you have understood the close collaboration that exists between man and God in the transmission of life. It would be inconceivable to your mind, enlightened by faith, that God could permit man to violate with impunity the dispositions of His providence and government—above all in relation to this bond so highly sanctioned from the first day of man's appearance on earth, a bond raised by Christ to a great Sacrament to call to the life here below souls destined by God

453a Cf. Gen. 38:10.

to sanctify themselves in the battle and in the victory over evil, to contemplate, to love and to praise Him in eternal happiness.

FATHERHOOD

All. to newlyweds, March 19, 1941.

(*The paternity of the Pope is a reflection of that of God.*)

What purpose then has fatherhood unless it be to communicate being; further still, unless it be to infuse into this being the mysterious ray of life? God is the Father of the Universe: *Nobis unus est Deus, Pater, ex quo omnia* (a). God the Father Who created heaven, the sun, the stars which shine in His presence and announce His glory. God is the Father Who created and modelled this earth, wherein He planted flowers and woods; He has made fertile and fruitful the airy nests of birds, the inaccessible haunts of fish, and the coral reefs, the sheep and cattle folds, the caves of wild beasts and the dens of roaring lions, ever ready to pounce on their prey. All this various and immense life is the child of God's love, directed, sustained, and enveloped in its growth and development by His Fatherly Providence. **454** *(20)*

But fatherhood is on a much higher plane: it means to communicate, along with being, with vegetable or animal life, the superior life of intelligence and love. The Angels also are the sons of God. Pure spirits, unburdened by the weight of flesh, sublime images of the Trinity which they contemplate and love, the Angels share in their own way in divine paternity. when, as St. Thomas points out, one Angel, illuminating and **455** *(20)*

454a I Cor. 8:6.

perfecting another Angel with intellectual light, becomes a father to him, something like a teacher who is a
father to his pupil and communicates to him ever new
impulses for the life of the mind (a).

456   Man is also a son of God, a knowing and loving image
(20) of the Trinity. Spirit united to matter—even if God has
made him a little inferior to the Angels—he is a father in
some ways even more than is an angel, who only communicates the luminous activity of his own intelligence,
while man brings to God his cooperation in the creation
and in the infusion itself of this intelligence in his children, by generating the body which will receive it.

457   Beloved Newlyweds, call to mind the great day of
(20) the creation of man and his companion. Before the great
work of uniting the spirit to the matter, the Divine Trinity
seems to take counsel and says: "Let us make man to our
image and likeness" (a). But if God forms the first man
from the slime of the earth note, since He wishes that
life to be propagated and multiplied, that He extracts the
second life not from inert mud but rather from the living
side of man, that second life which will be the woman,
his companion, a new ray of intelligence and love,
Adam's cooperator in the transmission of life, formed
from him and similar to him in all his posterity. When
God, leading and giving Eve to Adam, pronounces the
most high command, the source of life: "increase and
multiply" (b), does it not seem to you that the Creator
transfers to man himself His august privilege of paternity, entrusting henceforth to him and his companion the

455a Cf. St. Thomas, *Exposit. super Epist. ad Eph.*, c. 3.
        lect. 4.
457a Gen. 1:26.   457b Gen. 1:28.

duty of seeing to it that the river of life which springs from His love flow abundantly in the human race.

But the infinite love of God, which is charity, has a higher and most lofty means of diffusing its light and its flame by communicating as a Father a life similar to his own. Angel and man are the children of God and they reveal this by the image and likeness which in the natural order of simple creatures they have received from Him; but God possesses a more sublime fatherhood that begets children of adoption and of grace in an order that stands above the human and angelic natures, and that makes them partakers of, and sharers in, the divine nature itself, calling them to share His own happiness in the vision of His essence, in that inaccessible light, wherein He reveals to the children of grace Himself and the intimate secret of his incomparable fatherhood, together with the Son and the Holy Ghost. **458** *(21)*

In this sublime light rules God, Who creates, sanctifies and glorifies, Who, out of exceeding love for the last of His intelligent creatures, man, regenerates him from being a son of His wrath (a), as born from his guilty progenitor, Adam, and causes him to be born again here on earth with water and the Holy Ghost as a child of grace, brother of Christ, a new spotless Adam, making him joint heir to His glory in Heaven; and He willed that man himself cooperating with God might be the parent of such glory and supernatural life as well as of natural life; that he might be a parent in its transmission and in its preservation and perfection. **459** *(21)*

Beloved sons and daughters, this is the incomparable mystery to which your marriage leads you. Enter **460** *(20,*

459a Cf. Eph. 2:3.

21) such a state as you would enter a temple of the Most Holy Trinity, filled with respect, filial fear, and trusting love, with the consciousness of your responsibilities and of the greatness of the duty which you have to fulfill therein. You have also to pronounce the words: "Let us make man to our image and likeness." Divine words and human words which are fused on your lips and in your heart: ponder upon these words of paternity pronounced by God and by you: your children to your image and to your likeness.

461 Yes, your children will be similar to you in all things
(21) because you, by procreating them, will communicate to them their human nature. But will they also be similar to you as regards their supernatural life? We do not doubt your care to procure them that Baptism which has also regenerated you before God as children of grace and heirs of Adam; even if your little angel asks of your faith and love a sorrow or a sacrifice so that the gates of Paradise may be opened for him.   (*Christian education.*)

FAMILY PATRIMONY

R. M. to the world, June 1, 1941.

(*Fiftieth anniversary of* Rerum Novarum.—*Work and private property.*)

462 According to the Doctrine of *Rerum Novarum* (a),
(38) nature itself has closely linked private property with the existence of human society and with its true civilization, and, to a higher degree, has linked it with the existence and development of the family. Such a link shows itself most plainly. Must not private property secure for the

462a Cf. above, n. 210.

father of the family the healthy liberty which he needs if he is to be able to fulfil the duties assigned to him by the Creator in regard to the physical, spiritual and religious well-being of the family?

In the family the nation finds the natural and fecund **463** root of its greatness and power. If private property is to *(38,* lead to the good of the family, all public regulations, or *43,* rather all those of the State which govern the possession *44,* of it, must not only render possible and preserve such a *98)* function—a function which in the natural order under certain respects is superior to any other—but must perfect it evermore. The boasted civil progress would in fact be unnatural if—either through excessive taxes or through excessive direct interference—it should empty of all meaning private property, practically depriving the family and its head of the liberty of pursuing the purpose assigned by God for the perfecting of family life (a).

Among all the goods which may be the object of pri- **464** vate property, none is more natural, according to the *(38,* teaching of *Rerum Novarum,* than land, the homestead *42,* where the family lives and from whose fruits it derives, *60,* wholly or at least in part, its means of subsistence. And *97)*

463a *Se la proprietà privata ha da condurre al bene della famiglia, tuttte le norme pubbliche, anzi tutte quelle dello Stato che ne regolano il possesso, devono non solo rendere possibile e conservare tale funzione—funzione nell'ordine naturale sotto certi rapporti superiore a ogni altra,—ma ancora perfezionarla sempre più. Sarebbe infatti innaturale un vantato progresso civile, il quale—o per la sovrabbondanza di carichi o per soverchie ingerenze immediate—rendesse vuota di senso la proprietà privata, togliendo praticamente alla famiglia e al suo capo la libertà di perseguire lo scopo da Dio assegnato al perfezionamento delle vita familiare.*

it is in the spirit of *Rerum Novarum,* to affirm that as a rule only that stability which has its roots in a homestead makes of the family the most perfect and fecund living cell of society, marvellously uniting present and future generations united by its ever increasing cohesion. If today the idea and creation of living space is at the center of social and political goals, should it not be one's first concern to take thought for the living space of the family, and free it from the restricting conditions which do not permit the formation of the idea of one's own home?   (*Emigration.—A new social order.*)

THE CHURCH'S RICHES

All. to Newlyweds, August 13, 1941.

(*Heroism on the battle field.—Heroism of daily duty.—Heroism of married couples.*)

465
(9,
22,
29,
43,
104)
The intimate and inviolable wedding bond is a sign and a symbol of the indissoluble union of Christ with the Church (a); and Christian matrimony is a source of grandeur and perpetuity no less for the Church than for the Christian people. The union of Christian married people is also a path to sanctity; whence the Church together with the faithful exalts and venerates its heroes in her Churches and on her altars. The Divine Spouse of the Church gathers the children of God from Christian families, regenerating them with water and the Holy Ghost; elects His levites, calls His heroes of goodness, His consecrated virgins, His heroines of charity, His priests, the propagators of His Gospel, His knights and heroes of the cloister, the pastors and the Bishops of

465a Cf. Eph. 5:32.

His lambs, the Successors of His first Vicar in the universal government of His whole flock.

MARRIED HEROISM

All. to newlyweds, August 20, 1941.
(*Matrimony can demand heroic acts.*)

When Our Predecessors of happy memory, and in particular, the Supreme Pontiff, Pius XI, in the Encyclical Letter *Casti connubii* (a), recalled to mind the holy and fixed laws of married life, they reflected upon and were perfectly aware of the fact that in many cases a real heroism was required in Christian couples if they were to be observed faithfuly. Whether it be to respect the purposes of matrimony willed by God; or to resist the ardent and insistent stimulation of passions and the solicitations which lure a troubled heart to look elsewhere for that which it has not found in its lawful marriage, or does not believe itself to have found so fully as to repay all it had hoped. Again, if the bond of souls and mutual love is not to break or grow slack, the time may come when one must know how to forgive, to forget what is perhaps a serious discord, offence or wrong. How many intimate dramas lie hidden behind the veil of daily life! How many hidden heroic sacrifices! How many anxieties of the spirit in order that married couples may live together and remain constant in a Christian way to their own place of duty! (*Means to reach this heroism.*)

466
(33,
104)

MATRIMONIAL CASES

All. to the Tribunal of the Sacred Roman Rota, October 3, 1941.

466a Cf. above, n. 263 ff.

(*Universality of the Church's law.—Authority of the Tribunal of the Rota.*)

467
(51,
99)
So much the greater the authority it possesses, so much the more is the Sacred Roman Rota held to observe sacredly and interpret faithfully the norms of the law, according to the mind of the Roman Pontiff, under whose guidance it exerts its office as an instrument and organ of the Holy See. If this is so, no matter with what it has to deal, it is necessarily even more so in the ever frequent matrimonial cases, to which your illustrious Dean has just referred, and whose right solution demands that the sanctity and firmness of matrimony be upheld in the best possible manner, as is the natural right of the faithful, holding in due account the common welfare of human society and the private welfare of individuals.

The right to marriage

468
(12,
56,
109,
110)
In the first place, if the *right to marriage* is considered, Our glorious Predecesors, Leo XIII and Pius XI, already taught that "no human law can deprive man of the natural and primordial right to marriage". Such a right, indeed, since it was given to man directly by the Author of nature, the Supreme Legislator, cannot be denied to anyone, unless it be proved that he had either freely renounced it or that he be incapable of contracting marriage because of a mental or bodily defect (a). That

468a Çf. above n. 319ff.—Cf. C.I.C., can. 1068, §1.—
"*Impotentia antecedens et perpetua, sive ex parte viri, sivi ex parte mulieris, sive alteri cognita sive non, sive relativa, matrimonium ipso naturae iure dirimit.*
§2.—"*Si impedimentum impotentiae dubium sit, sive dubio iuris sive dubio facti, matrmonium non est impediendum*".
§3.—"*Sterilitas matrimonium nec dirimit nec impedit*".

in particular cases the marriage to be contracted can be impeded or, once contracted, can be declared null, it is necessary that this antecedent and perpetual incapacity be not merely doubtful or probable, but morally certain. Such a condition being ascertained, the marriage can neither be permitted, nor, if already celebrated, be declared valid.

Cases concerning this incapacity, whether psychic—that is of the mind—or somatic, since of their very nature they are delicate and often most intricate, are not rarely referred to the Sacred Roman Rota; and it redounds to its merit and glory to have treated such matters with diligent understanding and without respect to persons.

The Sacred Roman Rota has of late been concerned **469** with psychological incapacity based on certain patho- *(12)* logical defects. On such occasion the juridical sentence had to cite some very new theories presented by modern psychiatrists and psychologists. This is certainly a praiseworthy thing and a sign of assiduous and ample investigation; because ecclesiastical jurisprudence neither can nor must neglect the genuine progress of the sciences which treat of moral and juridical matters; neither can it be considered lawful and suitable to dismiss them merely because they are new. Is something new an enemy of science? How could human knowledge make any progress in the immense field of nature were it to stop at the discoveries already made? But there is need for examination and consideration, however, with discernment and accuracy, if there is to be a true science, whose certainty is based on sufficient experiments and proofs; not merely on vague hypotheses and theories which cannot be sustained by solid and positive arguments. In this last case they would be of no value to constitute a safe judgment which could exclude every prudent doubt.

470
(12,
30,
31)
More than once the Sacred Roman Rota has also had to deal with somatic incapacity. Two tendencies must be avoided in this difficult and, at the same time, delicate question. The first is that which in examining the constitutive elements of the generative act gives weight exclusively to the primary end of marriage, almost as if the secondary end did not exist or at least was not the *finis operis* established by the Creator of nature Himself. The second is that which considers the secondary end as an equally principal end, detaching it from its essential subordination to the primary end, which would logically bring about disasterous consequences. Two extremes, in other words, if truth stands in the middle, are to be avoided: on the one side to deny practically or to esteem too little the secondary ends of matrimony and the generative act; on the other, to set free and separate immoderately the conjugal act from the primary end to which in all its intrinsic structure it is primarily and principally ordained (a).

> 470a *Nella quale delicata altrettanto che difficile questione due tendenze sono da evitarsi: quella che nell'esaminare gli elementi costitutivi dell'atto della generazione dà peso unicamente al fine primario del matrimonio, come se il fine secondario non esistesse o almeno non fosse* finis operis *stabilito dall'Ordinatore stesso della natura; e quella che considera il fine secondario come ugualmente principale, svincolandolo dalla essenziale sua subordinazione al fine primario, il che per logica necessità condurrebbe a funeste conseguenze. Due estremi, in altre parole, se il vero sta nel mezzo, sono da fuggirsi: da una parte, il negare praticamente o il deprimere eccessivamente il fine secondario del matrimonio e dell'atto*

Declarations of nullity

As regards *declarations of nullity of marriages*, no **471** one is unaware that the Church is hesitant and averse *(14,* to granting them. Indeed, if the tranquillity, stability *51)* and safety of human commerce in general demands that contracts should not be declared null for every fickle reason, then all the more so must it be demanded of a contract of such importance as matrimony, whose firmness and stability are required by the common welfare of human society and by the private welfare of the wedded couples and of the children; while the dignity of the Sacrament forbids that what is sacred and sacramental be easily exposed to the danger of profanation. Who is unaware then that human hearts are frequently unfortunately inclined—for reasons of hardships of different kinds, or through disagreement and weariness with the other party, or to open the way to a union with another person sinfully loved—to study means to free themselves from the marriage union already contracted? For these reasons the ecclesiastical judge must not too easily be inclined to declare a marriage null, but rather to devote himself above all to see that what has been invalidly contracted be convalidated, especially when the circumstances of the case particularly suggest this course.

If convalidation is impossible, either because there **472** exists a diriment impediment from which the Church *(51)* cannot or is not accustomed to dispense, or because the parties refuse to give or renew their consent, then the

della generazione; dall'altra, lo sciogliere o il separare oltre misura l'atto coniugale dal fine primario, al quale secondo tutta la sua intrinseca struttura è primieramente e in modo principale ordinato.

sentence of nullity cannot be denied him who, according to canonical prescriptions, justly and legitimately asks for it, provided there be ascertained the asserted invalidity with a *certainty* which in human things goes under the name of *moral certainty*—that is, it excludes every prudent doubt and, moveover, is based on positive reasons. The *absolute* certainty of nullity cannot be demanded, that is, that certainty which not only excludes every positive probability, but even the mere possibility of the contrary. The norm of canon law, according to which *"matrimonium gaudet favore iuris; quare in dubio standum est pro valore matrimonii, donec contrarium probetur"* (a) must be understood as referring to the moral certainty of the contrary; but this certainly must be well established. No ecclesiastical court has the right and the power to exact anything more. By requiring more, the very right of the plaintiffs to marriage could be easily injured; since, not being in reality bound by any matrimonial bond, they enjoy the natural right to contract it.

Dissolving the bond

473
(16,
51,
57)
Finally, in reference to that which concerns *the dissolving of the bond* validly contracted, the Sacred Roman Rota in some cases is also called upon to investigate whether there has been completed all that is previously required for the valid and lawful dissolution of the bond and, in consequence, whether the concession of the relative favor can be sought from the Supreme Pontiff.

These preliminaries are concerned above all with the very dissolubility of matrimony. It is superfluous be-

---

472a C.I.C., can. 1014: *"Matrmonium gaudet favore iuris; quare in dubio stadum est pro valore matrimonii, donec contrarium probetur, salvo praescripto can. 1127"*.

fore a juridical court such as yours but not unsuitable to our discourse—to repeat that a marriage *ratum et consummatum* is indissoluble by divine law, inasmuch as it cannot be dissolved by any human power (a); while other marriages, even if they are of themselves intrinsically indissoluble, do not have, however, an absolute extrinsic indissolubility, but, given certain necessary conditions, can (here it is a matter of a relatively few cases) be dissolved, in addition to the Pauline privilege, by the Roman Pontiff in virtue of his ministerial power.

474
(51)
From the fact that the ecclesiastical judge is called upon to investigate whether such conditions exist, you will immediately understand how the importance of the subject sufficiently indicates that such an investigation must be conducted with all severity, rigor and diligence. This is all the more so because when it is a matter of the use of the vicarial power in a question of divine law, the validity itself of the dissolution of the bond depends on the existence of the necessary conditions. Moreover, in every such case, and in every step of the process, it is a duty to observe fully and strictly the rules which Christian modesty requires in such a delicate matter.

475
(51,
78)
On the other hand, there can be no doubt that the principle quoted above is of the highest importance here—that moral certainty is sufficient which excludes every prudent doubt to the contrary. It is very true that in our times, in which contempt of and carelessness about religion have again given birth to the spirit of a new paganism, pleasure-seeking and proud, there is manifested in not a few countries almost a mania for divorce,

473a C.I.C., 1118; cf. above, n. 297.

aiming at contracting and dissolving marriages with more facility and levity than is usual with contracts of leasing and hiring.

But such a mania, thoughtless and inconsiderate, cannot be counted as a reason why ecclesiastical courts should desist from the norms and practice dictated and approved sane judgment and a delicate conscience. In the Church no other norm and practice can have any value in the matter of the indissolubility or dissolubility of marriage except that established by God, the Author of nature and grace.

476
(51, 81)
Concerning this there are two passages in Holy Scriptures which in a certain sense indicate the limits between which the dissolution of the bond must remain and which exclude both the current laxity and the rigorism contrary to the divine will and mandate. The first is: *"Quod Deus coniunxit, homo non separet"* (a); that is to say, not man but God may separate the parties; hence there is no separation where God does not loose the bond. The other is: *"Non servituti subiectus est frater aut soror...; in pace autem vocavit nos Deus"* (b); which means that there is no longer servitude or bond where God has dissolved it and so permitted the parties to engage legitimately in a new marriage. In every case, the supreme norm according to which the Roman Pontiff makes use of his vicarial power to dissolve matrimony is that which We have pointed out at the beginning as the rule of the exercise of judicial power in the Church, namely the *salus animarum*, in the attainment of which both the common welfare of religious society, and of

476a Matt. 19:6.
476b I Cor. 7:15.

human kind in general, and the well being of individuals will receive due and proportionate consideration.

(*Good wishes for the New Year.*)

THE GOLDEN RING

All. to newlyweds, March 18, 1942.
(*Collaboration between husband and wife.*)

They are two persons—the man and woman who **477** walk together side by side and bind themselves with *(32)* the bond of a ring, a bond of love which even paganism did not hesitate to call *vinculum iugale* (a). What then is woman if not man's help, she to whom God gave the holy gift of bringing man into the world, she whose great sister, "more humble and higher than any creature, fixed term of eternal counsel" (b), was to give us the Redeemer of mankind, and with His first miracle was to render happy the nuptial bond at the wedding of Cana?

God ordained that the father and mother should co- **478** operate in the essential and primary end of marriage, *(19,* which is the procreation of children, with a freely under- *20)* stood and willing collaboration in submitting themselves to all the sacrifices which such a magnificent purpose could impose. For this end the Creator, as it were, makes the parents partakers of that supreme power with which he molded the first man from the slime of the earth, while He reserves to Himself the right to infuse into the body the *spiraculum vitæ*, the breath of immortal life, making Himself thus the Supreme Collaborator in the work of the father and mother, just as He is the Cause

477a *Aeneid,* 1. 4, v. 16 and 59.
477b Dante, *Paradise,* 33. 2ff.

of the working, and works in all those who work (a). His then is your joy, dear mothers, when forgetting all your pains, you joyfully exclaim at the birth of the child: *Natus est homo in mundum!* A man is born (b). There is completed in you that blessing which God had already given our first parents in the earthly paradise, and which He again after the flood repeated to Noah the second father of mankind: "Increase and multiply and fill the earth" (c).

479
(23, 24) But besides collaborating in the birth of the child in the physical life and in his health, you must also collaborate in his education in the spiritual life. All the more so, because in that tender soul the first impressions have lasting memories. The principal end of matrimony is not only to procreate children, but also to educate them (a), and have them grow in the fear of the Lord and in the faith, so that in the total collaboration which has to pervade and animate married life, you will find and enjoy that happiness, whose many seeds Divine Providence has prepared and nourished with His grace in the Christian family.

(*There must be a will to collaborate.*)

THE NUPTIAL BOND

All. to newlyweds, April 22, 1942.

480
(7, 10, 12, 99) ... It will not be difficult for you to raise your mind if with attention and helped by your prayer book you return in thought to consider the moving ceremonies of the marriage rite, in which the sacred liturgy is wholly

478a Cf. St. Thomas, *Contra gentes,* 1. 3, c. 66-67.
478b John 16:21.   478c Gen. 1:28; 8:17.
479a C.I.C., can. 1013, §1; cf. above n. 279.

concerned and occupied with the bond, which from that moment joins together the bride and the groom. What sweet thoughts, what desire led you to the holy altar! What hopes and happy visions illuminated your steps! But that bond is one and indissoluble. *Ego coniungo vos,* the priest said, an appointed witness of the union you have founded. The Church has taken that bond, contracted by you with the consecration and power of a Sacrament, under her protection and guardianship, writing your names in the great book of Christian marriages, and, at the conclusion of the nuptial rite, she then turned to God with the invocation: *ut qui te auctore iunguntur, te auxiliante serventur*: so that those who are united through Your authority, be saved by Your aid (a).

The marriage bond is one. Regard in the terrestrial paradise, the first image of domestic paradise, the first bond established by the Creator between man and woman, of which the Son of God Incarnate will say one day: *"Quod Deus coniunxit, homo non separet"*: "What God hath joined together, let no man put asunder"; because *"iam non sunt duo, sed una, caro"*: "they are not two but one flesh (a). In that union of our first parents in the garden of delights is the whole human race, all the future course of generations which shall fill the earth and struggle to conquer it, and will dominate it in the sweat of their brow to make it yield them bread soaked in the bitterness of original sin born from the stolen fruit of Eden. For what purpose has God brought man and woman together in pardise? Not only that they might be guardians of that garden of happiness but also, in the words of the great Doctor of Aquin, because they

481
(2, 13, 19, 29)

480a Roman Ritual, *De ritu nuptiali;*   481a Matt. 19:6.

were ordained for marriage so that they might procreate and educate offspring, and also for a common family life (b).

Indissoluble bond

482
(10,
12,
14,
16)
In the unity of the marriage bond you see stamped the seal of indissolubility. It is, indeed, the bond to which nature tends, but one which is not necessarily caused by the principles of nature, being instead brought about by the exercise of free will: but the mere will of the contracting parties, though it can form the bond, cannot dissolve it. This is true not only for Christian marriage but for every valid marriage contracted on earth through the mutual consent of the partners. The *"yes"* pronounced by your lips through the impulse of your will unites you by the marriage bond, and ties your wills together forever. Its effect is irrevocable: sound, the sensible expression of your consent, passes away but the consent, formally established, does not pass away; it is perpetual, because it is a consent established in the perpetuity of the bond, while a consent exchanged for only a certain period would not constitute between the parties true matrimony. The union of your "yes" is indivisible; so much so that there is no true marriage without indissolubility, nor indissolubility without a true marriage (a).

483
(7,
9,
16,
18)
Therefore, beloved Newlyweds, raise your thoughts on high and remember that matrimony is not only an institution of nature, but for Christian souls a great Sacrament, a great sign of grace and of a sacred thing, namely the union of Christ with the Church, made His

481b *Summa theol., Supplem.,* q. 44, a. 1.
482a Cf. St. Thomas, *Supplem.,* q. 41, a. 1; q. 49, a. 3.

and won with His Blood, to regenerate to a new spiritual
life the sons of men who believe in His name, born
not of blood, nor of the will of the flesh, nor of the will
of man, but of God (a). The seal and light of the Sacrament, which, let Us say, transforms the institution of
nature, give a nobility of sublime holiness to matrimony,
which encloses and reunites in itself not only the indissolubility, but in addition, all that concerns the significance of the Sacrament (b).

But if the will of husband and wife cannot dissolve the bond of matrimony once it has been established
can the authority which is above them and established
by Christ for the religious life of man do so? The bond
of a Christian marriage is so strong that if it has reached
full stability by the use of marriage rights no power on
earth, not even Our own as the Vicar of Christ, can dissolve it. It is true that we may recognize and declare that
a marriage contracted as valid was in reality void owing
either to some diriment impediment, or to an essential
flaw in consent, or to a substantial defect in the form.
We can also, in certain cases and for serious reasons,
dissolve marriages which lack a sacramental character.
We can even dissolve the bonds of a Christian marriage,
rescind the *yes* pronounced before the altar, if there is a
just and proportionate cause, when it has been established that the marriage has not been consummated
by the conjugal act. But once that has taken place,
that bond is beyond any human interference. Has
not Christ restored the matrimonial unity to that fundamental dignity which the Creator had given it at the

**484
(16,
49,
50)**

483a John 1:12-13.
483b Cf. St. Thomas, *Supplem.*, q. 42, a. 2, ad 4 et 7.

dawn of human life in Paradise, to the inviolable dignity of marriage, one and indissoluble?

Jesus Christ the Restorer of matrimony

485
(4)
Jesus Christ, the Redeemer of fallen humanity, did not come to take away but to fulfil and restore the divine law, to bring about as a law-maker above Moses, as one with wisdom beyond that of Solomon, as a prophet greater than the prophets, what had been predicted of Him, that He would be another Moses, chosen from the people of Israel, from whose lips the Lord would speak His word, while those who would not hear Him would have no part with God's people (a). Therefore Christ, through His word which is everlasting, elevated man in marriage and again raised up woman who had been cast down by the ancients to the role of slave and whom the most austere of the Roman censors had likened to an "unbridled nature and an unsubdued animal" (b). The Redeemer exalted in Himself not only man but woman also, taking human nature from a woman and exalting His Mother, blessed among women, as an immaculate mirror of virtues and grace for every Christian family throughout the centuries, crowned in Heaven Queen of the Angels and Saints.

486
(4,
9,
16)
Through their presence, Jesus and Mary sanctified the wedding feast of Cana; it was there that the Divine Son of the Virgin wrought His first miracle, as if to show at the outset that He was beginning His mission in the world and the kingdom of God by the sanctification of the family and the marriage union which is the origin of life. There He began the elevation of marriage which

485a Cf. Dt. 18:15-22; Acts 3:22-23.
485b Titus Livius, *Ab Urbe condita,* 1:34, c. 2.

was to stand out in the supernatural world of symbols
that produce sanctifying grace as the symbol of the union
of Christ with the Church (a); an indissoluble and inseparable union nourished by the absolute and endless
love that flows from the heart of Christ. How could
married love represent and be called the symbol of such
a union if it were deliberately limited, conditioned, dis-
soluble; if it were a flame of love for a time only? No:
having been elevated to the high and sacred dignity of
a Sacrament, imprinted and held in such close union
with the love of the Redeemer and the work of
Redemption, it can only be indissoluble and perpetual.

Indissolubility, rule of love

Faced with this law of indissolubility human passions, **487**
ever curbed by it and held back from the free satisfaction *(17,*
of their disordinate appetites, have sought in every way *61)*
to cast off its yoke, wanting to see in it only a hard
tyranny arbitrarily weighing down conscience with an
unbearable load, with a slavery repugnant to the sacred
rights of the human being. It is true that a bond may
sometimes constitute a burden, a slavery, like the chains
which fetter a prisoner. But it may also be a powerful
aid and a sure guarantee, like the rope which binds the
mountain climber to his companions in the ascent, or
like the ligaments which unite the parts of the human
body making it free and easy in its movements; and so
is clearly the case with the indissoluble bond of marriage.

This law of indissolubility will appear and will be **488**
understood as a manifestation of vigilant maternal love, *(14,*
especially if it is regarded in that supernatural light in *17)*

486a Cf. Eph. 5:32.

which Christ has placed it. In the midst of difficulties, trials and inordinate desires which will perhaps be strewn along your life's path, your two souls inseparably joined will not find themselves alone or helpless. God's omnipotent grace, an essential fruit of the Sacrament, will constantly be with these souls, to sustain them in the moments of weakness, to sweeten their sacrifice, to comfort and console them even in the hardest and longest trials. For if obedience to the divine law necessitates shaking off the allurements of prospective earthly joys in the hour of temptation, renouncing them to "begin life again," grace will still be there to recall the teachings of the faith in all their aspects: that is, that the only true life, that which must never be exposed to danger, is that heavenly life, precisely that life which such renunciations assure, no matter how difficult they be; renunciations which are, as all events of this present life, transitory things, designed merely to prepare the ultimate state of the future life, which will be all the more happy and glorious as the inevitable afflictions in life's pilgrimage here below have been boldly and generously accepted.

INDISSOLUBILITY IS DEMANDED BY NATURE

All. to newlyweds, April 29, 1942.

489
(9,
10,
16)
We see resplendent in you the dignity of husbands and wives, beings not only anointed with the mystical chrism common to all the faithful destined to be a chosen race and royal priesthood, according to St. Peter's words (a), but also raised up, in the holy act of your marriage by your free and mutual consent, to the dignity

489a I Peter 2:9.

of ministers of the Sacrament of Matrimony; Matrimony which represents the most perfect union of Christ and His Church and so cannot but be indissoluble and perpetual.

Natural harmonies

But what does nature say about this perpetuity? While grace with its salutary action does not change nature, even if it always and in every case perfects it, would it perhaps encounter an enemy that hinders it? No: God's art is wonderful and gentle: it is always in accordance with nature, of which He is the Author. That perpetuity and indissolubility, which the will of Christ and the mystical signification of Christian marriage require, is required by nature also. Grace fulfills the desires of nature and gives it the strength to be that for which it greatly longs (a). **490 (14, 16)**

The heart's desires

Question your heart's desires, beloved newlyweds. The heart is inscrutable to others but not to you. If you recall to mind the moment in which you felt your affection respond fully to another love, does it not seem to you, perhaps, as if from that instant to the "yes" pronounced by you both in front of the altar there had been an advance hour by hour, steps taken with anxious hope and fearful expectancy? Now, that hope is no longer in bud but a rose fully flowered, and that expectation awaits other joys. Has your dream vanished perhaps? No: it has become reality. What has transformed it **491 (14)**

490a *Quella perpetuitá e indissolubilità ... è voluta anche dalla natura. Di questa la grazia adempie le brame, e le dà la forza di essere ciò di cui il suo miglior sapere e volere le ispira il desiderio.*

into a reality of union before the altar? Love, which has not disappeared but has remained, has become stronger, firmer, and in its firmness it has made you cry out: this love must remain unchanged, intact, inviolate forever! If married affection knows beginnings and dawns, it need not know sunsets or seasons, cloudy and sad days, because love can be always youthful, unshaken by strong winds. Thus you attribute to your nuptial love without realizing it, We would say, with holy jealousy, that characteristic sign, which the Apostle Paul ascribed to charity when, exalting it, he exclaimed: *Caritas numquam excidit* (a): Charity never fails. Pure and true married love is a clear stream which through nature's impetuosity disgorges from the unbreakable rock of fidelity, flows calmly among the flowers and briers of life, until it loses itself in the urn of the tomb. The indissolubility of matrimony is therefore the fulfilment of an impulse of a pure and incorrupt heart, of the *anima naturaliter christiana,* and ceases only with death. In the future life there will be no marriages, but men will live in heaven as the Angels of God: *in resurrectione neque nubent, neque nubentur, sed erunt sicut angeli Dei in cælo* (b).

492
(14) If, however, married love in this its peculiar manifestation ends with the cessation of the purpose for which it was established on earth; nevertheless, inasmuch as it has acted in the souls of the married couples and has bound them to each other in that great bond of love which unites the hearts with God and to each other, such a love remains in the other life, as endure the souls themselves wherein such love had its abode here below.

491a I Cor. 13:8.   491b Matt. 22:30.

Indissolubility demanded by married couples' dignity

But the indissolubility of Matrimony is demanded **493** by nature for yet another reason. Such a quality is *(14)* needed to protect the dignity of the human person. Married cohabitation is a divine institution rooted in human nature as a union of two beings made to the image and likeness of God, Who calls them to continue His work in the preservation and propagation of mankind. From its most intimate expressions such cohabitation appears as something of extreme delicacy: it ennobles, sanctifies and makes souls happy when it rises above sensible things with a movement of mutual and simultaneous spiritual and unselfish devotion of the two married persons. There is rooted and living in the consciousness of both husband and wife a desire to belong totally one to the other, to remain faithful to each other in all the changes and chances of life, in the days of happiness and sadness, in health and sickness, in their first years together as in their later years, without limit or conditions, until God wishes to call them to eternity. In this consciousness, in these intentions, human dignity is exalted, matrimony is exalted, nature is exalted which sees itself and its laws respected; the Church rejoices because in such a community of married life it sees shining forth the dawn of the family order established by God, and the summit of its divine restoration in Christ. When this is not verified, common life runs the risk of sliding into the pit of selfish desire, which seeks nothing but its own satisfaction and thinks not of the personal dignity and honor of the partner.

Glance at modern society in the countries where **494** divorce is rife and ask yourself: Has the world the clear *(14,*

75,
78) knowledge and vision of how many times in those countries woman's dignity, outraged and offended, spurned
and corrupted, is cast aside and almost buried in degradation and abandonment? How many secret tears have
bathed certain thresholds, certain rooms; how many
have resounded in certain meetings, along certain streets
and byways, in certain corners and deserted haunts?

495
(14) No: the personal dignity of the husband and, even
more that of the wife has no better defense and safeguard
than the indissolubility of matrimony. They are in grave
error who believe that feminine culture and the dignity
of women can be maintained, protected and elevated
without basing it on the foundation of a matrimony one
and indissoluble.

496
(14,
52) If the Church, fulfilling the mission received from
the Divine Founder, with powerful and fearless use of
holy and invincible energy, has always affirmed and
spread abroad in the world inseparable marriage, give
praise and glory to her who so doing has greatly con-
tributed in safeguarding the right of the spirit before
the impulse of sense in matrimonial life, saving the dignity of the marriage no less of the woman than of the
human person.

Disastrous consequences of divorce

497
(32,
78) When there is not fixed in the will the intention to
guard perpetually and inviolably the marriage bond,
there also grows enfeebled and decreases the consciousness of tranquillity and future safety for the father,
mother and children, that sustaining feeling of uncon-
ditional reciprocal faith, that bond of strict and unchang-
able union (no matter what happens), in which one
great and essential element of domestic happiness is

rooted and nourished. Why, perhaps you will ask, do We extend such consequences to the children? Because they receive from their parents three great gifts: being, nourishment and upbringing (a), and they need a happy atmosphere for their healthy development; and it is certain a serene youth, a harmonious formation and education, are inconceivable without the undoubted fidelity of the parents. Do not the children nourish the bond of this married love? The rupture of this bond is cruelty towards them and contempt for their blood, a humiliating of their name, a division of their heart and a separation of brothers and home, a bitterness for their youthful happiness, and, what is worse still, moral scandal. How many are the wounds to the souls of millions of youths? In many cases, what sad and lamentable ruin! What implacable remorse is planted in souls! The Church and civil society place their hopes in spiritually upright, morally pure, happy and joyful men, who for the most part do not come from homes torn with discord and uncertain affection, but from those families wherein all is based on the fear of God and inviolate married fidelity.

Whoever wishes to know the reasons for the decay of contemporary morality and the poison which infects a great part of the human family will not be long in finding out that one of the most ill-omened and responsible sources is the legislation and practice of divorce. God's creations and laws always have a beneficial and powerful action; but when human neglect or malice intervenes and causes disorder and upheaval, an incalculable process of damage sets in, almost to the point where it seems that exasperated nature itself turns against man's

498
(14,
59,
75,
79,
103)

497a Cf. St. Thomas, *Supplem.,* q. 41, a. 1.

work. Who can ever doubt or deny that the indissolubility of marriage is both a creation and law of God,
most valid support for the family, for the greatness of
the Nation, for the defense of the fatherland, which in
the breast of its courageous youth will always find the
protection and strength of its fortunes?

499   Beloved Newlyweds, thank Our Lord for the upright
family, in which, surrounded by the love of God-fearing
parents, you have had the gift of growing to the full
maturity of Christians and Catholics. Value your honor
and glory in a time unfortunately characterized by such
a widespread deviation from God's laws, in order that
you may display, effect and profess the great idea of
matrimony in your married life as it was established by
Christ. Raise your heart to God in daily prayer, so that
He Who has graciously granted you the beginning of
your married life, may deign with the powerful efficacy
of His grace to give you its happy fulfillment.

THE FAMILY IS A SACRED THING

Radio Message to the World, May 13, 1942.
(*Sufferings of the present time.—The Church and
the world conflict.*)

500   But out of the anxieties and family hardships already
(60) mentioned by Us, there is rising up behind the battle
front, covering almost the entire world, another most
vast front, that of wounded and grieved families. Before
the conflict, some nations now in arms could not manage
to equalize births and deaths; and at the present time,
the war, far from remedying the matter, threatens to
force new families headlong into physical, economic and
moral ruin.

We would therefore like to direct Our paternal **501**
voice of warning to the leaders of the world. The family *(19,*
is sacred; it is the cradle not only of children, but also *21,*
of the Nation, of its power and glory. Let the family never *31,*
stray or deviate from the great purpose which was willed *42,*
by God! His desire is that husband and wife, in the *43,*
fulfillment of their marriage and family duties, should *44,*
transmit through the home to the new generation not *98)*
only the flame of corporal life but still more that of
spiritual and moral life, the Christian life. The Creator's
will is that there should grow up in the family under
the guide and guardianship of the parents men who will
be sincere and upright, men who in the future will be
valuable members of human society, free from stain,
virile in the face of happy and sad events, obedient to
those who command and to God. Let neither the family
nor the school become the vestibule of a battle field;
let the married couple not separate for a considerable
period of time; let the children not separate themselves
from the vigilant corporal and spiritual care of their
parents; let not the treasures of the family become
fruitless.

NEW DANGERS

All. to the young women of the Catholic Action,
April 24, 1943.

(*Transformation of family life.—Its dangers: for the
woman. . . .*)

Out of this is born another danger for matrimony. **502**
Young women such as those described up to now are not *(62)*

ordinarily destined for marriage, still less for matrimony according to Christ's law. Rather they themselves often throw it off as a chain. How many others are contaminated by the same evil even if not to the same extent! On the other hand, how even will the man who in the vigor of his youth has led a dissolute life be able to establish in married fidelity a holy and chaste marriage (a). You know the ideal of Christian marriage, which We seek to teach to those newlyweds who come to visit Us. How can this ideal shine forth and prosper if its presupposition, the Christian form of life and culture, tends to disappear ever more and more?

503
(42) Lastly, the third danger regards people, who have always drawn their vigor, growth and honor from a wholesome and virtuous family life. If this is withdrawn from its religious and moral foundations, the way is opened to worse dangers for social institutions and even for the country itself.

(*The program for the second 25 years of the Italian Young Women of Catholic Action—J.F.A.C.I.—Safeguard and defense of the Christian family.*) (a).

RESPECT FOR MATRIMONY

All. to the Parish priests and Lenten preachers of Rome, February 22, 1944.

502a Cf. Pius XI, Encycl. *Casti Connubii*, December 31, 1930; cf. above nn. 318 & 400.

503a According to chronological order followed in this book, the extract of a judgment passed by the Sacred Roman Rota should be inserted here, which was given on the 22nd of January 1944: see the Appendix, pp. 1⁰– 17⁰.

(God's commandments.—The sixth: "Thou shalt not commit adultery.")

Is it saying too much if we regret that viewed in the light of such a commandment those very countries who boast of an advanced civilization present a spectacle of the most profound moral devastation, and if We add that its traces are to be found even in the Eternal City? We know well—and We gave it Our full attention on another occasion—how even economic and social reforms can contribute to the preservation of matrimony and the family; but such preservation, in the final analysis, remains a religious duty and function which must attack the evil at its very root. **504** *(61, 97, 99)*

The entire conception of the scope of life which bears on the sixth commandment is infected by what could be called "marriages in the movies," which are nothing else but an irreverent and immodest display of matrimonial corruptions and married infidelity, which show marriage freed from any moral bond, as a scene and source of sensual pleasure, and not as a work of God, a holy institution, a natural function and pure happiness, in which the spiritual element is always sovereign and dominant, as a school and at the same time a triumph of love faithful to the tomb, even to the gates of eternity. Is it not perhaps a duty of the priests who have the care of souls to revive such a Christian concept of marriage among the faithful? **505** *(29, 62, 99)*

It is necessary that married life once again be clothed and surrounded by that respect with which healthy and uncorrupted nature and revelation adorned it: with respect for the forces which God has wonder- **506** *(103, 107)* fully infused into nature to create new lives, to build the family, to preserve the human race. Bringing young people up to have chaste thoughts and affections, to practice premarital continence, is not the ultimate goal to which Christian education looks and aims, but rather demonstrates its power to strengthen man's spirit against dangers which threaten virtue. The young person who faces and endures victoriously the battle for purity will also observe the other commandments of God and will be prepared to found a family according to God's designs. On the other hand, how could one ever hope for chastity and marital fidelity from a young person who can never dominate himself and rule his passions, nor despise bad invitations and evil examples, and who before marriage permitted himself every moral disorder?

507
(62,
87,
93,
99,
102,
107)
If the pastor of souls—as his sacred obligation before God and the Church obliges him—wants to conquer the two cancers of the family, the abuse of matrimony and the violation of marital fidelity, he must form, guide and instruct with the light of faith a whole generation, which from early life has learned to think spiritually, to live chastely, and to dominate itself.

THE ORIGIN OF MATRIMONY

All. to the Tribunal of the Holy Roman Rota, October 2, 1944.

(*Purpose of matrimonial trials; guiding principles.*)

508
(1,
Indeed, the nuptial contract is, of its very nature, and between baptized persons by reason of its elevation

to the dignity of a Sacrament, ordained and determined 5) not by human will, but by God. It is sufficient to recall to mind Christ's words: "What God hath joined together, let no man put asunder" (a), and the teaching of St. Paul: "Sacramentum hoc magnum est, ego autem dico in Christo et in Ecclesia" (b).

(Duties of all those who have a part in the trial.)

THE SANCTITY OF HUMAN LIFE

All. to the Biological-Medical Union of St. Luke, November 12, 1944.

(Duties of Catholic doctors.)

The fifth commandment—"Thou shalt not kill" (a), **509** this synthesis of the duties regarding the life and the (89) integrity of the human body, is rich in teaching both for the professor in his university chair and for the practicing doctor. As long as a man is not guilty, his life is sacrosanct, and every act which tends directly to destroy such a life is therefore unlawful, whether such destruction is intended as an end in itself or only as a means to an end, whether it is a matter of a life in embryonic form or already fully developed and at its peak. God alone is Master of the life of man not guilty of a crime punishable by death! The doctor has no right to dispose of the life either of the mother or of the child: and no one in the world, no private person, no human power, may authorize him to proceed to such a complete

508a Matt. 19:6.
508b Eph. 5:32.
509a Exodus 20:13.

destruction. His office is not to destroy life but to save
it. These are fundamental and unchangeable principles
which the Church, in the last ten years or so, has found
necessary to repeat and clarify in the face of such contrary opinions and methods.

The Catholic doctor will find a safe guide in this
respect both for his theoretical judgment and practical
conduct in the resolutions and decrees of the teaching
authority of the Church.

510 But there is a vast field in the moral order requiring
(19, of the doctor a peculiar clarity of principles and certainty
26) of action: that in which ferment the mysterious energies
placed by God in the organism of man and woman for
the procreation of new life. It is a natural process of
which the Creator Himself determined the structure
and the essential forms of activity, with a precise purpose
and corresponding duties to which man is subject in
every conscious use of that power. The primary purpose
(to which the secondary ends are essentially subordinated) desired by nature in this use is the propagation
of life and the bringing up of children. Only the marriage
regulated by God Himself in its essence and its properties assures both the one and the other according to the
dignity and welfare of the parents, no less than of the
offspring. Such is the unique principle which regulates
and enlightens all this delicate matter; the principle
which must necessarily be kept in mind in every actual
case and to which all special questions must be referred;
the rule, finally, whose faithful observance guarantees
on this point the moral and physical well being of society and the individual (a).

510a Cf. **THE HUMAN BODY,** n. 60.

THE FAMILY IS THE NATURAL PLACE
FOR EDUCATION

Letter *Au moment où,* January 6, 1945, to the French Episcopate.

(*It is necessary to create a new world from the ruins of war.*)

Above all, may We be able to see, thanks to the **511** combined forces of the Church, the State and family in- *(37,* stitutions, the family—the natural environment for the *98,* normal development of the human being, and of which *99,* the war, alas! has made one of its greatest victims—gain *105)* again in France as soon as possible its stability and fecundity.

(*Christian conditions for the renewal.*)

THE SACRAMENTAL "YES"

All. to Parish Priests and Lenten preachers of Rome, February 17, 1945.

(*Gravity of the duties of the pastoral office at the present time.—The Sacraments, a source of spiritual life.*)

Like the natural forces, but in an incomparably **512** superior degree, the Sacraments are realities, and active *(9,* realities. They have the power to raise man above him- *11,* self and the whole natural order to the divine sphere, *43)* to infuse a new life in him in order that he may live in a God-like manner. Not only do they have this power to infuse this life in him, but also to preserve and develop it, so that man born of God is no longer a creature only but a son of God in a true and real sense, a brother and co-heir of Christ, with a personal claim to eternal life, to the beatific vision and the perfect possession of God.

This characteristic is peculiar to the Christian Religion alone; it is the religion of personal friendship between God and man, the religion of the divine Sonship of man; and the Sacraments—Baptism first of all—are, as it were, the channels which communicate this new being, this hidden life to man.

513
(9,
11,
43) In Christian marriage the power of the Sacrament is united with the mutual consent of the parties; their "yes" becomes a source of grace. Thus that supernatural dignity which makes it a symbol of the union of Christ and His Church is conferred on the nuptial bond, while with the sanctification of matrimony there flows over to the family, and by means of the family to social life, the beneficial effects of the higher world of grace.

(*The teaching to give the faithful on the Sacraments.*)

FAMILY UNIONS

Radio Message to French families, June 17, 1945.

(*The moving ceremony of the consecration of French families to the Heart of Jesus.*)

514
(43) The value and prosperity of a people do not rest in the blind action of an amorphous multitude but rather in the normal organization of healthy and numerous families, under respected fatherly authority, wise and vigilant motherly care, and in the intimate and coopera-tive union of the children.

Every family extends itself, broadens itself, in the relationship which unites the bonds of blood. The alliances between the various families through their harmonious agreements constitute, little by little, a net whose harmony and solidarity assure the living unity of a nation, a great family of the great home which is their native land.

It is such a perfect and delicate net that every mesh that is broken or loosened tends to compromise, with the integrity of the net itself, the whole organism of society.

Now, this rupture or loosening, this weakness and degeneration, are produced with their deplorable consequences each time that an attack is made on the sanctity or indissolubility of matrimony, on married fidelity or fecundity; each time that the paternal authority, through the parents' abdication or the children's insubordination, is diminished. **515** *(36, 68, 78, 87, 93)*

The fragments of disorganized and broken families are no more able to construct a healthy and stable society than the amorphous conglomerations of individuals of whom We recently spoke (a). **516** *(43, 103)*

Certainly great, noble and pure is the happiness of a patriarchal hearth, intact in its integrity and dignity. But—who would dare to deny it?—this happiness is the fruit of attachment to austere duties; of victory over obstacles and allurements, over uncontrolled passions and temptations of the flesh or the heart. Therefore, courage is needed, a generous and, above all, constant and continuous courage over the years as long as life lasts.

516a All. to the Sacred College, 2nd June, 1945.—AAS 37, p. 159.

517
(101,
104)
Unless one wishes to ignore human weakness completely, obstinately to close his eyes to evidence, it is necessary to admit that such a courage cannot arise, still less sustain itself, from the sole power of arguments of simple and cold reason.

Pure doctrine, sublime morals, the eternal hopes of the religion of Christ, all greatly contribute to create such courage, but it is certainly not the external action that gives the Christian religion this salutary influence, this marvellous power of safeguarding the purity, the sanctity of matrimony and the family amid a corrupting civilization.

518
(104)
Christ works in souls through the infusion of grace even more than through His teachings, His exhortations, His promises: above all, He is through the Eucharist "the source of life and sanctity."

(*Picture of families consecrated to the Sacred Heart. —The consecration implies the duty of extending Christ's kingdom interiorly and exteriorly.*)

The duty of fathers of families

519
(105)
Christian fathers of families, you, the honor and vitality of France, have the right to speak and act in the name of your families, in the name of France, that France which on the morrow of sorrowful disasters has engraved on the pediment of the Basilica of Montmartre the moving humility of its sorrow, the flame of its love and devotion: *Gallia pœnitens et devota!*

520
(101,
105)
In the name of your families and of France, defend the sanctity of matrimony and the unity of the family lacerated by divorce; defend the authority of parents and their freedom to bring up their children in a Christian

manner; defend infancy and childhood against profane and dishonest propaganda, against the seduction of scandalous shows, against the pernicious license of an uncontrolled press and radio.

In the name of your families and of France, vindicate decency in your cities, dignity in the streets and public squares; the right for all your fellow citizens to practice their religion openly; for your clergy and religious to use kindness towards children, towards the ignorant, the poor and the dying.

In the name of your families and of France, prepare and bring about the Kingdom of God and of the Heart of Jesus for your country, the recognition of His divine Majesty in the sanctification of Sundays and holy days, in the exercise of public worship, in the practice of social justice and charity, in Christian fraternity among all the French people for reciprocal reconciliation, in calmness and order, in a word, in peace.

You have once more proclaimed that you believe in the Christian vocation of France; and the Author of this sublime vocation is faithful: *Fidelis Deus per quem vocati estis* (a).

Now the consecrated Christian families of France on their part must faithfully cooperate.

THE MATRIMONIAL STATE

All. to Italian Catholic Women, October 21, 1945. (*The Church and the dignity of woman.*)

The two sexes, by their peculiar qualities, are or- **521** dained one for the other in such a way that this mutual *(42)* coordination influences all the various manifestations of

520a I Cor. 1:9.

human social life. We shall here recall only two of these because of their special importance: the matrimonial state, and voluntary celibacy according to the evangelical counsel.

522
(42) The fruit of a true marital community comprises not only children, when God grants them, but also the material and spiritual benefits which family life offers mankind. All civilization, in all its branches, the peoples, the society of peoples, the Church itself, in short, all the true values of humanity feel the good effects, where this married life flourishes in good order, where youth is accustomed to contemplate it, to honor it and to love it as a holy ideal (a).

523
(68) On the other hand, where the two sexes, unconscious of the intimate harmony willed and established by God, abandon themselves to a perverse individualism; where they are reciprocally an object of egoism and cupidity; where they do not cooperate with mutual accord in the service of humanity according to the design of God and of nature; where youth, careless of its responsibilities, light and frivolous in its spirit and conduct, renders itself morally and physically unfitted for the holy life of matrimony; then the common welfare of human society, both in the spiritual and in the temporal order, is gravely compromised, and the very Church of God trembles, not

522a *Il frutto di una vera comunanza coniugale comprende non solo i figli, quando Iddio li concede agli sposi, e i benefici materiali e spirituali che la vita di famiglia offre al genere umano. Tutta la civiltà dei popoli, la Chiesa stessa in una parola, tutti veri beni dell'umanità ne risentono i felici efett, là ove questa vita coniugale fiorisce nell'ordine, ove la gioventù si abitua a contemplarla, a onorarla, ad amarla come un santo ideale.*

for her existence—it has divine promises!—but for the greater success of her mission among men.

(*Voluntary celibacy.—Woman in modern society.*) (a)

ENCROACHMENT OF THE STATE

Letter *Czestochoviensis Beatæ Mariæ*, January 17, 1946, to the Polish Episcopate.

(*Episcopal conference in Poland.—Denunciation of the Concordat.*)

Our fear is now justified and well founded: in fact, **524** in your country a new law has been promulgated which *(37,* places the sanctity and indissolubility of marriage in *42,* grave danger. In conformity with the duties of your of- *55,* fice, you have done everything possible to preserve intact *69,* the family—the foundation of all human society and *75,* nursery of the state—the family which naturally and by *80,* itself constitutes the place where the human being grows *100)* and is formed as is fitting to his state. Your plea never-theless went unheeded. Devote yourselves, therefore, as your pastoral zeal demands, to warning your faithful that the perverse decrees enacted by men have neither abolished the divine laws nor weakened them. The faith-ful must not, even if the law permits it, invoke provisions contrary to God's commandments to dissolve the mar-riage bond. (*Other matters which require the Bishops' attention.*)

THE TWO COLUMNS OF SOCIETY

Consist. All., February 20, 1946.

(*Church's duty: as regards the foundation of soci-ety, as regards cohesion.*)

523a Cf. **THE WOMAN IN THE MODERN WORLD,**

525
(37,
42)
Here, Venerable Brethren, is the deepest and mos'
active union that could ever exist—the Church living in
the heart of man and man living in the heart of the
Church. By this union the Church elevates man to the
perfection of his being and his life, to give to human
society men so formed: men constituted in their inviolable integrity as images of God; men proud of their personal dignity and their healthy liberty; men justly jealous
of their equality with their fellow men in all that reaches
to the more intimate depths of human dignity; men attached in a stable manner to their land and their traditions; men, in a word, characterized by this quadruple
element. This is what provides for human society its
solid foundation and procures its security, equilibrium,
equality and normal development in time and space.

(*Supra-nationality of the Church.*)

526
(37,
42,
98)
On such a foundation rest above all the two principal columns, the mainstay of human society as it has been
conceived and willed by God: the family and the State.
Based on such a foundation, both these columns can
surely and perfectly fulfill their respective functions: the
family as the source and school of life, the State as the
guardian of the law, a law which with society itself has
its proximate origin and its goal in the complete man,
the human being, the image of God. The Apostle addresses the faithful by two magnificent names: "citizens with
the saints" and "members of the family of God," *cives
sanctorum et domestici Dei* (a). Do we not see, perhaps,
that of these two words the first refers to the life of the
State and the second to that of the family? And is it
perhaps forbidden to discover there an allusion to the

526a Eph. 2:19.

manner in which the Church contributes in building the foundation of society according to its intimate structure, in the family and in the State?

Has this conception and this manner of acting lost *527* its value today? The two supporting columns of society, *(68)* falling away from the center of gravity, have shifted from their foundation. What has been the result? The family has seen its vital and educative force diminish, while the State, in its turn, is on the point of renouncing its role as defender of rights and has become as Leviathan of the Old Testament, dominating everything in wanting to draw all things to itself. Today, in the inextricable confusion in which the world is thrown, the State undoubtedly finds itself under the necessity of assuming an immense weight of duties and functions, but does this abnormal condition of things perhaps not threaten to compromise in a most serious manner the intimate force and efficacy of its authority?

(*Consequences for the Church.*)

WAR DAMAGES

All. to the Parish Priests and Lenten preachers of Rome, March 16, 1946.

(*Outline of the actual situation.*)

The consequences of war always present you with *528* serious and numerous duties. Our thought goes out *(16,* above all to the protection of abandoned children, to *50,* the healing of the wounds inflicted especially on the *60,* sanctity of marriage, on married fidelity. With reference *97)* to this, let Us repeat here what We said, about a year ago, on the question of divorce, that a marriage validly contracted and consummated by baptized persons can never be dissolved by any human power, not even by the Supreme ecclesiastical Authority. To these urgent duties there must be added another, no less serious, of reviving the sense of rights and of justice in the whole of social life and to promote further still the works of Christian charity.

(*The ministry of the Parish Priests.—Preaching the Faith.*)

FAMILY RIGHTS

All. to French journalists, April 17, 1946.

(*The mission of the true France, at home and abroad.—Journalists must enlighten public opinion.*)

529
(42,
45,
102) ... Public opinion should and must be enlightened on the nature and the extent of the inviolable sacred rights of the human person and the family, which are the natural and essential bases of society; on the duty of respecting in others and of defending and safeguarding for oneself the inalienable prerogatives of true and legitimate liberty, which, notwithstanding the diversity of objects, cannot subsist if even one of these objects is excluded. Now, these holy rights of the person and of the family, with the related duties, have as much value in international affairs as in national ones.

(*Reminder of the Pope's efforts in such matters.*)

THE STATE'S VIGOR

Radio Message to the Swiss nation, September 20, 1946.

(Congratulations for the balance of the Swiss Constitution and its notion of liberty based on two fundamental rules.—The first is equity....)

...The other is the absolute respect for the sovereign **530** law of God as regards matrimony and the family. *(43)*

If the profound sense of common welfare is the soul of the healthy and strong State, then the dignity and sanctity of nuptial and family life are as its vertebra. When this latter suffers a serious injury the State's power is finished, and sooner or later the people fall into disaster.

(Against Red atheism.—There is a need of Christians who believe and pray.)

MATRIMONIAL PROCESSES

All. to the Tribunal of the Holy Roman Rota, October 6, 1946.

(Cases proper to the Tribunal of the Rota.—Defense of the Catholic Faith.)

Another object, which clearly manifests the differ- **531** ence between the ecclesiastical and civil judicial order is *(6,* Matrimony. This is, according to the Creator's will, a *51,* *res sacra*. Therefore, when it is a matter of the union *55,* between baptized persons, it remains of its very nature *57)* outside the competence of civil authority. But even marriages legitimately contracted between non-baptized persons are a holy matter, so much so that civil courts have no power to dissolve them, nor has the Church in similar cases ever recognized the validity of their sentences of divorce. This does not alter the fact that simple declarations of the nullity of marriages themselves—relatively few in comparison to divorce judgments—can in determined circumstances be justly pronounced by civil courts, and therefore be recognized by the Church.

532
(46,
51,
54)
It goes without saying, as all know, that the purely civil effects of matrimony even between baptized persons are within the judicial competence of the civil authority (a). But much wider and deeper is the Church's competence in matrimonial questions, because on her depends, by divine institution, what concerns the guardianship of the nuptial bond and the sanctity of marriage.

You also, beloved sons, participate in this competence, called as you are to pass your sentences in matrimonial cases.

533
(46,
51,
54,
75)
If at the beginning of Our discourse We expressed Our paternal recognition of your assiduous work particularly in this field, We cannot now hide Our anxiety over the growing number of such cases, an anxiety which We know is shared by you also, as the considerations explained up to now by your worthy interpreter have openly manifested to Us.

534
(51,
60)
Indeed, are not the matrimonial cases to be dealt with by your Tribunal an indication and a measure of the progressive dissolution of married life?—a dissolution which threatens to poison and corrupt even the morals

532a C.I.C., can. 1016; cf. above n. 43.

of Catholic peoples. Both World Wars, but the second incomparably more than the first, have largely played their part in the development of such a disastrous disorder. No one can remain coldly insensible to the tragedy which still drags behind it its lamentable consequences, nor at the thought of millions of young married couples who have been forcibly separated one from the other for long months and years. What kind of courage, abnegation, patience, what a treasure of lovingly mutual faith, what a spirit of Christian confidence were necessary to maintain intact the vowed faith, to resist! Undoubtedly, with the help of grace implored in prayer, many have known how to remain strong. But, on the other hand, how many others were not so steadfast! How many ruins of destroyed domestic relations, how many souls wounded in their human dignity, in their conjugal delicacy, how many falls with fatal effects to family happiness.

Now it is a matter of repairing the ruins, of healing **535** these wounds, of curing these evils. The maternal heart *(16,* of the Church bleeds at the sight of the unutterable *61,* pains of so many of her children. The Church does not *97,* spare any means to come to their aid, and extends her *98,* condescension to the extreme limit. This extreme limit *99)* is found solemnly formulated in Canon 1118 of the Code of Canon Law: *"Matrimonium validum ratum et consummatum nulla humana potestate nullaque causa, præterquam mortem, dissolvi potest."*

No one doubts that at present one of the principal cares of the Church is that of halting by every means the growing decay of matrimony and of the family. The Church is fully aware of her duty, while at the same time she knows well that her preoccupation will only have effective results according to the measure in which the general economic, social and, above all, moral conditions make the conduct of a married life acceptable to God less difficult in practice. The responsibilities that weigh on the public authorities in such a matter are very great.

536 Meanwhile, beloved sons, in the expectation that this
(51) improvement in public morality will occur, you will have to endure and control with "labor and patience" (a) the incessant influx of matrimonial processes, because the action for the healing of conjugal and family life is one thing, and the judicial procedure as regards matrimony is another. To this latter belongs the duty of judging and deciding objectively the cases which are presented to it, according to the state of the facts and the norms of canon law. Continue the exercise of your office with the unalterable impartiality of the conscientious judge, with the knowledge that in this way you contribute greatly to the edification of the Church. The wise equity with which this Tribunal also considers the financial side of these cases in the difficult economic situations of today—equity to which there corresponds the generous cooperation of the advocates of the Rota—shows clearly the concept you have of your work: a service given for the true benefit of the faithful, for the welfare of souls.

(*Matters proper to the Tribunal of the Holy Office.—The obligation of secrecy.*)

536a Cf. Apoc. 2:2.

THE FAMILY IN DANGER

All. to the Sacred College, June 2, 1947.
(*The world is in a state of uncertainty.*)

What can be the fate of the family, this natural **537** nursery and this school, where the man of tomorrow *(43,* grows and is educated, in such a perpetual state of pre- *60,* cariousness and uncertainty? Heart-rending news reach- *97,* es Us from the territories more tested by trials in regard *104)* to the miserable conditions in which the family, young girls and women find themselves. More tragic still is the condition of those homes—if those wandering groups can be called such—in which the fidelity of the husband and wife to the law of God had gained for them the blessing of a rich crown of children. After having often paid, more than others, their contribution of blood during the war, today they must particularly suffer the consequences of a general scarcity of houses and food. Now it is certain that God will not break His Word, as the mocking laughter of egoists and of the prosperous insinuate; but the incomprehension, the hardness, the reluctance of others render life harder and more difficult and almost unbearable for the heroes of married fidelity. Indeed, only a true heroism, sustained by divine grace, can maintain in the heart of the young newlyweds the desire and the joy of a numerous family. But what a humiliation for the world to have fallen so low and into a social state so contrary to nature!

Before God, before the sorrowful truth, let Us invoke with all Our power a prompt remedy and let Us trust that this Our cry of sorrow will go out to the extremities of the earth and echo in the souls of those who, placed in positions of public authority, cannot be ignorant that without a healthy and vigorous family life the people and the nation are lost. There is perhaps nothing that so urgently demands the pacification of the world as the unutterable misery of the family and of women!

(*Collaboration for the renewal of the world.*)

CANONICAL FORM

Motu proprio *Decretum Ne temere,* August 1, 1948.

538 The decree *Ne temere* (a), issued by order of Our
(*12*) Predecessor, Pius X, of happy memory, established (article XI) that all those who had been baptized in the Catholic Church, even if afterwards they separated from it, were obliged to observe the form of Matrimony established by the Council of Trent.

To avoid the nullity of marriages contracted by persons born of non-Catholic parents, and baptized in the Catholic Church but continuously, from their infancy, living in heresy, schism or infidelity, or without any religion, it was established in the Code of Canon Law (b) that such baptized persons were not obliged to observe the canonical form of matrimony.

Now, after thirty years of experience, it has been clearly shown that the exemption from the canonical form of matrimony accorded to these persons baptized in the Catholic Church was of no benefit at all to the welfare of souls. Besides, it has very often multiplied the

538a Decree *Ne temere,* 2nd August 1907.—Cf. above n. 253.
538b C.I.C., can. 1099.—Cf. above n. 254, note (a).

difficulties in solving cases. For this reason it appears to Us to be an advantage to do away wth the said exemption (c).

(*Practical dispositions.—Abrogation of the last part of canon* 1099.)

FAMILY RIGHTS

All. to the Congress of the European Union, November 11, 1948.

(*To establish the European Union there must be reestablished the bond between religion and civilization.—The rights of God and the natural law on which are based the rights of man must be recognized.*)

And then among man's rights there must be inscribed those of the family, of parents and of children. United Europe cannot base itself on a simple abstract idea. It has to be supported by living men. Who will they be? Hardly the former leaders of the old European powers: they have disappeared, or do not have any other further influence. Still less the elements of a mass such as We defined in Our 1944 Christmas message: true democracy, with its ideal of healthy liberty and equality, has no greater adversary. **539** *(38, 43, 45)*

There remains therefore the question: whence will the most urgent appeal for European unity come? It will come from men who sincerely love peace, from men of order and calm, from men who—at least in their intention and their will—are not yet exterminators of

538c Cf. above, no. 254, note (a).

the family and who find in the life of the honest and happy family the first object of their solicitude and joy. They are those who will carry on their shoulders the building of United Europe.

For as long as their cry goes unheard nothing lasting can be done, nothing which will bear any proper relation to the present crisis.

(*The great problem*: *will the necessary comprehension be found?*)

FAMILY HOMES

All. to the Delegates of the "Bureau international du Travail," March 25, 1949.

540 On the one hand, indeed, We have often manifested
(97) Our preoccupation with the urgent and anxious need to procure thousands, nay, millions of homes for individuals and families, which will assure them a minimum of hygiene, welfare, dignity and morality. We see the work of the construction of houses as a matter of prime importance.

(*The present difficulties which hinder this undertaking.*)

541 The oft praised modern economy which is so proud
(60, of its ever more and better produced bargains has not
97) yet precisely succeeded in satisfying this real need of man and above all of the family, a need which is real and not merely ficticious as is sometimes insinuated, as if one could be contented either with the huts of primitives or nomads or with an elegant little apartment furnished with every modern comfort but where there is no place for a child.

If the building industry will therefore assist in stimulating the modern economy towards a production destined to satisfy the primordial needs of man, instead of letting itself be directed by the intermittent movement of prices, it will have well merited its title of social work, because it will have brought economy back from the deviations of a disordered competition to the main road of collaboration in a truly social order.

(*Other activities of the Bureau.*)

AN URGENT REMEDY

All. to Women of Catholic Action, July 24, 1949.
(*Disastrous conditions of the family and youth.*)

Let Us say first of all that whatever can contribute **542** to a healthy social policy for the welfare of the family *(97)* and Christian youth can always rely on the efficacious support of the Church.

What We said two years ago to the men of Catholic Action, We repeat to you: the Catholic Church firmly supports the demands of social justice (a).

Among such demands there is the necessity of dwelling places for the people, first of all, for those who want **543** to form a family or already have one. Could there be *(60,* conceived a more urgent social measure? How painful it *97)* is to see young people in those years in which nature inclines them all the more towards matrimony having to wait years and years owing to the shortage of houses, with the danger that after this unnerving and demoraliz-

542a Discourse of the 7th September 1947.—A.D. 9, 245-254.

ing waiting they finally give up! Do your utmost to promote as far as possible with your propaganda and action the preparation of houses, so that the dignity of matrimony and Christian upbringing will not have to suffer through such defect.

(*Materialism and education.*)

ORGANIC ELEMENT OF SOCIETY

All. to the International Union of family organizations, September 20, 1949.

544 Would it have been possible, Gentlemen, not to
(97) greet with lively satisfaction your desire to present to Us, together with your deferential homage, the report of your work and your activities in favor of a matter which is so close to Our heart, namely that of the family?

Right from the beginning of Our election to the Chair of St. Peter, in Our Encyclical *Summi Pontificatus,* We affirmed Our intention to regard as an imperious duty of conscience, imposed on Us by Our Apostolic ministry, the firm defense of family rights (a).

For more than ten years the world has heard Our cry of appeal, has noticed Our actions. But if these efforts of Ours have not been recognized by some, and Our intentions have been misinterpreted by others, it makes it much sweeter to receive from you, in your position as representatives of family organizations, the proof that you have known how to understand and appreciate the work of the common Father. For this We are grateful to you.

544a AAS 31 (1939) 434.

The dignity, rights and duties of the family **545** established by God as a vital cell of society are, in fact, *(34,* as ancient as mankind and are independent of the State's *42,* power (a); but, if they are threatened, the State must *43,* protect and defend them; rights and duties equally holy *44,* for every phase of history and in all countries; holier *60,* still in the tragic hours of calamity and wars, of which *68,* the family is always the greatest victim, the greatest *98)* to be sacrificed.

Now precisely because this is the organic element of society, every attempt to damage it is an attack on humanity. God has placed in the heart of man and woman as an innate instinct conjugal love, paternal and maternal love, filial love. To pretend to abolish, to paralyze, this triple love constitutes a profanation horrible in itself, and fatally leads one's native land and humanity into ruin.

The impotence of the family abandoned to its own **546** means is taken falsely as a pretext to subject it to full *(44,* dependence upon the State and public authorities and *66,* to make it serve a purpose not its own. This is deplorable *97,* disorder, in the more or less sincere illusion of a fictitious *98)* order, but a disorder that logically leads to chaos.

It is unfortunately too true that the family, reduced to relying solely upon its private resources, helpless and friendless, isolated . . . is, in the economic and social conditions of today, insufficient to provide for itself and to fulfill its function as a vital and organic cell. But is this a sufficient reason to adopt a remedy worse than the evil? What then must be done? That which for a long

545a Leo XIII, Enc. *Rerum Novarum,* 13th May, 1891; cf. above n. 210.

time just and sincere men have sought to promote; that which Our Predecessors and We Ourselves have never ceased to recommend, working with all the means at our disposal; that which you yourselves, Gentlemen, seek to actualize in a progressive manner thanks to the Union of family organizations.

Program of action

547
(45,
98,
101,
107)
The program of this action which aims at consolidating the family, to elevate its potentialities, to integrate it in the living mechanism of the world can be synthesized in a few precise points; to supply the insufficiencies of the family, procuring for it what it needs to fulfill its proper domestic and social function;—to unite families among themselves to form a solid front, conscious of its force;—to permit the family to make its voice heard in the affairs of every country, in every society, so that it will never have to suffer damage from them, but will instead be benefited by them as much as possible.

How different would be the path followed by economics and politics if this fundamental principle became the common guide of all men who dedicate themselves to politics!

What matters above all is that the family's nature, goal and life be regarded under their proper aspect, which is that of God, of the moral and religious law.

548
(61,
66,
68,
97)
How pitiful is the picture presented by the solutions of the most delicate problems deriving from a materialistic mentality: the shattering of the family as a result of the undisciplined use of habits based on the system of an unquestioned liberty; weakening of the family by means of eugenics supported in all its forms by legislation;

material or moral enslavement of the family as a conse_ quence of which in the education of children parents are almost reduced to the condition of condemned persons deprived of parental power! The concept of the family considered from God's point of view will necessarily result in return to the only principle of an honest solution: to use all means to place the family in a condition where it can be sufficient of itself and bring its own contribution to the common welfare.

Measures of family assistance

Methods of family assistance are well known to you. **549** Whether they are of public institution or private *(97)* initiative, they are always clothed in the most diverse forms. Since the first World War, family welfare has become a part of the official organizations of public health. The Popes in their social messages have striven earnestly in favor of the family or social wage, which helps the family to provide for the maintenance of the children as they grow up. What must be undertaken therefore, and which here and there has been attempted with great courage, is a policy of vast extent which would empty the properties where the lodgers are barracked and create family dwellings. Today after the second world war, such a demand must certainly be regarded as most urgent.

Let Us also add to this the formation of a more acute **550** sense of the responsibility involved in beginning a home, *(100,* the development of a more healthy family life in a *102,* respectable dwelling which will be of benefit for the soul *107)* as well as the heart.

Nor have We left unremembered the organizations suitable for preparing better for the duties and tasks of matrimony. What cooperation could the press, radio, cinema give, and how great is their responsibility towards the family! Should not the cinema, instead of immersing itself in the intrigues of divorce and separation, place itself at the service of matrimonial unity, married fidelity, family holiness and domestic happiness? People feel the need of a better and higher concept of domestic life. The unexpected success of some recent films is a sufficient proof of this.

551
(97,
105)
At the same time We want to note the aids for infancy, youth assistance, vacation places and rest homes for mothers, the very beneficial organizations of immediate help to particularly hard-pressed families, when for example, the mother of a family finds herself unable to look after her own house: an immense field of work open to the organizations of public welfare, but above all to private charity.

It is necessary of course to remember that even greater assistance is owed to large families; that tax reliefs, subsidies, indemnities are not a purely gratuitous gift, but rather a very modest contribution due to the social service with its great value given by the family, especially by the large family.

552
(45)
You opportunely affirm in your statutes the will to "strengthen the bonds of solidarity among all the families of the world," a most favorable condition for the fulfillment of their function as living cells of society. How many valuable moral forces would in such a way be united for the battle against war in the service of peace!

ARTIFICIAL INSEMINATION

All. to the International Congress of Catholic Doctors, September 29, 1949.

(*Duties of Christian doctors.*)

We have already had numerous other occasions of referring to a large number of particular problems in morals and medicine. But here is a problem no less urgent than the others which requires the light of Catholic moral doctrine. The problem is that of artificial insemination. We cannot let this occasion go by without pointing out, in general outline, the moral judgment which must be passed on this matter (a): **553** *(94)*

1) The practice of artificial insemination, when it refers to man cannot be considered either exclusively or principally from a biological and medical point of view to the neglect of morals and law.

2) Artificial fecundation practiced outside of marriage must be condemned purely and simply as immoral. **554** *(26, 37, 94)*

Indeed, natural law and divine positive law establish that the procreation of a new life must be the fruit only of marriage. Only marriage safeguards the married couple's dignity (principally of the woman in the present case) and their personal good. It alone provides for the welfare and education of the child.

553a To the following question: "Can artificial insemination be practiced?" the Holy Office had already at other times replied: "It is prohibited". Decree of the 26th April, 1897. Cf. *Questions actuelles*, 39, 157.

It follows that there can be no divergence of opinion among Catholics as regards the condemnation of artificial insemination outside of the married state. The child conceived in such conditions would be, by the very fact, illegitimate.

555
(23,
26,
94)

3) Artificial insemination in marriage—produced with the active element of a third person—is equally immoral, and as such is condemned without appeal.

Only husband and wife have a reciprocal right on each other's body to generate a new life—a right which is exclusive, inalienable and which cannot be ceded. And such it must be in consideration for the child. Nature imposes on whoever gives life to a small being—by reason of such a bond—the duty of its preservation and upbringing. But no bond of origin, no moral or juridical bond of conjugal procreation, exists between the legitimate husband and the child which is the fruit of an active element of a third person. This would be the case even if the husband consented to such a practice.

556
(12,
94)

4) As regards the legitimacy of artificial insemination in marriage, it will be sufficient for the moment to recall these principles of the natural law: the mere fact that the result which is desired is achieved by such a means does not justify the use of such means; nor does the desire to have a child—a perfectly legitimate desire of husband and wife—suffice to prove the legitimacy of resorting to artificial insemination which would fulfill such a desire.

It would be erroneous to think that the possibility of resorting to such a means could render valid the marriage between persons incapable of contracting it because of the *impedimentum impotentiæ*.

On the other hand, it is superfluous to point out **557**
that the active element can never be obtained in a law- *(30,*
ful manner by means of acts which are against nature. *94)*

Although new methods cannot be excluded *a priori*
merely because they are new, nevertheless, as regards
artificial insemination, it is not enough to be extremely
reserved, it must be absolutely excluded. Saying this
does not necessarily proscribe the use of certain artificial
means destined solely to facilitate the natural act, or to
assure the accomplishment of the end of the natural act
normally performed.

Only the procreation of a new life according to the
will and design of the Creator—and never let this be
forgotten—brings with it, in a wonderful degree of
perfection, the fulfillment of the proposed ends. It is, at
the same time, in conformity with bodily and spiritual
nature and the dignity of husband and wife, as well as
the normal and healthy development of the child.

THE HOME

Letter *Testes obsequii*, October 18, 1949, to the German Episcopate.

(*Efforts of the Bishops for religious and social restoration.*)

It is particularly comforting for Us to see you pro- **558**
moting, with your teaching, your exhortations, and your *(60,*
acts the very rapid—insofar as is possible—construction of *97)*
homes destined for the homeless. What can be more
necessary, indeed, then the home, in order to live a
life in conformity with the demands of human dignity?
It is the home which protects from the inclemencies of

the weather, serves for rest, guards honesty, preserves heartfelt peace and joy; it is the warm nest of children, the sacred depository of the examples and remembrances of ancestors, and further still, if there flourishes the grace of the Gospel, the domestic sanctuary and the smiling corner of the kingdom of God. If men are deprived of a home they are in their desperation assailed by violent irritation, and, led astray by the desire for novelty, go to the worst extremes.

(*Catholic Action.*)

CATHOLIC MAGISTRATES AND DIVORCE SENTENCES

All. to Catholic jurists, November 6, 1949.

(*Christian concept of law and juridical positivism.— Conduct to use regarding unjust laws.*)

559
(58) The unbridgeable contrasts between the noble concept of man and of the law according to Christian principles, which We have attempted to point out briefly, and juridical positivism can become the sources of deepest bitterness in professional life. Beloved sons, We know well how, not rarely, there arise conflicts of conscience in the soul of the Catholic jurist who wishes to remain true to the Christian concept of law. This is particularly so when he finds himself faced with having to apply a law which his conscience condemns as unjust. Thanks be to God, your duty is notably lightened here because in Italy divorce (the cause of so many interior worries even for the magistrate who must administer the law) has not gained acceptance. However, from the end of the eight-

eenth century—especially in those places where persecution against the Church was the order of the day—the number of cases has grown in which Catholic magistrates have found themselves faced with the tormenting problem of applying unjust law. Therefore, We take this opportunity of your gathering here to enlighten the conscience of Catholic jurists by pointing out some fundamental rules.

1) The principle that the judge cannot purely and **560** simply dismiss the responsibility of his decision by mak- *(58)* ing it fall back totally on the law and on its authors holds valid for every sentence. Certainly, these are principally responsible for the effects of the law itself. But the judge, who with his sentence applies it to the particular case, is the joint cause, and therefore shares the responsibility for those effects.

2) The judge may never with his decision oblige **561** anyone to commit an act intrinsically immoral, that is *(58)* to say, of its very nature contrary to the law of God or of the Church.

3) In no case may he expressly recognize or approve an unjust law (which indeed would never constitute the basis of a valid judgment in conscience and before God). Therefore he may never pronounce a penal sentence which would be equivalent to such an approval. His responsibility would be all the more grave were such a sentence to cause a public scandal.

4) Nevertheless, not every application of an unjust **562** law is equivalent to its recognition or its approbation. *(58)* In this case, the judge can—sometimes perhaps he must—let the unjust law run its course, whenever it is the only

means to hinder a much greater evil. He can inflict a penalty for the transgression of an iniquitous law if it is of such a kind that he who is blameworthy is reasonably disposed to undergo it to avoid that damage or to assure a benefit of much greater importance, and if the judge knows or can prudently suppose that such a sanction will be accepted by the transgressor for higher motives. In times of persecution, priests and lay people have often let themselves be condemned, without opposing resistance, even by Catholic magistrates, have paid fines or been deprived of personal liberty for an infraction of unjust laws, when in such a way it was possible to preserve an honest magistracy for the people and avoid greater calamities for the Church and the faithful.

563
(58,
80)
Naturally, the graver the consequences of the judicial sentence, so much the more important and general ought also to be the good to be achieved or the evil to be avoided. There are cases, however, in which the concept of a compensation bringing greater benefits or removing greater evils cannot apply, as in the case of the death sentence. In particular, the Catholic judge may never pronounce, except for greatly important reasons, a civil divorce sentence (where it exists) for a marriage which is valid before God and the Church. He must never forget that such a sentence, in practice, does not refer to the civil effects only, but in reality gives rise to an erroneous belief that the present bond is dissolved and the new one is valid and binding (a).

563a Following up the French law on divorce, the Inquisition, (to-day the Holy Office), had given on the 27th May, 1886, the following reply: *A nonnullis Galli-*

arum episcopis sequentia dubis S.R. et U. Inquisitioni proposita sunt: "In epistola S.R. et U.I. 25. Iunii 1885 ad omnes in Gallica ditione Ordinarios circa civilis divortii legem ita decernitur: Attentis gravissimis rerum, temporum ac locorum adiunctis tolerari posse, ut qui magistratus obtinent et advocati causa matrimoniales in Gallia agant, quin officio cedere teneantur, conditiones adiecit, quarum secunda haec est: Dummodo ita animo comparati sint tunc circa valorem et nullitatem coniugii, tum circa separationem corporum, de quibus causis iudicare coguntur, ut nunquam proferant sententiam, nesue proferendam defendant vel ad eam provocent vel excitent divino aut ecclesiastico iuri repugnantem".
Quaeritur:
1. An recta sit interpretatio per Gallias diffusa ac etiam typis data, iuxta quam satisfacit conditioni praecitatae iudex, qui, licet matrimonium aliquod validum sit coram Ecclesia, ab illo matrimonio vero et constanti omnio abstrahit, et applicans legem civilem pronuntiat, locum esse divortio, modo solos effectus civiles solumque contractum civilem abrumpere mente intendat, eaque sola respiciant termini prolatae sententiae? Aliis terminis, an sententia lata dici possit divino aut ecclesiastico iuri non rejugnans?
II. Postquam iudex pronuntiavit locum esse divortio, an possit syndacus (gallice: le maire) et ipse solos effectus civiles solumque civilem contractum intendens, ut supra exponitur, divortium pronuntiare, quamvis matrimonium validum sit coram Ecclesia?
III. Pronuntiato divortio, an possit idem syndacus coniugem ad alias nuptias transire attentantem civiliter cum alio iungere, quamvis matrimonium pruis validum sit coram Ecclesia vivatque altera pars?
Responsum est:
Negative ad primum, secuundum et tertium.
(AAS., 22 (1889/1890) 635s).—Cf. Denz., 1865.

THE BACKBONE OF SOCIETY

Radio Message to the faithful of Haiti, December 8, 1949.

(*The faith of the people of Haiti.*)

564 But, doing her utmost with all the possibilities and
(*43,* means at her disposal, without ever tiring of or pausing
53) from pursuing this goal the Church makes a very great
contribution also to the common welfare and prosperity
of the State. This is so because in reality the true secret
of the moral power of the Church rests in the sources
of grace of which she disposes, above all in the principal source which are the Sacraments. Through this the
Church contributes—indirectly, but efficaciously—to the
welfare of civil society. In what way? Especially by forming Christian families, in which fidelity and loving peace
reign between husband and wife, where children are
brought up in the filial fear of the Lord to respect legitimate authority, to be loyal, honest and pure. Conjugal
chastity, the joys of family life, the vigor of a morally
healthy youth, are the mainstay and, as it were, the
backbone of the national community.

(*Social duty of the Church.*)

CATHOLIC AND FAMILY ACTION

Letter *Après des années,* May 7, 1950, to the J.A.C.
of France.

(*Ideal of Catholic Action: to be a presence of the
Church.*)

565 Let Our dear sons and daughters also pay heed to
(*99,* the pressing exhortation which We address them in

favor of the Christian family! Faithful to the centuries' *103,* old tradition of the Church the Catholic Action youth *107)* movement from its beginning proposed to elevate, in the complete sense of the word, those who are consecrated to its cause. It took on the duty of forming young people in the apostolic and civic duties in the rural world. Now We recall to mind what has first place in this educative action, the regeneration of the institution of the family. Already, at their age, the necessary means are the reform of habits which are too free, respect for young women, serious preparation for marriage and, later still, the foundation of Christian homes of which numerous children will be the normal adornment and in which the sense of parental authority and the practice of prayer in common will flourish again.

But often these reforms thus awaited are depen- **566** dent, in the temporal order, on conditions of life still *(97)* so imperfect or incompatible with the aspirations of a true Christian community. It is, then, in the rural world which they know so well from experience and whose economic and social structures are attempting to renew themselves, that young Catholic militants and their elders must communicate the evangelical leaven.

(*Invitation to interior life.*)

RUINS OF THE MORAL ORDER

All. to Cardinals, Archbishops and Bishops, November 2, 1950.

(*Persecution against the Church.*)

We finally consider more closely the social condi- **567** tions of the present times. Our attention and our con- *(67,*

68, sideration are recalled above all to the great question of
101, matrimony and the family. We believe that We do not
103) err if We speak of the disorder in this field as the cancer
of modern human society, gravely prejudicial to souls
themselves. It is incredible how much has been written
theoretically and practically about marriage and the
family. Nevertheless, the evil is aggravated and made
worse in both. Nor can it be otherwise while those who
wish to find a remedy and those to whom a remedy
must be given separate matrimony from God's command
as it is proclaimed by genuine nature under all its aspects, and equally by the doctrine of the Church.

568   Human language is unable to describe the muddy
(62, torrent of books and pamphlets, magazines and papers
97) of all kinds, whereby, through words and pictures full
of frivolity and sensuality, the healthy and rightful
thoughts and sentiments of the people are corrupted.

We are not unappreciative of nor do We undervalue
the progress that medicine, psychology and sociology
have made; rather, We desire that ethics and moral theology, the practice of the care of souls, consultations in
matrimonial matters and the institutes of family assistance take advantage of the results of these sciences.
What We do deprecate is that, along with honest and
serious investigation, there is developed a pseudo-scien-
tific literature, which induces the incompetent and in-
expert reader to enjoy the attractions of what is morbid,
or even to cover with pretended scientific reasons the
dark instincts of one's own immorality.

569   Nor is it fitting that a scientist or a professional
(61, practitioner should communicate imprudently to his
62) clients with danger to soul or body knowledge which is

useful to him. We want to put you on guard against the repetition of the error diffused at the time of the so-called illuminism, the belief, that is, that mere knowledge renders man and his work good. Such an error, if always dangerous, is particularly disastrous in this field.

Perversion of opinion

No less dangerous is the influence of propaganda in creating artificially a false public opinion, which, with moral and often economic pressures, dominates the practical conduct of the relations between both sexes in matrimony and in the formation of the family. **570 (62, 68, 102)**

Is it not perhaps an overturning of every moral order to make man, the image of God, in that which is in him most personal and intimate, the object of a base utilitarian calculation? Healthy public opinion about matrimony and the family is undoubtedly a force which influences the principles and the rules of life and as such is indispensable. But inasmuch as it is called, and in reality is, healthy, it is not, or is not only, a rule imposed from outside, but is always and above all a rule which derives from man's whole nature and binds him to God and to the divine law.

Now We have arrived at the decisive point of Our considerations: matrimony and the family are intimately bound to the law of God. Only such a bond can give the necessary protection to matrimonial life during life's trials and in the face of human frailty, inconstancy and changeableness. And this protection, without offending the personal character of that society and without making it false and dishonest—even in the most unhappy circumstances—confirms the bond which binds husband and wife to each other. **571 (17, 61, 96, 103)**

572   There are not a few Catholics, as well, who express
(61, inexact and confused opinions on such an argument. A
101, false philosophy led the way in despising and rejecting
103) the objective norm, the law, as something extraneous
to true being, as an enemy and a dissolvent of fertility
and the force of life. In this one sees the danger of such
a philosophy for the sanctity of matrimonial and family
morality, which flourish if and where the Church's doctrine is in force. Therefore, a timely and general education is necessary, directed to teaching man that both the
temporal and eternal happiness for which he longs can
be found only in the bond of duty and in the law of God.

573   If this bond is rejected, there are things which can-
(61, not be understood or established: the right of everyone
87, to defend and perfect his person, the liberty of the person
97, itself, the consciousness of having to render an account
99, of our actions. To wish to release man from the bond of
101, the divine order, appealing to the liberty given by God, is
103) a hidden contradiction. This path is sinful and injurious
even when it is a matter of coming to the aid of man in
the more difficult circumstances of his married life. It
is as disastrous for the Church as for human society when
pastors of souls in teaching and practice habitually
and almost as a rule keep silent when the laws established by God for matrimonial life are violated, laws
which are always binding in every case.

       If they fall back for an excuse on the difficulties,
especially economic, to which matrimony and the family
are exposed today, We strongly deplore and have pity
for such difficulties with all Our paternal heart. Nevertheless, We must remain firm on the principle of the
fulfillment of the divine order. This principle must never

in any place be compromised; but social conditions must correspondingly be bettered. If justice and love must always urge the Christian to work for this betterment, even more so must they when it is a matter of aiding thousands and thousands of persons who are otherwise able to lead a worthy, upright and happy married life only with heroic sacrifices.

Social security

At the present time there is much talk of "social security." It gives Us reason to fear for matrimony and the family if that phrase must mean: security by means of society; for there would then not only be the danger that society might undertake something which does not as a rule concern it, but also that the sense of Christian life and the good ordering of this life would be diminished or eliminated completely. Indeed, neo-Malthusian demands have already been exalted in the name of "social security"; already there is an attempt to abate, in the same name even the rights proper to matrimony and to children, as has been done with regard to other rights of the human person or at least to the exercise of such rights. For the Christian, and in general for the man who believes in God, "social security" can only mean safety in a society and with a society in which the natural life of man and the natural development of the family are the essential foundations upon which society itself must depend to exercise properly and safely all its functions and obligations. **574** *(42, 66)*

The experience of the last terrible years has taught what force of resistence the family possesses, notwithstanding all its frailties. In that it is above all other in- **575** *(60, 100,*

103, stitutions. If therefore, there is a true desire to benefit
105) human society, there must be an indefatigable will to
do everything to save the family, to support it and make
it possible for the family to defend itself. This is the
third great request which We constantly beg of the
Virgin assumed into Heaven. Where sad and unjust conditions for matrimony and the family make it harder to
overcome difficulties may the powerful intercession of
Mary to God the Creator secure that men may find
the path to return to the ideal of matrimony as He desired and established it, and that the children of the
Church always unite themselves only by sacramental
marriage and that their chaste wedlock may worthily
symbolize the wonderful union of Christ with the
Church (a).

576   Where there blossoms the Christian life of matri-
(110) mony there also blooms, in mutual accord and progress,
virginal chastity for love of Christ. Therefore We pray
you, exhort your clergy to foster for themselves in a
lively manner the greatest esteem for this ideal which
makes men equal to angels, and to persuade others to
walk in such a noble path of virtue, especially women,
without whose increasing cooperation the Church's apostolate would suffer great damage.

(*Exhortation to the Bishops.*)

575a Cf. Eph. 5:25-33.

PRAYER IN COMMON

Encycl. *Ingruentium malorum,* September 15, 1951.
(*The tragic conditions of our time.—The Rosary.*)

But it is above all in the midst of the family that **577**
We desire that the custom of the holy rosary be spread*(105,*
everywhere, be religiously guarded and always further *106)*
developed. Indeed, in vain is there sought a remedy to
the vacillating destiny of civil life, if domestic society,
the principle and foundation of human society, is not
led back to the laws of the Gospel. We insist that to
develop such an arduous duty the Family Rosary is a
more than efficacious means. What a pleasant sight and
highly pleasing to God it is when, at eventide, the Christian house resounds to the frequent repetition of praise
in honor of the great Queen of Heaven!

(*Beauty of the recitation of the Family Rosary:
power of this prayer.*)

FATHERS

All. to the Fathers of families, September 18, 1951.

What a heartfelt joy it is for Us to see this pilgrim- **578**
age of fathers of families! How many times—in connec- *(43,*
tion with the most varied questions—have We insisted *105)*
on family sanctity, on its rights, on its duties as the fundamental cell of human society? Its life, health, vigor
and activity ensure the life, health, vigor and activity
of society as a whole. Since God has given the family its
existence, its dignity, its social function, it must answer
to God for them. Its rights and its privileges are inalienable, sacrosanct; it has the duty, primarily before God

and secondarily before society, to defend, to vindicate and to promote effectively these rights and these privileges, not only for its own good, but for the glory of God and the welfare of the community.

579
(40) How many times have been sung the praises of the mother, hailing her as the heart, the sun of the family? But if the mother is the heart, the father is the head of the family, and consequently its health and efficiency depend on the vigor, the virtues and activity of the father.

Beloved sons, you understand—and for this reason you have come here—the necessity for the fathers of families to know individually, socially, and in a Christian manner the function confided to them and their inherent duties. You are here and it is your intention to ask the advice and the blessing of the Common Father, the Head of the great human family.

580
(40,
105) It is clear that your first duty in the sanctuary of the family home is to provide—with due respect and the perfection, humanly possible, of its integrity, of its unity, of the natural hierarchy which unites the members among themselves—for the preservation of the physical, intellectual, moral and religious sanctity of the family. Evidently, this obligation includes that of defending and promoting its sacred duties; in the first place that of fulfilling the obligations due to God, to constitute a Christian society in the full sense of the word; secondly to defend the rights of the family against all attacks or external influences which could attack its purity, faith, and holy stability.

Promote these same rights by demanding from the civil, political and cultural society the means, at least those which are indispensable, for their free exercise.

The cell of society

The Christian has a rule which permits him to determine with certainty the extent of the rights and duties of the family in the community of the State. It is thus conceived: the family is not made for society; rather it is society which is made for the family. The family is the fundamental cell, the constitutive element, of the community of the State, because—to use the expression of Our Predecessor, Pius XI, of happy memory—"the State is what it is made to be by the individuals and families which compose it, as a body is composed of its members" (a). The State then, should, as it were, in virtue of the instinct of self-preservation fulfill that which, essentially according to the design of God, Creator and Savior, is its first duty, namely guarantee in full measure the values which ensure to the family order, human dignity, health, and happiness. These values, which are also the very elements of the common good, may never be sacrificed for what may apparently be the common advantage.

Let Us point out, as an example, some of these benefits which are greatly threatened today: the indissolubility of matrimony; the protection of prenatal life; suitable housing for the family, and that not merely for the family composed of one or two children or a childless family, but for the normal larger family; the possibility of finding work, for a father lacking employment is one of the bitterest worries of a family; the rights of the parents over their children in the eyes of the State; their full freedom to raise them in the true faith, and, consequently,

581
(42,
43,
44,
98,
105)

581a Enc. *Casti connubii*, 31st December, 1930; cf. above, n. 300.

the right of Catholic parents to Catholic schools; a condition of public life, and above all, public morals such that the families and especially young people will not have the moral certainty of being corrupted.

582
(105) On this and other points which concern family life more intimately there are no differences between family and family. On other questions of an economic or political nature they may find themselves in very different conditions, and sometimes in competition or even in opposition. Here there is a great need—and Catholics should be the first to give a good example— to promote a balance of interests, even at the cost of sacrificing particular interests, but having in view an internal peace and stable economy.

583
(53, 105) But when it is a question of the essential rights of the family, the true faithful of the Church will pledge themselves in support from beginning to end. It may be that on this or that particular point, there must be a retreat before the superiority of political forces. But here it is not capitulation but a matter of patience. In such cases it is necessary that doctrine be safeguarded, that all efficacious means be adopted to arrive little by little at the goal which has never been given up.

The union of fathers of families

584
(102, 105) Among these efficacious means, even of those which look to a distant future, certainly one of the most powerful is the union between fathers of families who are guided by the same convictions and the same desires. Your presence here is a testimony that such is even your thought.

Even before obtaining a desired result, in the absence of or while awaiting the success which your group continues to pursue, the aim of this association of fathers is to use fruitful means of enlightening public opinion and little by little to pervade it to favor the triumph of truth and justice. No effort to act upon public opinion must be disdained or neglected.

Sexual initiation

There is another field in which this education of **585** public opinion is needed and this with tragic urgency. *(62,* It is in this field perverted by propaganda which one *107)* does not hesitate to call evil, even if at times it takes its origin from Catholic sources and aims at making headway among Catholics,—and even if those who promote it do not seem aware that they are deluded by the spirit of evil.

Here We intend to speak of writings, books, and articles regarding sexual initiation, which today very often achieve fame as "best sellers," and flood the whole world, taking possession of infancy, submerging the new generation, and disturbing engaged couples and the newly married.

The Church has treated this question regarding **586** instruction on this matter, both as concerns the physical *(62,* development and normal psychology of adolesence, and *107)* as concerns particular cases arising from different individual conditions, with all the gravity, attention, and decency that the argument permitted. The Church can rightly declare that, profoundly respectful of the sanctity of marriage, she has in theory and in practice left husband and wife free in that which the impulse of a wholesome and honest nature concedes without offence to the Creator.

587 One becomes terrified by the intolerable impudence
(62, of certain literature; and while paganism itself seemed
107) to halt in respect before the secret of married intimacy, it is our lot to see the mystery violated and its vision, sexual and degraded, offered as a meal to the public and even to youth.

One must ask oneself if there still remains sufficiently marked out the boundaries between the initiation which is called Catholic, and the press with its erotic and obscence illustrations, which, with serious deliberation, aims at corruption, and basely exploits the lowest instincts of fallen nature for despicable interests.

588 Would that it ended here. Such a propaganda also
(19, threatens Catholics with a double calamity, not to use
31, a stronger expression. First of all, it exaggerates out of
62) all proportion the importance and significance of the sexual element. It may be admitted that these authors, under the purely theoretical aspect, keep within the limits of Catholic morals. But no less true is it that their manner of explaining sexual life is such that it acquires in the mind and conscience of the average reader the idea and value of an end in itself, making him lose sight of the true primordial purpose of matrimony, which is the procreation and upbringing of children, and the grave duty of married couples as regards this purpose—something which the literature of which We are speaking leaves too much in the background.

Secondly, this literature—if it deserves such a title— **589**
seems to hold in no account the universal experience of *(61,*
past, present and future ages, although such experience *62,*
is based on nature itself, which attests that in moral edu- *104,*
cation neither initiation nor instruction offers of itself any *107)*
advantage; that indeed, it is seriously harmful and prejudicial where it is not firmly restrained by constant discipline, by a vigorous self-control, above all, by the use of
the supernatural means of prayer and the Sacraments.
All Catholic educators, worthy of the name and their
mission, are fully aware of the overwhelming importance
of supernatural forces in man's sanctification—youth or
adult, married or single. But in the writings mentioned,
hardly a word is said about these things, even when the
whole matter is not passed over in complete silence. Even
the principles so wisely explained by Our Predecessor,
Pius XI, in the Encyclical *Divini illius Magistri*, regarding sexual education and the related problems (a), are
pushed aside with a smile of compassion: Pius XI, it is
said, wrote these things twenty years ago for his own
times! The world has gone a long way since then!

Fathers here present: in every corner of the globe, **590**
in every country, there are other Christian fathers of *(105)*
families such as yourselves, who share your sentiments.
Unite yourselves therefore with them—naturally under
the direction of your Bishops. Call to your help all
Catholic mothers and with their powerful support fight
together, without timidity or human respect, to halt and
curtail these movements which authorize and mask themselves under any name or patronage. Not without reason

589a The Enc. *Divini illius Magistri,* of Pius XI, is dated
  December 31, 1929.

you have placed your pilgrimage under the special care of the great Pope of the Eucharist, Blessed Pius X. Have faith in the help of the Immaculate Virgin, Mother most pure, Mother most chaste, Help of Christians; have faith in the grace of Christ, source of all purity, Who never abandons those who work for the coming and establishment of His kingdom.

MATRIMONY AND VIRGINITY

All. to Discalced Carmelites, September 23, 1951.
(*Religious virtues.—Obedience.—Chastity.*)

591 Let him who chooses virginity not hold of little value
(108, or despise matrimony. Matrimony is good and virginity
110) is better; matrimony's goal is noble, that of virginity, as the Gospel attests, is much higher, because virginity is embraced for love of Christ and is made productive by the fruit of charity. Above all, perpetual virginity is a pure host offered to God, a holy victim; and besides it is a flower which gives honor and joy to the Church, and is a great source of strength which the Church cannot exclude nor neglect.

592 Being under a duty to treat of virginity and give in-
(33) structions related to it, let all, from the beginning, keep well in mind that perfect chastity, and conjugal chastity also, cannot be preserved constantly without the aid of God's grace and this heavenly aid is even more necessary when it is a matter of preserving chastity until the last breath of life. Therefore, he who has made a vow to God of virginal integrity must struggle with prayer and with the exercises of penance, as Jacob with the Angel, so as to be always victorious.

THE LAWS OF CONJUGAL RELATIONS

All. to midwives, October 29, 1951.
(*Nature of their profession.*)

When one thinks of this admirable collaboration of **593** the parents, of nature and of God, from which is born a *(20)* new human being in the image and likeness of God (a), how can the precious contribution which you give to such a work be not appreciated? The heroic mother of the Machabees admonished her children: "I know not how you were formed in my womb, for I neither gave you breath, nor soul, nor life, neither did I frame the limbs of every one of you. But the Creator of the world that formed the nativity of men ..." (b).

Therefore, he who approaches this cradle of life's **594** origin and exercises his action in one way or another *(20)* must know the order which the Creator wishes maintained and the laws which govern it. For here it is not a case of purely physical or biological laws which blind forces and irrational agents obey, but of laws whose execution and effects are entrusted to the voluntary and free cooperation of man.

This order, fixed by the supreme intelligence, is **595** directed to the purpose willed by the Creator. It em- *(20,* braces the exterior work of man and the internal assent *87,* of his free will; it implies action and dutiful omission. *101)* Nature places at man's disposal the concatenation of the causes from which will rise a new human life; it is for man to release its loving force, for nature to develop

593a Cf. Gen. 1:26-27.
593b 2 Mac. 7:22.

its course and lead it to its completion. When man has completed his part and placed in action the marvellous evolution of life, his duty is to respect its progress in a religious manner, a duty which forbids him to arrest nature's work or halt its natural development (a).

596 In such a way nature's part and man's part are dis-
(102) tinctly determined. Your professional formation and experience place you in a position to know the action of nature and that of man, no less than the rules and the laws to which both are subject; your conscience, illuminated by reason and faith, under the guidance of the Authority established by God, teaches you how far lawful action extends, and when, instead, there is strictly imposed the obligation of omission.

The inviolability of human life

597 You, more than others, can appreciate and realize
(89, what human life is in itself, and what it is worth in the
101, eyes of sane reason, before your moral conscience, before
102) civil society, before the Church and, above all, what it is worth in the eyes of God. God created all earthly things for man; and man himself, as regards his being and his essence, has been created for God and not for any other creature, even if, as regards his actions, he has obligations towards the community as well. The child is "man," even if he be not yet born, in the same degree and by the same title as his mother.

598 Besides, every human being, even the child in the
(89) womb, has the right to life *directly* from God and not from his parents, not from any society or human author-

595a *Dovere che gli vieta di arrestare l'opera della natura o d'impedirne il naturale sviluppo.*

ity. Therefore, there is no man, no human authority, no science, no "indication" at all—whether it be medical, eugenic, social, economic, or moral—that may offer or give a valid judicial title for a *direct* deliberate disposal of an innocent human life, that is, a disposal which aims at its destruction, whether as an end in itself or as a means to achieve the end, perhaps in no way at all illicit. Thus, for example, to save the life of the mother is a very noble act; but the direct killing of the child as a means to such an end is illicit. The direct destruction of so-called "useless lives," already born or still in the womb, practiced extensively a few years ago, can in no wise be justified. Therefore, when this practice was initiated, the Church expressly declared that it was against the natural law and the divine positive law, and consequently that it was unlawful to kill, even by order of the public authorities, those who were innocent, even if, on account of some physical or mental defect, they were useless to the State and a burden upon it (a). The life of an innocent person is sacrosanct, and any direct attempt or aggression against it is a violation of one of the fundamental laws without which secure human society is impossible. We have no need to teach you in detail the meaning and the gravity, in your profession, of this

598a To the doubt: "Is it lawful to kill directly, by order of the public authority, a person. who although innocent of every crime worthy of death, cannot however by reason of psychical or physical deformities be useful to the nation, but rather seems to hinder its vigor and force?" was given the reply: *"It is not allowed,* because this is an act contrary to the natural and positive law". Decree of the Holy Office, 2nd. December, 1940, (AAS, 32, pp. 553-554).

fundamental law. But never forget this: there rises above every human law and above every "indication" the faultless law of God.

599   The apostolate of your profession imposes on you
*(101,*the duty of passing on to others the knowledge, esteem
102) and respect for human life that you foster in your heart by reason of your Christian convictions. You must, when called upon, be prepared to defend resolutely, and when possible, protect the helpless and hidden life of the child, basing yourselves on the divine precept: *Non occides*: do not kill (a). Such a defensive function is sometimes presented as most necessary and urgent. It is not, however, the nobler and more important part of your mission; this in fact is not merely negative, but above all constructive, and tends to promote, edify and strengthen.

Welcoming the newly born

600   Infuse into the spirit and heart of the mother and
(27, father the esteem, desire, joy, and the loving welcome of
102) the newly born right from its first cry. The child, formed in the mother's womb, is a gift of God (a), Who entrusts its care to the parents. With what delicacy and charm does the Sacred Scripture show the gracious crown of children united around the father's table! Children are the recompense of the just, as sterility is very often the punishment for the sinner. Hearken to the divine word expressed with the insuperable poetry of the Psalm: "Your wife, as a fruitful vine within your house, your children as olive shoots round about your

599a Exod. 20:13.
600a Ps. 127:3.

table. Behold, thus is that man blessed, who fears the Lord!" (b), while of the wicked it is written: "May his posterity be given over to destruction; may their name be blotted out in the next generation" (c).

Immediately after birth, be quick to place the child **601** in the father's arms—as the ancient Romans were wont *(27)* to do—but with a spirit incomparably more elevated. For the Romans, it was the affirmation of the paternity and the authority which derived from it; here it is grateful homage to the Creator, the invocation of divine blessings, the promise to fulfill with devout affection the office which God has committed him. If the Lord praises and rewards the faithful servant for having yielded him five talents (a), what praise, what reward will He reserve for the father, who has guarded and raised for Him a human life entrusted to him, greater than all the gold and silver of the world?

Your apostolate, however, is directed above all to **602** the mother. Undoubtedly nature's voice speaks in her *(27,* and places in her heart the desire, joy, courage, love and *102)* will to care for the child; but to overcome the suggestions of fearfulness in all its forms, that voice must be strengthened and take on, so to say, a supernatural accent. It is your duty to cause the young mother to enjoy, less by your words than by your whole manner of acting, the greatness, beauty and nobility of that life which begins, is formed and lives in her womb, that child which she bears in her arms and suckles at her breast; to make

600b Ps. 128:3-4.
600c Ps. 109:13.
601a Cf. Matt. 25:21.

shine in her eyes and heart the great gift of God's love for her and her child. Sacred Scripture makes us understand with many examples the echo of suppliant prayers and then the songs of grateful happiness of many mothers who, after having longingly and tearfully implored the grace of motherhood, were finally answered.

603
(27) Even the pains which, after original sin, a mother has to suffer to give birth to her child only make her draw tighter the bond which unites them: the more the pain has cost her, so much the more is her love for her child. He who formed mothers' hearts, expressed this thought with moving and profound simplicity: "A woman about to give birth has sorrow, because her hour has come. But when she has brought forth the child, she no longer remembers the anguish for her joy that a man is born into the world" (a). Through the pen of the Apostle, St. Paul, the Holy Ghost also points out the greatness and joy of motherhood: God gives the child to the mother, but, together with the gift, He makes her cooperate effectively at the opening of the flower, of which He has deposited the germ in her womb, and this cooperation becomes a way which leads her to her eternal salvation: "Yet women will be saved by child bearing" (b).

604
(27) This perfect accord of reason and faith gives you the guarantee that you are within the real truth and that you may continue your apostolate of respect and love for incipient life with unconditioned security. If you succeed in carrying out your apostolate at the cradle where rests the newly born child, it will not be too diffi-

603a John 16:21.   603b 1 Tim. 2:15.

cult for you to obtain what your professional conscience, in harmony with the laws of God and of nature, obliges you to prescribe for the welfare of mother and child.

On the other hand, it is not necessary for Us to show you who are well experienced, how much this apostolate of respect and love for the new life is necessary today. Unfortunately, cases are not rare in which it is sufficient only to hint at the fact that children are a "blessing" to provoke contradiction and even derision. More often in word and thought the idea of the great "burden" of children is predominant. Inasmuch as this mentality is opposed to God's plan and to Scripture, so is it also contrary to sane reason and the sentiments of nature! If there are conditions and circumstances in which parents without violating God's law can avoid the "blessing" of children, nevertheless these unavoidable and exceptional cases do not authorize anyone to pervert ideas, to despise values and to treat with contempt the mother who had the courage and honor to give life. **605** *(68, 90)*

Supernatural life

If what We have said up to now concerns the protection and care of natural life, much more so must it concern the supernatural life, which the newly born receives with Baptism. In the present economy there is no other way to communicate that life to the child who has not attained the use of reason. Above all, the state of grace is absolutely necessary at the moment of death; without it salvation and supernatural happiness—the beatific vision of God—are impossible (a). An act of love **606** *(21)*

606a *Senza di esso non è possibile giungere alla felicità soprannaturale, alla visione beatifica di Dio.*

is sufficient for the adult to obtain sanctifying grace and to supply the lack of baptism; to the still unborn or newly born this way is not open. Therefore, if it is considered that charity to our fellowman obliges us to assist him in the case of necessity, then this obligation is so much the more important and urgent as the good to be obtained or the evil to be avoided is the greater, and in the measure that the needy person is incapable of helping or saving himself with his own powers; and so it is easy to understand the great importance of providing for the baptism of the child deprived of complete reason who finds himself in grave danger or at death's threshold.

607   Undoubtedly this duty binds the parents in the first
(21) place; but in case of necessity, when there is no time to lose or it is not possible to call a priest, the sublime office of conferring baptism is yours.

(*Loveliness of this act of spiritual mercy.*)

The mother's duties

608   At the moment she understood the Angel's message
(27) the Virgin Mary replied: "Behold the handmaid of the Lord! Be it done unto me according to thy word" (a). A "fiat," a burning "yes" to the call to motherhood! A virginal maternity, incomparably superior to any other; but a real maternity, in the true and proper sense of the word (b). Therefore, when reciting the *Angelus,* after having recalled to mind Mary's acceptance, the faithful immediately reply: "And the Word was made flesh" (c).

609   One of the fundamental demands of the true moral
(27) order is that to the use of the marriage rights there

608a Luke 1:38.   608b Cf. Gal. 4:4.   608c John 1:14.

corresponds the sincere internal acceptance of the function and duties of motherhood (a). With this condition the woman walks in the path traced out by the Creator towards the goal which He has assigned His creature; He makes her, by the exercise of this function, partaker of His goodness, wisdom and omnipotence, according to the Angel's message: *"Concipies in utero et paries*—you will conceive and bear forth a child" (b).

If such then is the biological foundation of your **610** professional activity, the urgent object of your apostolate*(102)* will be: to maintain, reawake and stimulate the sense and love of the function of motherhood.

When husband and wife value and appreciate the **611** honor of producing a new life, whose coming they await *(27)* with holy impatience, your part is a very easy one: it is easy enough to cultivate in them this interior sentiment: the readiness to welcome and cherish that nascent life follows spontaneously. This is unfortunately not always the case; often the child is not wanted; worse still, it is dreaded. How can there be a ready response to the call of duty in such conditions? Your apostolate must in this case be exercised both efficiently and efficaciously: first of all, negatively, by refusing any immoral cooperation; secondly, positively, by turning your delicate care to the task of removing those preconceived ideas, various fears or faint excuses, to removing as far as possible the obstacles, even if external, which may make the acceptance of motherhood painful.

609a *All'uso dei diritti coniugali corrisponda la sincera accettazione interna dell'ufficio e dei doveri della maternità.*
609b Cf. Luke 1:31.

612 If recourse is had to you for advice and help to
(87, facilitate the birth of new life, to protect it and set it on
101) its way towards its full development, you can unhesitatingly lend your help; but in how many cases are
you, instead, called upon to prevent the procreation and
preservation of this life, regardless of the precepts of the
moral order? To accede to such requests would be to debase your knowledge and your skill by becoming accom-
plices in an immoral action; it would be the perversion
of your apostolate. This requires a calm but unequivocal
"no" that prevents the transgression of God's law and of
the dictates of your conscience. Hence your profession
obliges you to a clear knowledge of this divine law, so
that it may be observed without excess or defect.

The conjugal act

613 Our Predecessor, Pius XI, of happy memory, in his
(27, Encyclical *Casti Connubii, of* December 31, 1930, once
87) again solemnly proclaimed the fundamental law of the
conjugal act and conjugal relations: that every attempt
of either husband or wife in the performance of the conjugal act or in the development of its natural consequences which aims at depriving it of its inherent force
and hinders the procreation of new life is immoral; and
that no "indication" or need can convert an act which is
intrinsically immoral into a moral and lawful one (a).

This precept is in full force today, as it was in the
past, and so it will be in the future also, and always,
because it is not a simple human whim, but the expression
of a natural and divine law.

613a *Nessuna "indicazione" o necessità può mutare un'azione intrinsecamente immorale in un atto morale e lecito;*
cf. Encycl. *Casti Conubii,* n. 263.

Let Our words be a sure rule for all those cases which require of your profession and your apostolate a clear and firm decision.

Sterilization

It would be more than a mere lack of readiness in the service of life if an attack made by man were to concern not only a single act but should affect the organism itself to deprive it, by means of sterilization, of the faculty of procreating a new life. Here, too, you have a clear rule in the Church's teaching to guide your behavior both interiorly and exteriorly. Direct sterilization— that is, whose aim tends as a means or as an end at making procreation impossible—is a grave violation of the moral law and therefore unlawful. Not even public authority has any right, under the pretext of any "indication" whatsoever, to permit it, and less still to prescribe it or to have it used to the detriment of innocent human beings. This principle is already proclaimed in the above mentioned Encyclical of Pius XI on marriage (a). Thus, when ten years or so ago sterilization came to be more widely applied, the Holy See saw the necessity of expressly and publicly declaring that direct sterilization, either perpetual or temporary, in either the male or

614
(50, 56, 88)

614a Cf. Encycl. *Casti connubii;* above, n. 328 .ff.—Cf. Degree of the Holy Office, Feb. 24, 1940: "The doubt proposed to the Supreme Sacred Congregation of the Holy Office: *If direct sterilization, either perpetual or temporal, of a man or a woman is allowed;* received the following reply: *It is not allowed,* because it is prohibited by the natural law; as regards eugenic sterilisation, it had already been condemned in a decree of the same Congregation of the Holy Office, 21st March, 1931". (AAS. 32 (1940) 73). Cf. Denz. n. 2283.

the female, is unlawful according to natural law (b), from which, as you well know, not even the Church has the power to dispense.

As far as you can, oppose, in your apostolate, these perverse tendencies and do not give them your co-operation.

Birth control

615   Today, besides, another grave problem has arisen,
(28) namely, if and how far the obligation of being ready for the service of maternity is reconcilable with the ever more general recourse to the periods of natural sterility (the so-called "agenesic" periods in woman), which seems a clear expression of a will contrary to that precept.

616   You are expected to be well informed, from the
(28, medical point of view, in regard to this new theory and
52, the progress which may still be made on this subject,
102) and it is also expected that your advice and assistance shall not be based upon mere popular publications, but upon objective science and on the authoritative judgment of conscientious specialists in medicine and biology. It is your function, not the priest's, to instruct the married couple through private consultation or serious publications on the biological and technical aspect of the theory (a), without however allowing yourselves to be drawn into an unjust and unbecoming propaganda. But in this field also your apostolate demands of you, as women and

614b *La sterilizzazione diretta, sia perpetua che tempo-ranea, sia dell'uomo che della donna, è illecita.*

616a *E' ufficio non del sacerdote, ma vostro, d'instruire i coniugi, sia in consultazioni private, sia mediante serie pubblicazioni, sull'aspetto biologico e tecnico della teoria.*

as Christians, that you know and defend the moral law, to which the application of the theory is subordinated. In this the Church is competent.

It is necessary first of all to consider two hypotheses. **617** If the application of that theory implies that husband and *(28)* wife may use their matrimonial right even during the days of natural sterility no objection can be made. In this case they do not hinder or jeopardize in any way the consummation of the natural act and its ulterior natural consequences. It is exactly in this that the application of the theory, of which We are speaking, differs essentially from the abuse already mentioned, which consists in the perversion of the act itself. If, instead, husband and wife go further, that is, limiting the conjugal act exclusively to those periods, then their conduct must be examined more closely.

Here again we are faced with two hypotheses. If, **618** one of the parties contracted marriage with the intention *(12,* of limiting the matrimonial right itself to the periods *28)* of sterility, and not only its use, in such a manner that during the other days the other party would not even have the right to ask for the debt, than this would imply an essential defect in the marriage consent, which would result in the marriage being invalid, because the right deriving from the marriage contract is a permanent, uninterrupted and continuous right of husband and wife with respect to each other (a).

However if the limitation of the act to the periods **619** of natural sterility does not refer to the right itself but *(28)*

618a *Il diritto derivante dal contratto matrimoniale è un diritto permanente, ininterrotto, e non intermittente, di ciascuno dei coniugi di fronte all'altro.*

only to the use of the right, the validity of the marriage does not come up for discussion. Nonetheless, the moral lawfulness of such conduct of husband and wife should be affirmed or denied according as their intention to observe constantly those periods is or is not based on sufficiently morally sure motives. The mere fact that husband and wife do not offend the nature of the act and are even ready to accept and bring up the child, who, notwithstanding their precautions, might be born, would not be itself sufficient to guarantee the rectitude of their intention and the unobjectionable morality of their motives.

620
(19,
27,
28)
   The reason is that marriage obliges the partners to a state of life, which even as it confers certain rights so it also imposes the accomplishment of a positive work concerning the state itself (a). In such a case, the general principle may be applied that a positive action may be omitted if grave motives, independent of the good will of those who are obliged to perform it, show that its performance is inopportune, or prove that it may not be claimed with equal right by the petitioner—in this case, mankind.

621
(22,
26,
28,
43,
102)
   The matrimonial contract, which confers on the married couple the right to satisfy the inclination of nature, constitutes them in a state of life, namely, the matrimonial state. Now, on married couples, who make use of the specific act of their state, nature and the Creator impose the function of providing for the preservation of mankind. This is the characteristic service which gives rise to the

620a *Il matrimonio obbliga ad uno stato di vita, il quale, come conferisce certi diritti, cosi impone anche il complimento di un'opera positiva, riguardante lo stato stesso.*

peculiar value of their state, the *bonum prolis* (a). The individual and society, the people and the State, the Church itself, depend for their existence, in the order established by God, on fruitful marriages. Therefore, to embrace the matrimonial state, to use continually the faculty proper to such a state and lawful only therein, and, at the same time, to avoid its primary duty without a grave reason, would be a sin against the very nature of married life (b).

Serious motives, such as those which not rarely arise from medical, eugenic, economic and social so-called "indications," may exempt husband and wife from the obligatory, positive debt for a long period or even for the entire period of matrimonial life. From this it follows that the observance of the natural sterile periods may be *lawful,* from the moral viewpoint: and it is lawful in the conditions mentioned. If, however, according to a reasonable and equitable judgment, there are no such grave reasons either personal or deriving from exterior circumstances, the will to avoid the fecundity of their union, while continuing to satisfy to the full their sensuality, can only be the result of a false appreciation of life and of motives foreign to sound ethical principles (a). **622** *(28, 88, 91)*

621a *E'questa la prestazione caratteristica, che fa il valore proprio del loro stato, il* bonum prolis.
621b *Abbracciare lo stato matrimoniale, usare continuamente la facoltà ad esso propria e in esso solo lecita, e, d'altra parte, sottrarsi sempre e deliberatamente, senza un grave motivo, al suo primario dovere, sarebbe un peccare contro il senso stesso della vita coniugale.*
622a *Non può derivare che da un falso apprezzamento della vita e da motivi estranei alle rette norme etiche.*

The heroism of continence

623
(33,
102)
Perhaps you will now press the point, however, observing that in the exercise of your profession you find yourselves sometimes faced with delicate cases, in which, that is, there cannot be a demand that the risk of maternity be run, a risk which in certain cases must be absolutely avoided, and in which as well the observance of the agenesic periods either does not give sufficient security, or must be rejected for other reasons. Now, you ask, how can one still speak of an apostolate in the service of maternity?

624
(33,
89)
If, in your sure and experienced judgment, the circumstances require an absolute "no," that is to say, the exclusion of motherhood, it would be a mistake and a wrong to impose or advise a "yes." Here it is a question of basic facts and therefore not a theological but a medical question; and thus it is in your competence. However, in such cases, the married couple does not desire a medical answer, of necessity a negative one, but seeks an approval of a "technique" of conjugal activity which will not give rise to maternity. And so you are again called to exercise your apostolate inasmuch as you leave no doubt whatsoever that even in these extreme cases every preventive practice and every direct attack upon the life and the development of the seed is, in conscience, forbidden and excluded, and that there is only one way open, namely, to abstain from every complete performance of the natural faculty (a). Your apostolate in this matter requires that you have a clear and certain judgment and a calm firmness.

624a *Una sola via rimarne aperta, vale a dire quella dell'astinenza da ogni attuazione completa della facoltà naturale.*

It will be objected that such an abstention is im- 625
possible, that such a heroism is asking too much. You *(11,*
will hear this objection raised; you will read it every- *33)*
where. Even those who should be in a position to judge
very differently, either by reason of their duties or
qualifications, are ever ready to bring forward the following argument: "No one is obliged to do what is impossible, and it may be presumed that no reasonable
legislator can will his law to oblige to the point of impossibility. But for husbands and wives long periods of
abstention are impossible. Therefore they are not
obliged to abstain; divine law cannot have this meaning."

In such a manner, from partially true premises, one 626
arrives at a false conclusion. To convince oneself of this *(11,*
it suffices to invert the terms of the argument: "God *33,*
does not oblige anyone to do what is impossible. But *101,*
God obliges husband and wife to abstinence if their *104)*
union cannot be completed according to the laws of
nature. Therefore in this case abstinence is possible."
To confirm this argument, there can be brought forward the doctrine of the Council of Trent, which, in
the chapter on the observance necessary and possible of
the commandments, referring to a passage of St. Augustine, teaches: "God does not command the impossible,
but while He commands, He warns you to do what you
can and to ask for the grace for what you cannot do,
and He helps you so that you may be able" (a).

Do not be disturbed, therefore, in the practice of 627
your profession and apostolate, by this great talk of im- *(33,*

626a Council of Trent, sess. 6, c. 11.—Denz. n. 804.—
St. Augustine, *De natura et gratia,* c. 43, n. 50.—Migne,
P.L., 44, 271.

104) possibility. Do not be disturbed in your internal judgment nor in your external conduct. Never lend yourselves
to anything which is contrary to the law of God and to
your Christian conscience! It would be a wrong towards
men and women of our age to judge them incapable
of continuous heroism. Nowadays, for many a reason,
—perhaps constrained by dire necessity or even at times
oppressed by injustice—heroism is exercised to a degree
and to an extent that in the past would have been thought
impossible. Why, then, if circumstances truly demand it,
should this heroism stop at the limits prescribed by the
passions and the inclinations of nature? It is clear: he
who does not want to master himself is not able to do
so, and he who wishes to master himself relying only
upon his own powers, without sincerely and perseveringly
seeking divine help, will be miserably deceived.

628   Here is what concerns your apostolate for winning
(102) married people over to a service of motherhood, not in
the sense of an utter servitude under the promptings of
nature, but to the exercise of the rights and duties of
married life, governed by the principles of reason and
faith.

The final aspect of your apostolate concerns the
defense of both the right order of values and of the dignity of the human being.

The order of values

629   "Personal values" and the need to respect such are
(91) a theme which, over the last twenty years or so, has been
considered more and more by writers. In many of their
works, even the specifically sexual act has its place assigned, that of serving the "person" of the married couple.
The proper and most profound sense of the exercise of

conjugal rights would consist in this, that the union of bodies is the expression and the realization of personal and affective union.

Articles, chapters, entire books, conferences, especially dealing with the "technique" of love, are composed to spread these ideas, to illustrate them with advice to the newly married as a guide in matrimony, in order that they may not neglect, through stupidity or a false sense of shame or unfounded scruples, that which God, Who also created natural inclinations, offers them. If from their complete reciprocal gift of husband and wife there results a new life, it is a result which remains outside, or, at the most, on the border of "personal values"; a result which is not denied, but neither is it desired as the center of marital relations. **630 (61, 62, 91)**

According to these theories, your dedication for the welfare of the still hidden life in the womb of the mother, and your assisting its happy birth, would only have but a minor and secondary importance. **631 (61, 91)**

Now, if this relative evaluation were merely to place the emphasis on the personal values of husband and wife rather than on that of the offspring, it would be possible, strictly speaking, to put such a problem aside. But, however, it is a matter of a grave inversion of the order of values and of the ends imposed by the Creator Himself. We find Ourselves faced with the propagation of a number of ideas and sentiments directly opposed to the clarity, profundity, and seriousness of Christian thought (a). Here, once again, the need for your aposto- **632 (31, 63, 91)**

632a *Una grave inversione dell'ordine dei valori e dei fini posti dallo stesso Creatore. Ci troviamo dinanzi alla propagazione di un complesso d'idee e di affetti, diretta-*

late. It may happen that you receive the confidences of the mother and wife and are questioned on the more secret desires and intimacies of married life. How, then, will you be able, aware of your mission, to give weight to truth and right order in the appreciation and action of the married couple, if you yourselves are not furnished with the strength of character needed to uphold what you know to be true and just?

The primary end of marriage

633
(19,
29,
30,
31)
Now, the truth is that matrimony, as an institution of nature, in virtue of the Creator's will, has not as a primary and intimate end the personal perfection of the married couple but the procreation and upbringing of a new life. The other ends, inasmuch as they are intended by nature, are not equally primary, much less superior to the primary end, but are essentially subordinated to it (a). This is true of every marriage, even if no offspring result; just as of every eye it can be said that it is destined and formed to see, even if, in abnormal cases arising from special internal or external conditions, it will never be possible to achieve visual perception.

634
(19,
31,
It was precisely to end the uncertainties and deviations which threatened to diffuse errors regarding the scale of values of the purposes of matrimony and of

mente opposti alla chiarezza, alla profondità e alla serietà del pensiero cristiano.

633a Il matrimonio, come istituzione naturale, in virtù della volontà del Creatore non ha come fine primario e intimo il perfezionamento personale degli sposi, ma la procreazione e l'educazione della nuova vita. Gli altri fini, per quanto anch'essi intesi dalla natura, non si trovano nello stesso grado del primo, e ancor meno gli sono superiori, ma sono ad esso essenzialmente subordinati.

their reciprocal relations, that a few years ago (March *104)*
10, 1944) (a), We Ourselves drew up a declaration on
the order of those ends, pointing out what the very internal structure of the natural disposition reveals. We
showed what has been handed down by Christian
tradition, what the Supreme Pontiffs have repeatedly
taught, and what was then in due measure promulgated
by the Code of Canon Law (b). Not long afterwards,
to correct opposing opinions, the Holy See, by a public
decree, proclaimed that it could not admit the opinion
of some recent authors who denied that the primary
end of marriage is the procreation and education of the
offspring, or teach that the secondary ends are not
essentially subordinated to the primary end, but are
on an equal footing and independent of it (c).

634a It seems as though this declaration was not published, but it must have been similar to the Decree of the
Holy Office quoted here above, n. 643c. (Cf. *De re
matrimoniali,* Romae, *apud aedes Pont. Universitatis
Gregorianae,* 1951, p. 424, n. 30).
634b C.I.C., can. 1013, §1; cf. above, n. 279.
634c Sacred Congregation of the Holy Office, 1st April
1944; AAS 36 (1944) 103; Dez. n. 2295:
—To the query: "Is it possible to admit the opinion of
some authors who deny that the primary end of matrimony is the procreation and education of the offspring, or teach that the secondary ends are not essentially subordinated to the primary ends, but are with them
parallel *(aeque principales)* and independent?" the Holy
Office decreed: *"It cannot be admitted."* This reply,
given on the 29th March, 1944, was approved by H.H.
Pope Pius XII on the 30th March, 1944 and published on
April 1st, of the same year.—This question and its answer,
are preceded by their motivation; below are the words
which form the first part of the decree: *De finibus
matrimonii.—De matrimonii finibus eorumque relatione*

635   Would this lead, perhaps, to Our denying or dimin-
(20, ishing what is good and just in personal values resulting
25,   from matrimony and its realization? Certainly not, be-
30)   cause the Creator has designed that for the procreation
of a new life human beings made of flesh and blood,
gifted with soul and heart, shall be called upon as men
and not as animals deprived of reason to be the authors
of their posterity. It is for this end that the Lord desires
the union of husband and wife. Indeed, the Holy Scripture says of God that He created man to His image and
He created him male and female (a), and willed—as is
repeatedly affirmed in Holy Writ—that "a man shall
leave mother and father, and shall cleave to his wife:
and they shall be two in one flesh" (b).

636   All this is therefore true and desired by God. But,
(19, on the other hand, it must not be divorced completely
20,   from the primary function of matrimony—the procreation

et ordine his postremis annis nonnulla typis edita pro-
dierunt, quae vel asserunt finem primarium matrimonii
non esse prolis generationem, vel fines secundaros non
esse fini primario subordinatos, sed ab eo indipendentes.
"Hisce in elucubrationibus primarius coniugii finis
alius ab aliis designatur, ut ex. gr.,: coniugem per om-
nimodam vitae actionisque communionem complementum
ac personalis perfectio; coniugem mutuus amor atque
unio fovenda ac perficienda per psychicam et somaticam
propriae personae traditionem; et huiusmodi alia plura.
"In iisdem scriptis interdum verbis in documentis Ecclesiae occurrentibus (uti sunt v. gr. finis primarius,
secondarius) sensus tribuitur, qui cum his vocibus,
secundum communem theologorum usum, non congruit.
"Novatus hic cogitandi et loquendi modus natus est ad
errores et incertitudines fovendas; quibus avertendis..."
(AAS 36 (1944) 103).
635a Gen. 1:27.   635b Gen. 2:24; Matt. 19:5; Eph. 5:31.

of offspring (a). Not only the common work of external 29,
life, but even all personal enrichment—spiritual and intel- 30,
lectual—all that in married love as such is most spiritual 31)
and profound, has been placed by the will of the Creator
and of nature at the service of posterity (b). The perfect
married life, of its very nature, also signifies the total
devotion of parents to the well-being of their children,
and married love in its power and tenderness is itself a
condition of the sincerest care of the offspring and the
guarantee of its realization (c).

To reduce the common life of husband and wife and 637
the conjugal act to a mere organic function for the (20,
transmission of seed would be but to convert the domes- 31,
tic hearth, the family sanctuary, into a biological labora- 94)
tory. Therefore, in Our allocution of September 29, 1949,
to the International Congress of Catholic Doctors, We
expressly excluded artificial insemination in marriage.
The conjugal act, in its natural structure, is a personal
action, a simultaneous and immediate cooperation of
husband and wife, which by the very nature of the agents
and the propriety of the act, is the expression of the reciprocal gift, which, according to Holy Writ, effects the
union "in one flesh" (a).

> 636a *La fuzione primaria del matrimonio, cioè dal servizio
> per la vita nuova.*
> 636b *Non soltanto l'opera comune della vita esterna, ma
> anche tutto l'arricchimento personale, lo stesso arricchi-
> mento intellettuale e spirituale, perfino tutto ciò che vi
> è di più spirituale e profondo nell'amore coniugale come
> tale, è stato messo, per volontà della natura e del Crea-
> tore, al servizio della discendenza.*
> 636c Cf. St. Thomas, *Summa th.*, p. 3, q. 29, a. 2, in c.;
> *Suppl.* q. 49, art. 2, ad 1.
> 637a *L'atto coniugale, nella sua struttura naturale, è
> un'azione personale, una cooperazione simultanea e im-*

638
(11,
20)
That is much more than the union of two genes, which can be effected even by artificial means, that is, without the natural action of husband and wife. The conjugal act, ordained and desired by nature, is a personal cooperation, to which husband and wife, when contracting marriage, exchange the right.

639
(12,
19,
20,
31,
94)
Therefore, when this act in its natural form is from the beginning perpetually impossible, the object of the matrimonial contract is essentially vitiated. This is what we said on that occasion: "Let it not be forgotten: only the procreation of a new life according to the will and the design of the Creator carries with it in a stupendous degree of perfection the intended ends. It is at the same time in conformity with the spiritual and bodily nature and the dignity of the married couple, in conformity with the happy and normal development of the child" (a).

640
(30,
31,
107)
Advise the fiancée or the young married woman who comes to seek your advice about the values of matrimonial life that these personal values, both in the sphere of the body and the senses and in the sphere of the spirit, are truly genuine, but that the Creator has placed them not in the first, but in the second degree of the scale of values.

> mediata dei coniugi, la quale, per la stessa natura degli agenti e la proprietá dell'atto, è l'espressione del dono reciproco, che, secondo la parola della Scrittura, effettua l'unione "in una carne sola"—cf. above, n. 555.
>
> 639a "Solo la procreazione di una nuova vita secondo la volontà e il disegno del Creatore porta con sè, in un grado stupendo di perfezione, l'attuazione dei fini intesi. Essa è al tempo stesso conforme alla natura corporale e spirituale e alla dignità degli sposi, allo sviluppo normale e felice del bambino (AAS, XLI, 560, 1949, cf. above, n. 557).

Free renunciation to fatherhood

To these considerations must be added another **641** which tends to be forgotten. All these secondary values *(19,* of the procreative sphere and activity are included in *23,* the ambit of the specific function of husband and wife, *26,* which is to be authors and educators of a new life (a). A *31,* high and noble duty! Yet one which does not pertain to *110)* the essence of a complete human being, because, if the natural generative tendency does not come to its realization, there is no diminution of the human person, in any way or degree. The renunciation of this realization is not—especially if made for more sublime purposes— a mutilation of personal and spiritual values (b). Of such free renunciation for the love of God's kingdom the Lord has said:*"Non omnes capiunt verbum istud, sed quibus datum est*—Not all can accept this teaching; but to those to whom it has been given" (c).

To exalt beyond measure, as it is often done today, **642** the generative function, even in the just and moral form *(110)* of married life, is therefore not only an error and an aberration; it also bears with itself the danger of intellectual and affective error, capable of preventing and stifling good and lofty sentiments, especially in youth which is still without experience and ignorant of life's delusions. For what normal man, healthy in body and

641a *Tutti questi valori secondari della sfera e dell'attività generativa rientrano nell'ambito dell'ufficio specifico dei coniugi, che è di essere autori ed educatori della nuova vita.*

641b *La rinunzia a quell'attuazione non è—specialmente se fatta per i più nobili motivi—una mutilazione dei valori personali e spirituali.*

641c Matt. 19:11.

soul, would like to belong to the number of those deficient in character and spirit?

May your apostolate enlighten the minds and inculcate in them this just order of values, there where you exercise your profession, so that men may conform to it in their judgments and conduct!

Human dignity in the conjugal act

643
(30,
33)
This explanation of Ours on the functions of your professional apostolate would be incomplete, if We did not add further a few more words about the defense of human dignity in the use of the procreative faculty.

The same Creator, Who in His bounty and wisdom willed to make use of the work of man and woman, by uniting them in matrimony, for the preservation and propagation of the human race, has also decreed that in this function the parties should experience pleasure and happiness of body and spirit. Husband and wife, therefore, by seeking and enjoying this pleasure do no wrong whatever. They accept what the Creator has destined for them.

644
(26,
33)
Nevertheless, here also, husband and wife must know how to keep themselves within the limits of a just moderation. As with the pleasure of food and drink so with the sexual they must not abandon themselves without restraint to the impulses of the senses. The right rule is this: the use of the natural procreative disposition is morally lawful in matrimony only, in the service of and in accordance with the ends of marriage itself. Hence it follows that only in marriage with the observing of this rule is the desire and fruition of this pleasure and of this satisfaction lawful. For the pleasure is subordinate to the law of the action whence it derives, and not vice

versa—the action to the law of pleasure. And this law, so very reasonable, concerns not only the substance but also the circumstances of the action, so that, even when the substance of the act remains morally safe, it is possible to sin in the way it is performed (a).

The transgression of this law is as old as original sin. But in our times there is the risk that one may lose sight of the fundamental principle itself. At present, in fact, it is usual to support in words and in writing (and this by Catholics in certain circles) the necessary autonomy, the proper end, and the proper value of sexuality and of its realization, independently of the purpose of procreating a new life. There is a tendency to subject to a new examination and to a new norm the very order established by God and not to admit any other restraint to the way of satisfying the instinct than by considering the essence of the instinctive act. In addition there would be substituted a license to serve blindly and without restraint the whims and instincts of nature in the place of the moral obligations to dominate passions; and this sooner or later cannot but turn out to be a danger to morals, conscience and human dignity.

645
*(31,
33,
61,
62,
68,
91,
103)*

If nature had aimed exclusively, or at least in the first place, at a reciprocal gift and possession of the married couple in joy and delight, and if it had ordered that act only to make happy in the highest possible

646
*(19,
23,
25,*

644a *Poichè il godimento sottostà alla legge dell'azione, dalla quale esso deriva e non viceversa, l'azione alla legge del godimento. E questa legge, così ragionevole, riguarda non solo la sostanza, ma anche le circostanze dell'azione, di guisa che, pur restando salva la sostanza dell'atto, si può peccare nel modo di compierlo.*

31, degree their personal experience, and not to stimulate
91) them to the service of life, then the Creator would have
adopted another plan in forming and constituting the
natural act. Now, instead, all this is subordinated and
ordered to that unique, great law of the *"generatio et educatio prolis,"* namely the accomplishment of the primary
end of matrimony as the origin and source of life (a).

647   Unfortunately, unceasing waves of hedonism invade
(61, the world and threaten to submerge in the swelling tide
91) of thoughts, desires and acts the whole marital life, not
without serious dangers and grave prejudice to the
primary duty of husband and wife.

648   This anti-Christian hedonism too often is not
(61, ashamed to elevate itself to a doctrine, inculcating the
91) ardent desire to make always more intense the pleasure
in the preparation and in the performance of the conjugal
union; as if in matrimonial relations the whole moral
law were reduced to the normal performance of the act
itself, and as if all the rest, in whatever way it is done,
were to be justified by the expression of mutual affection,
sanctified by the Sacrament of Matrimony, worthy of
praise and reward before God and conscience. There is
no thought at all of the dignity of man and of the Christian—a dignity—which restrains the excess of sensuality.

649   No; the gravity and sanctity of the Christian moral
(33, law do not admit an unchecked satisfaction of the sexual
61) instinct tending only to pleasure and enjoyment; they
do not permit rational man to let himself be mastered

646a *Ora invece è insomma tutto subordinato e ordinato a
quell' unica grande legge della* "generatio et educatio
prolis", *vale a dire al compimento del fine primario del
matrimonio come origine e sorgente della vita.*

to such an extent, neither as regards the substance nor the circumstances of the act (a).

There are some who would allege that happiness **650** in marriage is in direct proportion to the reciprocal *(61,* enjoyment in conjugal relations. It is not so: indeed, *34,* happiness in marriage is in direct proportion to the *103)* mutual respect of the partners, even in their intimate relations; not that they regard as immoral and refuse what nature offers and what the Creator has given, but because this respect, and the mutual esteem which it produces, is one of the strongest elements of a pure love, and for this reason all the more tender.

In the performance of your profession, do your ut- **651** most to repel the attack of this refined hedonism void *(31,* of spiritual values and thus unworthy of Christian mar- *62,* ried couples. Show how nature has given, truly, the in- *103,* stinctive desire for pleasure and sanctions it in the lawful *107)* marriage, not as an end in itself, but rather for the service of life. Banish from your heart that cult of pleasure, and do your best to prevent the spreading of a literature which considers as its duty the description in full of the intimacies of married life under the pretext of instructing, guiding and reassuring. In general, common sense, natural instinct and a brief instruction on the clear and simple maxims of Christian moral law, are suffcient to give peace to the tender conscience of married people. If, in certain circumstances, a fiancée or a young married woman were in need of further enlightenment on some particular point, it is your duty to give them tactfully

649a *Essa non permette all'uomo ragionevole di lasciarsi dominare sino a tal punto, nè quanto alla sostanza, nè quanto alle circostanze dell'atto.*

an explanation in conformity with natural law and with a healthy Christian conscience.

652 This teaching of Ours has nothing to do with
(199) Manichaeism and Jansenism, as some would have people believe in order to justify themselves. It is only a defense of the honor of Christian matrimony and of the personal dignity of the married couple.

(*Conditions for a fruitful apostolate on the part of midwives.*)

ABUSE OF SPORT

All. to the representatives of the Sporting Press, November 11, 1951.

(*Conditions of a good influence of sport.*)

653 Sport should never compromise the marital couple's
(96) intimacy or the holy joys of family life. Still less must it enlarge its demands, inasmuch as the hard necessities of life, separating by necessity father, mother, sons and daughters for daily work, already make their load excessively felt. Family life is so precious that it cannot be refused this protection.

RESPECT FOR LIFE

All. to the Associations of the large families, November 26, 1951.

654 In the order of nature, among social institutions
(99, there is no other that is dearer to the Church than the
105) family. Christ has elevated Matrimony to the dignity of a Sacrament, which is as it were the root of the family. The family itself has always found, and will always find, in the Church a defender, a support, a protector in all

that concerns its inviolable rights, its liberty, the exercise
of its high function.

Therefore, We feel a particular happiness, beloved
sons and daughters, in giving a welcome in Our home
to the national Congress of the "Family Front" and of
the large family, and in expressing Our satisfaction for
your efforts towards the ends at which you aim, and
Our paternal blessing for their successful realization.

A family movement such as yours, whose aim is to **655**
produce fully in the people the idea of the Christian fam- *(105,*
ily, cannot fail, under the impulse of the interior force *109)*
which animates it and of the necessities of the people
itself, in the midst of which it lives and grows, to place
itself at the service of that threefold aim which forms the
object of your cares: the influence to be exercised on
legislation in the vast field which immediately or mediate-
ly affects the family; solidarity between families; Christian culture of the family. This third object is the fundamental one, the first two must contribute to second it and
promote it.

We have often and on the most varied occasions **656**
spoken on behalf of the Christian family, and in most *(60,*
cases to come to its help or to call others thereto to save *97)*
it from the most serious dangers; above all to succor it
in the calamity of war. The damage wrought by the
First World War was far from being fully repaired, when
the second even more terrible conflagration came to
increase it to the uttermost. There will be need of time
and efforts on the part of men and of an even greater
divine help before the deep wounds inflicted on the family
by these two wars begin to heal extensively. Another
evil, also partly due to devastating wars, but a conse-

quence of over-population and of individual tendencies inexpedient and self-interested, is the housing crisis; all those, legislators, statesmen, members of social welfare, who endeavor to find a remedy accomplish, even if only indirectly, an apostolate of eminent value.

657
(97,
105)
The same is true for the struggle against the scourge of unemployment, for the establishment of a sufficient family wage, so that the mother is not obliged, as too often happens, to look for work outside the home, but may devote herself to a greater extent to her husband and children. Work for schools and for religious education is also a precious contribution towards the welfare of the family; as is also the encouraging in it of a healthy naturalness and simplicity of manners, a reinforcement of religious beliefs, a development of an atmosphere of Christian purity, suitable for protecting it from those harmful external influences and from all those morbid excitements that arouse the sordid passions in the minds of adolescents.

658
(44,
66)
But there is an even deeper misery, from which the family must be preserved; it is that debasing slavery to which it is reduced by a mentality tending to make it a mere organism at the service of the social community, in order to procreate for such a community a sufficient mass of "human material."

Conjugal morality

659
(52,
61)
Another danger threatens the family, a danger no means recent, but having its roots in the past, which, however, is growing rapidly, and can become disastrous because it attacks the family in its very germ; We mean the extensive revolution in conjugal morals.

In the course of the last few years, We have taken every opportunity to expound one or other of the essential points of that morality, and more recently to indicate it in its entirety, not only by confuting the errors which corrupt it, but also by showing positively its meaning, duty, and importance, its values for the happiness of the married couple, the children and the whole family, for stability and greater social benefit from the domestic hearth even to the State and to the Church herself.

At the center of this doctrine matrimony appeared as an institution at the service of life. In strict relation with this principle, in accordance with the constant teaching of the Church, We expounded a thesis which is one of the essential foundations not only of conjugal morality, but also of social morality in general, that is, that the direct attack on innocent human life, as a means to an end—in the present case to the end of saving another life—is illicit (a). **660**
(19, 52, 89)

Respect for life

Innocent human life, in whatever condition it may be, from the first moment of its existence, is to be preserved from any direct voluntary attack. This is a fundamental right of the human person, of general value in the Christian concept of life; valid both for the still hidden life in the womb and for the new born babe; and opposed to direct abortion as it is to the direct killing of **661** *(89)*

660a *Noi, secondo l'insegnamento costante della Chiesa, abbiamo illustrato una tesi che è uno dei fondamenti essenziali non solo della morale coniugale, ma anche della morale sociale in genere: cioè che il diretto attentato alla vita umana innocente, come mezzo al fine,—nel caso presente, al fine di salvare un'altra vita,—è illicito.*

the child, before, during, and after birth (a). No matter what the distinction between those different moments in the development of the life, already born or still to be born, for profane and ecclesiastical law and for certain civil and penal consequences—according to the moral law, in all these cases it is a matter of a grave and illicit attempt on inviolable human life.

662
(89) This principle holds good both for the mother as well as the child. Never and in no case has the Church taught that the life of the child must be preferred to that of the mother. It is erroneous to place the question with this alternative: either the life of the child or that of the mother. No; neither the life of the mother nor of the child may be submitted to an act of direct suppression. Both for the one and the other the demand cannot be but this: to use every means to save the life of both the mother and the child (a).

663
(89) To seek always new ways to assure the life of both is one of the most beautiful and noble aspirations of medicine. If, notwithstanding the progress of science, there still remain, and will remain in future, cases in which the mother's death is certain, when she desires that the life in her womb continue its life's course, and does not desire to destroy it, thus violating God's com-

661a *E' questo un fondamentale diritto della persona umana, di valore generale nella concezione cristiana della vita; valido così per la vita ancora nascosta nel seno della madre, come per la vita già sbocciata fuori di lei; così contro l'aborto diretto, come contro la diretto uccisione del bambino prima, durante e dopo il parto.*

662a Cf. Pius XI, Encycl. *Casti Connubii,* December 31, 1930; cf. above, n. 322 ff. Cf. AAS, 22, pp. 562-563.

mandment: do not kill! (a)—there remains for man, who to the last moment shall have attempted to help and to save, only to bow down with respect to the laws of nature and to the dispositions of divine Providence.

But—it is objected—the life of the mother, especially **664** the mother of a large family, is far superior in value to *(89)* that of the still unborn child. The application of the theory of the scale of values to the case which here concerns us has already been favorably received in juridical discussions. The reply to this tormenting objection is not difficult. The inviolability of the life of an innocent person does not depend on its greater or lesser value (a). More than ten years ago, the Church formally condemned the killing of a life deemed "useless" (b); and those who know the sad antecedents that provoked such a condemnation, those who know how to ponder the disastrous consequences that would follow were the sanctity of an innocent life to be measured according to its value, can easily appreciate the motives which led to such a disposition. On the other hand, who can judge with certainty which of the two lives is in reality the more precious? Who can know what path that child will follow and to what heights of perfection and of work it will reach? Here, two greatnesses are compared, about one of which nothing is known. (*An example.*)

It has been Our intention here to use always the **665** expressions "*direct* attempt on the life of the innocent *(90)*

663a Cf. Exodus 20:13.
664a *L'inviolabilità della vita di un innocente non dipende dal suo maggiore o minor valore.*
664b Decree of the Holy Office, 2nd December, 1940; see above n. 598a.

person", "*direct* killing." The reason is that if, for example, the safety of the life of the future mother, independently of her state of pregnancy, might call for an urgent surgical operation, or any other therapeutic application, which would have as an accessory consequence, in no way desired nor intended, but *inevitable,* the death of the foetus, such an act could not be called a *direct* attempt on the innocent life. In these conditions the operation can be lawful, as can other similar medical interventions, provided that it be a matter of great importance, such as life, and that it is not possible to postpone it till the birth of the child, or to have recourse to any other efficacious remedy (a).

666
(19) Therefore, since the primary office of matrimony is to be at the service of life, Our special regard and Our paternal gratitude go to those generous husbands and wives who, for the love of God and trusting in Him, courageously raise a numerous family.

Birth control

667
(28, The Church, on the other hand, can understand, with sympathy and comprehension, the real difficulties

665a *Noi abbiamo di proposito usato sempre l'espressione "attentato diretto alla vita dell'innocente", "uccisione diretta". Poichè se, per esempio, la salvezza della vita della futura madre, indipendentemente dal suo stato di gravidanza, richiedesse urgentemente un atto chirurgico, o altra applicazione terapeutica, che avrebbe come conseguenza accessoria, in nessun modo voluta nè intesa, ma inevitabile, la morte del feto un tale atto non potrebbe più dirsi un diretto attentato alla vita innocente. In queste condizioni l'operazione può essere lecita, come altri simili interventi medici, sempre che si tratti di un bene di alto valore, qual è la vita, e non sia possibile di ricorrere ad altro efficace rimedio.*

of matrimonial life in these our days. For this reason, in *90)*
Our last address on conjugal morality (a), We affirmed
the legitimacy and at the same time the limits—truly
very wide—of that controlling of births which, unlike
the so-called "birth control," is compatible with God's
law. It can be hoped (but in such matters the Church
naturally leaves the judgment to medical science) that
for such a lawful method a sufficiently certain basis can
be found, and recent research seems to confirm this hope.

To overcome the many trials of conjugal life there **668**
is above all the most powerful aids of a lively Faith and *(11,*
a frequenting of the Sacraments, whence emerge tor- *60,*
rents of strength whose efficacy is hardly clearly known *61,*
by those who are outside of the Church. We wish to *104)*
close Our speech by recalling these sublime aids. It may
also happen to you, beloved sons and daughters, that,
one day or another, you may feel your courage being
troubled by the violent storm raging about you, and,
even more dangerously, in the midst of your family, by
the doctrines which subvert the wholesome and normal
concept of Christian marriage. Be trustful! Nature's energies and, above all, those of grace with which God
has enriched your souls by the means of the Sacrament
of matrimony are like a solid rock, against which the
waves of a stormy sea break up powerless. And, if the
tragedies of the war and post-war period have inflicted
upon matrimony and the family wounds which are still
bleeding, nonetheless during those years also, the constant fidelity, the sound perseverance of married couples,
and maternal love standing firm in the face of innumer-

667a Cf. above, n. 615.

able difficulties, have in many cases truly and splendid-
ly triumphed.

IN DEFENSE OF MATRIMONY

Radio Message to Austrian Catholics, September
14, 1952.

(*Religious renewal.—Defending the school.*)

669
(8,
Intent on preserving your faith, guard the sanctity
of "matrimony"!

74,
99,
103)
Let the "conclusion" of matrimony be holy for you.
For a Catholic, only a religious marriage, and never an
exclusively civil marriage, is a true marriage. If the
"people's will" has any meaning in the national life, insist
that, in matrimonial legislation, there be held in due account the will which animates the greater majority of
your people.

670
(43,
103)
Let conjugal "life" be holy for you. Let what Our
Predecessor, Pius XI, of happy memory, pointed out in
his Encyclical "Casti connubii" (a), and what We said
last autumn, in an allocution on the moral postulates of
married life, be a rule for you, keeping in mind—as far
as is possible—the circumstances of the present time.
You know, beloved sons, that the most elementary care
for the existence and future of your people coincides,
here, with the demands of the natural law and of the
Church.

671
(60,
96,
Let "family" life be holy for you: for you, parents,
the Christian education of your children; for you, children, respect and obedience towards your parents; for

670a Cf. above, n. 263ff and 593 ff.

all of you, family prayer in common and the Christian *103)*
celebration of Sunday. Let Sunday be and always remain
the Lord's day, the day of rest for the body and soul,
the family day. Wherever there is good will, the serenity and Christian pleasure of Sunday can still give the
family that cohesion which daily work with its separating tendencies cannot provide. Take a stand to prevent
physical culture, pagan exaggerations, and the desire of
pleasure succeeding in secularizing the Sunday and
shattering the family once and for all.

(*Social questions.*)

CHOICE OF STATE OF LIFE

All. to women Religious Superiors, September 15,
1952.

(*Crisis of female vocations.*)

We do not wish to treat in detail of this crisis which **672**
causes Us grave anxiety. The occasion will be given us *(110)*
in other circumstances. Today We wish to address Ourselves to those only who, priests or lay persons, preachers,
speakers or writers, have no longer a word of approval
or praise for virginity consecrated to Christ; who for
years, notwithstanding the warnings of the Church and
contrary to her thought, have conceded to matrimony
preference in principle over virginity; who go so far as
to present it as the only means capable of assuring the
development and natural perfection of the human personality: let those who write and speak in such a way
be conscious of their responsibility before God and the
Church. They must be numbered among the prime causes
responsible for the phenomenon which We recalled above
with sadness: that while in the Christian world and even

outside of it, the call for Catholic Sisters is louder today than ever, time after time there must be given a negative answer; matters have reached a stage where it is necessary to abandon ancient activities, hospitals and educational institutions—all because vocations are not sufficient for their needs.

(*Practical proposals.*)

MECHANIZED SOCIETY

Radio Message to the World, December 24, 1952. (*Modern problems.—Industrialization.*)

673
(37) ... The impersonal character of such a world is in sharp contrast with the completely personal character of those institutions which the Creator has given to human society. Matrimony, in fact, and the family, the State, private property, all tend by nature to form and develop man as a person, to protect him and render him capable of contributing, with his voluntary contribution and personal responsibility, towards the maintenance and the development, likewise personal, of social life.

(*Problems of conscience in modern society.*)

674
(23,
56,
66,
88) Modern society, in fact, wishing to plan and organize, comes into conflict, owing to its mechanical conceptions, with all that lives and that cannot, therefore, be subjected to quantitative calculations; more precisely, with those rights which man exercises in accordance with nature, on his own personal responsibility, as author of new lives, of which he is always the principal guardian. Such intimate conflicts between systems and conscience are veiled under the names: the problem of the birth rate and the problem of emigration.

When husband and wife intend to remain faithful **675**
to the inviolable laws of life established by the Creator, *(66,*
or when to safeguard this fidelity they seek to detach *88)*
themselves from the straitened circumstances which oppress them in their own country, and find no other
remedy than emigration—in other times prompted by
the desire of gain, today often inflicted by misery—
behold, they come up against an inexorable law, against
the precautions of organized society, the bare calculation
which has already determined how many persons in
given circumstances a country can or must support, at
present or in the future. And as part of the preventive
calculations an attempt is made to mechanize consciences:
lo and behold! public meetings advocating birth control, the pressure of the administrative apparatus of
so-called social security, and the influence exerted on
public opinion in the same sense, and finally the natural
right of the person not to be hindered in emigration or
immigration not recognized or practically annulled under
the pretext of a common welfare falsely understood or
applied, but which legislative or administrative measures
sanction and make available.

These examples are sufficient to show how organi- **676**
zation inspired by cold calculation, in the attempt to *(66,*
force life between the narrow frames of fixed laws, al- *88)*
most as if it were a static phenomenon, becomes a nega-
tion of and offense to life itself and to its essential character which is one of unceasing dynamism, communicated
to it by nature and manifested in the most varied range
of individual circumstances. Its consequences are very
serious Numerous letters which We receive reveal the
affliction of worthy and good Christians, whose con-

science is tormented by a rigid incomprehension of a society inflexible in its orders; which like a machine is moved according to calculations, and without pity bears hard upon and passes over the problems which personally and profoundly touch them in their moral life.

677   We certainly won't deny the fact that this or that
(88) country is at present burdened by relative overpopulation. But wishing to escape from embarrassment by using the formula that the number of inhabitants must be regulated according to the public economy is equivalent to upsetting the order of nature and the whole psychological and moral world with which it is bound up. What an error it would be to blame the natural laws for the present anxieties, when it is obvious that these derive from the lack of solidarity between men and peoples themselves!

(*Persecutions.—Miserable state of the poor.—Appeal in their favor.*)

PREPARATION FOR MARRIAGE
.

All. to the Italian association of Catholic Teachers, March 19, 1953.

(*The problems of adult education.*)

678   The importance of politics and the far-reaching in-
(37, fluence of economics in the world of today naturally
42, stimulate the teachers of adults to give preference to
43) these subjects. But is it not perhaps too often forgotten that the basis of society, the very center of education and of every culture, is the family? Does not the "depersonalization" of social relations which We recently lamented in Our Christmas message arise particularly from this unawareness? The worker is not primarily a

producer or a voter, but a human being, eager for affection and the opportunity of self-education, who strongly desires to transmit to others the most intimate treasures of his heart, and not only the work of his hands.

Could one believe that it is not necessary to learn **679** the supreme art of governing the family unit, wherein *(37,* man uses, as far as possible, all his faculties of mind and *107)* heart, all his qualities and resources? The bad outcome of many marriages, the waywardness of unhappy children neglected by their families, prove the contrary. It is essential that adult education should not lose sight of the importance of preparing young people for matrimony and for the serious obligations of fathers and mothers of families. Before choosing a life's work, the young should subordinate their choice of an occupation and a place to live to considerations of human and Christian wisdom which foresee and appraise spiritual, economic, and physical possibilities, and not take such an important step without careful thought. Adult education ought to aid and enlighten them on the needs and difficulties of marriage and the setting up of a home.

If the worker is aware of the dignity of his function **680** as a father, and if the mother devotes herself to her *(43,* mission as educator, giving suitable instruction and *107)* guidance, the life-cell of society will be healthy and strong. Mothers must acquire the elementary knowledge necessary for the government of a family, the art of keeping a house in order, of balancing a budget, useful ideas about bringing up children, and, above all, enough understanding of the rules of pedagogy to profit by the experience of others, without placing too much confidence in their maternal instinct, which, of itself, will not always and surely keep them from harmful mistakes.

681 As for the father of the family, one of his principal
*(107)*functions undoubtedly is to procure for his wife and children the financial means indispensable for life. Is he not, however, above all, the enlightened and wise guide, strong in his own personal experience, a prudent counsellor in matters regarding the important laws of life and the intimate aspirations and difficulties of those dear to him, to whom he gives a spiritual support more valuable and more necessary than material protection? If the schools of popular education should even succeed in initiating their pupils properly in the art of education, what inestimable service they would render to the family, to society and to the Church!

SEXUAL EDUCATION

All. to the V Congress of Clinical Psychotherapy, April 13, 1953.

(*Man as a psychical, organic and social entity.*)

682 A word also on the method sometimes employed by
(61, the psychologist to set "ego" free from its inhibitions,
107) in the case of aberrations in the sexual field. We refer to complete sexual initiation, which would not pass over anything in silence, leave nothing obscure. Is there not therein a harmful exaggeration of the value of knowledge in these matters? There is, however, an effective sexual education which, quite safely, teaches calmly and objectively what the young person should know for his own personal conduct and his relationship with those with whom he is brought into contact. For the rest,

special stress will be laid, in sexual education, as indeed, in all education, upon self-mastery and religious
training. The Holy See published certain norms in this
connection shortly after the Encyclical of Pius XI on
Christian Marriage (a). These have not been rescinded,
either expressly or "via facti" (b).

(*Man as a transcendent unity tends towards God.*)

GOAL OF RELIGIOUS ACTION

Radio Message to the Catholic Congress of Denmark, May 24, 1953.

(*Past action of the Church in Denmark.—Necessity
of present action.*)

682a Cf. above, n. 407a.
682b On the 30th June, 1952, the Supreme Congregation
of the Holy Office, published the following Monitum:
—"*Gravi cum sollicitudine Apostolica Sedes animadvertit
non paupos scriptores his ultimis temporibus, de vita
coniugali agentes, passim palam et minute ad singula
eam spectantia inverecunde descendere*: *praeterea non-
nullos actum quemdam,* amplexum reservatum *nuncupa-
tum, describere, laudare et suadere.*

"*Ne in re tanti momenti, quae matrimonii sanctitatem et
animarum salutem respicit, munere suo deficiat, Suprema
Sacra Congregatio S. Officii, de expresso mandato SS.
mi D.N.D. Pii, divina Providentia Pp XII, omnes prae-
dictos scriptores graviter monet, ut ab huiusmodi agendi
ratione desistant. Sacros quoque Pastores enixe horatur
ut in his rebus sedulo advigilent et quae opportuna sint
remedia sollicite apponant.*

"*Sacerdos autem, in cura animarum et in conscientiis
dirigendis, nunquam, sive sponte sive interrogati, ita
loqui praesumant quasi ex parte legis christianae contra
amplexum reservatum nihil esset obiicendum*". Cf. AAS
44 (1952) 546.

683
(23,
43,
103
104)
If We had to point out to you a work worthy of particular attention, We would recall to your mind the perfect Christian family, whose fertile soil is constituted by the conjugal life lived in purity, whose sun is constituted by the wife and the mother who in self-abandonment and love is capable of reaching the complete sacrifice of herself; the family in which children grow up unstained, proud of their father in the sense that he precedes them in the fear of God, gives them the example of the fulfillment of his vocation and the faithful care of those dear to him; the family which is based on its consecration by prayer in common each day and which is surrounded by that peace which only Christ can give. Beloved sons and daughters, you could not desire a better gift from the Church, for yourselves and your country than the perfect Christian family.

(Best wishes and blessings.)

.

RIGHT TO MATRIMONY

All. to the "Primum Symposium Geneticae Medicae," September 7, 1953.

(Recent progress in genetics.—Heredity and evolution.—Exigencies of scientific knowledge.—Practical genetics.)

684
(56,
88,
109)
In fact, there are certain defensive measures in genetics and eugenics which moral common sense, and especially Christian morals, must reject both in principle and in practice.

Amongst the methods contrary to morality, there must be included "racialism," mentioned above, and *eugenic sterilization.* Our Predecessor, Pius XI (a), and We Ourselves (b), were obliged to declare contrary to the natural law not only eugenic sterilization but every direct sterilization, whether temporary or permanent, of an innocent person, either man or woman. Our opposition to sterilization has been, and still remains firm, for although racialism has come to an end, there are persons who are still desirous to suppress by sterilization a lineage affected by hereditary diseases, and indeed attempt to do so.

Another method leading to the same end, *A ban on marriage,* namely making marriage physically impossible through segregation of those whose heredity is defective, must also be rejected. The purpose intended is good in itself, but the means of attaining it violate a person's right to contract and use marriage. When a person with an hereditary defect is unable to behave like a human being, and in consequence, is unfit to contract marriage, or when, later, he becomes incapable of claiming by an act of free will the right he has acquired through valid marriage, then he can be prevented by lawful means from procreating a new life. Outside these cases, the banning of marriage or of marital intercourse for biological, genetical or eugenical motives, is an injustice, no matter who it is who issues that prohibition, whether a private individual or a public authority. **685** *(12, 56, 88, 90, 109)*

Certainly it is right, and in the greater number of cases it is a duty, to point out to those whose heredity is beyond doubt very defective, the burden they are **686** *(12, 56,*

684a Cf. above n. 406—407.
684b Cf. above, n. 614.

88, about to impose on themselves, upon their partner in
109) marriage and upon their offspring. That burden might
perhaps become unbearable. To advise against, however,
is not to forbid. There might be other motives, especially
of a moral or personal nature, which are of such importance as to authorize the contracting of marriage and its
use even in the circumstances just mentioned.

687   In order to justify direct eugenic sterilization, or the
(12, alternative of segregation, it is claimed that the right
56,   to marriage and to the marriage act is not affected by
88,   sterilization, even though it be prenuptial, total, and
109) certainly definitive. This attempt at justification is
doomed to failure. If, in the judgment of a prudent
person, the fact in question is doubtful, the unsuitableness
for marriage is also doubtful, and then one must apply
the principle that the right to marry persists until such
time as the contrary is proved with certainty. In this
case, too, marriage must be permitted; but the question
of its objective validity remains open. If, on the contrary,
there is no doubt about the above-mentioned fact of
sterilization, it is premature to say that the right to
marry remains unimpaired notwithstanding, and, in any
case, this statement leaves room for most serious doubts.

688   There remains to be mentioned other mistaken
(56, attempts to avoid hereditary defects, which the text
89,   quoted above calls "preventive means and abortive
109) practices." These do not even come under consideration
in eugenics, because by their very nature they are to be
rejected.

689   That, Gentlemen, is what We had to say to you.
(56, The practical aims being pursued by genetics are noble

and worthy of recognition and encouragement. Would 88,
that your science, in weighing up the means devised 89,
to achieve those ends, could remain always conscious 109)
of the fundamental difference that exists between the
animal and vegetable world on the one hand and man
on the other! In the first case the means of bettering
species and race are entirely at the disposal of science.
But where man is concerned, genetics are always dealing
with personal beings, with inviolable rights, with
individuals who, for their part, are bound by inflexible
moral laws, in using their power to raise up a new life.
Thus the Creator Himself has established certain barriers in the moral domain, which no human power has
authority to remove.

PREPARATION FOR MARRIAGE

All. to the Chaplains of the Italian Youth of Catholic
Action (G.I.A.C.), September 8, 1953.

(*Dangers encountered by youth.—Drive out the
enemy, wherever he may have already penetrated into
the inner circle of youth associations.—Instruction and
education.—Selecting and forming priestly vocations.*)

Other youths, and they are the vast majority, are **690**
called by God to cooperate with Him in the procreation of *(20,*
new life. Put before them the beauty of Christian love, *107)*
and, in order to prepare them to bring up an honest and
happy family, let them taste the happiness of purity un-
spoiled.

(*Youth must be ready to spurn mediocrity.*)

TRANSMISSION OF HUMAN LIFE

Letter of Msgr. Montini to His Eminence Cardinal Siri, on the occasion of the XXVI Social Week of Italian Catholics, September 27, 1953.

(*Demography and economics.*)

691
(23,
26,
27,
37,
89,
103)
So that the treatment of such a delicate theme may have useful results, it will be of benefit to the speakers of the Congress to reflect on a few teachings of the magisterium of the Church which will be a guide and light for them in the course of the work.

Let them remember first of all that no solution of demographic problems will ever be able to be considered as corresponding to justice and truth if it does not hold in due count the holy and sacred values of human life, or if in some way it prescinds from the respect of those rules which govern its orderly transmission. This finds its natural application in the family circle, in the dignity of conjugal relations and embraces the procreation and education of the children.

692
(43,
87,
89)
It is criminal, therefore—in no matter justified by a reason of the State or eugenic or economic argument— to make any attack on the life of the child from the womb to the cradle, and here must be included not only the direct killing of the innocent, but also the fraud against the plans of nature which, as such, express the will of the Creator. "If a profound sense of common welfare is the soul of the healthy and strong state," warned the Holy Father in his Radio Message to the Swiss people, on September 20, 1946 (a)—"the dignity and sanctity of

692a Cf; above, n. 530.

conjugal and family life is its backbone. When this suffers great damage, the healthy condition of the State is over and the people sooner or later fall into ruin." For this reason, speaking to the midwives, he inculcated "the apostolate of esteem and love for new life" and defined as "opposed to God's plan and the sentiments of Scripture and to sane reason and the sentiment of nature" (b), the modern mentality hostile to the ideal of a fruitful family.

(The distribution of created gifts among all men.)

MEDICAL PROBLEMS

All. to the XXVI Congress of Urology, October 8, 1953.

(The Holy Father welcomes the members of the Congress.—The question of the amputation of a healthy organ to suppress the disease which afflicts another organ.)

Three things condition the moral permission of a **693** surgical operation requiring an anatomical or functional *(88,* mutilation: firstly, that the preservation or functioning *90)* of a particular organ provokes a serious damage or constitutes a threat to the complete organism; secondly, that this damage cannot be avoided, or at least notably diminished, except by the amputation in question and that its efficacy is well assured; lastly, that it can be reasonably foreseen that the negative effect, namely,

692b Cf. above, n. 605.

the mutilation and its consequences, will be compensated by the positive effect: exclusion of a damage to the whole organism; mitigation of the pain, etc.

694
(88,
90)
The decisive point is not that the amputated or paralyzed organ be itself diseased, but that its preservation or functioning directly or indirectly cause a serious threat to the whole body. It is quite possible that by its healthy functioning a healthy organ exerts a harmful action on a diseased organ, capable of aggravating the evil and its repercussion on the body as a whole. It can also happen that the removal of a healthy organ and the arrest of its normal function halts the evil, for example, growth in the case of cancer; or at all events essentially changes its conditions of existence. If no other means are available, surgical intervention on the healthy organ is permitted in both these cases.

695
(88,
90)
The conclusion at which We have arrived is deduced from the right of disposal which man has received from the Creator as regards his own body, in conformity with the principle of totality, also involved here, by which every particular organ is subordinated to the body as a whole and must be subordinated to it in case of conflict. As a consequence, he who has received the use of the complete organism has the right to sacrifice a particular organ if its preservation or functioning causes a notable damage to the whole, impossible to be avoided in any other way. Since you are sure that, in the case stated, only the removal of the seminal glands permits the disease to be conquered, there is no objection from the moral point of view to this removal.

(At this point, the Holy Father spoke of a special case of surgery, to prevent an erroneous application of the above principle) (a).

We must, however, call your attention to a false application of the principle explained above. **696** *(88)*

It happens often, when gynecological complications call for a surgical operation, or even independently of such an operation, that healthy oviducts are excised or rendered incapable of functioning in order to prevent another pregnancy and the serious dangers which would result therefrom for the health or even the life of the mother, dangers which stem from other diseased organs, such as kidneys, heart, lungs, but which are aggravated in the case of pregnancy. To justify the excision of the oviducts, recourse is had to the principle quoted above, and it is stated that it is morally permissible to operate on healthy organs when the good of the whole requires it.

Here, however, recourse is wrongly made to this principle. For in this case the danger which the mother undergoes does not come either directly or indirectly from the presence or the normal functioning or the oviducts, nor from their influence upon the diseased organs, kidneys, lungs, heart. The danger is verified only if free sexual activity leads to a pregnancy which could threaten these organs already too weak or diseased. The conditions which would justify disposing of a part in favor of the whole in virtue of the principle of totality are lacking. It is not therefore morally permissible to operate on healthy oviducts. **697** *(88)*

696a The complete text of the discourse can be found in AAS 45 (1953) 673-679.

The impediment of impotence

(The second question: the duty of the medical expert in the processes where there is raised the question of nullity of marriage arising from impotence.)

698
(12) To give an accurate reply to this question, it may be useful first to dispel misunderstandings surrounding the concept of "impotentia" or "potentia generandi." Potentia generandi takes on at times such a wide meaning that it includes all that both partners must possess to procreate new life: the internal or external organs, as well as the aptitude for the functions which correspond to the finality of these organs. The term is also used in a narrower sense and includes then only that which is required on the part of the personal activity of the spouses in order that this activity may really engender life, at least by itself and in a general way. In this sense "potentia generandi" is not the same as "potentia coëundi."

699
(12,
27) The conditions required for "potentia coëundi" are determined by nature and are deduced from the mechanism of the act. In this the action of the spouses, from a biological point of view, is at the service of the seminal fluid which it transmits and receives. How can we tell whether the "potentia coëundi" really exists and that consequently the act of the spouses is vested with all its essential elements? A practical criterion, although it is not valid without exception in all cases, is the capacity of performing the external act in a normal way. It is true that an element can be lacking without the partners being aware of it. However, this "signum manifestativum" (indication) must suffice in practice in life, for life requires that for an institution as wide as marriage,

men should possess in normal cases, a sure and easily recognizable means of ascertaining their aptitude for marriage; this is sufficient because nature is wont to build the human organism in such a way that the internal reality corresponds to the external form and structure.

Further, the "potentia coëundi" includes on the part **700** of the husband the capacity to transmit in a natural way *(12)* the liquid of the seminal glands; it is not a question of each of the specific and complementary elements which constitute this liquid. The lack of active sperm is not ordinarily a proof that the husband cannot exercise the function of transmission. Thus, azoospermia, oligospermia, asthenospermia, necrospermia have nothing to do by themselves with "impotentia coëundi" because they concern the constitutive elements of the seminal fluid itself, and not the faculty of transmitting it.

In all this one must hold that this action of the **701** spouses is and remains at the service of a finality: the *(12,* bringing forth of new life. It is erroneous to state that *19)* medicine and biology have a different concept of "potentia coëundi" than theology and canon law, and that the latter means, by this term, something other than what nature and the Creator have determined. You have but to read the text of canon 1068 (a) on the physical power to see that it is dealing not with positive law, but with natural law.

Certainly the good sense of men and the practice **702** of the Church leave no doubt on the fact that personal *(12,* values are involved in marriage and its consummation; *20,* values which surpass by far mere biology and which the *23,* spouses often understand much better than the imme- *26,*

701a Cf. above, n. 468a.

31, diately biological ends of nature. But reason and Reve-
32, lation suggest also and imply that nature introduces this
102) personal and supra-biological element because it calls
to marriage not sensitive beings deprived of reason, but
men endowed with intelligence, heart and personal dignity, and charges them to procreate and educate new
life: because, in marriage, the spouses devote themselves
to a permanent task and to a community of life which
is indissoluble.

Biology and medicine have, today more than ever,
the mission of leading contemporary man toward a
heightened concept of the biological meaning of the collaboration of the spouses and of the reason why nature
authorizes this act only in marriage.

In our day, people heed the physician more readily
than they do the priest. But the physician himself must
possess a sure judgment, guided by nature, and enough
personal independence to remain faithful to it.

703 This being said, We can reply to your question: The
(12, expert examination required by the ecclesiastical tribunal
49, in cases "de nullitate ex titulo impotentiae" generally
51, does not consist in ascertaining the "impotentia gene-
87) randi," but the "impotentia coëundi." "Impotentia generandi," as opposed to "impotentia coëundi," is not sufficient, according to ordinary jurisprudence, to warrant
a sentence of nullity. In the very large majority of the
cases, therefore, the microcospic examination of the
sperms could be omitted. It can be shown in another
way, if there is any usefulness to it, that the seminal
tissue still possesses some functional aptitude and, likewise, that the canals that link these glands with the organs of evacuation are still functioning, are not entirely

deteriorated or definitely obstructed. The examination of the sperm, by itself alone, can hardly give sufficient security.

Besides, the Holy Office has already decided, on August 2, 1929 (a) that "masturbatio directe procurata— ut obtineatur sperma" is not licit, and this, whatever may be the purpose of the test.

(*Duty of the medical expert.*)

MATRIMONIAL CRISIS

Letter to the President of German Catholic Women, November 6, 1953.

(*The dangers of the feminine world.—The multiplicity of the works undertaken.*)

Your association is well aware of two of the gravest **704** problems of our times, the hardship of matrimony and *(59,* social hardship. The hardship of matrimony does not *(101,* diminish nor disappear with the relaxation of teaching *103)* concerning Christian wedlock, rather it is increased. Thereby if there is required for the removal of this hardship the harmonious action of a series of natural and supernatural forces, then they will certainly be provided in the first place by men and women willing to regulate their matrimonial life in perfect conformity to the order established by God.

(*Social crisis.*)

703a AAS 21 (1929), 490.

THE PROBLEM OF HOUSING

All. to a society for low cost dwellings, November 21, 1953.

(*The praiseworthy aim of the association.*)

705
(38,
60,
96,
97)
In the last hundred years, after the industrial progress and the consequent development of great cities gave to the question of housing a special aspect, the Popes, Bishops and Catholic Associations have unceasingly dedicated their special consideration to this important and unfortunately often distressing problem.

The problem was difficult from the beginning and such it has remained up to the present time; indeed, the consequences of the war have rendered the conditions more difficult and the need of help more urgent. Even nowadays We must make Ours the works of Our Predecessor Pius XI, of glorious memory, in the Encyclical *Quadragesimo Anno*: "It is horrifying to consider the impediments to the union and intimacy of family life caused by a most unsuitable dwelling place" (a).

This is the main point, in view of which the Church in virtue of her pastoral office praises and earnestly asks for your work. She cannot cease to admonish and recall to mind that, according to the will of the Creator and the natural order established by Him, the family must be a spiritual and moral, juridical and economic unity, and that strict and unchangeable laws regulate the birth and development of a new life. What a burden poses itself therefore for Christian consciences, when future husbands and wives, new domestic societies, and

705a   AAS 23 (1931) 221.

growing families are either unable to find any shelter or only insufficient and often very expensive dwelling places! Only the Lord knows in how many similar cases human weakness has been shipwrecked in the conduct of its Christian life and then even in the Faith!

(*The duty of private property and that of public authorities.*)

THE TECHNICAL SPIRIT AND THE FAMILY

Radio Message to the World, December 24, 1953.
(*Technical progress and the dangers of the technical spirit.*)

Undoubtedly a great part of humanity has not yet **706** been touched by such a "technical concept of life"; but *(42,* it is to be feared that wherever technical progress pene- *43,* trates uncontrolled, the danger of the above-mentioned *96)* deviations will not be long in rearing its head. And We think with particular anxiety of the danger for the family, which in the life of society is the strongest principle of order, inasmuch as it knows how to inspire in its members innumerable personal services, binds them to the home and the hearth with the bonds of affection, and awakens in each of them the love of the family tradition in the production and preservation of good habits. On the contrary, where there penetrates the technical concept of life, the family loses the personal bond of its unity, it loses its warmth and its stability. It only remains united to the degree that mass production imposes on it, and such production is employed more and more frequently. No longer is the family a work of love and a refuge for souls, but a soulless depot, according to the circumstances, either for manpower for such mass production, or for consumers of the material benefits produced.

(*Gravity of the present time.—Call to European unity; to the internal order of peoples.*)

MATRIMONY AND VIRGINITY

Encycl. *Sacra Virginitas*, March 25, 1954.
(*Virginity in history.*)

The motive of the encyclical

707   As, however, some of our contemporaries are in error
(110) on this subject and are exalting the married state to the point of placing it above virginity, thereby disparaging consecrated chastity and ecclesiastical celibacy, Our apostolic sense of duty compels Us to proclaim and defend the excellence of virginity, at the present moment in particular, with the object of shielding Catholic Faith from mistaken ideas of this kind.

(*Virginity: motives that lead to its choice.*)

Life-long celibacy frees people from the heavy cares and responsibilities of married life

708   The teaching of Christ, quoted above, already sug-
(29, gests that lifelong celibacy frees people from the heavy
110) cares and responsibilities of married life. The Apostle of the Gentiles, divinely inspired, tells in the following passage why celibacy is a liberation: "And I would have you free from concern. . . . The married man is concerned with the world's claim, asking how he is to please his

wife; and thus he is at issue with himself" (a). But here it must be noted that the Apostle is not blaming husbands because they are concerned with their wives. Nor is he taking wives to task for trying to please their husbands. He is merely pointing out that their hearts are divided between love of the partner and love of God, that they are too distracted by the anxieties and obligations of married life to be able readily to give their minds to the affairs of God. They are subject to the duty of wedlock, which clearly commands that "the two become one flesh" (b). Man and wife are yoked to one another in all the gladdening and saddening circumstances of their lives (c). Hence it will readily be appreciated why those who wish to give themselves to the service of God embrace the state of virginity as a state of emancipation, which enables them to serve God more completely and to devote their undivided energies to the welfare of their fellowmen.

(*Examples from the lives of the Saints.*)

There is a further reason why all who are set on **709** devoting themselves entirely to God and the spiritual *(108,* welfare of their neighbor adopt the state of virginity. It *(110)* is the reason stressed by the Holy Fathers when they dwell on the benefits available to those who observe absolute continence for the purpose of becoming better fitted for the enjoyment of the higher states of the spiritual life. Certainly, as the Fathers themselves point out quite frankly, the gratifications which are the lawful property of marriage are not to be condemned in them-

708a 1 Cor. 7:32-33.
708b Gen. 2, 24.—Cf. Matt. 19:5.
708c Cf. 1 Cor. 7, 39.

selves. On the contrary, chaste wedlock has been hallowed by being raised to the dignity of a special sacrament. But at the same time it has to be confessed that, owing to the misfortune of Adam's fall, the lower powers of human nature pit themselves against right reason and even at times incite a man to do wrong. As the Angelical Doctor writes, the use of marriage "restrains the soul from thorough-going absorption in the service of God" (a).

So that sacred ministers may achieve spiritual freedom of soul and body and avoid entanglement in earthly concerns, the Latin Church requires them to submit, of their own free will, to the obligation of perfect chastity (b).

(*This obligation is to render them more worthy to serve at the altar.*)

Superiority of virginity

710
(110) This is the chief reason why it must be maintained, in accordance with the clear teaching of the Church, that holy virginity is more excellent than matrimony. Our divine Savior had previously spoken to His disciples in favor of its advisabilty as a higher way of life (a). Then St. Paul the Apostle, after stating that a man who gives his ward in marriage "is well advised," hastens to add "and still better advised not to give her in marriage" (b). When comparing marriage with virginity, the Apostle more than once discloses his own sentiments, especially when he declares that "I wish you were all in

709a Cf. St. Thomas, *Summa theol.*, 2.a 2.ae, q. 186, a. 4.
709b Cf. C.I.C., can. 132, § 1.
710a Cf. Matt. 19:10-11.
710b 1 Cor. 7:38.

the same state as myself.... To the unmarried, and to the widows, I would say that they will do well to remain in the same state as myself" (c). The superiority of virginity to marriage which We have been asserting is, then, due, beyond doubt, to the superior purpose which it envisages (d) and to the supremely effective contribution which it brings towards complete self-dedication to God. On the other hand, the mind and heart which is involved in the ties and tasks of marriage is more or less "at issue with itself" (e).

(*The results of virginity consecrated to God.*)

Virginity and the symbolism of matrimony

It is particularly gratifying to dwell on another delightful outcome of virginity. Consecrated virgins present a vivid picture of the perfect virginity of Mother Church herself and bring out the holiness of their own intimate union with Christ. The words used by the Bishop, when addressing supplication to God, during the rite for the consecration of virgins, are inspired by a deep sense of this truth: "to the end that there might be more noble souls who care nothing for the connubial commerce of man and wife, yet desire what it mystically denotes, and instead of imitating what is done in marriage esteem what it represents..." (a). **711** *(110)*

Errors contrary to the Church's doctrine

The higher excellence of virginity and celibacy, as compared with the married state, is, as We have already **712** *(110)*

710c 1 Cor. 7:7-8; cf. 1 and 26.
710d Cf. St. Thomas, *Summa theol.*, 2. a 2. ae, q. 152, a. 3-4. 710e Cf. 1 Cor. 7:33.
711a *Pontificale Romanum*: De benedictione et consecratione virginum.

noted, a doctrine taught in the first instance by Our
Divine Savior and by the Apostle of the Gentiles. It was
solemnly defined as an article of divine faith by the
Holy Council of Trent (a). It has always been taught
by the Fathers and Doctors of the Church. Like Our
Predecessors before Us, We Ourselves have taken every
possible opportunity to expound the doctrine and to give
it Our warm endorsement. Since, however, certain folk
have recently been subjecting the traditional teaching
of the Church to unfavorable criticism which carries
with it the risk of harm to the faithful, Our sense of duty
gives Us to think that it will be well to take the matter
up once again in this Encyclical and to expose and censure these mistaken views, which are often camouflaged
in the colors of truth.

Chastity is not harmful
to physical equilibrium

713   In the first place, people who regard man's natural
(110) sex instinct as the dominant factor in his make-up, and
infer from this that he can master it for a lifetime only
at the imminent peril of upsetting his physical and, still
more, his mental equilibrium, with consequent harm to
the balance of his human personality, are simply going
counter to the common judgment of sane and conscientious men, for which the Church has ever entertained the
greatest respect.

As St. Thomas so justly and rightly states, the most
deep-seated of all human instincts is the instinct of self-
preservation, whereas the sex instinct lies on a more
superficial level. It belongs to the controlling power of

712a Sess. 24, can. 10.

human reason, which is the singular prerogative of our nature, to govern these fundamental impulses and to sublimate them by exercising due mastery over them (a).

It is unfortunately true that, as a result of the first **714** sin, committed by Adam, our bodily powers and passions *(110)* have been upset and tend to domineer, not only over our senses, but also over our souls. They darken the mind and weaken the will. But the grace of Jesus Christ is forthcoming, principally through the Sacraments, to enable us to let the Spirit be our rule of life and to make the body our slave (a). The virtue of chastity does not mean insensibility to the promptings of the flesh. It requires us rather to make them the servants of high reason and subjects of the kingdom of grace, as we strain with all our might towards what is noblest in human and Christian life.

In order to acquire this perfect sway over our bodily **715** passions, it is not enough to refrain from any direct *(110)* violation of chastity. Willing and generous avoidance of everything that is more or less distantly opposed to the practice of this virtue is indispensable. Then the soul can completely rule the body and lead the life of the spirit in peace and freedom. Anyone, therefore, who acts on Catholic principles cannot fail to see that, so far from arresting the natural progressive development of men and women, perfect chastity furthers and ennobles it to the highest degree.

713a St. Thomas, *Summa theol.*, 1. a 2. ae, q. 94, art. 2.
714a Cf. Gal. 5:25; 1 Cor. 9:27.

It is no easier to sanctify oneself in matrimony than it is in virginity

716
(11,
110)
It was with regret that We recently had to pass censure on a view which goes so far as to maintain that marriage is indispensable for the due and proper expression and fulfillment of human personality (a). It is asserted in some quarters that the grace of God given by the sacramental agency of Matrimony hallows the use of matrimony in such a way as to make it a more powerful instrument of a personal union with God than virginity itself, since, We are told, Christian wedlock is a sacrament, whereas virginity is not. We must denounce this doctrine as a dangerous error. True it is that the sacrament gives husbands and wives the grace worthily to fulfill the duties of married life. True it is that it strengthens the bond of mutual love. But the sacrament was not established precisely for the purpose of making the use of marriage an instrument of its nature better calculated directly to strengthen the bond of union in charity with God Himself (b). Why does the Apostle Paul recognize that the parties are entitled to observe continence for a time in order to give themselves to prayer (c), if not because continence is a release for one who wishes to devote himself to heavenly things and to raise his mind and heart to God?

717
(11,
Finally, it cannot be asserted, as some would have it, that the mutual assistance (a) which the parties look

716a All. of the 15th September, 1952; cf. above, n. 672.
716b Decree of the Holy Office, 1st April, 1944; cf. above, n. 634c.
716c Cf. 1 Cor. 7:5.
717a Cf. C.I.C., can. 1013, § 1.

for in marriage is a better aid to self-sanctification than **29,** what they call the virgin's or celibate's "loneliness of *(101)* heart." For, despite their renunciation of this particular kind of human love, it is not true to say that those who have embraced the state of perfect chastity have thereby dwarfed and denuded their human personality. They receive from God, the Giver of gifts descending from above, something in the spiritual order which utterly transcends the "mutual assistance" rendered to each other by man and wife. As they give themselves entirely to the one who is the source of their being and who imparts to them His divine love, they are not contracted but amplified to a degree. Those wonderful words of St. Paul: "I live; now, not I; it is Christ that lives in me" (b); can anyone apply them to himself with more justice than these virgins?

Hence the Church is very wise in taking the view that priestly celibacy is to be maintained. She knows full well that for her priests it is, and will continue to be, a source of ever closer union with God.

The apostolate is not made any more fruitful in matrimony than in virginity

We also deem it expedient to refer to another mis- **718** take, the mistake made by advisers who wish to dis- *(110)* courage young men from entering seminaries and young women from entering convents, by trying to make them believe that the Church of today stands in greater need of the help that can be given by good practicing Catholics living an ordinary married life in the world than of priests and nuns who are supposed to be withdrawn

717b Gal. 2:20.

from human society by their vows of chastity. This, Venerable Brethren, is nothing but palpable and dangerous make-believe.

719
(107, 110)
Needless to say, We do not mean to deny that the witness borne by the exemplary Christian life of Catholic husbands and wives, wherever they may be and whatever their circumstances, is capable of doing a great deal of good. But to make this a ground for saying that marriage is preferable to complete self-dedication is sheer topsy-turvydom and confusion. We do, indeed, strongly desire, Venerable Brethren, that husbands and wives and brides and bridegrooms be given a timely reminder that they are seriously bound, not only duly and diligently to rear their actual or prospective families, but also to do everything they can to help others, by bearing witness to their faith and giving good example. But We must sharply reprove anyone who tries to dissuade young people from entering seminaries or religious orders or other institutions in which vows are taken, by putting it to them that they will be doing greater spiritual good if they get married and make open and public profession of their Christian life in the capacity of mothers and fathers of families. The energies of such counsellors would assuredly be better spent if, instead of being directed towards restraining the unfortunately all too few young people of today who wish to give themselves to the service of God, they were devoted with all possible earnestness to urging the thousands upon thousands who are already married to lend an eager helping hand in the work of the apostolate.

(*Those who make the vow of chastity do not estrange themselves from society.*)

Practical consequences
The choice of virginity is free

It must be clearly stated at the outset that because **720** virginity is to be deemed more perfect than wedlock *(108,* we are not to conclude that it is necessary for the at- *110)* tainment of Christian perfection. Holiness of life can also, in fact, be achieved without consecrated chastity. This is proved by the illustrious example of the many canonized men and women who were loyal husbands and wives and excellent fathers and mothers of families. It is no exceptional thing to meet with married folk who are striving very earnestly after perfection.

(Difficulties which chastity encounters.—Conditions which rule its choice.—Means to be used to remain faithful.)

FAMILY PROBLEMS

Letter of Monsignor Montini to His Eminence Cardinal Siri, on the occasion of the XXVII Social Week at Pisa, September 19, 1954.

(Happy choice of the theme to be studied during the social week: family problems.)

The family is the cell of society

Society's cell and the first community constituted **721** by God Himself for the development of the human per- *(22,* son, the family remains always, today as in the past, *42,* among the highest, most serious and telling arguments, *44,* as much for the social order as for the very life of the *53)* Church. Christ's Bride looks to it for the origin and formation of her children; to it likewise looks the nation, which measures in the family's vigor its stability, power and greatness, since: "the city is what the families and the men by which it is formed make it, as the body is formed by the members" (a).

722
(42,
43,
60)
If attention is directed on the great crises and instabilities to which society has been subjected over the last few years on the economic, political and religious plane and from which the institution of the family has not evidently been able to withdraw itself, it will not be too difficult to discern another reason, which renders the most noble theme more than ever a response to the needs of our times. In reality, the family is the great sufferer from this last war; for on the family still weigh, sometimes in a tragic manner, the disastrous consequences of the last conflict. The family must be reintegrated again as the Supreme Pontiff timely observed: "if the world is to arise at last from the present crisis" (a) otherwise all will be in vain. The invitation launched during the war by His Holiness still resounds urgently: "We would therefore like to direct Our paternal voice of warning to world leaders: The family is sacred; it is the cradle not only of children, but still more of the nation and of its power and glory. Let the family never stray or deviate from the great aim which was willed by God! ... If you have at heart the future of humanity, if your conscience before God gives some importance to what the names of father and mother mean for man and to what makes for the true happiness of your children, reinstate the family in its work of peace" (b).

721a Pius XI, Enc. *Casti connubii,* 31st December, 1930; cf. above, nn. 263-400.
722a All. 26th June 1940; cf. above, n. 430.
722b All. 14th May 1942; cf. above, n. 500 ff.

Perils that threaten the family

It must be asserted that Italy still remains among **723** the nations which resist in large measure the attacks of **(60,** evil morality and the sad work of breaking up domestic **(62,** life. Stable in its Christian foundation, deeply rooted in **68,** the traditions of its people, safeguarded by providential **87)** laws, the family constitutes one of the more resplendent glories and more spiritual resources of Italy. It would, however, be a great danger to be deluded to thinking that the family taken in the fullness of its dignity and its rights is so considered by everyone. Still more fatal would it be not to oppose a powerful remedy to certain theoretical and practical errors which prepare the way to always expanding concessions in regards to family morality. The truth is that also in Italy in many circles there can be noticed a progressive disrupture of family unity, which is favored by insane entertainments, materialistic theories and shameful fashions. It is sufficient to call to mind the tendency of some to recur to fraud in order to evade those laws which so well defend family stability; of others to have recourse to the spreading of neo-malthusian practices which violate the divine laws governing the transmission of life; of others still, and of certain elements of the press, who publish public scandals which deaden that one and indissoluble, faithful and fruitful married love. To this may be added the uneasy economic conditions of modern life, which, more or less common to every country, are also causing modifications of a social and ethical character even in Italy and giving rise to new and complex family problems which require on the part of Catholics no longer only a general respect for the family and a vague knowledge of its traditional prerogatives.

Truly providential are these days of study at Pisa, because listening to the more qualified persons of Italian Catholic life, public opinion can be enlightened on such a vital matter.

The needs of the family

724 But these efforts, if they are to equal expectation, **(97,** cannot be limited to defending an inheritance of values **105)** which are passively preserved. The organizers of the Week have realized—and the theme of the works to be treated demonstrate it—that the social structures are today rapidly being transformed in the direction of a new order, which will be living and vigorous only if it is based on the social doctrines of the Church. In the presence of such a change, the position of the family must be rapidly modernized, so that the cell of society shall not remain outside the rising flow of future life.

725 Called on to place the stones of renewed family **(21,** building in this work of reconstruction, the speakers of **105)** the Week cannot be unmindful of the importance of the magisterium of the reigning Pontiff, who has made family questions the chosen theme of his apostolate of the spoken word, and who has so admirably known how to harmonize the stability of principles with the technical evolution of the problems.

Enlightened by such valuable teachings the "Relators" will know how to keep constantly in mind both the purpose proper to family life, whose office is that of transmitting "the flame of corporal life, and with it the spiritual and moral life, the Christian life to new generations" (a); and again, "the only measure of progress" which consists in strengthening under every aspect the solidarity of domestic society; and that is, "to create always greater and better public conditions, so that the family can exist and develop itself as an economic, juridical, moral, and religious unit" (b). Keeping this in mind, it will be easy to trace the directives assigned by the Pontifical documents corresponding to the various needs of the physical, moral, and supernatural life of the family.

Economic safety

The family has primarily a need of a certain economic security. As long, indeed, as man is compelled to lead a desolate and miserable life, and to live in repulsive and unhealthy dwellings; while he is not assured of a certain tranquillity of work, of the possibility to marry at a young age, and a salary that will permit him to save and to acquire a small piece of property; in such conditions, family life will always become disorganized and evermore open to the germs of social and moral corruption. On this point it is worth calling to mind the words of the Holy Father regarding housing problems, which are certainly among the most affecting: "How painful it is to see young people in those years in which nature inclines them strongly towards matrimony forced to wait years and years owing to the shortage of houses, with the danger that in this unnerving expectation they wither morally in the end!" (a)

726
(60, 97, 98)

725a All. 13th May 1952.
725b Christmas Message, 1945.
726a All. July 24, 1949; above, n. 542 ff.

Moral sanity

727
(15,
60,
77,
78,
99,
100,
107)
It is necessary, moreover, to give back to the family its moral sanity; for in fact it is an ethical organism no less than a social one, because it is destined to promote the perfection of the moral qualities of its members. The indispensable condition for this is its stability. On this matter His Holiness believes that the time has come to exhort Italian Catholics to greater vigilance before the advocates of divorce, who are preparing new attacks and advancing always more impudent pretexts and, what is worse still, finding less resistance than in the past in the eyes of public opinion. True Catholics know—and when the time arises they must concentrate on such matters to the full—that the bond of matrimony is of its very nature indissoluble. To give way to these pressures in the name of a liberty which is open rebellion to divine laws, would be, for those responsible for public life, a launching of the country into a fearful decadence. On the other hand, there is strictly connected with family life the problem of education, the hinge on which the moral sanity of the family itself depends, and which today demands a revision of methods, in order to be able to confront the possibilities, difficulties and risks of the new conditions of life. How is it possible not to take into consideration the greater autonomy which youth today claim from their parents, their tendency to seek outside of the family satisfaction for those needs which were one time entrusted to family life, and finally the increased responsibilities in the field of education which the State nowadays attributes to itself? This becomes more evident if woman's social position is considered, which lately, according to the expression of the Holy Father, "has

undergone an evolution no less rapid than profound. She has seen herself moved from the recollected sanctuary of the family to the vastness and excitement of public life. She has part today in the same professions, bears the same responsibilities, even enjoys in the field of politics an equal footing with man" (a). If therein there are undoubted perils, on the other hand it would be unjust, even injurious, not to value the advantages that could at times arise from these new relations.

As regards the increasing invasion of civil society **728** in the field of education, one can never sufficiently call *(98,* to mind that "parents have a primary right by natural *105)* law to the education of their children ... inviolable, and antecedent to that of society and of the State" (a). The State must therefore safeguard the free exercise of this right and supply any occasional insufficiency of the family, but it must never unduly replace the family itself. Where there is a need to intervene, instead of creating new organizations—which could encourage in the parents a tendency to rid themselves of the work of education originally belonging to them—the State should rather promote such conditions of life, work and assistance as are suitable for encouraging the family to exercise better its function of bringing up children. This could be done by repression of evil habits, by elevating to the level of family morality the means used for propagating ideas, and particularly by promoting the more frequent presence of husband and wife in the home, both by diminishing the necessity for the woman to stay out of the house and "by providing a place of work not distant from the home;

727a All. 12th May, 1946.
728a All. 8th September 1946, Cf. **EDUCATION.**

otherwise the head of the family and educator of the children will become almost a stranger in the home" (b). This would also allow a deeper collaboration between husband and wife, which, if good in all fields, would be particularly so in that of education.

Strengthening religious sentiment

729
(6,
7,
9,
11,
29)
The revival of the family should be begun on the *religious plane* in the first place, because it is precisely from the weakening of religious sentiment itself that there derive, as from a main source, all the evils which afflict modern families. Born from a contract "essentially sacred" (a), which the Redeemer has elevated to the dignity of a Sacrament, symbolizing His union with the Church, the family finds, in the goal assigned to it by the New Law, its highest perfection and the most secure safeguard of its unity, dignity and stability. In this light, the life of husband and wife led in a Christian family is not only an exchange of human rights and the performance of natural functions, but the participation in heavenly realities; a means of spiritual elevation and sanctification, since the Sacrament has provided so great a source of divine energies to which the married couple can have access during their whole matrimonial life, to draw help and comfort for the fulfillment of their duties. This reveals the preeminent function that belongs to the family in the vast reality of the Mystical Body, and at the same time opens horizons of limitless perfection to the family organisms whenever they become more intimately united in the life of the Church.

728b Christmas Radio Message, 1945.
729a Leo XIII, Encycl. *Arcanum*, 10th Feburary 1880; cf. above, nn. 143-198.

From all this appears the need for married couples **730** to recognize more and more the spiritual bond that unites *(43,* them to the parish, where their union has been blessed, *65,* in order to draw the light of faith and heavenly strength *97,* to complete the supernatural education of their children, *103)* and to give themselves consciously to the various forms of religious and social apostolate that form part of parish life. Thus sanctified, the family will find once again the peace, serenity, and joy which modern materialistic and secularistic ideas extinguish when they deprive the family of its sacred character. Family life will develop love towards the home that will preserve its members from dangerous accidents on the roads of life, and through the family the Church will spread over all social life the beneficial gifts of the higher world of grace.

(*Blessing of the Holy Father.—Best wishes for good results.*)

FAMILY AND WORK

Letter *Am bevorstehenden Pfingstest,* to the Bishop of Passau, May 19, 1955.

(*Centenary of the Kolping Society.—Two directing principles of the Kolping Associations:* I) *religion and life form an indivisible whole....*)

The second principle which guided Adolph Kolping **731** was: the family is the originating cell and prototype *(42,* of all social life. Kolping further opposed a decisive *43,* refusal to any social ideology which regards individuals *107)* and members of society under the sole aspect of producers and consumers of wealth, and which therefore exhausts itself solely in the process of production and in consumption; thus he saved the soul from a materialistic social life. For Kolping, the Christian family, its condition and its moral vocation, the good cohabitation of two parties, are the foundations of social life. The family above all else! The Constitution and the laws, no matter how perfect, are of no value if the family is torn asunder and made unfit for its duty (a). How many times Adolph Kolping expressed this thought! His creation, the so-called "Gesellenverein," was to be in great and small matters, in its totality and in its parts a family to prepare young people to become founders and fathers of genuine Christian families.

(*Directives for the future apostolate of the Kolping Association.*)

We likewise invoke the blessings of Heaven on the young newlyweds who accompany you: may their family life, happy and fruitful, spread that love of Christ which has united them in the Sacrament of Matrimony, that it may be always light and power in the moments of joy and sorrow.

ARTIFICIAL INSEMINATION

All. to the members of the II World Congress of fertility and sterility, May 19, 1956.

(*Welcome to the members of the Congress.*)

732 You prepare to study a difficult and delicate ques-
(19, tion, because it pertains to one of the principal functions

731a Cf. Pius XII, *All. to the X National Congress of Swiss Catholics*, 16th May, 1954: The difficulties of matrimony and of the family increase at the same rate in as much as they defect from the essential precepts and the commandments of God." (DR 16:23; A.D. 16:118).

of the body and because the results of your work can 94)
have serious and significant consequences for the life
of many men and women and for the evolution of
society.

Involuntary conjugal sterility, to which you propose
to seek a remedy, is a hindrance to the fulfillment of the
primary end of marriage and provokes profound distress
for the married couple, oftentimes veiled by an instinct
of modesty, but harmful to the stability of the marriage
itself.

(*Technical studies undertaken in relation to this
problem.*)

Social aspect of the problem

Your previous Congress signalled out in its final **733**
report the fact that involuntary conjugal sterility con- (43,
stitutes an economic and social problem of great im- 94)
portance, that it helps to lower the index of fertility of
peoples and can therefore influence the life and destiny
of mankind. It sometimes happens that one stops at this
more apparent and more easily controlled point of view.
It will be said, therefore, that there is need to increase
the birth rate to assure the nation's vitality, its expansion
in all its fields. It is true that a high birth rate manifests
the creating energies of a nation and of the family; it
reveals the courage of men in the face of life's risks
and difficulties; it underlines their will to construct and
to make progress. It is right to assert that the physical
impossibility to exercise fatherhood and motherhood
easily becomes a motive of discouragement and of with-
drawing into oneself. Life, which ardently desires to
be transmitted, to be perpetuated, falls back, so to say,
on itself, and many homes, alas, are tried in this manner.

Spiritual and moral aspect

734   It is with pleasure that We offer a consideration
(20, here which you yourselves have already mentioned. It
94) is very true that if your zeal to do research work on
marital sterility and the means to overcome it, presents a scientific subject worthy of attention, it involves
high spiritual and ethical values also, which must be
held in due account. We shall point them out to you.

It is profoundly human for husband and wife to
see and to find in their offspring the true and full expression of their reciprocal love and their mutual gift.
It is not difficult to understand how the unsatisfied
desire of motherhood and fatherhood is felt as a painful
and sorrowful sacrifice by parents animated with noble
and healthy sentiments. Besides, the involuntary sterility
of marriage may become a serious danger to the union
and very stability of the family.

735   But this social aspect in reality only hides a more
(21, intimate and grievous matter. Indeed, matrimony unites
23, two persons in an identical destiny, in their voyage
29, towards the realization of an ideal which implies not
31) the fullness of an earthly happiness but the conquest of
spiritual values of a transcendent order, which Christian
revelation in particular presents in all their grandeur.
Husband and wife arrive at this ideal by consecrating
themselves to the fulfillment of the primary end of marriage, in other words, the procreation and rearing of
children.

The ends of matrimony

736   Several times it has been necessary for Us to recall
(31) how the peculiar intentions of the married couple, their

life in common, their personal perfection, cannot be conceived unless they are subordinated to the primary end, namely, fatherhood and motherhood. In an address to midwives, on October 29, 1951, We said: "Not only the common work of external life, but even all personal enrichment—spiritual and intellectual—all that in conjugal life as such is most spiritual and profound, has been placed, by the will of the Creator and of nature, at the service of posterity" (a). This is the constant teaching of the Church. She has rejected all those concepts of matrimony which threatened to enfold it in itself or to make it an egoistic search for affective and physical satisfaction in the sole interest of husband and wife.

But the Church has likewise rejected the opposite **737** attitude which pretended to separate, in procreation, the *(20,* biological activity from the personal relations of hus- *25,* band and wife. The child is the fruit of the marriage *26,* union, when it finds full expression by the placing in *30)* action of the functional organs, of the sensible emotions thereto related, and of the spiritual and disinterested love which animates such a union; it is in the unity of this human act that there must be considered the biological conditions of procreation. Never is it permitted to separate these different aspects to the point of excluding positively either the intention of procreation or the conjugal relation.

The relation which unites mother and father to their child is rooted in the organic fact, and further still in the deliberate action of husband and wife, who give themselves one to the other and whose will to surrender themselves is revealed and finds its true result

736a See n. 636.

in the being they bring into the world. Only this consecration of self, generous in its principle and arduous in its realization, with the conscientious acceptance of the responsibilities it carries, can guarantee that the work of educating the children will be followed with all the diligence, courage and patience required. It can therefore be affirmed that human fertility, beyond the physical plane, is vested with essentially moral aspects which must be considered, even when this question is treated from the medical viewpoint.

Human significance of generation

738 It is evident that when the scientist and the doctor (20, undertake a study of a problem within their competence, 94) they have the right to concentrate their attention on its precise scientific elements and solve it with these facts alone. But when the way is opened for practical application to man, it is impossible not to hold in due account the repercussions which the proposed methods will have on the person and his dignity. The greatness of the human act consists precisely in surpassing the moment itself in which it is completed to involve the whole orientation of a life and lead it to take its position before the absolute. That is already true for daily activity: *a fortiori* it is true for an act which involves, with the reciprocal love of husband and wife, their future, and that of their posterity.

We believe it is for you, Gentlemen, a matter of the greatest importance not to overlook this aspect when you consider the methods of artificial insemination. The means with which a new life is to be produced acquires an essential human significance, inseparable from the

end which is foreseen, and capable of damaging gravely
this end itself if it is not in conformity with reality and
with the laws written in the nature of beings.

Artificial insemination

On this subject also We have been asked to give **739**
some directives. As regards the experiments of human *(94)*
artificial fecundation "in vitro," let it suffice to observe
that they must be rejected as immoral and absolutely
unlawful. As regards the various moral problems which
surround artificial insemination, We have already expressed Our thought in a special address to doctors on
September 29, 1949; for the details We refer you to what
We said then, and here We limit Ourselves to repeating
the judgment given as a conclusion: "As regards artificial insemination, not only must one be extremely
reserved, but rather one must condemn the matter absolutely. Speaking thus, one does not necessarily condemn the use of some artificial means destined solely to
facilitate the conjugal act and to achieve the attainment
of the natural act normally performed" (a).

But since the use of artificial insemination is becoming more and more widespread, and in order to
correct some erroneous opinions which are spreading
about what We have taught, We add the following:

Artificial insemination exceeds the limits of the **740**
right which the married couple has acquired by the mat- *(11,*
rimonial contract, namely, the right to exercise fully *19,*
their natural sexual capacity in the natural accomplish- *87,*
ment of the matrimonial act. The contract in question *94)*
does not confer on them the right to artificial insemina-

739a See nn. 553-557.

tion, for such a right is in no way expressed in the right to the natural conjugal act and cannot be thence deduced. Less still can it be derived from the right to offspring, the primary end of marriage. The matrimonial contract does not confer this right, because it has for its object not the offspring but the natural acts capable of procreating a new life and which are destined to this. So it must be said that artificial insemination violates the natural law and that it is contrary to justice and morality.

(*The Pope, speaking in French, now continues in Latin, and condemns certain forms of masturbation. The following is left in Latin, because it concerns above all doctors and confessors.*)

Illicit use of the generative faculty

741
(87,
94)

Alia nunc occurrit quaestio, ad quam pertractandam magis addecet latinam linguam adhibere (a).

Quemadmodum rationalis animus noster artificiali inseminationi adversatur, ita eadem ethica ratio, a qua agendi norma sumenda est, pariter vetat, quominus humanum semen, peritorum examini subiciendum, masturbationis ope procuretur.

Hanc agendi rationem attigimus Nostra quoque allocutione coram Urologiae doctoribus caetum participantibus, die VIII mensis Octobris anno MDCCCCLIII prolata, in qua haec habuimus verba: "Besides, the Holy Office has already decided (August 2, 1929) (b), that a '*masturbatio directe procurata ut obtineatur sperma*', was by no means allowed, no matter what the result of

741a Cf. above nn. 693-703.
741b Cf. n. 703. AAS 21 (1929) 490 II.

the examination" (c). *Cum vero Nobis allatum sit, pravam huiusmodi consuetudinem pluribus in locis invalescere, opportunum ducimus nunc etiam, quae tunc monuimus, commemorare atque iterum inculcare.*

Si actus huiusmodi ad explendam libidinem ponantur, eos vel ipse naturalis hominis sensus sua sponte respuit, ac multo magis mentis judicium, quotiescumque rem mature recteque considerat. Iidem actus tamen tunc quoque respuendi sunt, cum graves rationes eos a culpa eximere videntur, uti sunt: remedia iis praestanda qui nimia nervorum intentione vel abnormibus animi spasmis laborant; medicis peragenda, ope mircroscopii, spermatis inspectio, quod venerei vel alius generis morbi bacteris infectum sit; diversarum partium examen, ex quibus semen ordinarie constat, ut vitalium spermatis elementorum praesentia, numerus, quantitas, forma, vis, habitus aliaque id genus dignoscantur. **742** (87, 94)

Eiusmodi procuratio humani seminis, per masturbationem effecta, ad nihil aliud directe spectat, nisi ad naturalem in homine generandi facultatem plene exercendam; quod quidem plenum exercitium, extra coniugalem copulam peractum, secum fert directum et indebite usurpatum eiusdem facultatis usum. In hoc eiusmodi indebito facultatis usu proprie sita est intrinseca regulae morum violatio. Haudquaquam enim homo ius ullum exercendi facultatem sexualem iam inde habet, quo facultatem eandem a natura recepit. Homini nempe (secus ac in ceteris animantibus rationis expertibus contingit) ius et potestas utendi atque exercendi eandem facultatem tantummodo in nuptiis valide initis tribuitur, atque in **743** (2, 10, 26, 87, 94)

741c Cf. above n. 703.

iure matrimoniali continetur, quod ipsis nuptiis traditur et acceptatur. Inde elucet hominem, ob solam hanc causam quod facultatem sexualem a natura recepit, non habere nisi potentiam et ius ad matrimonium ineundum. Hoc ius tamen, ad obiectum et ambitum quod attinet, naturae lege non hominum voluntate discribitur; vi huius legis naturae, homini non competit ius et potestas ad plenum facultatis sexualis exercitium, directe intentum, nisi cum coniugalem copulam exercet ad normam a natura ipsa imperatam atque definitam. Extra hunc naturalem actum, ne in ipso quidem matrimonio ius datur ad sexuali hac facultate plene fruendum. Hi sunt limites, quibus ius, de quo diximus, eiusque exercitium a natura circumscribuntur.

744 *Ex eo quod plenum sexualis facultatis exercitium*
(23, *hoc absoluto copulae coniugalis limite circumscribitur,*
87, *eadem facultas intrinsece apta efficitur ad plenum matri-*
94) *monii naturalem finem assequendum (qui non modo est generatio, sed etiam prolis educatio), atque eius exercitium cum dicto fine colligatur. Quae cum ita sint, masturbatio omnino est extra memoratam pleni facultatis sexualis exercitii naturalem habilitatem, ideoque etiam extra eius colligationem cum fine a natura ordinato; quamobrem eadem omni iuris titulo caret atque naturae et ethices legibus contraria est, etiamsi inservire intendat utilitati per se iustae nec improbandae.*

745 *Quae hactenus dicta sunt de intrinseca malitia cuius-*
(87, *libet pleni usus potentiae generandi extra naturalem*
94) *coniugalem copulam, valent eodem modo cum agitur de matrimonio iunctis vel de matrimonio solutis, sive plenum exercitium apparatus genitalis fit a viro sive a muliere, sive ab utraque parte simul agente; sive fit tacti-*

bus manualibus sive coniugalis copulae interruptione:
haec enim semper est actus naturae contrarius atque in-
trinsece malus.

Matrimony—its educative role

If fecundity corresponds to certain demands of the **746**
organism and satisfies powerful instincts, it immediate- *(23,*
ly involves, as We have already pointed out, the moral *42)*
and psychological plane. The work of education exceeds
by far, in its importance and its consequences, that of
generation.

The communications of one soul with another,
which come about between parents and children, with
all the seriousness, delicacy and self-denial which they
require, cause the parents to go beyond the stage of
affective possession in order to give thought to the personal future of those who have been entrusted to them.

Very often, having reached a certain age, children
leave the family and depart in order to correspond to
the necessities of life or to the call of a more sublime
vocation.

The thought of this normal separation, so full of
distress for them also, must help the parents to have a
nobler concept of their mission and give them a clearer
vision of the meaning of their efforts.

Under pain of a partial failure, the family is destined to become part of society, to extend the limits of
affection and interests, to direct its members towards
wider horizons so that they care not only for themselves
but especially for the service of humanity.

Virginity is the highest fecundity

The Catholic Church, therefore, guardian of the **747**
Divine intentions, points out the highest fecundity of *(102,*

110) those lives entirely consecrated to God and to their neighbor. Here the complete renunciation of a family must permit a spiritual action, wholly disinterested and springing not from any fear of life and its duties, but from the knowledge of man's true destiny, man created to the image of God and in search of a universal love, to which he is not forced by any attraction to the flesh. This is the most sublime fecundity, and the most enviable, which man can achieve and which transcends the biological plane to enter completely that of the spirit.

It was not Our intention, Gentlemen, to close this speech without pointing out these horizons. To some of you these may seem to be far from the object of your present occupation. Such is not the case, however. Only these horizons will permit you to place your work practically in its true light and to keep in sight its value. What you propose is not only to increase the number of individuals but to raise the moral level of humanity, its beneficial forces, its will to grow physically and spiritually. You wish to bring a new fervor to the affection of so many married couples saddened by an empty home; far from hindering their full growth, you aim to place all your knowledge at their service so that there may be awakened in them those admirable resources which God hid in the heart of fathers and mothers to help them and all their family tend towards Him.

(The responsibility of doctors in this scientific work and in its practical realization.—Blessing.)

FIDELITY TO THE CHURCH

All. to Austrian law students and their professors, June 3, 1956.

(Place of canon law in the Church.—The Church re-proached with an "excess of juridicism.")

The Church has often been reproached with the inflexibility with which she remains attached, and firmly attached, to the indissolubility of the Christian marriage which has been validly contracted and consummated. However, this is not a case of insensibility, or of hardness of heart on the part of jurists acting as if they were incapable of understanding the tragedy of more than one conjugal situation: what is here at stake is quite simply the fidelity of the Church to maintain the rights of marriage such as her Divine Founder instituted them Himself, without her having, on her side, the right to pass judgment on them. **748** *(15-16, 50)*

(Necessity for more laws as the extension of the Church becomes greater.)

ABORTION

Radio Message to the International Congress of Catholic physicians, September 11, 1956.

(Law and medical ethics.)

Medical law is subject to medical ethics, which expresses the moral order willed by God. **749** *(89-90)*

Therefore, medical law can never permit either the physician or the patient to practice direct euthanasia, and the physician can never practice it either on himself or on others. This is equally true for the direct suppression of the foetus and for medical actions which go counter to the law of God clearly manifested. In all this medical law has no authority and the doctor is not obliged to obey it. On the contrary, he is obliged not to take it into consideration; all formal assistance is forbidden him, while material assistance falls under the general norms of *cooperatio materialis.*

(*Collaboration of physicians on the international plane.*)

THE MIND OF THE CHURCH

All. to the participants in the 6th Week of Pastoral Adaptation, September 14, 1956.

(*Our Lord's preaching: its character.—Its content: preparation to receive the action of God.—Faith in Christ. —The duties of a Christian.*)

750 Among these duties We find in the first place the
(15, duty of prayer; the duty of interior and exterior humili-
32) ty, with the rejection of every sort of pride or arrogance; the duty of abnegation and sacrifice; the duty to control one's passions; the duty to bear one's cross and follow a crucified Lord; the duty to tend towards perfection; the great duty of love of neighbor, which is like to the first and greatest commandment of the love of God; the duty of submission to the Church and to the authority instituted by Christ; the duty of the sanctity and indissolubility of marriage; the doctrine and the fact of the superiority of virginity over the married state.

(*Other points in Christ's teaching.—The preaching of the clergy.—Mission of the Church with regard to preaching.—Its adaptation to the questions of the moment.—Among them:*)

751 The very recent encyclical *De Sacra Virginitate* of
(110) March 25, 1954 (a) has shown you, among other things,

751a Cf. above nn. 707-720.

the Church's mind on the interminable debates of our contemporaries, especially the young, on the importance and even the absolute necessity—so some maintain—of marriage for the human person (who, without marriage would remain—according to them—a spiritual cripple), as also on the pretended superiority of Christian marriage and the conjugal act over virginity (which is not a sacrament producing *ex opere operato* effects).

(*Other questions recently explained in the Church's teaching.—The leaven in the mass.*) (b)

THE PILLARS OF HUMAN SOCIETY

All. to the President of Liberia, September 23, 1956.
(*Links between the Holy See and Liberia.*)

Family, Church, and State, these potent pillars of human society and of its varied cultures, in your native Africa and in every other clime as well, owe their institution, as they must owe their stability, to the creative power and the sustaining mercy of God. Well have you had occasion to realize, from your earliest political beginnings on the sunny shores of the South Atlantic, the truth of the Master's warning that to build any othei foundation is to build upon the sand (a). **752** *(36, 42)*

(*The proven loyalty of the Catholics of Liberia.*)

VIRGINITY AND MARRIAGE

All. to hospital nuns, April 24, 1957.

(*The mission of the nuns.—Above all, be true religious.*)

751b For parts of this all. omitted here, see **THE CHURCH.**   752a Cf. St. Matt. 7:24-27.

753 It is a truth of faith, recently recalled by Us in the
(110) encyclical *Sacra Virginitas* under date of March 25,
1954, that virginity is superior to the married state because the virgin soul contracts bonds of absolute and
indissoluble love directly with God, even more, with
God Incarnate, Jesus Christ. In fact, all that she has
received as a gift of God to be a wife and mother, is
offered by her as a holocaust on the altar of a complete
and perpetual renunciation. To reach the heart of God,
to love Him and be loved by Him, the virgin soul does
not go through many other hearts, does not stop to treat
with other creatures; nothing comes in between her and
Jesus, no obstacle, no medium.

754 On the contrary, marriage, while it is a real sacra-
(9, ment, one of the seven sources of grace instituted by
11, Christ Himself; while it comprises the reciprocal offer-
110) ing of each of the parties to the other; while it brings
about a real fusion of life and destiny, nonetheless includes, in God's eyes, something which is held back,
something which is not completely given. Only virgin
souls offer what for other souls who love is an inaccessible goal; for them the first rung of their ascent is also
the last; and the term of their *ascesis* is at once a summit and a profound abyss.

(*Religious spirit.—See Jesus in each invalid.*)

THE FAMILY AND THE STATE

Letter from the Secretariate of State to M. Charles
Flory, July 9, 1957.

(*The subject of the "Semaine Sociale" at Bordeaux:
The Family, 1957.—Present situation of the family.*)

(*The "Week" is dominated*) by the imperative duty **755** of safeguarding with the greatest firmness the institu- *(38,* tion of the family—this is both natural law and divine *66,* law—against the growing encroachment of socialization, *101)* without, for that matter, placing any *a priori* obstacles in the way of a sane transformation of society. There lies the major problem which must be treated by the "Semaine Sociale" ° of Bordeaux.

"For the Christian," the Holy Father has declared, **756** "there is a rule which permits him to determine with *(36,* certainty the measure of the rights and duties of the *44)* family in the community of the State. It is stated in the following terms: 'the family does not exist for the State (or society); it is the State (society) which exists for the family' (a)." Once this has been said, the Holy Father only continues the constant teaching of his predecessors: "Domestic society, immediately instituted by God for its proper end . . . , has for that reason a priority of nature, and consequently a priority of right, with respect to civil society," so Pius XI wrote (b). And Leo XIII before him had taken up the defense of the family against socialism: "(the family is), doubtless, a very tiny society, but it is a real one, and anterior to all civil society, and for that reason of necessity certain rights and certain duties absolutely independent of the State must be attributed to it" (c); and he concluded that "it is a grave and pernicious error to wish the civil power to penetrate at will into the sanctuary of the family."

° A week of lectures, conferences, seminars on the problems of modern society.

756a All. of September 18, 1951; Cf. above n. 581.

756b Pius XI, *Divini illius Magistri*, cf. **EDUCATION**.

756c Leo XIII, *Rerum novarum*, Cf. above nn. 210, 213.

(Complexity of social machinery.—Action of the State.)

757
(44,
98)
Certainly the State must protect the family, but it must first of all respect it. As the Holy Father has already said to the International Union of Family Associations, "they retreat behind the fallacious pretext that the family left to its own devices is powerless, to make it totally dependent on the State and on public welfare" (a).

(Research proposed to the "Semaine sociale.")

758
(65,
97-
98,
101)
Therefore, let public institutions and private enterprise make common cause with their efforts in order to consolidate the society of the family, uplift its potential of life and action, and support it without substituting themselves for it. Above all, let the family have once more the knowledge of God; forgetfulness of Him, alas! has been, in many cases, at the root of the evils from which the family is suffering.

THE END OF THE UNION

All. to the Congress of Family Associations, September 15, 1957.

(Widowhood.—Its spiritual and moral problems.)

759
(9,
34)
Although the Church does not condemn remarriage, she has a marked predilection for the souls who wish to remain faithful to their spouses and to the perfect symbolism of the sacrament of matrimony. She rejoices to see the cultivation of the spiritual riches proper to this state. The first of these, it seems to Us, is the conviction

757a All. September 20, 1949, Cf. above, n. 546, ff.

carried out in life that, far from destroying the bonds of human and supernatural love contracted in marriage, death can perfect and reenforce them. Doubtless on the purely juridical plane and on the plane of sensible realities the institution of matrimony no longer exists; but what constituted its soul, what gave it vigor and beauty, conjugal love with all its splendor and its eternal vows, subsists, as the spiritual and free beings who pledged themselves to one another subsist. When one of the partners, freed from the bonds of the flesh, enters into the divine intimacy, God liberates him from all weakness and from all the disfigurement of selfishness; he also invites the partner who remains on earth to stability in a purer and more spiritual disposition of soul. Since one of the spouses has consummated his sacrifice, should not the other one accept a greater detachment from this earth, a renunciation of its intense—but fugitive—joys, of the sensible and carnal affection which bound the spouse to the home and absorbed heart and energy? By accepting the cross, the separation, the renunciation of the presence of the loved one, he becomes concerned now with winning through to another presence, stronger, more intimate, more profound. A presence which will be also a purifying presence; for he who sees God face to face cannot tolerate in those whom he loved most while on earth, self-preoccupation, discouragement, inconsistent attachments.

If the sacrament of matrimony, symbol of the redemptive love of Christ for His Church, already applies to husband and wife the reality of that love, transfigures them, makes them resemble, the one Christ, Who gives Himself to save humanity, the other the redeemed **760**
(9, 34)

Church who accepts her share in the sacrifice of Christ, then widowhood beomes in some sort the goal and end of this mutual consecration; it is the figure of the present life of the militant Church deprived of the vision of her heavenly Spouse, but with whom she remains indefectibly united, journeying towards Him in faith and hope, living on that love which sustains her in all her trials, and waiting impatiently for the final accomplishment of the initial promises.

Such is the grandeur of widowhood when it is lived as the prolongation of the graces of marriage and the preparation of their full flowering in the light of God.

(*The life of the widow, at home and in the Church.*) (a)

DIGNITY OF THE SPOUSES

All. to the World Union of Women's Organizations, September 29, 1957.

(*The woman belongs to God.—The woman belongs to Christ.*)

761 The fact that the woman belongs to Christ takes
(7, on a special meaning in marriage, and a meaning which
34, the Apostle St. Paul establishes vigorously. He writes
39) to this effect to the Ephesians: "Husbands, love your wives, as Christ also loved the Church and delivered himself up for it" (a); "let women be subject to their husbands, as to the Lord. . . . As the Church is subject to

760a For the parts of this discourse omitted here, cf. **THE WOMAN IN THE MODERN WORLD**, nn. 561-576.
761a Eph. 5:25.

Christ: so also let the wives be to their husbands in all things" (b). In raising to the dignity of a sacrament the marriage of baptized persons, Christ conferred on the spouses an incomparable dignity and assigned a redemptive function to their union. When he affirms that women must be subject to their husbands as the Church is to Christ, St. Paul establishes a very clear difference between the spouses, but, by that very fact, he illustrates the force of the bond which unites them with one another and maintains the indissolubility of the link which joins them.

(*The woman belongs to the Church.*) (c)

A PRECIOUS TREASURE

Radio Message to the faithful of Bolivia, September 29, 1957.

(*Closing of the mission exercises.—To assure the fruits of the mission: a resolution.*)

And if you were to ask Us in what this resolution **762** should consist fundamentally, by reason of the paternal (42- affection which We have for you and the desire We 43) have for your real good, We would tell you that it should consist in a generous will ever to bear in mind the grandeur of Christian marriage, a sacrament of incalculable transcendence, even socially, and whose neglect is generally followed by terrible consequences of every kind; in a very firm determination to safeguard the

761b Eph. 5:24; cf. Col., 3:19.
761c For parts here omitted, cf. **THE WOMAN IN THE MODERN WORLD**, nn. 577-619.

sanctity of the family, which you ought to look on as one of your most precious treasures and from which so many other benefits should flow, because in a truly holy home, the family prays and works in an ordered fashion. Each of the members observes with care his duties with regard to men, the Church, and God. A more solid, more stable, surer basis could not be given to the modern world in its instability and its restlessness, the sources of such very real anxiety. Finally, from a holy home emerges, as a natural consequence, a youth which should renew society, as well as pure and pious souls, the indispensable good soil in which the Lord can plant the seeds of the priestly and religious vocations which you feel the need of so intensely.

(Hope that the mission will be the dawn of an era of Christian life.)

LARGE FAMILIES

All. to the Italian Association of Large Families, January 20, 1958.

(Welcome.—Large families are the sign of a nation's health.)

Birth control

763
(28,
61,
88)
It is fitting to class among the most harmful aberrations of modern neo-pagan society the opinion of certain men who dare to term the fruitfulness of marriage a "social ill" from which the "infected" nations should endeavor by every means to be cured. Whence the propaganda of what is called "rational birth control" ("planned parenthood"), supported by individuals and

associations, sometimes distinguished for other reasons, but in this one unfortunately blameworthy. But if it is painful to speak of the spread of such teaching and practices, even in traditionally wholesome milieus, it is at the same time comforting to note in your country the symptoms and the facts of a healthy reaction, in the juridical as well as the medical domains. As everyone knows, the present Constitution of the Italian Republic—to cite only this source—grants (Article 31) "special consideration to large families," and as for the most current teaching of Italian doctors, it is more and more in opposition to birth control. But for all that, it must not be thought that the danger is past, or that prejudices are at an end which tend to enslave marriage and its wise norms to culpable selfishness, individual and social.

The press is particularly to be reproved: it comes **764** back on the question from time to time with the obvious *(61-* intention of sowing confusion in the minds of good people *62,* and leading them astray by one-sided documentation, *88)* by questionable surveys, and even by statements falsely attributed to one or another ecclesiastic. On the Catholic side, efforts must be made to spread the conviction based on truth that the physical and moral health of the family and of society can be protected only by a generous obedience to the laws of nature, that is to say, of the Creator, and, above all, by fostering a deep and sacred respect for them. In this matter everything depends on the intention. Laws might be multiplied and sanctions increased, irrefutable proofs might be used to demonstrate the foolishness of these theories of "limitation" and the evils which spring from their application; but if the sincere will to allow the Creator to accomplish his work freely is lacking, human egoism will always be able to find new sophisms and expedients to silence the conscience, if this be possible, and to perpetuate abuses.

The testimony of parents

765
(27,
61,
103)
Now the testimony of parents of large families is valuable from the fact that not only do they reject outright and in practice all intentional compromise between the law of God and the egotism of man, but they are also prompt to accept with joy and gratitude the inestimable gifts of God which children are, as many as He pleases to send. While it frees the spouses from intolerable nightmares and remorse, this disposition of mind assures—and this is the opinion of competent medical authority—the most favorable physical premises for a wholesome development of the fruits proper to marriage, while it avoids at the very origin of the new lives that trouble and anxiety which become so many blemishes in the mother as also in the child. In fact, outside of exceptional cases about which We have had occasion at other times to speak, the law of nature is an essentially harmonious one: therefore, it does not create discord or contradiction, except in so far as it is interfered with by circumstances which are for the most part abnormal, or by the opposition of the human will. No eugenics can do better than nature, and eugenics is good only when, after having profoundly penetrated these laws, it respects them, although in certain cases of defective subjects, it is advisable to dissuade them from contracting marriage (a).

765a Cf. above, n. 329.

Popular good sense

For the rest, the good sense of the people has always **766** and everywhere seen in large families the sign, the proof, *(27)* and the source of physical health, while history makes no mistake when it sees in the tampering with marriage laws and the laws of procreation the first cause of a nation's decadence. Large families, far from being a "social ill," are the guarantee of the physical and moral well-being of a people. In homes where there is always a cradle from which rise an infant's cries, virtue flourishes spontaneously and vice stays at a distance, as if driven away by childhood which is renewed there like the fresh and life-giving breath of springtide.

Let the pusillanimous and the egotistical, therefore, take you as their example; let the country show you its gratitude and its predilection for the sacrifices you have accepted in bringing up and educating its citizens. As for the Church, she is grateful to you for the power of being able, thanks to you and with you, of presenting to the sanctifying action of the Divine Spirit multitudes of souls, ever more numerous and more healthy.

(*The large family is witness to lively faith in God.— Happy and fruitful holiness of large families.*) (a)

Action to instigate

Finally, a word for you, Directors and representatives **767** of the Association of Large Families at Rome and in *(103,* Italy. Take care to inject an ever more vigilant and ef- *105)* fective dynamism in the action which you propose to undertake to promote the dignity of large families and

766a Parts of this discourse here omitted will be found in the volume on **THE CHRISTIAN HOME.**

their economic protection. For the first objective, work in conformity with the precepts of the Church; for the second, you will have to rouse from its lethargy that part of society which is not yet conscious of its duties to its fellow men. Providence is a divine reality, but it loves to use human collaborators. Ordinarily, it moves and acts when it is appealed to and, so to say, is guided by the hand of men; it loves to hide behind human action. If it is just to recognize that Italian law has the honor of very advanced positions in the area of family protection, especially in the protection of large families, we must not hide from ourselves that there are still very many families struggling, without any fault on their part, in the midst of economic difficulties and privations. Well!—your action should propose to extend to these families in particular the protection of the laws, and, in the most urgent cases, the succor of charity. Every positive result obtained in this field is a solid stone set in the edifice of country and Church; it is the best thing anyone can do as a Catholic and a citizen.

PERMANENT VALUES

Radio Message to the faithful of Sardinia, April 24, 1958.

(*Social and religious evolution of Sardinia.*)

768 There is every reason for hope, as long as the Sardin-
(61, ian people and their rulers keep the spirit of restoration
205) alive in the rules of the wise prudence of which they have given proof up to this time, resisting the seduction of vain mirages and badly understood progress. It would be a vain and pernicious mirage, for example, to attempt

to "modernize" spiritual, family, and social values which have, up to the present, been preserved from materialistic and hedonistic contamination. Even among you, in fact, there are some who dare to consider traditional Christian values as henceforth "outmoded" and consequently irreconcilable with modern progress. If such an outlook should prevail—and God forbid that it should—your Sardinia would receive greater harm than the sterility and abandonment which were the result of the depredations and incursions of the past. Therefore, you must promote what is wholesome in order to reenforce, develop, and root more firmly the good traditions of the past: for example, the sanctity of marriage and the unity of the family, the moral education of youth inspired by Christian norms of purity, modesty, obedience to parents, simplicity (and almost austerity) of life, harmony between clergy and laity, zeal for work, attachment to the locality as a living and active part of the common fatherland. To wish to destroy these qualities of the Sardinian people is to wish to efface their special features, to obscure the splendor of their nobility, to strip them of their most precious treasures.

(Choice of guides.—Wishes for a full life.)

AT THE SOURCES OF TRUTH

Message to the World Congress on the Family, June 10, 1958.

(Welcome.)

Whoever wishes to erect the civic and social structure on strong and stable bases must found it on a conception of marriage and the family in conformity with the order **769** *(42, 61,*

101) established by God. Guardian of the truths of the natural law, and at the same time interpreter of the divine revelation which confirms and prolongs them, on these questions the Church has given precise teachings of permanent value. We Ourselves on many occasions have recalled the intangible principles touching upon the indissolubility of marriage, its essential ends, the sacred character of life, and many other points of moral too often the subject of attack in our times. Beloved Sons, draw from the clear, pure sources of the truth. From the teaching authority of the Church gather the divine words which do not change. Lift up your hearts and your thoughts during this vigil of prayer!

770 For it is from the summits of a sure and immutable
(100- teaching that you will see the true perspectives in which
101, it will be possible for you to bring light to many of the
105) present problems concerning the family in the world. The stability of the home is often compromised, and for many reasons; in many cases living conditions are difficult; the magnificent mission of husband and wife, which is not without its sacrificial aspect, is far from being understood by all; and the children are, alas! the first victim of this state of affairs. You will pray and you will work, beloved Sons, so that plans can be made and possibilities mapped out which will permit the greatest number possible to have a wholesome and fruitful union, an honest and happy family life, in which the exigencies of morality are not sacrificed to individual pleasure or to the enjoyment of individual well-being. And you yourselves will have at heart to be examples of fidelity to this Christian ideal.

Legislation which favors the family

God grant that so many men of good will who desire **771** to serve the true interests of the family in the world may *(44,* bring to it the support of friendly public opinion and *100,* favorable legislation! Where the institution of the family *105)* is still honored and prosperous, may it be protected against every undermining influence. If the force of circumstances has severely shaken it, let it be reestablished in its rights and its just functions. And everywhere where the difficulties of contemporary life threaten its equilibrium, let the family receive opportune support from the power of the state for the good of society itself, but always with a respect for the true character of this natural institution, raised by Our Lord to the dignity of a sacrament.

To this common task, Fathers and Mothers of Catholic families, workers in the family associations of your respective countries, you will bring an effective contribution.

GENETICS OF THE BLOOD

All. to the members of the International Congress on Blood Transfusion, September 5, 1958.

(*Medico-biological aspects.—Problems with regard to conjugal morality.*)

We will speak of some of these problems, following **772** the information which has been furnished to Us, and *(108)* of the solutions which it is proposed to apply to the problems, considering at the same time the moral implications involved. In general, we should emphasize in the first place the necessity of furnishing the public with indispensable information on the subject of blood and heredity, so as to allow individuals and families to be on guard against terrible accidents. To this end, it would be possible to organize, after the manner of the American "Dight Institute," clinics for information and consultation which engaged couples and married persons could consult with confidence on the subject of heredity, the better to assure the happiness and security of their union.

The function of medical consultation

773
(88,
102,
108)
These clinics would not give information merely, but would assist interested parties to apply effective remedies. In a work which, We have been assured, is authoritative in this area (a), We have read that the principal function of the consultation is to make clear to the interested parties the problems of genetics presented by their respective families (b). In almost every home, it seems, difficult situations can be met with concerning the heredity of one or more of the members. It might even happen that husband and wife accuse each other of an anomaly which becomes manifest in their child. Often the specialist who is consulted can intervene successfully to attenuate the difficulty. Advised of the danger and of its scope the parents will then make a decision which will be "eugenic" or "disgenic" with regard to the hereditary character in question. If they decide to have no more children, their decision is "eugenic," that is to say, they will not propagate further the defective gene by engendering either defective children or

773a Sheldon C. Reed, *Counseling in Medical Genetics.*
773b *Ibid.*, III, p. 12.

normal "carriers." If, as it usually happens, the probabilities of engendering an infant carrier of this defect are fewer than they fear, it may be that they will decide to accept other children. This decision is "disgenic" because they propagate the defective gene instead of arresting its progress. Definitely, the effect of consultation in genetics is to encourage parents to have more children than they otherwise would have, since the probability of an unfortunate case is less than they thought. If consultation may seem "disgenic" with regard to the abnormal gene, it must be considered that persons sufficiently concerned about the future to ask advice have a high conception of their duties as parents: from the point of view of moral, it would be desirable that such cases should be multiplied.

Consultation and religious duties

The "Dight Institute" is frequently asked if there **774** is any relationship between consultation and the reli-(102, gious duties of the consultant (a). In reality, genetic consultation leaves out of account religious principles. It does not provide an answer for parents who ask if they should have more children, and it abandons to them the responsibility of the decision. The Dight Institute is not, therefore, a clinic organized to circumvent fecundity; they do not furnish information on "planned parenthood," for this question does not enter into their field.

The work from which We have taken this material **775** emphasizes clearly and forcefully the importance of the (102, work which remains to be done in this area: "Death," 108)

774a *Ibid.*, p. 15-16.

it states, "is the price of ignorance of the genetics of blood groups." Happily, the physician now has at his disposal information sufficient to assist men to a surer realization of the desire—so deep and so powerful among large numbers—to have a happy family of healthy children! If the couple be sterile, the physician will try to assure their fecundity; he will put them on guard against dangers they would not suspect; he will help them to engender normal, healthy children.

Moral implications

776
(88,
108)
Better advised on the problems posed by genetics and on the gravity of certain hereditary illnesses, men today have, more than in the past, the duty of taking these acquisitions into account so as to avoid, for themselves and others, numerous physical and moral ills. They must be attentive to all that might cause their posterity permanent damage and involve it in an endless succession of misfortunes. Let us recall on this point that community of blood, whether in families or in groups, imposes certain duties. Although the formal elements of every human community are of the psychological and moral order, the succession of generations forms the material basis, and this must be respected and in no way harmed.

What We say of heredity may be applied in a larger sense to the communities which make up the races of humanity. But the danger becomes all the greater here of an exaggerated insistence on the meaning and value of the racial factor. It is only too well known, alas! to what excesses pride of race and racial hatred can lead; the Church has always opposed them energetically, whether they appear as attempts at genocide, or as practices inspired by what is called the "color-bar." She disapproves also of every experiment in genetics which would hold cheap the spiritual nature of man and would treat him as the equal of some insignificant representative of an animal species.

(*Assistance to the sick.*)

PROBLEMS OF HEREDITY

All. to the members of the Seventh Congress on Hematology, September 12, 1958.

(*Discourse of September 5, 1958 recalled* [a].—*Problems of defective heredity.—Different cases foreseen.*)

Artificial insemination

The first case mentioned envisages, as a solution to the problem of the sterility of the husband, artificial insemination, which obviously supposes a donor who is a stranger to the married couple. We have already had occasion to take a position against this practice in the allocution addressed to the Fourth International Congress of Catholic Physicians, September 29, 1949. On that occasion We absolutely condemned insemination between unmarried persons and even between spouses (b). We returned to this question in Our allocution to the World Congress on Fertility and Sterility, May 19, 1956 (c), to condemn once more every type of artificial insemination, because this practice is not included in the rights of spouses and because it is contrary to natural law and to Catholic morality.

777
(94)

777a Cf. above, nn. 772-776.
777b Cf. above, nn. 553-557.
777c Cf. above, nn. 732-747.

As for artificial insemination between celibates, already in 1949 We had declared that it violates the principle of natural law that no new life can be procreated outside the bonds of a valid marriage.

778
(93) The solution by voluntary adultery condemns itself, whatever be the biological, eugenic, or juridical reasons by which people seek to justify it. No married partner can permit his or her conjugal rights to be placed at the disposition of a third party, and every attempt to renounce these rights remains ineffectual; nor can such an attempt be based on the juridical axiom: *volenti non fit inuria.*

Direct sterilization

779
(53,
61,
88) Another solution is envisaged, namely sterilization, whether of the person, or simply of the action. For biological and eugenic reasons these two methods are now viewed with increasing favor and are being spread more widely by reason of new drugs which are growing in effectiveness and convenience. The reaction of certain groups of theologians to this state of affairs is symptomatic and somewhat alarming. It reveals a deviation in moral judgment which goes hand in hand with an exaggerated promptness to revise commonly received positions in favor of new techniques. This attitude proceeds from a laudable intention which, in order to help those who are in difficulty, refuses to exclude too summarily new possibilities of solution.

780
(61) But the effort of adaptation is here applied in an unfortunate manner, because certain principles have been badly understood, or they have been given a meaning and a scope which cannot be theirs. The Holy See then

finds itself in a situation similar to that in which Blessed Innocent XI was: more than once he found himself obliged to condemn theses advanced by moral theologians who were animated by an indiscreet zeal and an ill-judged boldness (a).

Several times We have taken a position on the subject of sterilization. In substance, We have stated that direct sterilization is not authorized by man's right to dispose of his own body, and cannot, therefore, be considered a valid solution to the problem of transmitting unhealthy heredity. **781** *(88)*

Direct sterilization, We said on October 29, 1958, that is to say, sterilization which aims, either as a means or an end, at rendering procreation impossible, is a grave violation of the moral law and therefore is illicit. Even the authority of the State has not the right under any pretext whatever to permit it, still less to prescribe sterilization or to inflict it upon innocent persons. This principle has already been enunciated in the encyclical of Pius XI on marriage, *Casti connubii* (a). Thus, when sterilization began to be much more widely used (about ten years ago), the Holy See was obliged to declare openly and explicitly that direct sterilization, permanent or temporary, whether of men or women, is illicit in virtue of the natural law, from which the Church herself, as you know, has no power to dispense (b). **782** *(88)*

Indirect sterilization

By *direct sterilization* We wish to designate the action of one who proposes, as end or means, to render **783** *(90)*

780a Denz., nn. 1151-1216; 1221-1288.
782a Cf. above, n. 328.   782b Cf. above, n. 614.

procreation impossible; but We do not apply this term to every action which renders procreation impossible in fact. Man, in fact, has not always the intention of doing what results from his action, even if he has foreseen it. Thus, for example, the removal of diseased ovaries will, as a necessary consequence, render procreation impossible; but this impossibility may not be intended (or willed) either as end or means. We took up in detail these same explanations in Our allocution (October 8, 1953) to the Congress of Urologists (a). The same principles apply to the present case and prohibit considering as licit the removal of glands or sex organs with a view to impeding the transmission of defective hereditary characteristics.

784
(88) These principles allow us also to resolve a question much discussed today by physicians and moralists: is it lawful to prevent ovulation by means of pills employed as remedies against exaggerated reactions of the uterus and the organism, although this medication, in preventing ovulation, also renders fecundation impossible? Is it permissible for the married woman who, in spite of this temporary sterility, wishes to have relations with her husband?

785
(88,
90) The response depends upon the intention of the person. If the woman takes this medication not with a view to preventing conception, but solely on the advice of her physician, as a necessary remedy because of a uterine or organic disorder, she brings about an *indirect* sterilization which remains licit according to the general principle of "actions with a double effect." But a *direct—*

783a Cf. above, nn. 693-703.

and therefore an illicit—sterilization is brought about when ovulation is arrested in order to preserve the uterus and the organism from the effects of a pregnancy which it is not capable of bearing. Certain moralists hold that it is lawful to take medication with this end in view, but wrongly. It is also necessary to reject the opinion of several physicians and moralists who permit the use of these remedies when medical indications render undesirable a conception in the near future, or in other similar cases which it would not be possible to mention here: in these cases the use of medication has as its end to prevent conception by impeding ovulation; therefore, we are here dealing with direct sterilization.

To justify it, a moral principle—just in itself, but incorrectly interpreted—is sometimes invoked: *licet corrigere defectus naturae,* they say, and since in practice it is sufficient to have reasonable probability to make use of this principle, it is pretended that here a natural defect is being corrected. If this principle had an absolute value (or validity), eugenics could unhesitatingly employ drugs to prevent the transmission of a defective heredity. But it is also necessary to see in what way the natural defect is being corrected and to take care not to violate other principles of morality. **786 (88)**

Ogino-Knaus Method

Finally, as a means of arresting defective hereditary characteristics, the use of the preventatives and of the Ogino-Knaus method has been proposed. Specialists in eugenics who condemn their use absolutely when it is simply a question of giving free rein to passion, approve **787 (27, 88)** these two systems when serious hygienic reasons warrant. They consider them a lesser evil than the procreation of defective children. Even if others approve this position, Christianity has followed and continues to follow a different tradition. Our predecessor Pius XI has given a solemn exposition of it in his encyclical *Casti connubii* of December 31, 1930.

788
(27,
88)
He calls the use of preventatives a violation of the natural law; an act to which nature has given the power to raise up a new life is deprived of it by the human will: *quemlibet matrimonii usum*—he wrote—*in quo exercendo, actus, de industria hominum, naturali sua vitæ procreandæ vi destituatur, Dei et naturæ legem infringere, et eos qui tale quid commiserint gravis noxæ labe commaculari* (a).

789
(28)
On the other hand, taking advantage of the temporary natural sterility in the Ogino-Knaus method does not violate the natural order as the practice described above does, since conjugal relations respond to the will of the Creator. When this method is used for motives of serious proportions—and the indications of eugenics can assume a grave character—it is morally justified. We have already spoken of it in Our allocution of October 29, 1951, not to set forth the biological or medical point of view, but to put an end to the conscientious concern of many Christians who have been using the method in their conjugal life. Moreover, in his encyclical of December 31, 1930, Pius XI formulated the statement of principle: *Neque contra naturae ordinem agere ii dicendi sunt coniuges, qui iure suo recte et naturali*

788a Cf. above, n. 316.

ratione utuntur, etsi ob naturales sive temporis sive quorundam defectuum causas nova inde vita oriri non possit (a).

We have stated definitely in Our allocution of 1951 **790** that spouses who make use of their conjugal rights have *(27-* the positive obligation in virtue of the natural law proper *28)* to their state not to exclude procreation (a). In fact, the Creator has willed that the human race is to be propagated precisely by the natural exercise of the sexual function. But to this positive law We applied the principle which is valid for all laws: they do not oblige in the measure that their accomplishment would bring about notable disadvantages, which are not inseparable from the law itself, nor inherent in its fulfillment, but come from without, and which the legislator, therefore, had no intention of imposing upon men when he promulgated the law.

Adoption

The last means mentioned above and upon which **791** We wish to express Our opinion is that of adoption. *(26)* When it is necessary to advise against natural procreation because of the danger of hereditary taint, the system of adoption can be suggested to married couples who wish all the same to have children. It is noteworthy, moreover, that this advice is usually crowned with happy results and gives to the parents the joy, peace, and serenity which they desire. From the religious and moral point of view there is no objection to adopting children; it is an institution recognized in almost every

789a Cf. above, n. 319.
790a Cf. above, nn. 593-652.

civilized country. If certain laws contain morally un-
acceptable provisions, this does not militate against the
institution as such. From the religious point of view it
is necessary to stipulate that the children of Catholics
be committed to Catholic foster parents; in the great majority of cases in fact parents impose upon their adopted
children their own religion.

Response to certain questions

792   After having discussed the solutions currently proposed to the problem of hereditary defects, it still remains for Us to answer the questions you have proposed
to Us. They all spring from the desire of defining the
moral obligation which stems from results which
eugenicists can consider as verified.

793   In the different cases which have been presented,
(87) the question is focused on the general obligation of
avoiding every danger or damage, more or less grave,
as much for the interested party as for his partner and
their posterity. This obligation is in proportion to the
gravity of the possible damage, to its greater or lesser
probability, to the intensity and the proximity of the
pernicious influence at work, to the gravity of the motives for committing the actions which may be dangerous and for permitting their ill-fated consequences.
Now these questions are for the most part questions of
fact, in which only the interested party, the physician,
and the specialists who have been consulted can give
an answer. From the point of view of moral, it can be
said in general that no one has the right not to take
into account the real risks which are in the realm of
the known.

Prenuptial examination

According to this basic principle, we may answer **794** in the affirmative to the first question which has been *(108)* asked: *should the prenuptial examination be advised in general, and the blood test in particular, in Italy and the Mediterranean countries?*

This examination should be advised, and even, if the danger is really grave, it can be made obligatory in certain provinces or regions. In Italy, in the entire Mediterranean basin, and in the countries which receive groups of emigrants from these countries, special attention must be paid to the "Mediterranean" blood disease. The moral theologian will avoid pronouncing, in individual cases, an apodictic *yes* or *no;* only scrutiny of all the data makes it possible to determine whether there is grave obligation or not.

Is it permissible to advise against marriage?

You ask next *whether it is permissible to advise an* **795** *engaged couple not to contract marriage in a case where* *(88)* *the blood test has revealed the presence of the "Mediterranean disease"?*

When one party is the carrier of the Mediterranean blood disease he may be advised not to marry but he cannot be forbidden to marry. Marriage is one of the fundamental rights of the human person which may not be tampered with. If it is sometimes difficult to understand the Church's generous point of view, it is because men too easily lose sight of the presuppositions laid down by Pius XI in the encyclical *Casti connubii* on marriage: men are created not first and foremost for this earth and for a temporal existence, but for heaven and for eternity. This essential principle is foreign to the concerns of eugenics, and yet it is just; it is even the only one which is fully valid. Pius XI stated further, in the same encyclical, that no one has the right to prevent a person from marrying or from exercising his rights in a marriage legitimately contracted, even when, in spite of every precaution, the couple cannot have healthy children. In fact it will often be difficult to reconcile the two points of view, that of eugenics and that of moral. But to guarantee the objectivity of the discussion, each one must know the other's point of view and become familiar with his reasoning (a).

May a couple be advised not to have children?

796
(30) The same principles will lead to the solution of the third problem: *if, after marriage, the presence of the Mediterranean blood disease is recognized, is it permitted to advise the married couple not to have any children?*

They may be advised against having children, but they cannot be forbidden to do so. Moreover, it remains to be seen what method the counselor (be he doctor, hematologist, or moralist) will suggest to them for this end. Here the works of specialists refuse to answer and they leave to the couple their entire responsibility. But the Church cannot be satisfied with this negative attitude; she must take a position. As We have explained, there is no opposition to the method of perfect continency, to the Ogino-Knaus system, or to the adoption of a child.

795a Cf. above, n. 328.

Nullity of marriage?

The next question concerns the validity of a marriage contracted by partners who are carriers of the Mediterranean blood disease. *If the contracting partners are not aware of their state at the time of the marriage, is this fact a reason for the nullity of the marriage?* **797 (12)**

Setting aside the case where it is laid down as one of the conditions (a) that there be no hereditary taint, neither mere ignorance, nor fraudulent concealment of defective heredity, nor even positive error which would have prevented the marriage if it had been discovered, is sufficient to cast doubt on the validity of the contract. The object of the marriage contract is too simple and too clear for anyone to be able to allege ignorance of it. The bond contracted with a specific person must be considered as willed, because of the sanctity of marriage, the dignity of the spouses, and the security of the children engendered, and the contrary must be proved clearly and beyond a doubt. Grave error having been the cause of the contract (b) is not deniable, but it does not prove the absence of the real will to contract marriage with the person in question. What is decisive in the contract is not what would have been done if one or another circumstance had been known, but what was willed and done in reality, because, in fact, the circumstance was not known.

Is the Rh factor sufficient cause for nullity?

In the seventh question you ask *if the Rh-factor can be considered a valid reason for declaring the mar-* **798 (12)**

797a C.I.C., can. 1092.
797b C.I.C., Can. 1084.

*riage null and void, when it causes the death of the
child, from the very first pregnancy?*

You are supposing that the parents have not wanted
to commit themselves to have children who would be
the victims of a premature death caused by a hereditary
defect. But the simple fact that hereditary defects bring
about the death of the child does not prove the absence
of the intention to conclude the marriage. This situation
is obviously a tragic one, but the argument rests upon
a consideration which has no weight. The object of the
matrimonial contract is not the child but the accomplishment of the natural marriage act, or, more precisely, the right to accomplish this act; this right remains
entirely independent of the heredity of the child
who is engendered, and even of his ability to live.

Is it necessary to wait for the first "incident"?

799   *In a situation involving the Rh-factor,* you ask fur-
(30) ther *whether it is lawful to advise against the procreation
of children, or whether it is necessary to wait for the
first incident?*

Specialists in genetics and eugenics are more competent than We are in this field. In effect, we are here
dealing with questions of fact, which depend on many
factors of which you are the competent judges. From
the moral point of view, it is sufficient to apply the
principles, with the necessary distinctions, which We
have proposed above.

Marriage between blood-relations

800   Finally, you ask *if it is lawful to initiate a campaign
(92, of propaganda at the technical level to emphasize the
107) dangers inherent in marriage contracted by blood-relations.*

There can be no doubt that it is useful to inform the public of the serious risk involved in marriages of this type. Here, too, account must be taken of the gravity of the danger in order to judge of the moral obligation.

With wisdom and perseverance you are attempting to explore every possible outcome to so many difficult situations; you are engaged without respite in preventing and curing an infinity of human sufferings and miseries. Even if clarifications or modifications seem desirable on certain points, this does not diminish in any way the unquestionable merit of your labors. We gladly encourage them. We have the highest appreciation of the active and serious collaboration which permits differing opinions a free expression, but never stops at negative criticism. This is the only way opening to real progress, as well in the acquisition of fresh theoretical knowledge as in its clinical application.

SOCIAL NECESSITIES OF THE CHURCH

Encycl. *Mystici corporis,* June 29, 1943 (a).

(*The Church is the Mystical Body of Christ.—I. The Church is a social body, organic in constitution, and provided, in the sacraments, with vital means of sanctification.—The five first sacraments are ordered to the good of each member.*)

801a Following an overlooked citation in the original French edition, this passage was inserted here in this English translation, but belongs on page 354.

801
(19,
22-
23)
Christ provided in a special way for the social necessities of the Church by the institution of two sacraments. By matrimony, in which the contracting parties are themselves the ministers of grace, He procured the exterior and ordered increase of the Christian community, and, what is even better, the good religious education of the children, without which His Mystical Body would be exposed to the greatest dangers. By Holy Orders, men are consecrated to the service of God: men charged with immolating the Eucharistic Victim, with feeding the flock of the faithful with the Bread of Angels, and the food of doctrine; with directing them by the commandments of God and the counsels; finally, with strengthening them by the other supernatural gifts (b).

(*The members of the Church.—II. The Church is the Body of Christ.—III. The Church is a Mystical Body.—The Union of the faithful with Christ.*)

801b For passages here omitted see **THE CHURCH,** nn. 1002-1112.

JOHN XXIII
1958-1963

THE TRIBUNAL OF THE CHRISTIAN FAMILY

All. to the Prelates of the Sacred Rota, *Avete voluto far Ci cognoscere*, October 1, 1959 (a).

Beloved Sons, you have desired to make known to Us, in a clear and matter-of-fact report, the number and the complexity of the causes you have treated in the course of the past year. In the multiplicity of your present duties, the one which is more meritorious than any other is that which you perform in safeguarding the most sacred of human ties—the marriage bond. Our Predecessor Pius XII in a felicitous statement contained in one of the first discourses he addressed to you said that "the Sacred Roman Rota has the glory of being *the Tribunal of the Christian family,* humble or noble, rich or poor, in which justice enters to bring about the triumph of the divine law in the conjugal union, as avenger of the indissoluble bond, of the full liberty of consent in unity of life, of the sanctity of the sacrament" (b).

It is very natural that you should carry out with diligence and discretion this delicate mission of safeguarding the sanctity and indissolubility of matrimony, of defending it against the subtle attacks of a hedonistic egotism; and, at the same time, you are the protectors of the sacred rights of the human person when you

a AAS, LI (1959), pp. 824-825.
b All., October 1, 1940, Cf. above, n. 434.

acknowledge and declare, after long and profound examination, the lack of validity, namely, the non-existence of the marriage bond.

IMPORTANCE OF THE INSTITUTION
OF THE FAMILY

All. to the Prelates of the Sacred Rota, *E motivo di intima consolazione*, October 25, 1960 (a).

In fact, from the account which has been presented to Us there emerges very clearly the truth that matrimonial cases are almost the predominant cause of the work of the Sacred Rota. And it is easy to see how it can happen that in the juridical process—which here imposes very grave study and the most delicate exactitude—the interested parties, more or less consciously, not only bring forward motives which militate in favor of or against the existence of the bond, but sometimes use to their own advantage the more sacred aspects of the Christian life.

There is certainly in our day something which insensibly increases the perils to which the institution of the family is subject, and accentuates the dangers which weaken it: and this is happening in a way which is more insistent, more seductive, and more subtle than in the past.

The Church has never failed to raise her voice in warning about these dangers which are laying siege to the individual and collective conscience in so delicate

a AAS, LII (1960), pp. 899-903.

a matter, and which are so fraught with consequences for the life of society: encyclicals, documents, discourses are there to bear witness to the maternal and prevenient anxiety of the Church. Again today she will not abandon the mission which she has received from Christ Himself. First and foremost she will speak out; she will enunciate more clearly and more completely her teaching, always as appropriate as it is severe.

In this way, Beloved Sons, We wish to draw the attention of all men of good will—jurists, sociologists, educators, and the simple faithful—to the grave problem of the sanctity of marriage, so that they may be ever more effectively warned of those dangers which We have pointed out. These are brief reflections which We confide with simplicity to the consideration of all men. They touch on three points of the practical and authentic apostolate and the care of souls: I. the duty of instruction for all; II. strong doctrine in those who must educate, counsel, and guide; III. constant recourse to the fatherhood of God.

I. In the first place, *the duty of instruction* on the dignity and the obligations of the conjugal life.

Speaking to a group of newlyweds on April 22, 1942, Pius XII reminded them that "marriage is not only an act of nature, it is for Christian souls a great sacrament, a great sign of grace and of a sacred reality: namely, the espousals of Christ with the Church, made His Own and bought by His blood, to regenerate to the new life of the spirit the sons of men who believe in His name. . . . The sign and the light of the sacrament which, so to say, transform the act of nature, give to matrimony a nobility of sublime integrity, which comprises and unites within itself not only indissolubility, but also all that is concerned in and signified by the sacrament" (a).

Today the luminous beauty of the Christian doctrine on the nature of matrimony is required first of all in the constant and persuasive teaching given to the faithful, which will reach every level of society. In particular is it necessary—nay, it is even urgent—that this teaching reach the youth; as they approach matrimony it must arouse the conscience and make them aware of the grave duty of religious instruction in this very delicate matter.

Yes, We know that in many quarters various enterprises are on foot to serve as means, means which the press and technology today place at our disposition to make more effective, and even more attractive, this obligation of instruction: scientific publications, dispensaries, study courses, specialized preaching. We express a lively approval for such initiatives which, undertaken with caution, tested with discretion, and duly approved by the supreme ecclesiastical authority, kindle the sweet hope of an ever more consoling harvest of good fruit.

It is necessary to proceed in this sense with all energy and sincerity: the conditions of the times require us to move without delay. The period of youth—and especially the period of the engagement—sometimes wraps in the clouds of a badly understood and insufficiently disciplined sentiment and expression of love, the limpid clarity of the ideal. In saying this We are not far from the truth: it is confirmed by the suggestions of the press, of the radio, of the cinema—in their more

a Cf. above, n. 483.

or less empty expressions which lack a moral foundation. It must be noticed, too, what a complex of pleasure-inducing manifestations is created by an artificial environment, how they impose themselves by a thousand seductive means—which, in reality, do violence to the conscience—changing for the worse traditional customs, and the first and most ruinous effect of which is to undo the education of youth.

To consider the gravity of the peril, amounting not so much to many individual and specific episodes as on the contrary to a widespread letting down of firm moral barriers, there arises spontaneously the invitation, which We repeat with ardor *in visceribus Jesu Christi* first of all to pastors of souls to adopt every means—in instruction classes and catechesis, or: in preaching and writing, by word and by writing—in as extensive a manner as possible to enlighten the consciences of parents and children with regard to their duty.

And We extend this invitation also to as many as have the will and the means to influence public opinion, so that by their intervention there may always be clarification—not confusion—of ideas: rectitude, respect for the greatest and most precious of the good things of social life: the integrity of marriage.

II. This duty requires a particular *strength of doctrine* in those who, by their specific vocation and profession, must frequently turn their attention to these problems.

And first of all in you jurists: a strength nourished at the sources of the natural and positive law, which does not yield to any flattery or weakness, and at the same time is accompanied by a perfect equilibrium of judgment stemming from knowledge of the conditions of the times in which we live.

Again, strength in educators and physicians. We can never sufficiently deplore the damage caused in this area by naturalistic conceptions, first, and then by materialistic conceptions of life, with particular reference to marriage and the family. In seeking to withdraw them from the sphere and the defense of the Church's maternal vigilance, in reducing their value to that of a purely human institution, men have come little by little to an increasing weakness in their structure and consistency.

While, on the other hand, We can never sufficiently emphasize that purity of manners, sane education of the emotions, esteem of human values seen in harmony with the supernatural—all these prevent and resolve at the start this unfortunate situation; while neglect of the law inflicts on the soul wounds which do not heal. And here it is as necessary to state that the present state of things is caused by original sin as it is to hold that recourse to grace is necessary; this alone can restore the lost equilibrium of man's damaged nature; and if he wanders from this grace, wilfully neglects it, he deprives conjugal life of its most worthwhile and effective support.

Today it is still the duty of the educator and of the Christian physician not to look upon their professions in a one-sided manner, but in the fullness of the reality of man's situation: the concurrence in fruitful harmony of the natural and the supernatural has been won back for him.

The levity with which on so many occasions the subject of marriage is treated, and the frightening weakening of moral standards, are caused not only by defective religious instruction—as We have pointed out—but still more by the lack of clear and precise ideas on the part of those who, by their profession, ought to be the light and guide of the young. By the vacillation of their convictions, the superficiality and even the errors of their philosophical and religious foundation, and—We say it with sorrow—sometimes even by their perverse will in opposing the action of the Church, they aim the first blow at the firmness of many consciences, for whom the encounter with anti-Christian educators and physicians stands often as the occasion and the cause of a sad apostasy.

Strength, therefore, of convictions, of doctrine, of will, drawn from continuous study, from a humbly sincere attitude of soul: this is the straight line, this is the profound science which never goes, nor ever can go counter to the dictates of Revelation and the teachings of the Church.

III. A third means We deem very timely in its stabilizing effect on the security of the family, and this is connected with what We have already said. It is always to recall the fatherhood of God, *"ex quo omnis paternitas in caelis et in terris nominatur"* (a).

The interior and eternal fecundity which is in the bosom of God is, in a certain way, reflected beneficent and active in the sons of men, elevated as they are to the very high dignity and duty of procreators.

In the family is to be seen the marvelous and very close cooperation of man with God: two human persons, created to the divine image and likeness, are called not only to the great mission of continuing and prolonging

a Eph. 3:15.

the creative work, in giving physical life to new beings in whom the life-giving Spirit infuses the powerful principle of immortal life; but also to the more noble office which perfects the first: the civil and Christian education of their offspring.

This firm conviction, based on so high a truth, is enough to secure to each matrimonial union the stability of the bond, and make the parents aware of the responsibility which they assume before God and man.

Educators and pastors of souls know by experience what vigor of holy enthusiasm and of joyful gratitude to God such considerations raise in the hearts of the young who are preparing themselves for matrimony, and what touching seriousness of assent and of purpose are roused in their generous souls.

Therefore, let all these means be used with a joyous consciousness of the august nobility of man, of the father and the mother of the family as the first collaborators of God in the prosecution of his work in the world, in giving new members to the Mystical Body of Christ, in peopling heaven with the elect who will sing forever the glory of the Lord.

CHRISTIAN TEACHING ON MARRIAGE

All. to the Prelates of the Sacred Rota, *E anzitutto, nello incertezze dottrinali,* December 13, 1961 (a).

1. And above all, in the doctrinal uncertainty which, here and there in various expressions, threatens to disorientate public opinion, it is necessary to issue a grave

a AAS, LIII (1961), pp. 818-820.

and solemn summons to return to the solidity of the principles from which the Church draws her inspiration in the defence of matrimony. In safeguarding with jealous care the indissolubility of the bond and the sanctity of the *Sacramentum magnum,* the "great sacrament," the Church is defending a right, not solely ecclesiastical and civil, but above all natural, and a right of divine positive law. These two great and necessary goods, which the veil of the passions and of prejudice sometimes obscures until finally it makes men forget them, are commanded, the one by the natural law engraven in indelible characters in the human conscience, the other in the divine law of Our Lord Jesus Christ. Therefore, it is not a question of prescriptions and norms which circumstances impose and which can change in the course of generations, but of the divine will, of the intangible order established by God Himself to safeguard the first and fundamental nucleus of civil society. It is a question of the primordial divine law which in the fullness of time the words of Christ, *"ab initio autem non fuit sic," "but from the beginning it was not so"* (b), have brought back to its genuine integrity.

The Church is not defending the interests of class or of outmoded custom. Her glorious song, her title of nobility reverberates in the *Pater noster*: *Fiat voluntas tua ... in terra.* This is what she proposes and defends in the world: the will of God, in which is peace, serenity, and even prosperity for all her sons.

2. And, therefore, it is imperative that the doctrine of the Church on the sacrament of matrimony be better understood and more widely known in all its aspects.

b St. Matt. 19:8.

This is what We sigh for and what We confided to you with paternal hope in Our allocution last year.

"When We consider the gravity of the danger"—We said then—". . . there arises spontaneously the invitation, which We repeat with ardor *in visceribus Jesu Christi,* first of all to all pastors of souls to adopt every means—in instruction classes and catechesis, by word and by writing—in as extensive a manner as possible to enlighten consciences. . . . And We extend this invitation also to as many as have the will and the means to influence public opinion, so that by their intervention there may always be clarification—not confusion—of ideas; rectitude, respect for the greatest and most precious of the good things of social life: the integrity of marriage."

The invitation is renewed today with greater intensity, because the widespread feeling of danger persists, deriving in the first place from the lack of solid teaching and the dearth of correct information. Whether written or delivered orally, generally speaking these arguments require preparation, maturity of judgment, sincerity of conscience: nevertheless, there is need for the faithful, as well as the whole of human society, to be enlightened, forewarned, and well directed.

What is needed then, what is irreplaceable, is a vast work of catechesis and of illustration of the truth: by the traditional means which the Church has at her disposal, as also by those which are made available by the press and the new audio-visual techniques. New forms must be sought to bring this teaching to those who are contemplating marriage, in particular to young people and to engaged couples.

You see, therefore, what a vast pastoral horizon opens out before your work. To the obligation of teaching which it presupposes, you can add the work of collaboration in a variety of ways which your sacerdotal functions will not fail to supply.

3. There is only one reason for all that We have said. It is the motive power for the whole of the spiritual action of the Church in time: the salvation of souls: *salus animarum.* Her mother's heart leads her to act and to decide for the good of all her children. And this is the spirit which informs the action of the Tribunals of the Church; and, in consequence, of the ecclesiastical judge, of the defender of the bond, as of the promoter of justice and of the lawyers. It is a *ministerium veritatis,* because it tends primarily to the salvation of the souls who have to do with this court.

Yes, the Church has ever in view the eternal salvation of each one, even when she limits the rights of the accused and when she delivers sentence of guilt: nay, to the guilty party she never refuses the means to flee from the peril of eternal damnation.

In the perspective of a significance which is other than temporal and contingent, all the care and the safeguards with which, in this delicate matter, the Church surrounds your labors undertaken for the good of her children, acquire their true value: the hidden prudence with which each case is examined, the great number of cases which are treated with gratuitous legal assistance—in this past year about the same as any others.

This, therefore, is the way your labors contribute to strengthening the supreme work of the Church, and with the incontrovertible evidence of truth and of justice they remind us of the salvific will of the Heavenly Father and the incessant yearning of the Heart of Christ: *non enim misit Deus Filium suum in mundum ut iudicet mundum, sed ut salvetur mundus per ipsum*: for God sent not His Son into the world to judge the world, but that the world might be saved by Him (a).

a St. John 3:17.

APPENDIX

THE ORDER OF THE
PURPOSES OF MATRIMONY

Extract from the sentence of the Holy Roman Rota, January 22, 1944 (a).

(Exposition of the case.

I. — Discussion of the request for nullity based on the motive of violence and fear.)

II. — *Simulation of Matrimonial consent*

9. — The Law.

Since the asserted simulation of matrimonial consent, in the present case, is strictly connected with the ends of Matrimony, and the Holy Father gloriously reigning, inaugurating on October 3, 1941, the new juridical year of the Roman Rota, having spoken in regard to the ends of matrimony, inviting the Auditors,

(a) This is a translation of a judgment of the Holy Roman Rota which refers, according to its attributions and conforming to the will of the Supreme Pontiff, to the principles themselves of Canon Law. The publication of this sentence in the *Acta Apostolicae Sedis* (36th year [1944] pp. 179-200), and the constant use which seems to have been made of it in the addresses of the Holy Father, stress the importance of this document, which, though occasioned by a particular case, constitutes an official interpretation of previous texts and the most authoritative act of ecclesiastical jurisprudence as regards to the matter.

as it seems, to go deeper into this question and to study it more carefully, it is useful to point out what follows.

Matrimony has a primary and a secondary end. This is evident from the Constitutions and the numerous Encyclicals of the Supreme Pontiffs, from the common doctrine of theologians, canonists and moralists, and from the explicit words of Canon Law. Canon 1013, #I, says: "The primary end of Matrimony is the procreation and education of the children; the secondary end is mutual aid and a remedy for concupiscence." The word *finis* ("end") in the above-mentioned sources is taken in a technical sense and means a benefit which is meant to be obtained both on the part of nature and by deliberate intention of the agent. There must also be used in matrimony the well-known distinction between the *finis operis* and the *finis operantis* (which can be one or several). The *finis operis* in matrimony is that benefit which matrimony tends of its very nature to obtain, and which God the Creator gave to the institution of matrimony. If is is true that matrimony "by its very nature is a divine institution" and that "it was governed by laws, confirmed, and elevated by God, the Author Himself of nature, and by the same Restorer of nature, Christ Our Lord," it follows that "the very institution of matrimony, *the ends,* the laws and the benefits also come from God" (a). Beside this the *finis operantis* is that benefit to obtain which the will of the contracting parties tends. It is evident that the *finis operantis* can coincide with the *finis operis;* indeed, Pius XI of happy memory expressly warns the contracting parties "to seek in matrimony those very ends for which

9a Encycl. *Casti connubii;* cf. n. 267.

it was instituted by God" (b). The Roman Catechism, treating of the causes which direct men to matrimony, stress in the first place one of the *finis operis,* saying: "The prime cause is the society itself between the different sexes, sought by natural instinct and established in the hope of mutual help, so that each one may withstand, more easily with the help of the other, life's hardships and support the weakness of old age" (c). But these two ends do not always coincide. Indeed, it can happen that the *finis operantis* is completely *extra* or *praeter* to the *finis operis.* For example, if the contracting party proposes as the primary end of matrimony the acquirement of riches or the freedom from an evil which would otherwise threaten him. The *finis operantis* can also be contrary to the *finis operis* and this happens every time that a person contracting matrimony has in mind a benefit or an end which is repugnant to one or all of the *fines operis,* namely of matrimony. But now the *finis operis* must be treated separately.

10. — Matrimony, considered as a work and institution of nature, is a natural society, one and indivisible, specifically distinct from every other human association. It must have therefore a natural *finis operis,* one and indivisible, specifically proper and distinct from every other end. Now the end, as the Angelic Doctor testifies, *"est causis formalis, qua plurium unio peragitur atque specificatur talis qualis est."* It follows that when *several fines operis* are assigned to the one and same society, one of these must be *prime* and *principal,* by reason of its formal cause, in which the other ends are contained

9b Ibid., n. 385.
9c Cf. n. 287, note (a).

or to which others are added so that the prime cause can the more easily, surely and fully be achieved. It is necessary therefore that among the ends of matrimony there be determined the order, according to which the other *fines operis* be subordinated to the principal end, which determines the specific nature of matrimony.

11. — A) *The primary end of Matrimony.*

The primary and principal, one and indivisible *finis operis* of matrimony which uniquely specifies its nature is the procreation and education of the offspring. This end can be considered a) *active,* b) *passive,* c) *sub utroque respectu.* Considered as *active* it regards the activity of the wedded couples, namely, the wedded couple inasmuch as they procreate and educate the offspring; intended as *passive* it regards the offspring inasmuch as they are procreated and educated; taken *sub utroque respectu* it considers the wedded couple and the offspring together. The secondary ends, then, which are ordained to the primary end, can regard rather one aspect than another—active or passive—but they can also regard in an equal measure both aspects.

12. — a) This *objective ordination* of matrimony to the primary end which is included in its nature, if it is considered in the order of execution, consists in this that the conjugal union (as much *in fieri* as *in facto esse*) contains of its very nature and can supply all that is demanded on the part of human activity and is sufficient to obtain the procreation and the education of the offspring (in a manner suitable to and worthy of human nature). Indeed, Christian marriage, of its very nature, comprises the *destination, aptitude* and *sufficiency* to obtain this end, since all those who contract marriage

or are already married are united and bound by a reciprocal right, exclusive and perpetual, to effecting acts
capable of themselves to generate offspring. Therefore,
having placed this right in its true light, considering the
vehement urge of the sexual appetite to exercise the
generative power, and keeping in mind that it is not
lawful to satisfy this appetite outside of marriage, it
must necessarily be concluded that the end which is
the procreation and the education of the offspring is
sufficiently and efficaciously provided for.

13. — This natural ordination to the primary end,
this aptitude and sufficiency is achieved in *every* valid
matrimony (even those of the sterile and of the aged)
and is so essential that lacking this no marriage can
exist or continue to exist. No marriage can be contracted, no marriage can exist if the basic right over the
partner's body relative to the generative acts is not established or does not exist in the wedded couple. If this
basic right is wanting or ceases, marriage cannot be
contracted, or if it were already contracted, it ceases
with the ceasing of this basic right (this happens following a dispensation of a matrimony *ratum et non
consummatum*).

14. — b) No less so than marriage itself, even
the *conjugal act* is subordinated and bound to the primary end, and to such a degree, that the exercise of this
act is only permitted if and inasmuch as there is verified and is observed its essential subordination to the
primary end of matrimony. This subordination is secured
by the fact that husband and wife, when completing
the natural conjugal act, can give all that is requested
and suffices on the part of human activity for the generation of offspring (the sentence of the Rota, April 25,

1941, before Wynen should be consulted, where there is treated fully this subordination of the conjugal act and of the essentially required elements *in copula* so that this subordination can be said to be of itself apt for the generation of the offspring).

15. — This subordination to the primary end which exists through its natural structure in the naturally completed conjugal act, is observed and is verified even in the wedded union of sterile persons and of others who for causes extrinsic to the act cannot generate offspring with the natural use of marriage. The following words of Pius XI of happy memory, taken from the Encyclical *Casti connubii,* refer to such persons: "Nor are husband and wife to be accused of acting against nature if they make use of their right in a proper and natural manner, even though natural causes (owing to circumstances of time or to certain defects) render it impossible for new life to originate. Both matrimony and the use of the matrimonial right have secondary ends—which husband and wife are quite entitled to have in view, so long as *the intrinsic nature of the act, and therefore its due subordination to its primary end, is safeguarded*" (a).

16. — The Supreme Pontiff gloriously reigning, in his allocution to the Holy Rota, mentioned above, also stresses that the conjugal act is subordinated to the primary end of matrimony; indeed he reproves the manner of those whose writings and judgments either completely separate or isolate beyond due measure the conjugal act from the primary end of matrimony. In the same error fall also those who hold that for the essence of the matrimonial act it is sufficient that such an act be

15a Encycl. *Casti connubii,* cf. n. 319.

completed in the natural manner in conformity to its external species, even if in its fulfillment it lacks one of the elements which on the part of conjugal activity itself are wholly necessary, and whose absence, if antecedent and incurable, render man incapable of matrimony, according to the constant jurisprudence of the Holy Rota, (cf. the above stated sentence): "for example if the male has not the faculty or the power to emit *true seed,* namely that which is produced in the genital organs, even if it be deprived of spermatozoa. These are the words of Pius XII: "Two extremes ... are to be avoided: on the one hand, to deny practically or to abase excessively the secondary ends of matrimony and the generative act; on the other, to dissolve and separate beyond measure the conjugal act from the primary end, to which according to all its intrinsic structure it is primarily and principally ordained" (a).

17. — B) *The secondary end of Matrimony*

The previously mentioned canon 1013 assigns a double secondary end to matrimony, namely, the *mutuum adiutorium* and the *remedium concupiscentiæ.* These ends are *fines operis* and not only *fines operantis.*

18. — a) Only a few things need be said of the other secondary end, the *remedium concupiscentiæ* and of its relation to the primary end.

It will be easily understood that of its very nature this end is subordinated to the primary end of generation. Indeed, concupiscence is remedied *in* matrimony and *by means of* matrimony with the lawful use of the generative faculty—a use destined, proportioned and

16a Discourse to the Members of the Tribunal of the Holy Roman Rota, October 3, 1941; cf. n. 470.

subordinated to the primary end of matrimony, in the above mentioned manner. Therefore, even the *sedatio concupiscentiæ* as a result of conjugal acts, is together with these acts subordinated to the primary end of matrimony.

19. — b) The other secondary end is the *mutuum adiutorium*, which includes various services and mutual aids between the contracting parties, for example, co-habitation, the same table, the use of material benefits, the acquirement and the administration of the means of subsistence, the most personal help in the various conditions of life, in the pyschic and somatic exigencies of life, in the use of the natural faculties and also in the exercise of the supernatural virtues (a).

20. — Recently, some authors when treating of the ends of matrimony, explain this *mutuum adiutorium* in a different manner. They hold that inasmuch as "the personal being" of the married couple receives a help and a complement, this *evolution and perfection* "of the person" of husband and wife is not a secondary but a primary end of matrimony. However, not all of these authors consider the matter in the same light. These newcomers to matrimonial matters stray from true and certain doctrine, without being able to apply solid and proven arguments in favor of their opinions. Putting aside these teachings of some recent authors, therefore, we must now examine the order and the interdependence between the primary and the secondary ends of matri-mony, omitting the *remedium concupiscentiæ*, which we have already treated briefly above.

19a Cf. Leo XIII, Encycl. *Arcanum*, n. 156; Pius XI, Encycl. *Casti connubii*, nn. 285-287.

21. — C) *Relation of the secondary end of matrimony with the primary end.*

Even outside of matrimony there can be a reciprocal help and common life between two persons of different sex either in the simple case of brother and sister living together, or in virtue of an explicit agreement to lend each other reciprocal help. This reciprocal help and common life, inasmuch as they are called and are *proper to matrimony* and its *secondary finis operis* must be considered according to a special property, which distinguishes them from any other community of life, united to reciprocal help. They are, then, distinguished *by their internal relation to the primary end,* which differentiates the conjugal union from every other human association.

22. — a) This relation between the secondary and the primary end is found first of all in the *origin* of this primary end in the origin of the corresponding right to mutual aid. It can be demonstrated thus: The immediate and essential object of the matrimonial contract is the exclusive and perpetual right over the body of the partner as regards the acts capable of generating offspring (a). As a consequence and natural complement of this right, there follows the right to all that without which the right to generate—and consequently to educate—the offspring, cannot be satisfied in a manner suitable to the dignity of human nature. Now it is not possible to satisfy in the above mentioned manner the right to generate and educate the offspring if the right to mutual help is not added to such a principal right, which includes the right to common life, in other words the right to cohabitation, bed and board, and help in all the neces-

22a C.I.C., can. 1081, par. 2; cf. n. 268, note (b).

sities of life. Let it be noted, however, that it is not a question here of the help lent by fact, but of the *right* to this mutual *adiutorium,* indeed, as the *principal* object of the matrimonial contract is not the "offspring", but the "right" to beget offspring, so the secondary object is not the *mutuum adiutorium* but the right to it.

23. — From what has been said up to now it follows that the right to life in common and mutual help is a result of the contracting parties' primary right to beget offspring. It also follows that a matrimonial contract cannot be concluded, which aims at mutual help and which prescinds at the same time from the given and accepted right to the body: such a contract (not conceding any right on the body) cannot be stipulated between two persons of different sex unless it be outside of marriage. A matrimonial contract *attempted* (a) in such a manner would be null and would not establish in the contracting parties either a principal or a secondary basis of matrimonial rights. On the contrary, every matrimonial consent to give and accept the right over the body of its very nature, gives rise to the married couple's right to a life in common and to reciprocal help.

24. — However, since this secondary right does not enter into the principal right as its constitutive part, nor is united to it as its prerequisite condition *sine qua non,* a matrimonial contract can be concluded which regards the principal right and explicitly denies the secondary end. In particular, as regards *cohabitation* which is one of the principal benefits united to the secondary end, and

23a *Contractus matrimonialis taliter* attentatus *esset nullus nullumque conderet ius matrimoniale in contrahentibus, neque principale neque secundarium.*

of its exclusion in the contract, Wernz-Vidal has to say: "Husband and wife, not being able to satisfy regularly and conveniently the conjugal debt without cohabitation, are, owing to this fundamental right and duty of marital life, also held by an onerous duty not only to observe cohabitation in the same house, but also to participate at the same table and have the same bed, except in cases contemplated by law. This assiduous cohabitation, common bed and board, belongs to the integrity of individual life, not to the essence of conjugal life, and therefore, sometimes, in a particular case, for a reasonable cause, they may be wanting, as in a marriage of conscience, and the obligation of justice to observe these matters admits a certain elasticity" (a). Gasparri on the matter teaches: "The greater number of authors maintain that the condition never to live together is against the substance of matrimony; but if the matrimonial right is truly observed by both parties, we do not think that such a doctrine corresponds to truth, because habitation, bed and board in common do not form part of the substance of matrimony; and indeed, a marriage of conscience is permitted, with such a tacit or expressed condition" (b).

25. — These rules are to be taken into account also in the case in which the contracting parties, renouncing the secondary end of cohabitation and the mutual aid connected to it, by common consent agree not to make use of the right given and accepted to the body of the other partner. "Just as it is not contradictory to receive a right already suspended as concerns its use in the very

24a *Ius can.*, Vol. V, n. 600.
24b *De matr.* 1932, ed., n. 905.

acceptance of the right, as happens when two persons bound by the vow of chastity contract matrimony, so there is no contradiction in giving a right whose use is excluded, with the consent given by the other party to such an exclusion" (a). The inner reason which renders the matter admissible is this "Husband and wife are not obliged *ad copulam,* unless one or the other party asks for the debt, and one of the parties can renounce to claim this right, obliging himself not to request it; nor are husband and wife obliged to generate offspring positively, but it is sufficient that they do not hinder it positively or kill the offspring" (b). De Smet thus expresses himself: "Nothing prevents on the one hand that reciprocal matrimonial consent, or full mutual power over the other's body be given, and on the other, that the engaged couple agree between themselves and promise by a distinct act *not to use* the right they have, in order to preserve chastity. What is excluded is not the right to use this right, but only its exercise" (c).

While this opinion, according to approved authors, as regards the agreement made by the engaged couple is to be held as common teaching, nevertheless, the authors are not of one mind if the pact not to exercise this right is bound to the consent as a *condition sine qua non.* Whatever the outcome of this question, the matrimonial contract cannot in this case be declared null, because the question of law is not certain (d). But, notwithstanding the matters explained above, the following

25a Wernz-Vidal n. 521, note 46.
25b Wernz-Vidal n. 521.
25c *De spons. et matri.,* Third ed., n. 156, note 2.
25d On this subject cf. Cappello, *De matr.,* Third ed., n.

must be added: as in determined circumstances, the firm and definite will not to fulfill can be a sign of defect of will to contract and oblige oneself (this defect must be however demonstrated in another way), likewise the serious and definite will not to concede in any way or at any time the right to common life or mutual help, can be a sign more or less well-founded of the lack of intention in the contractant to concede to the other party the principle right over the body, although from this sign alone there can never arise the moral certainty of the lack of will to contract matrimony and to oblige oneself.

26. — From what has been said the following must be concluded. As the *right* to life in common and all mutual help is in its origin intrinsically dependent on the principal *right* to the acts of generation and not vice versa; and as in matrimonial rights there exists a determined order, and a determined dependence: likewise must it be said of the ends of matrimony—to which these rights are ordered and in view of which they are conceded by nature—that by reason of their origin they are arranged in a given order and connected between themselves. After having determined the principal and primary end of matrimony, the Author of nature gave matrimony, as an institution of nature, a secondary and complementary end, so that *in* and *by* the same institution called marriage, there could and must be satisfied that primary end in a suitable manner.

27. — By way of a corollary it may be added that the well known definition or, more to the fact, description, which *Modestinos* gave of Matrimony: "Matrimony is the union of a man and a woman in a life-long union,

the participation of divine and human law" (a), groups together the elements, essentially constitutive and naturally consequent, without clarifying the order and the dependence between them. Therefore, it is not possible to study the ends of matrimony from this famous description of matrimony, without proceeding with caution and allowing room for necessary distinctions. In reality, as it has been noted above, as in the matrimonial contract "the right to the body" and the "right to aid" are not coordinated on the one plane but remain between themselves as the principal or super-ordered object and the secondary or subordinated object, so the ends as well, corresponding to the rights, are not equally principal or coordinate, but one is principal and the other is secondary and subordinate.

28. — b) The order of dependence and subordination which is described here is not only found in the origin of the secondary right, which is destined to the attainment of the secondary end and which assures this attainment but the same order is pointed out when the marriage is considered *in facto esse*.

Every man, indeed, being of his very nature a "social being," needs the help of his fellow man. He finds this help inasmuch as he is a member both of human society in general, and of a determined civil and domestic society in particular. In this common help of all men, there must also be considered the help and complement which one sex (even without any carnal affection and activity) receives from the nature of the other sex. Human society is formed of men and women

27a Dig., lib. XXIIII, II, *De ritu nuptiarum*, lib. I, Regularum.

who exert a reciprocal influence. But this common help cannot constitute the *finem operis* of matrimony. To constitute this, it must be further determined by a *specific element,* whence it appears why "mutual help" was assigned to matrimony by the Creator as its *finis operis.* This specific element again is and must be *in relation to the primary end and to the principal right.* Hence husband and wife, by the very nature of matrimony, are bound to the primary end of this institution, because, by matrimony, they acquired the right and destination to become "authors of a new life," procreating and educating children, even if in fact this is not verified.

But to satisfy in a due manner this specific destination, they need a multiple reciprocal help, and that not only as regards generative activity properly so-called, but even as regards the primary end in a complete sense, that is, taken both actively and passively. Indeed, nature desires that those should become "the authors of a new life" who are burdened by numerous demands of nature and life, yet adorned with human dignity. Such being the case nature aids this principal right with various assistances and life in common. This *specific note* of mutual matrimonial aid, which emanates from the innermost structure of matrimony, is also had in those marriages in which husband and wife do not wish or are unable to reach effective generation. What the Creator placed *in natura rei,* namely in marriage, does not depend on human will nor is it abolished by an external impediment.

29. — This specific mutual matrimonial aid added to the institution itself of matrimony comprises directly only *the aptitude and the destination* for every necessary help, assured by means of the transfer of the right

properly so-called to such help, and not the actual assistance in itself. On the other hand, however, to contract a valid marriage the transfer of the right to such help is not required (a): thus it appears clear that there can be a true marriage, even if husband and wife in reality do not enjoy this assistance which nature intends to give to matrimony. It is, moreover, apparent, why the actual use of mutual aid is not by its nature reserved to the service of the primary right. Mutual matrimonial aid is given by nature rather as a comfort to the person of husband and wife, inasmuch as they are destined to become, not in any kind of way, but in a suitable and worthy manner, "the authors of a new life," by whom so sustained by due help, the generative activity itself as a result is favored. Indeed, if the persons who generate are placed in a safe position, both themselves and the children, as regards life's difficulties and necessities (which grow further still with the birth of children), then the generative activity is well founded for by that fact. Hence it is clear that every reciprocal help, which emanates from marriage without damage to the primary end, is contained within the limits of the secondary end, and, because of the help and comfort which it gives to the person of husband and wife, it possesses a specific attitude, destination and subordination to the primary end (notwithstanding a certain relative independence which, according to what was said, belongs to the secondary end).

30. — The matters spoken of up to now of the secondary end of matrimony, considered *in facto esse* can be thus briefly summarized.

29a Cf. n. 24 of this *Appendix*.

1⁰ The destination and corresponding right to "mutual aid" derive from the very nature of matrimony and from God's will, and constitute its secondary *finis operis*. Therefore they can never be wanting in a true and perfect domestic society, nor are they ever frustrated as long as there exists the marriage itself with it primary end and its principal right.

2⁰ The "mutual assistance," considered as a secondary end of matrimony *in facto esse,* is called a dependent end, subordinate in respect to the primary end, since it was an addition made by the Creator to marriage, in view of the primary end. But it is an adjoined and non-constitutive element *ab extra* only by reason of the *primary end,* but not in respect to marriage *itself,* as if it were an *extra-matrimonial end;* it is an "intra-matrimonial" end, although not of the same degree as the primary end.

3⁰ The aptitude and the right to *mutuum adiutorum* are not restricted to *generative activity* nor do they regard it in the first place, but rather they regard the *persons who generate,* inasmuch as these persons, by the marriage contract, are destined to be able to become *authors of a new life.*

4⁰ The secondary end has a certain independence, in that in the person of husband and wife it can be verified and brought to effect in those cases in which either temporarily or perpetually the accomplishment of the primary end is impeded. The reason is that the *mutuum adiutorium* (and equally so the right to it) does not constitute an essential part of the primary right and the primary end. It is rather *extra essentiam* of the primary right and the primary end, though it be something *naturale consequens* of it and properly called matrimonial *right*.

5⁰ Whoever separates the matrimonial *mutuum adiutorium* taken in the widest sense, from its intrinsic subordination to the primary end not only offends objective truth and the intention of the Creator Himself, but necessarily opens the way to disastrous consequences.

(*Discussion of the fact.*)

III. — Discussion of the *inconsummatio* of the marriage. — The Tribunal's conclusions.

INDEXES

ABBREVIATIONS

References

AAS	*Acta Apostolicae Sedis,* Romae, Typis Polyglottis Vaticanis, 1909-1956.
AD	*Atti e Discorsi di Pio XII,* Roma, Edizioni Paoline. XVII Volumes from 1939 to 1955.
AG	*Acta Gregorii Papae XVI,* Romae, ex Typographia polyglotta S.C. de Propaganda Fide, 1900-1904.
AL	*Leonis XIII Pontificis Maximi Acta,* Romae, Typographia Vaticana, 1881-1905.
A.P.IX.	*Pii IX Pontificis Maximi Acta,* Roma, ex Typographia Bonarum Artium - ex Typographia Vaticana, 1854 ff.
A.P.X.	*Pii X Pontificis Maximi Acta,* Romae, ex Typographia Vaticana, 1905-1914.
ASS	*Acta Sanctae Sedis,* Romae, 1865-1908.
Atti	*Atti di Leone XIII, Mondovì,* Tipografia dell'Immacolata, 1910. Second edition;
BB	*Sanctissimi Domini Nostri Benedicti Papae XIV Bullarium.* T. 1, 2, 3, 4. Venetiis, J. Gatti, 1778.
BRC	*Bullarii Romani Continuatio,* Prati, 1845-1854.
CC	*La Civiltà Cattolica.*
CIC	*Codex Iuris Canonici.*
Denz.	*Enchiridion Symbolorum.* Friburgi Brisgoviae, 1942. Edition 24-25.
DR	*Discorsi e Radiomessaggi di Sua Santità Pio XII,* Milano, "Vita e Pensiero", 1939-1946. - Roma, Tipografia Poliglotta Vaticana, 1946-1956. XVII volumes: one for each year of Pontificate.
ES	*Le Encicliche sociali dei Papi da Pio IX a Pio XII* (1864-1941). Under the direction of Igino Giordani. Roma, Studium, 1942.

Ft.	*Iuris Canonici Fontes,* Romae, 1923-1939. The documents are cited in order of number.
PG	*J.P. Migne, Patrologiae cursus completus, series graeca.* Lutetiae Parisiorum, 1857 ff.
PL	*J.P. Migne, Patrologia cursus completus, series latina.* Lutetiae Parisiorum, 1844 ff.
MT	*J.P. Migne, Theologiae cursus completus, Paris,* 1839-1845.
OR	*L' Osservatore Romano.*

Nature of the Documents

All.	*Allocution.*
Can.	*Canon*
Ch.	*Chirograph.*
Apost. Const.	*Apostolic Constitution.*
Encycl.	*Encyclical.*
Apost. Letter	*Apostolic Letter.*
R.M.	*Radio Message.*

Numbering of the text

In the margin of the text or in footnotes:

The numbers in heavy print refer to paragraphs of the papal pronouncements.

The numbers in italics, given in parentheses, refer to the divisions of the analytical index, which in turn indicates the parallel texts.

In the indexes:

See the explanation at the head of each index.

ALPHABETICAL INDEX

The numbers in parentheses refer to the division of the Analytical Index; the numbers in heavy black print refer to the paragraphs of the papal pronouncements.

ANALYTICAL INDEX

PLAN OF THE ANALYTICAL INDEX

Introduction: Origin and Institution of Matrimony: *(1)-(5)*.

PART ONE

THE DIVINE IDEA OF MATRIMONY

Nature and Property of Matrimony: *The good of the Sacrament*.
    The Sacrament of Matrimony: *(6)-(12)*.
    Its properties:
      Unity: *(13)*.
      Indissolubility: *(14)-(17)*.
    The good of the sacrament: *(18)*.
The ends of Matrimony:
    The principal end: *(19)-(25)*.
      the good of fecundity: *(26)-(28)*.
    The secondary ends: *(29)-(31)*.
      the good of fidelity: *(32)-(35)*.
Matrimony, First social bond:
    Matrimony and the family: *(36)-(41)*.
    Matrimony and civil society: *(42)-(45)*.
Corollary: *Competent authority in Matrimonial matter*:
    The Church: *(46)-(53)*.
    The State: *(54)-(58)*.

PART TWO

THE CORRUPTION OF THE DIVINE IDEA

Institutions decay in the measure in which they estrange themselves from the divine idea that gave them birth: *(59)*.
    General causes:
    Economic and moral causes: *(60)-(62)*.
    Ideological causes: Naturalistic philosophy:
      exposition: *(63)-(66)*.
      confutation: *(67)-(68)*.

PART THREE

THE RETURN TO THE DIVINE IDEA

ANALYTICAL INDEX

The numbers in italics and in parentheses indicate the divisions of the present Index or refer the reader to these divisions.

The numbers in heavy print refer the reader to the paragraphs of this volume.

The numbers which are underlined refer the reader to particularly important passages of the text.

The numbers followed by an asterisk, for example: 9°, refer to the paragraphs of the Appendix.

The titles in bold type, for example, **EDUCATION**, indicate a subject treated in numerous pontifical documents already published or to be published in another volume of this Papal Teaching Series.

Introduction

ORIGIN AND INSTITUTION OF MARRIAGE

(1) Matrimony was instituted:
   not by men: **130, 267, 508,**
   but by God: **142, 267, 268, 343, 411, 508.**

(2) God desired it from the beginning of the human race: **147, 481,**
   one and indissoluble: **1, 3, 127, 148, 295,** cf. *(13)*, *(14)*,
   as a function of nature: **3, 252, 743,**
   destined for the propagation of the human race: **127, 130, 147, 174, 481,** cf. *(19)*,
   and for the constitution of the family: **130, 174, 481,** cf. *(36)*.

(3) The divine institution of Matrimony undergoes profound disorders,
   in pagan society: **149-152,**
   and even among the Jews: **21, 149, 282, 295.**

(4) Jesus Christ, from the beginning of His Mission: **152, 263, 486,**

restored the conjugal bond to the former conditions of its unity and indissolubility: **23, 43, 148, 152, 154, 242, 295, 440, 485,**
and brought it to its full complement: **152, 161, 252,**
raising it to the dignity of a Sacrament: **43, 123, 127, 130, 153, 165, 247, 440,** cf. *(6)* ff.

(5) Matrimony as with all institutions, will be so much more perfect inasmuch as it conforms to God's idea: **360,** cf. *(6)* ff,
Who has declared its ends and its laws: **64, 155, 267, 272, 508,** cf. *(19)* ff,
Whose goodness has enriched it with three gifts that constitute its moral value: **273, 274:**
the offspring: cf. *(26),*
conjugal fidelity: cf. *(32),*
the sacrament: cf. *(18);*
gifts which can be endangered by the errors and vices contrary to the divine idea of Matrimony: **314, 332, 340,** cf. *(59)* ff,
and which cannot be restored unless Matrimony returns to its divine ideal: **360,** cf. *(97).*

First Part

THE DIVINE IDEA OF MATRIMONY

THE NATURE AND THE PROPERTIES OF CHRISTIAN MATRIMONY

The Sacrament of Matrimony.

(6) Matrimony is by its very nature, an institution of juridically moral character: **50, 409,**
and sacred: **50, 64, 164, 217, 343, 531, 729,**
as regards its origin: **142, 164, 217, 343,**
as regards its end: **343,**
as regards its laws: **267, 343,**
as regards its symbolism: **130, 343, 344.**

(7) Among Christians, this sacred character is further emphasized by the elevation of Matrimony to a sacrament: **4, 49, 101, 123, 127, 130, 153, 154, 165, 247, 263, 293, 344, 439, 480, 483, 729, 761-762,** cf. *(4);*
this elevation constitutes a dogma of faith: **10, 43, 91, 94, 106, 129, 218, 241.**

(8) In Christian Matrimony, the sacrament is not an accidental quality, added to the contract: **91, 94, 107, 170,**

which would be constituted by the nuptial blessing only: **91, 107;**

but it is inseparably identified with it: **101, 132, 169, 170, 218, 247, 252,**

in such a manner that outside of the sacrament there cannot be a true Matrimony for Christians: **101, 114, 169, 192, <u>241</u>, 302, 669.**

(9) The Sacrament of Matrimony is the symbol of unity between Christ and His Church: **84, 127, 170, 258, 298, 400, 465, 483, 486, 512, 513, 729, 754, 759-760.**

(10) It is conferred on the spouses,

who are the ministers of the sacrament: **<u>445</u>-448, 489,**

with the expression of their mutual consent: **268, 270, 448,**

which cannot be substituted by any human power: **15, 50, <u>268</u>, 451,**

that refers to their exclusive and perpetual gift: **49, 51, 269, 437, 482,**

and not the nature and the conditions of their union: **269, 743;**

and the exchange of which

freely: **268, 434, 448, 482,**

and validly expressed: **302,** cf. *(12),*

with the "yes" pronounced by them: **482,**

constitutes the sacramental rite of Matrimony: **170, 480.**

(11) The exchange of the matrimonial consent

confers on the spouses the conjugal rights: **51, 638, 729, 740-743;**

binds them with a permanent bond: **27, 304, 378,**

analogous to the sacramental character: **304.**

Efficacious sign of grace, it confers on them habitual grace: **301, 303, 512, 513, 754,**

together with the right to actual graces: **303, 304, 417,**

and assures them the necessary power: **372,**

to sanctify themselves: **174, 311, 729,**

and to fulfil their obligations: **123, 128, 240, 301, 303, 425, 428, 716, 717,** even the most difficult ones: **363, 429, 625, 626, 668,**

particularly the difficulties of educating their children: **157, 443,** cf. *(25).*

The grace of Matrimony flows over to the family and society: **240, 512, 513.**

(12) In order to be valid, the consent must be exchanged between persons who are physically and morally capable of contracting Matrimony: **116, 468-470, 556, 639, 685-687, 698-703, 797-798,**

and not juridically hindered: **116;**

but even for minors the parents' consent is requested: **61.**

Must not include conditions which are contrary to the nature or to the essential properties of the sacrament: **46, 47, 60, 267-269, 272, 409, 618,**

in particular against its indissolubility: **49, 51, 184, 296, 482.**

It must be, save for the exceptions foreseen by law: **249, 254, 538,**

contracted in the prescribed form: **4, 92, 112, 142, 169, 249, 253, 254, 480;**

and, unless there are serious reasons: **8, 222,**

with the notoriety requested by a public act: **4-7, 11, 13, 225, 226.**

Essential properties of Christian Matrimony.

Unity.

(13) Unity is an essential property of Christian Matrimony: **148, 154, 267, 282, 283, 423, 437, 481,**

from which no human will can dispense: **283.**

Indissolubility.

(14) Indissolubility, seal of unity: **482,**

is, by divine law, essential for every true marriage: **1, 43, 48, 49, 103, 108, 126, 127, 148, 154, 267, 296, 409, 482;**

it is proposed by the ends of Matrimony: **3, 148, 490,**

by the welfare of the offspring: **248, 471, 498,**

by that of the spouses: **248, 471, 488,**

by the nature of their love: **248, 491, 492,**

by their personal dignity: **493-496,**

and by the welfare of society itself: **248, 471, 498.**

and under a certain aspect, it is the greatest of its three gifts: **340**.

Errors and crimes against the goodness of the Sacrament: cf. *(69)*.

THE ENDS OF MATRIMONY

The offspring.

(19)   The procreation of the offspring is the principal end: **210, 271, 274, 279, 319, 588, 633, 646, 732, 740,** for which purpose matrimony, an institution at the service of life: **501, 636, 660, 666, 701,**

was ordained by its very nature: **315, 452, 478, 510, 620, 634, 639, 641, 646, 801,**

from its very beginning: **210, 481,** cf. *(2)*,

as can be certified by Sacred Scripture, and by the teaching and Tradition of the Church: **274, 279, 634.**

(20)   Procreation is not a simple biological function: **594, 595, 637, 702,**

which could be realized by artificial insemination: **636—639,** cf. *(94)*;

but it demands the total gift of the spouses: **636, 734,**

expressed by the conjugal act completed in the normal manner: **637, 737,**

with a free and personal cooperation: **448, 451, 478, 595, 635, 637, 638, 702, 738,**

who collaborate in the work of creation: **275, 425, 438, 447, 448, 450, 690,**

and the redemption: **425, 438, 478, 593,**

and in the paternity of God: **454-457, 460.**

(21)   In a Christian matrimony, this cooperation must be extended to the communication of the spiritual life: **431, 438, 458, 460, 501, 725, 735,**

which the parents do not directly transmit to their children: **276,**

but which they must assure them of by presenting them to be

baptized: **276, 461, 606, 607,**

thus transmitting to them the heredity of the faith: **421, 432 433.**

(22)   Christian matrimony in fact,

in conformity with its model: **65,**

has the scope of giving children to God: **65, 277, 343,**

> so that He be adored: **65, 276, 442,**

and to the Church, so as to be her members: **155, 276, 416, 441, 465, 621, 683, 721, 801,**

and future citizens of Heaven: **329, 416.**

And it is to this sublime end that the Sacrament of Matrimony has been raised to its new dignity: **65, 155, 275.**

(23) The principal end of matrimony also demands the education of the children: **3, 278, 279, 411, 479, 588, 646, 744-746, 801,**

> bound naturally with procreation: **211, 278, 279, 555, 641, 674, 691, 702, 735.**

It is therefore a law and a rigorous duty for the parents to provide for the education of the children: **157, 207, 213, 234, 277, 278, 747,**

(24) and for Christian parents to educate them in matters of their religion: **65, 77, 207, 441-443, 479,**

> with the help of the priest: **442,**

> and the Catholic school: **207.**

This is the first mission of the parents in Catholic Action: **421.**

The education of children: cf. **EDUCATION.**

(25) It is for this work of procreation and education of the children that the spouses were united: **450,**

> and received the graces of the sacrament: **443,** cf. *(11).*

It is for this work that the conjugal act is essentially ordained: **646, 737,**

> without a diminishing of personal values: **635,**

> since the spouses cooperate inasmuch as they are human beings: **635,** cf. *(20),* 9° ff.,

> and besides the children are an extension of the person of the parents: **211-213.**

The goodness of fecundity, cf. (5).

(26) Children occupy the first place among the gifts on which is based the moral value of matrimony: **273, 274, 621;**

> it is the specific accomplishment of the spouses: **620, 621, 641,**

> which gives the value to their act: **621,**

and which is strictly reserved for them alone: **15, 280, 510, 554, 555, 621, 644, 702, 737, 743,**
the intimate design being that of the orderly transmission of human life: **691.**
Corollary: The delivery: cf. **THE HUMAN BODY**
Legitimacy of adoption: **791.**

(27) The law of fecundity submits the use of the conjugal rights to the acceptance of the burdens that can derive from them: **273, 277, 452, 453, 600, 609, 613, 620, 691, 699, 765-766, 787-788, 790.**
such as those of maternity: **604, 609, 611,**
a duty often times heroic: **318,**
but glorious: **273, 453, 602, 603.**
Cf. **THE WOMAN IN THE MODERN WORLD**

(28) Birth control, restricting the fulfilment of the conjugal duties to those periods when the woman is infertile; (Rhythm Control—Ogino Method): **615-622;**
discretion imposed on the priest: **616;**
competence of the Church in this matter: **616;**
the problem: **615, 616, 787-790.**
The use of matrimonial right is not prohibited in the infertile periods: **617, 667.**
The limitation *of the conjugal right* to the infertile periods placed as a condition in giving matrimonial consent renders the matrimony invalid: **618.**
the limitation of *the use* of the right is licit or illicit according to the value of the motives which determine the spouses to use this method: **619, 621, 622, 787-790.**
The offspring, the principal end of matrimony: cf. Appendix, 9° ff.
Judgment of the Tribunal of the H. R. Rota.
Crimes and errors against the offspring: cf. (87) ff.

THE SECONDARY ENDS OF MATRIMONY.

(29) Matrimony has as its secondary ends:
a remedy for concupiscence: **272, 319,**
a mutual help for the spouses: **156, 174, 319, 343, 708, 717, 729,**
to conserve Christian love: **174, 282, 319, 505, 636,**
through the work of common life: **6, 153, 174, 347, 481, 636, 735,**
and the common search for perfection: **153, 174, 286, 287, 465, 636,**

it exacts a just moderation in the things permitted: **284, 643-645, 649;**

in certain cases it can demand an heroic continence on the part of the spouses: **428, 466, 623, 624,** which is possible with the help of grace: **592, 625-627,** cf. *(11)*.

(34) Mutual love: irradiation of chastity: **156, 285,**

placed in man's heart as an inborn instinct: **444, 545,**

is elevated in Christian matrimony by supernatural charity: **153, 444,**

and mutual respect: **650, 761,**

to render the mutual affection of the spouses in conformity with that of its divine model: **285, 305.**

Conjugal love in widowhood: **759-760.**

(35) Conjugal love implies:

reciprocal help: **35, 286, 287, 436,** cf. *(29),*
the fulfillment of the conjugal duty: **287,**
the submission of the wife: **288,** cf. (39).

MATRIMONY, FIRST SOCIAL BOND

Matrimony and family.

(36) By the institution of matrimony, God has provided:

for its constitution: **130.**

and for the benefit of the family: **126, 217, 752, 756.**

of which matrimony is the source and foundation: **146, 162, 229, 237, 260.**

The family is therefore based on a sacrament: **412, 417,**

and its staying power depends on the sanctity of matrimony: **126, 175, 205, 234, 259, 260, 515.**

(37) The family is the natural place:

for the transmission of life: **691,**

for the development and education of the human person:

206, 207, 211, 501, 511, 524-526, 673, 678, 679, an integral part of the primary end of matrimony: *(23)* ff.

It has its place in the apostolate and in Catholic Action: **421.**

(38) The family is a true society: **210,**
      with spiritual, moral, juridical and economic unity: **705,**
      of which God has fixed the constitution and the rights: **126, 212, 411, 412, 418, 539, 755.**
      in particular that of property: **210, 211, 462-464.**
      at least uniform to those of civil society: **212.**

(39) as such, it has a hierarchy: **289, 290, 338, 761.**
      arranged for its benefit: **289, 337,**
      in conformity to that of its divine model: **127, 221, 437,**
      and enlivened by charity: **156, 291,** cf. *(35).*

(40) Man is the head of the family which he governs in the name of God: **128, 156, 213, 259, 289, 291, 579,**
      and whose preservation he must assure: **580.**

(41) Woman is the heart of the family: **156, 289, 734;**
      her noble and worthy obedience: **156, 290, 291,**
      does not suppress her rights nor take away her freedom: **289, 290, 337.**
      The family hierarchy: cf. **THE WOMAN IN THE MODERN WORLD** and the volume on the Christian family.

Matrimony and civil society.

(42) Matrimony is directed also to the growth and preservation of human society: **174, 186, 262, 521-522, 525-526, 746,**
      of which the family is the mother cell: **126, 175, 257, 258, 300, 412, 464, 501, 545, 574, 581, 721-722, 731,**
      and the foundation: **237, 404, 503, 529, 534, 574, 678, 706, 731, 752, 762, 769;**
      And which gathers together individuals, not by themselves, but through families: **213, 299, 430.**

(43) The State therefore depends on the family
      for its existence: **416, 621,**
      for its prosperity: **199, 205, 207, 209, 214, 463, 501, 514, 578, 683, 692,**
      which is the result of the integrity of the family: **125, 126, 214, 234, 260, 300, 390, 430, 501, 514, 516, 530, 539, 545, 578, 670, 678, 680, 706, 721, 722, 731, 733, 762,**

(53) The Church cannot renounce her mission: **199**, **225**, **243**, **248**, **583**,
   which she knows how to adapt to the needs of the times: **186**, **779**,
   and which is resolved in various benefices: **145-146**, **160**, **184**,
      for individuals: **125**, **145**,
      for families: **126**, **145**, **246**, **564**, cf. *(99)*,
      and for society as a whole: **126**, **145**, **198**, **564**, **721**.

The State and Matrimony.

(54) The Church does not dispute the State's competence: to sanction the natural law: **271**,
   and to arrange the civil effects of matrimony for the common good: **61**, **98**, **135**, **186**, **193**, **218**, **237**, **241-242**, **247**, **532-533**,
   which must be in harmony with and subordinated to the Church: **19-20**, **83**, **187**.

(55) But the State has no power as regards Matrimony itself: **43**, **45**, **61**, **135**, **218**, **241**, **242**,
   neither as regards the sacrament, which as such, is outside of its competence: **43**, **45**, **164-165**, **242**, **531**,
   nor as regards the contract, inseparable from the sacrament in a Christian marriage: **169**, **240**, **241**, **242**, cf. *(8)*,
   nor as regards the bond contracted between infidels: **49**, **50**,
   nor as regards the engagement: **19**, **52**, **115**.
   The State's interventions have no value: **252**,
      and are sacrilegious: **83-85**, **218**.

(56) In particular, the State cannot, especially with diriment impediments: **53**, **61**, **91**, **109**, **685**,
   restrict the right to matrimony: **218-219**, **223**, **271**, **328**, **468**, **685-689**,
   a right anterior to civil society: **229**,
      as matrimony itself: **50**, **241**, cf. *(44)*;
   to limit the principal end of matrimony: **210**, **271**, **674**, **684**,
   or to intern the deficient: **685**.
   The State cannot judge matrimonial cases: **91**, **110**, **115**,
      nor dispense with the impediments established by the Church: **8**, **54**, **117**.

(57) The State cannot dissolve a Christian matrimony by a divorce sentence: **57, 135, 193, 242, 296, 351, 423, 473,**

nor dissolve a legitimate marriage between non-baptized persons: **48, 50, 531,**

but the simple declaration of the nullity of the marriage itself can be given in certain circumstances: **271, 531,**

and the civil effects of the separation decreed by the Church: **354.**

(58) The duties of Catholic magistrates and legislators faced with unjust marriage laws: **560-562,**

particularly in divorce cases: **355, 559-563,**

and with laws that impose direct sterilization: **328, 330,** cf. *(88).*

SECOND PART

THE CORRUPTION OF THE DIVINE IDEA

(59) Institutes decline in the measure in which they defect from the divine idea which conceived them: **360, 498;**

the Creator's designs over matrimony are hindered by errors and vices: **359,**

and by the forgetfulness of Christian doctrine: **704.**

GENERAL CAUSES

Economic and moral causes.

(60) The last wars: **257, 500, 528, 534, 537, 668, 722,** insufficient wages and needs: **320, 386-387, 390, 401, 419, 534, 575, 723, 726,**

obliged the woman to work outside of the home: **390, 671, 727,** cf. **THE WOMAN IN THE MODERN WORLD,**

and especially the housing problems: **464, 541-545, 558, 656, 705, 726,**

(61) the corruption of morals: **81, 178, 223, 357, 361, 363, 367, 548,**

especially in the more civilized countries: **504,** encouraged by the spreading of false moral theories: **265, 487, 535, 548, 630, 659, 668, 768-769,**

even amongst the faithful: **265, 308, 571-572, 645, 779,**

by divorce: **200, 245, 430,**
and legal concubinage: **105, 200, 201.**

(66) Socialism helps to destroy the family: **126, 546, 755,**
with its absorption in the totalitarian State: **409-410, 418-419, 548, 658, 674, 676.**

Risks presented under this relation for the social safety of the State: **574, 675.**

Confutation.

(67) The naturalistic doctrine of Matrimony is contrary to the nature of matrimony: **161, 164, 173,**
and to that of society: **173, 567;**
it is injurious to the Church: **93, 100, 161, 185, 217,**
and heretical: **40-43, 100, 567;**
it is contrary to the teachings of history: **164,**
and is refuted by the exposition of Catholic doctrine: **164, 311,** cf. *(6)* ff.

(68) It aims:
to weaken the laws of matrimony: **81, 176, 311-313, 374, 515,**
to reverse its ends: **172, 177, 245, 311-313, 605, 632, 645,**
and all moral order: **260, 392, 567;**
to legalize divorce: **177-178,**
to allow extra-marital intercourse: **311,**
to feign matrimony: temporary, friendly and trial marriages: **312,**
to relax fatherly authority and education: **126, 255-257, 515, 548,**
to the ruin of families and nations: **171, 177, 205, 209, 260, 311, 313, 357, 393, 521, 545, 548, 723.**

ERRORS AND CRIMES AGAINST THE SACRAMENT

"Civil Matrimony"

(69) The progress of secularization, the realization of the naturalistic plan, cf. *(63)*, *(65)*:
"civil matrimony" among the infidels: **12,**
introduced by Protestant countries and the abuse of mixed marriages: **17 ff, 83 ff,**
to penetrate:
the Catholic countries of Europe: **43, 94, 105, 119, 129, 199, 216, 236,**
and Latin America: **100, 238, 247, 250.**
Generalization: **161-163, 245, 340-341,**
especially in Communist countries: **409, 524.**

The law of divorce.

of the efforts of neo-paganism and Freemasonry: **200**, **340-341 348-350**, **413**, cf. *(65)*, *(66)*.

Admitted once by infidels alone: **14,**

it penetrated into Protestant countries: **48, 57, 71, 182, 235, 423,**

and extended to Catholic countries: **100, 178, 242, 245, 247, 348, 350, 494-498, 533,**

and is a normal matter in Communist countries: **405, 409, 524,**

(76) Divorce cannot be justified by the example of those nations which have adopted it: **243,**

nor by the difficulties of married life: **349-350,** which can be sufficiently remedied by the separation of the wedded couple: **10, 194, 354,**

which the Church authorizes for legitimate reasons: **10, 354,**

of which she is the judge: cf. *(49)*.

(77) The law which authorizes divorce is unjust: **405,** is contrary to the natural and divine law: **48, 242, 727,**

and the doctrine of the Church: **71, 108, <u>199</u>, 248, 352,** cf. *(14)* ff.

and its rights: **100, 243.**

(78) It is disastrous for the family: **179, <u>183</u>, 199, 201, 237, 244, 356-358, 405, 515, 727,**

by dissolving the union between husband and wife: **244, 355-356,**

by diminishing respect for matrimony: **244, 340, 475,**

debasing woman: **<u>201</u>, <u>244</u>, 356, 494,**

causing disastrous effects for the children: **<u>179</u>, 201, 244, 356, 497.**

(79) It is ruinous for society: **<u>179</u>, 183, 199, 235-237, 244, 355-357, 405, 423,**

because of its contagious character: **180, 243, 357,** already experimented: **181, 182, 358.**

(80) Divorce, being null in its effects, cannot dissolve a marriage between Christians: **57, 183, 242, 351, 524,**

nor can it dissolve any legitimate marriage: **21-22, 242, <u>351</u>,**

It cannot authorize the wedded parties to begin a new union, which would be nothing else than adultery: **57, 80, 242, 351, 563.**

(81) The Church does not prohibit that re-married divorcees be admitted to the Sacrament of Penance, provided, repentant, they consent to separate: **58-59.**

The Church does not confound divorce with the recognition of the nullity of a matrimony, contracted invalidly: **62, 435, 476,**

nullity which must not be too easily admitted: cf. *(51).*

Duties of magistrates and legislative men who are Catholics, in divorce cases: cf. *(58).*

Disparity of worship and mixed marriages.

(82) The principle of liberty of mixed marriages, between Catholics and non-Catholics, is a mistaken opinion: **70, 85, 341.**

Unless there has been granted a dispensation, such marriages, if contracted between a Catholic and a non-baptized person, are null: **60,**

if contracted between a Catholic and a baptized non-Catholic, are valid: **27, 42, 60,**

but prohibited by ecclesiastical law: **41-42, 204, 345,**

as a communication interdicted in holy matters: **86, 233,**

as contrary to the complete significance of the sacrament: **346,**

and to the intimate union between the wedded parties: **63, 196, 347, 423;**

and further—if they are not furnished with the prescribed guarantees to avoid the danger of perversion—they are prohibited by the divine law itself: cf. *(86).*

(83) Mixed marriages in contradiction with the obligation of safeguarding the faith, indispensable for salvation: **32-33, 68, 71-78, 196,**

place in danger: especially if the woman is the heretic: **32, 42,**

the faith of the Catholic party: **35, 42, 63, 86, 345, 424,**

that of the children: **32, 34, 63, 68, 78, 85, 86, 196, 238, 346,**

and lead to religious indifference: **34, 36, 84-85, 196, 205, 238, 346.**

(84) Besides the Church asks her ministers to persuade the faithful not to contract mixed marriages: **27, 67-68, 76-77, 204, 233, 345,**

which she has always abhorred: **25-26, 30, 31, 55, 60, 62, 66, 69, 85-86,**
and whose every approval would only multiply their number: **67, 90, 204.**

(85) The Church grants dispensations only reluctantly: **28-30, 41, 55-56, 63, 66,**
without wanting to give an approval: **56,**
but to avoid even greater evils: **69, 88-89.**

(86) The dispensation given to contract a mixed marriage supposes that the danger of perversion is avoided: **85, 345;**
the natural law exacts guarantees against this danger: **30, 66-69, 87, 345,**
in particular the promise to work for the conversion of the non-Catholic partner: **27, 66, 69, 87,**
and the Catholic education of the children: **66, 77, 87.**

Mixed marriage must not have in normal cases the nuptial blessing: **79, 88, 90.**

ERRORS AND CRIMES AGAINST THE OFFSPRING

The offspring, cf. *(19).*

Perversion of the conjugal act.

(87) The perversion of the conjugal act, with onanistic practices, is one of the greatest calamities of the family: **314, 404, 413, 453, 507, 515, 723;**
it is an act contrary to the natural law: **314-316, 692, 703,**
and intrinsically evil: **315-316, 320, 451, 595, 613, 745,**
which no human power can legitimate: **314-315, 318, 320, 573, 613, 740-745.**

Measure of guilt of the parties: **319, 612, 793.**

Duties of the parish priest and the confessor: **317.**

Eugenics and sterilization.

(88) Presented as a remedy for over-population: **674-677,**
and hereditary traits: **684, 795,**
the eugenic condition is not contrary to reason, unless it recommends unlawful practices: **326, 328, 622, 689, 763-765, 773-776,** cf. *(28),*
it can never authorize the mutilation or the sterilization of an innocent person: **328-331, 406-407, 614, 684-689, 693-697, 779, 781-782, 784-786,**
nor the use of preservatives: **787-788.**

Attempting the life of the child.

(89)　Today it is considered by some as lawful, at least in the case of medical indication: **322, 509, 688,**
　　　but abortion can never be authorized, if it is a direct attempt on the life of an innocent creature: **323-327, 597-598, 660-661, 664-665, 692, 749,**
　　　　at any stage of its development: **509, 597, 624, 661, 664, 691,**
　　　　and even in the case of eugenic indication: **323-326, 598, 688,**
　　　　　to save the mother: **598, 624, 662-664,**
　　　　　or on an order of the State: **509, 598, 688.**

(90)　However things not forbidden are:
　　　a regulation of births with legitimate means: **605, 667,** cf. *(28),*
　　　an intervention which would only indirectly cause the death of the child: **665, 749,**
　　　　or result in sterilization: **693-695, 783, 785,**
　　　the prevention of marriage to one who is not capable of conducting himself in a human manner: **685.**

Errors against the hierarchy of the ends of Matrimony.

(91)　The Church also rejects all those theories which do not respect the subordination of the other ends of Matrimony to the principal end: **622, 634,** cf. Appendix, 9° ff;
　　　in particular those theories which draw arguments from the value fo sexuality: **645-648,**
　　　　or from the relation of personal values alone: **629-632, 646.**

Marriages between blood relations and mixed marriages.

(92)　Abuse of marriages between blood-relations: **9, 116, 118.**
　　　Mixed marriages are contrary to the Christian education of children: cf. *(83).*

ERRORS AND CRIMES AGAINST FIDELITY

Fidelity cf. *(29)* ff.

(93)　The crimes against fidelity are as numerous as the virtues required by it: **331-332,** cf. *(32)* ff.;
　　　every sin against the offspring is also a sin against fidelity: **332.**

Intimacy with third persons.

　　　The too-easily admitted liberties which are admitted

Their intimacy, which cannot be completed in cases of mixed marriage: cf. *(82)*,

in particular by the family which permits the must not be compromised by the abuse of sport: **653, 671,**

or by the technical concept of life: **706,**

of by the lack of houses: **705.**

RELIGIOUS ACTION

THE ACTION OF MARRIED COUPLES

PREPARATION FOR MARRIAGE AND
CHOOSING MATRIMONY

INDEX OF QUOTATIONS

The numbers in heavy type refer to the paragraphs in the Papal documents.

SACRED SCRIPTURE

COUNCILS

SUPREME PONTIFFS

CODE OF CANON LAW

SACRED CONGREGATION OF THE HOLY OFFICE

INDEX OF DOCUMENTS AND SOURCES

ALPHABETICAL INDEX
OF WRITTEN DOCUMENTS

The numbers in bold type refer to the paragraphs of this volume. The numbers in bold type followed by a letter refer to a footnote corresponding to the paragraph indicated by the number.

The abbreviations in the last column (see explanation of abbreviations, pp. 561-562), refer to the original language sources of the English texts prepared by the translator of this volume. The translations of three Encyclicals: "Arcanum Divinae Sapientiae," "Casti Connubii," and "Sacra Virginitas," are used with the kind permission of the Catholic Truth Society, London.

CHRONOLOGICAL INDEX OF ORAL DOCUMENTS

The numbers in bold type refer to the paragraphs of this volume.
The abbreviations in the last column (see explanation of abbreviations, pp. 561-562), refer to the original language sources of the English texts prepared by the translator of this volume.

THE DAUGHTERS OF ST. PAUL

In Massachusetts
       50 St. Paul's Avenue
       Jamaica Plain,
       Boston 30, Mass.
       172 Tremont St.,
       Boston 11, Mass.
       381 Dorchester St.
       So. Boston 27, Mass.
       325 Main St.
       Fitchburg, Mass.
In New York
       78 Fort Place,
       Staten Island 1, N.Y.
       625 East 187th Street
       Bronx, N.Y.
       39 Erie St.,
       Buffalo 2, N.Y.
In Connecticut
       202 Fairfield Ave.,
       Bridgeport, Conn.
In Ohio
       141 West Rayen Ave.,
       Youngstown 3, Ohio
       Cleveland, Ohio
In Texas
       114 East Main Plaza,
       San Antonio 5, Texas
In California
       1570 Fifth Ave.,
       San Diego 1, Calif.
In Florida
       2700 Biscayne Blvd.
       Miami 37, Florida
In Louisiana
       86 Bolton Ave.,
       Alexandria, La.
In Canada
       8885 Blvd. Lacordaire,
       St. Leonard Deport-Maurice,
       Montreal, Canada
       1063 St. Clair Ave. West,
       Toronto, Canada
In England
       29 Beauchamp Place,
       London, S.W. 3, England
In India
       Water Field Road Extension,
       Plot N. 143,
       Bandra, India
In Philippine Islands
       No. 326 Lipa City,
       Philippine Islands
In Australia
       58 Abbotsford Rd.,
       Homebush N.S.W., Australia